# CHILD DEVELOPMENT AND LEARNING 2–5 YEARS

## Georgia's Story

## CATH ARNOLD OF PEN GREEN EARLY YEARS CENTRE

### SERIES EDITOR TINA BRUCE

Reprinted 2001, 2002

Paul Chapman Publishing Ltd
A SAGE Publications Company
6 Bonhill Street
London EC2A 4PU

SAGE Publications Inc
2455 Teller Road
Thousand Oaks, California 91320

SAGE Publications India Pvt Ltd
32, M-Block Market
Greater Kailash - I
New Delhi 110 048

*British Library Cataloguing in Publication data*
A catalogue record for this book is available from the British Library

ISBN 0 7619 72994

Library of Congress catalog card number

Reprinted for SAGE publications by the Alden Group, Oxford

*British Library Cataloguing in Publication Data*
A catalogue record for this title is available from The British Library

First published 1999
Impression number   10   9   8   7   6   5   4   3
Year                      2005   2004   2003   2002

Copyright © 1999 Cath Arnold

Typeset by Wearset, Boldon, Tyne and Wear.

Only a child –
Yet I am nearer to creation
My colours new and vivid
Chaotic and joyful
Give me the means and let me be free
To make sense of the world
As it unfolds around me
I will learn from you
But you can learn from me, if you
Cherish the life that I bring
And listen.

Di Brewster, 1996

# ᴀCKNOWLEDGEMENTS

I would like to acknowledge the huge contribution that Georgia and her parents, Ian and Colette, have made to this book. I have learnt a great deal from them during our discussions about Georgia. They have been very committed to gathering the diary record and to reflecting on and analysing what happened. They have both given me critical feedback on my representation of our discussions.

I would also like to thank Eloise for her meticulous proof reading of the manuscript, helpful critical feedback and for her witty comments.

I want to thank Tina Bruce as an editor and friend for encouraging me to write this book and for her frequent feedback on every aspect of the work. All of my colleagues at Pen Green have been supportive and interested, but a special mention must go to Margy Whalley for constantly inspiring me and for believing in my ability to write well.

Last, but not least, I want to thank Terry for shopping, cooking and sorting out the computer, and Paul for our Sunday afternoon chats about the wider world.

Cath Arnold

# CONTENTS

# Series Preface – 0–8 years

At most times in history and in most parts of the world, the first eight years of life have been seen as the first phase of living. Ideally, during this period, children learn who they are; about those who are significant to them; and how their world is. They learn to take part, and how to contribute creatively, imaginatively, sensitively and reflectively.

Children learn through and with the people they love, and the people who care for them. They learn through being physically active, through real, direct experiences, and through learning how to use and make symbolic systems, such as play, language and representation.

Whether children are at home, in nursery schools, classes, family centres, day nurseries, playgroups (now re-named preschools), workplace nurseries or primary schools, they need informed adults who can help them.

The 0–8 series will help those who work with young children, in whatever capacity, to be as informed as possible about this first phase of living.

From the age of 8 years old, the developing and learning can be consolidated, hopefully in ways which build on what has gone before.

In this series, each book emphasises a different aspect of the first stage of living (0–8 years).

*Getting To Know You: A Guide to Record Keeping in Early Childhood Education and Care* by Lynne Bartholomew and Tina Bruce is based on principles of good practice in the spirit of Stephen Isaacs. It explores the relationship between observation, assessment, evaluation and monitoring in a record keeping system. It takes account of legal requirements in the different parts of the UK. The book is full of examples of good practice in record keeping. Unless we know and understand our children, unless we act effectively on what we know, we cannot help them very much.

*Learning to be Strong: Integrating Education and Care in Early Childhood* by Margy Whalley is an inspirational book. Pen Green Centre for Under-fives and their Families in Corby, Northamptonshire, is an acknowledged beacon of excellence, emulated throughout the UK and internationally. When adults come together as a team – parents, educators, carers, those in Social Services and Health experts using their energy on behalf of the child – then education and care become truly integrated. Just as it was important that Margaret McMillan's pioneer work at the turn of the century in integrating education and care should be recorded, so this book has become a classic of the 1990s.

Beacons of excellence, like Pen Green, when documented in this way, can continue to illuminate principles which influence quality practice through the ages, transcending the passing of time.

*Helping Children to Draw and Paint in Early Childhood: Children and Visual Representation* by John Matthews gives a fascinating insight into the early drawings, paintings and models that children make. The book shows how these begin and traces development from scribbles to later drawings in the period of the first eight years. A wealth of real life examples is given, together with practical stategies that adults can use to help children develop their drawings and paintings with quality.

In *Helping Children to Learn through a Movement Perspective*, Mollie Davies, an internationally respected movement expert with years of practical experience of working with young children, writes about the central places of movement within the learning process. In a lively, well-illustrated book, with lots of real examples, she makes a case for movement as a common denominator of the total development of children, and in this draws our attention to its integrating function. A whole chapter is devoted to dance – the art form of movement. The provision of a readily accessible movement framework gives excellent opportunities for adults to plan, observe and record their children's development in movement terms.

*Self-Esteem and Successful Early Learning* by Rosemary Roberts is about the importance of being positive, encouraging and gently firm in bringing up and working with young children. Whilst every family is different, every family shares some aspects of living with young children. These are taken up and given focus in the book in ways that are accessible and lead to practical strategies. The reader meets a variety of situations with the family and explores successful ways of tackling them so that the theories supporting the practice become meaningful and useful.

*The Development of Language and Literacy* by Marion Whitehead emphasises the importance of adults being sensitive to the child's culture, feeling and ideas as language develops and early attempts to communicate in writing and reading emerge. Bilingualism and its indications are looked at in depth. Children need to spend time with people who care about them, enjoy being with them, and sensitively support their early language and literacy.

*Resources for Early Learning: Children, Adults and Stuff* by Pat Gura takes a critical look at the materials that are given to children in early years settings and examines the conventional wisdom and assumptions that early years workers make about resources such as sand, water, paint, blocks, the home area and others. The book encourages practitioners to be reflective.

*Effective Early Learning* edited by Christine Pascal and Tony Bertram is about practitioner research. It shows how nine very different early childhood settings experienced the Effective Early Learning project. This research project is about empowering practitioners to develop their own practice and is having a great influence and impact on the quality of practice in the UK.

Clinging to dogma, 'I believe children need. . .' or saying 'What was good enough for me . . .' is not good enough. Children deserve better than that. The pursuit of excellence means being informed. This series will help adults to increase their knowledge and understanding of the 'first phase of living', and to act in the light of this for the good of children.

TINA BRUCE

# Introducing Georgia

This book is the story of Georgia. It is about her development and learning between the ages of 2 and 5 years. Of course, no two children develop and learn in exactly the same way, but it is still helpful to follow one child in depth. Looking at Georgia's unique ways of learning, can lead us to discover the similarities between her and other children growing up in the UK today. As Bruce (et al, 1995) comment,

> By exploring differentiation, or differences between children, there is the possibility of making progress in teasing out the essentials, the universals.

There are many things to consider. These include Georgia's gender, her position in the family, and her likes and dislikes. Each of these features provides learning opportunities for Georgia – this is true of every child in every family. When Georgia starts nursery at 3 years of age, she brings with her a wealth of experience. The nursery workers can use these experiences as a base on which to build and to plan further learning experiences.

In order to tell Georgia's story, this book uses narrative observations, gathered over time by her parents at home (parent diary) and by workers at nursery. Narrative observations are useful because they:

- help us to analyse in many different ways

- encourage discussion, in retrospect, about Georgia's learning; discussions take place between her parents, a worker (who is the author) and Georgia herself

- help us to plan for Georgia's future learning.

In order to help us get to know Georgia, in Chapter One we will meet Georgia and her family. We will learn about Georgia's home context in some detail and about her transition to nursery.

Before we can begin to look at Georgia's development and learning, we need to make sure we are equipped to make sense of what we see. Theories help us to do this. For this reason, Chapter Two begins by outlining the theories and traditions in early childhood education and care. We will draw on these as we observe Georgia's development and learning. This chapter also explores two possible ways of analysing observations of Georgia and suggests the types of staff training necessary to help us to learn about children's development and learning.

Chapter Three is a record of Georgia learning to write and read, acknowledging her early mark-making, stories, rhymes and role play as part of that process.

Chapter Four traces Georgia's understanding of some mathematical concepts, such as number, quantity, division, size, fit, time and chronology.

Chapter Five charts Georgia's developing scientific concepts including food allergy, childbirth and changes in state.

Chapter Six examines Georgia's emotional development by looking at issues of power, change and uncertainty in her life and at how adults help her to cope with and to learn from periods of change.

Chapter Seven concludes the book by describing how adults help Georgia to make connections across the curriculum during her year at nursery. We also build a picture of Georgia as she starts school and we consider her interests at 7 years of age.

# IMPORTANT EVENTS IN GEORGIA'S LIFE

| Georgia's age | Event |
| --- | --- |
| 2 years 3 months | Harry (Georgia's brother) is born |
| 2 years 7 months | Georgia starts playgroup |
| 2 years 10 months | Harry has his first allergic reaction |
| 2 years 10 months | Dad changes job – works for Kai |
| 3 years 5 months | Dad changes job – works for Jane |
| 3 years 7 months | Georgia starts nursery |
| 3 years 8 months | Mum starts working evenings |
| 3 years 11 months | Dad is made redundant and is out of work for 2 months |
| 3 years 11 months | Mum begins working mornings and extra hours |
| 4 years 1 month | Dad begins training then working evenings |
| 4 years 7 months | Georgia starts school |
| 5 years | Parents decide to separate |
| 5 years 1 month | Mum begins full-time work |
| Over next 5 months | Parents negotiate and establish pattern of care, which is only possible because dad's working hours are flexible. |
| 5 years 6 months | Mum buys house and moves out – children sleep at mum's from Monday to Friday and at dad's Saturday and Sunday. Dad collects children from mum's each weekday morning and takes them to school or carer. At the end of the day, dad collects children from school or carer and either he brings them to her at work or she collects them from him at home. Mum continues working days and dad continues working evenings. |

# 1 INTRODUCING GEORGIA AND HER FAMILY

*It is when we are dealing with people and things in the context of fairly immediate goals and intentions and familiar patterns of events that we feel most at home.* (Donaldson, 1978)

In this chapter we meet Georgia, aged 2 years, and learn about her experiences in her family.

> - Georgia's home.
>
> - Who Georgia knows.
>
> - Where Georgia goes.
>
> - Georgia's play, both at home and at nursery.

Before we explore these ideas, we might remember what Margaret Donaldson wrote about the kinds of learning that will make human sense to Georgia at this point. In the 1970s Donaldson extended Jean Piaget's theory. She and her colleagues discovered that, often, problems did not make any 'human sense' to children (Donaldson, 1978). Unless problems make human sense, they are 'isolated from the rest of existence'. Young children, in their quest for knowledge and understanding of the world, are seeking to make connections between experiences. They continuously bring their earlier, familiar experiences to bear on new situations and problems. So, using problems disconnected from a child's previous experiences, is neither fair to the child nor likely to provide information about what a child knows or wants to know. If we are to give each child an equal chance in education, we must actively seek to discover what experiences they already have, in order that we might help them to make connections between new knowledge and their earlier experiences.

This discovery, that children function at a much higher level when what they learn makes human sense to them, along with renewed interest in Vygotsky's ideas about the importance of the social context of learning, sit well together. This is called a **social constructivist** or **interactionist approach**. This approach acknowledges that each child must explore and discover things for him or herself (**Piagetian theory**), while attributing equal importance to the people with whom the child interacts (**Vygotskerian theory**).

# GEORGIA'S HOME

When Georgia was born, her dad had lived in the same house for 10 years. For three of those years, her mum shared the house with him. It is a detached house. It has an open plan garden at the front and a back garden which can be accessed either through the garage or through the living room of the house. The back garden is big enough for a sandpit, paddling pool and small slide as well as other toys. Georgia's family garden consists of a small patio and grass. There are 10 houses in the close. They are in a circle facing inwards. The front gardens are not enclosed and several are used by children to play together. When Georgia was born there were already seven children living in the close, all girls. The only cars that come into the close either belong to the families who live there or to people who are visiting those families.

## Looking back with Georgia's parents

Looking back on Georgia's early life, Georgia's parents realise something that only now seems significant, happened soon after Georgia was born. Some of the older children in the close began to take an interest in her.

>**Dad:** *'The older girls paid her a lot of attention – they used to ask to come into the house.'*
>**Mum:** *'Amy and Jennifer came and asked to play with Georgia because they liked babies.'*

Amy and Jennifer are non-identical twins, at the time aged 7, who live next door but one.

Georgia's parents took her out into the close from the time that she was four or five months old. That way, she got to know other people and they got to know her.

>**Dad:** *'You just have to take a baby or toddler out and other children come.'*
>**Mum:** *'The older children kept her amused.'*

Georgia seemed to enjoy the company of other people, particularly the children. Soon, two other children, only months younger than her, are born: James (next door) and Little Emma (three houses away). Later, Georgia, James and Little Emma all start school together at 4 years old.

Gradually, Georgia begins to play outside in the close. At first her parents go outside with her. Soon they begin keeping an eye on her from the house. Again the physical layout of the house is important.

> **Dad:** *'Most kitchens look out on the close.'*

Other parents are either out with or watching out for their children who are playing in the close.

### The advantages of living in a close

> **Mum:** *'If you live in a street, you can only let your child play in the garden. If other children come into the garden, then I would be responsible for them as well as my own child. The close is a sort of public place. I only have to be responsible for my own child there, although I would look out for the others.'*

In the close the adults can take some joint responsibility for what happens. Georgia's parents consider the close to be 'a safe environment'. It's not just the parents who help to create this atmosphere: the older children are genuinely interested in including a younger child in their play.

## How Georgia's home affects her development and learning

The physical layout of the close enables each family to observe what other families are doing when they come out of their houses or when they look out of a window which faces the close. In a small close like this, the various activities of the people seem to take precedence over everything else. The layout of the houses in a circle facing in helps to foster a spirit of a community among the people who live there. Going out into the close enables Georgia, not only to get to know the people, but also to begin to understand the 'social meanings' of the cultural context in which the family live (Blanck, 1990).

Georgia is the firstborn child in her family and, therefore, it is fairly quiet in her house. However, step outside the front door and there is a great deal of stimulation, mostly from the people who live in the close. Georgia gains knowledge early on about the latest trends, for example, friendship bracelets and braids. She knows about the games currently being played, for example 'tig'. At 3 years 7 months she listens carefully to what the older children tell her.

*Georgia plays with older children out in the close*

*Georgia has had two friendship bracelets on for about two weeks now. They're the current trend – Nicola made them for her. When she came in with them on she said,'have to keep them on at bath time, shower time, bed time and all the time. Them allowed wet, them just dry.' Obviously trying to repeat what Nicola had told her.*
(Parent Diary)

# WHO GEORGIA KNOWS

## Attachment

Georgia gets to know her immediate family (mum and dad), extended family – grandparents, aunt and uncle – and the people who live in the close. She is very closely attached to her mum, dad, aunty Eloise and Jennifer. Jennifer is one of the 7-year-old twins, who live next door but one. Attachment to important people 'spells security' for Georgia (Schaffer, 1995).

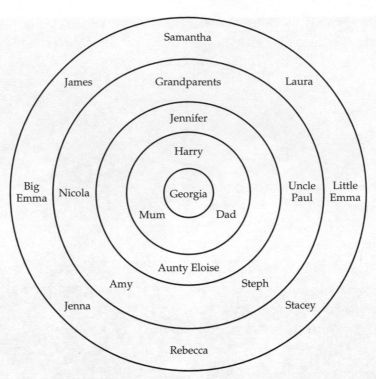

Adapted from Bronfenbrenner's Ecology of Human Development (Henry, 1996)

When Georgia learns to talk, she calls Eloise 'Aya', her maternal uncle Paul 'Pob', Jennifer 'Gaga' and Amy (the other twin) 'Meemy'. She also attempts to say James (3 months her junior and living next door). She calls him 'Mem'. Pinker (1994) speculates that babies and young children communicate words connected to their interests just as adults do. The diagram above shows how closely attached Georgia is to the people in her life. So, Georgia is most closely attached to her parents and brother (when he is born) and merely acquainted with Samantha (who is placed in the outer circle of the diagram).

## Harry is born

When her brother, Harry, is born Georgia is 2 years 3 months old. She frequently engages in role play which includes babies and buggies. Georgia likes to be the 'mummy' or the 'baby'. Her role seems to depend on who else is playing. Faulkner (1995) describes George Herbert Mead's theory:

*He claimed that the experience of role-play and pretence in early childhood was vital for the development of the self.*

As well as getting to know those people with whom she has frequent, direct contact, Georgia is interested in and has knowledge of people her parents speak about but whom she sees rarely. When she was born her dad had worked at the same toy firm for over 10 years. He took her to the office when she was a baby. Georgia's dad's boss of 10 years gave Georgia what turned out to be a very special gift. It was a small cloth doll, wearing a velvet dress. She is called Nancy.

## Georgia and her transitional objects

Georgia becomes very attached to Nancy and soon will not go anywhere without her dummy and the doll. Dummy and Nancy become 'transitional objects' which she uses for comfort and security (Winnicott, 1975). Sometimes young children use inanimate objects such as blankets, cuddly toys or dummies for comfort in new situations or at times when they separate from the people to whom they are closely attached (Bowlby, 1991). It is as though having a familiar and loved object to cuddle helps Georgia to feel safe.

## Georgia uses role play

Georgia's dad leaves his firm and gets another job in a different toy company. Although she does not ever meet his new boss, Kai, Georgia incorporates him into her role play. This helps her to understand who Kai is. When she is 2 years 11 months Georgia chats to her grandmother:

> **Grandmother:** *'I must get ready for work soon.'*
> **Georgia:** *'Work . . . me been to daddy's work.'*
> **Gran:** *'Who was there?'*
> **Georgia:** *'Bill.'*
> **Gran:** *'Anyone else?'*
> **Georgia:** *'Kai's called the boss.'*
>
> *Later Eloise gave Georgia a small case with some things in. She carried it around for a while and then said 'This is a briefcase . . . me be the boss too.'*
> (Parent diary)

## Before Georgia was born

As well as being interested in people who she does not see but hears about, Georgia is also intrigued by family events that took place before her birth. At 2 years 5 months her favourite story is about the car crash her parents were involved in before she was born.

**Grandmother:** *'She wants to know what happened when Ian and Colette had a car accident. She can relate the story and likes to see the newspaper cutting of the crashed car. When they are out in the car, she says she is looking for the car that was involved in the accident. (Her mum explains that both cars were so broken they could not be used again).'*

## Looking back with Georgia's parents

Georgia's parents and her nursery worker talk together about her when she was 2 to 3 years old. Her mum describes Georgia as a 'people person'.

**Mum:** *'She is always interested in people and in what they are doing. Even on holiday she always seems to link up with other children. They are often older than her.'*

Her mum believes that at 2 or 3 years old Georgia played with children who were several years older because 'they let her have her own way'. The twins, for example, 'were into looking after babies'. Georgia could fulfil a role in their games. Schaffer (1996) says that for cognitive (intellectual) change to occur, although there is no conclusive evidence yet, it seems that 'at younger ages children require a person of greater competence than themselves' while 'later on, a person of equal or even lesser capability will suffice'. Gradually Georgia begins to play with children nearer her own age.

**Mum:** *'She began playing with Samantha at around three or four and Big Emma at five or six.'*

Georgia's dad sees Georgia at 7 years as being very like the twins (Jennifer and Amy) were at the same age.

**Dad:** *'Georgia likes older girls or babies – she loves to play with James' baby cousin.'*

The other children that Georgia meets are the children of her parents' friends, some of whom begin playgroup and nursery when she does.

# How people affect Georgia's development and learning

It is difficult to work out whether Georgia was born 'a people person' or becomes 'a people person' because of her early experiences. Research into temperament indicates that some children tend to be high on 'sociability' (Buss and Plomin, 1984). It appears that the important factor is the 'goodness of fit between the child's temperament and the context in which the child finds itself' (Oates, 1994). Georgia, who is sociable, seeks out and reacts positively towards other people. If people respond to this sociability, then Georgia will continue to be sociable.

The 'goodness of fit', in this case, is between Georgia's personality and the context in which she has the opportunity to get to know the range of people of varying ages and interests.

Her attachments to the people in the close as well as to her extended family, offer her a great deal of stability and security. This is a predictable environment for her and one that stays the same throughout other changes in her life. She is 7 years old and the same people are all still living there.

## Georgia and her role models

Georgia gets ideas about what she wants to do from the people she knows. She seems to build up a story of her own possible future by using people she admires as role models. For example, Jennifer and Amy have been going to gymnastics for as long as Georgia has known them. She spends a lot of time trying out handstands and other movements that they have been practising in the close. Georgia begins a gymnastic class when she is old enough.

At 2 years 11 months Georgia speaks confidently about going to school.

> **Georgia:** *'When me five or six me go to school with Amy, Jennifer and Nicola, same school.'*

Georgia seems to choose others to play with when she and they are at a similar stage developmentally, or when they have shared interests. She and Samantha gravitate towards one another when Georgia is 3 years 6 months and Samantha is 5 years. Both are interested in drawing and writing. The three months between Georgia and James seems a big age gap until both children are 4 years old. He is physically taller than her and both children are riding two wheeled bicycles. They swap bikes and race against each other.

# WHERE GEORGIA GOES

Georgia's mum likes to go out each day so, over time, she adopts a routine. She might go to her local under-fives centre (to attend groups, baby massage or drop-in), visit or be visited by friends, shop or go to see Georgia's grandparents. At weekends Georgia might be taken to the zoo, a local park or go swimming.

Before Harry is born, the family go on holiday to Tenerife and twice to Majorca. The holiday photographs show that on each holiday Georgia makes friends with other children and adults.

## Looking back with Georgia's parents

Her dad cannot remember Georgia having particular preferences for places. He can remember that she 'loved Wicksteed Park, especially the swings. We used to go there every week.' When her brother is being born, her grandmother and uncle take her to Wicksteed Park and push her on the swings because they know they can keep her happy and amused there.

> **Mum:** *'She liked going to people's houses. She liked being with people.' I never worried about what she would be like in public – she was always good.'*

(Her mum explains that Georgia was always well-behaved and happy when she was with people outside her immediate family.)

Georgia's parents take her swimming occasionally.

> **Dad:** *'She always loved the water – she spent half of her life in the bath or at the sink.'*

## How going places affects Georgia's development and learning

### Going to the shops

When Georgia is around 2 years, she spends a lot of time playing with money, dishing out 'tickets' and playing shops. Although shopping, to her parents, is routine, Georgia seems to learn a great deal from her trips to the shops. Her early understanding that 20p buys her a ride on a toy train at the supermarket, prompts her to call a 20p coin a 'choo choo'.

*Georgia's dad says that she loves playing with and in water!*

## Going to the creche

When her mum attends groups at the under-fives centre, Georgia goes to the creche. This gives her a new experience with different people, away from the familiarity of the close. Often she is with children she knows well – the children of her parents' friends. Attending creche helps Georgia to trust that her mum will come back for her and also helps her to learn a sense of what a 'couple of hours' means. A creche session is one and a half hours long.

## Going to the playgroup

Several of the children from the creche start playgroup at the same time. Georgia is familiar with the physical layout of the building, so 'playgroup' is not a strange, new place – it is very close to the creche which she knows well. Her transition to playgroup seems to be smooth, possibly because she understands what happens and knows several other children. Georgia begins attending playgroup five mornings a week when she is 2 years 7 months. Each session lasts 2 hours.

# GEORGIA'S PLAY

## Georgia's interests

Georgia is 3 years 7 months when she starts nursery. The chart below shows her main interests at home and at nursery and is based on observations made around the time of starting nursery.

| WHAT GEORGIA DOES | WHO WITH? | WHERE? |
|---|---|---|
| Plays on the rocking-horse | Alone or with Harry | Nursery |
| Playing with water | Alone or with children outside | Home |
| Using dough or clay | Alongside peers | Nursery |
| Playing with dolls | Alone or with Jennifer and Harry | Home |
| Taking part in role play | With Big Emma or Harry | Home |
| | With Steph, Laura and Harry or with peers | Family Room* Nursery (occasionally) |
| Drawing and writing | With Samantha or older children | Home |
| | Alongside peers or adults | Nursery |
| Listening to stories | With adults | Home |
| | With adults | Nursery |
| Using the computer | With adults | Grandparents' house |
| | With adults | Nursery |
| Painting | With older children or Harry | Home |
| | With peers | Nursery |
| Sticking/collage | Alone or with Harry | Home |
| | With Steph, Emma and Laura | Nursery |
| Building/using construction materials | Alone or with Harry | Home or at grandparents' |
| | Alone or with Steph | Nursery |
| Woodwork | Alongside adult | Nursery |

| WHAT GEORGIA DOES | WHO WITH? | WHERE? |
|---|---|---|
| Playing outside with bikes, trailers and climbing equipment | Children in close | Home |
| | Steph, Laura and others | Nursery |

\* The Family Room is a room at the under-fives centre. Families can drop in and stay as long as they wish. There are toys for the children, drinks and sometimes lunch.

While this table cannot give a completely comprehensive list, it does show where Georgia makes links between what she does at home and what she chooses at nursery.

Shortly after Georgia starts nursery, her mum begins evening work. This change knocks her confidence a little – Chapter 6 describes how Georgia deals with change and uncertainty.

## Looking back with Georgia's Parents

### Different things to do

Georgia's dad is struck by his observation that she seems to do 'different things in different places'. He wonders '. . . maybe she categorised them.'

> **Mum:** *'Was she using nursery for things she did not get at home or in the Family Room?'*

### Different people

Role play seems to be the predominant play both at home and in the Family Room, where the children who play together are from a wider age range. Often games are initiated by the older children in the group. Maybe at home in the close, older children initiate games, and in the Family Room, Georgia, as one of the older children there, can take the lead? Her mum is certain that '. . . she does get something from playing with older children.' The size of the group may influence what happens. In the close, there are usually five or six children playing together. In the Family Room, it is probably about the same number or less. In nursery, about 35 children attend each session. Although there is plenty of space and 'cosy areas' have been created in which children can develop more complex play, (Bruner, 1980), Georgia is new to nursery and may feel more secure near an adult. It may not be a coincidence that she frequently chooses to have stories and to go on the computer, as each guarantees having an adult alongside.

When Georgia does move away from adults, she is usually alongside Steph and other children she knows from creche and playgroup.

### Making links

When Georgia plays with blocks she seems prepared to build alone or with a partner. Her dad recalls that, as a baby, Georgia played for long periods with her babywalker and blocks. She may find playing with maple blocks intrinsically more satisfying than other lone activities.

## Bringing experiences from home to nursery

### Trying new experiences

Getting to know the people and how things work seems to be important for Georgia at nursery. She is not always prepared to try out something new without first observing what happens. For example, although she has been massaged by her mum since she was a baby, when foot massage is offered in nursery, she is most comfortable observing Steph having her feet massaged before taking part herself.

### Learning the system

Georgia very quickly understands the system for getting a turn on the computer. There is a book in which an adult (or the child) writes the child's name. You are called when it is your turn. Adults try not to limit children's learning by deciding how long each child needs on the computer. Georgia understands taking turns. Some of the street games in which Georgia has participated use turn-taking. Taking turns physically precedes the abstract idea of being in a queue which is written down in a book.

Going out on the minibus is organised in a similar way. Adults or children write down the names of the children who want to go out on the minibus in a special book. If your name is down and there is not room, you get a turn the next time there is a trip. Again, Georgia very quickly works out the system.

### Having a laugh

Although Georgia likes to be alongside familiar people and to know what is going to happen next, one of the exciting things about people is their unpredictability. Georgia is also excited and attracted by this unpredictability. She likes to watch and sometimes do things which are slightly risque. She loves to have fun and to laugh raucously. Whereas at home she might be instigating the laughter by deliberately saying something funny or humorous, at nursery she is more likely to be watching and listening.

### Georgia's Family Worker

Georgia's nursery has a Key Worker system (Whalley, 1997). Alison is Georgia's Family Worker. Alison visited Georgia and her family at home prior to Georgia starting nursery and Georgia is in Alison's 'group' at nursery. Once Georgia has established that there is a regular, predictable routine whereby she joins her Family Group for the last 20 minutes each day, she begins to choose to go with different Family Workers. This is a sign of being settled and wanting to explore what happens in other Family Groups.

## Different equipment

There is a great deal of equipment out of doors at nursery for children to extend their development and learning (there are co-operative vehicles and trailers as well as climbing equipment). Georgia makes good use of the equipment. She enjoys the trailers at nursery so much that her parents buy her a trailer for Christmas.

Georgia's transition from home to nursery is a gradual one, involving brief sessions spent in creche, then a year in playgroup before joining nursery. During her year at playgroup Georgia tries to master the monkey bars (in the playgroup playground). This is adjacent to the nursery playground and is used by nursery children and staff too. Georgia is able to continue her strive to master the monkey bars while she is at nursery.

*Getting to grips with the monkey bars*

## SUMMARY

- When Georgia is born, her family live in a small, intimate close.

- Georgia gets to know several people who are important to her.

- Georgia's transition to nursery is via creche and playgroup, which are situated on the same site.

We have been introduced to Georgia and the people who are important to her. In the next chapter we shall begin to look at her from many different angles – through different theories and how what she does links with research. We shall begin to see how we can assess and evaluate what she is learning and the implications this has for the way we work with children and their families.

# 2 EARLY CHILDHOOD EDUCATION, CARE AND TRADITIONS

*'I dunno,' Arthur said, 'I forgot what I was taught. I only remember what I've learnt.'*
(White in Cohen, 1993)

*Not enough attention is paid to how children learn most effectively and consequently how teachers can teach most effectively.*
(Athey, 1990)

Whether the 'teacher' is a parent, health visitor or classroom assistant, their aim is generally to help children to learn effectively. The ways in which adults have a shared view of children and the childhood they want for them, may be a suitable starting point for thinking about Georgia and how she learns. Learning and teaching are inextricably linked together.

- **Different views of Georgia** – looking at Georgia through the theories of Piaget, Vygotsky and in the light of current research of Laevers, Goleman, Gardner and neuroscientists.

- **Assessing what Georgia is learning** – seeing her as a whole child, listening to her parents and gathering narrative observations of her spontaneous actions.

- **Analysing observations** – by using AIRSS (autonomy, involvement, relationships, schemas and strategies: Arnold, 1997) or by using traditional subject areas.

- **Staff training** – linking theory and practice, developing skills in gathering and analysing narrative observations.

## VIEWS OF EARLY CHILDHOOD

We can look at Georgia through various different theoretical perspectives. Both Piaget and Vygotsky were born in 1896, so their's are not new ideas. However, aspects of their original theories, which we can use in trying to understand Georgia's learning, continue to influence and to be developed by others.

# Jean Piaget

Piaget had a background in genetic epistemology (how knowledge grows), so it is not surprising that he began his investigations by observing his own three children in naturally occurring situations, in exactly the same way that he might have observed shellfish in their natural habitats! In his early work, Piaget did not set up experimental situations. These early naturalistic observations were the basis for formulating his theories.

## Piaget's major ideas

1 Knowledge is constructed by the learner.
2 Learners pass through stages of development.
3 Children display **schemas** (or patterns of behaviour) that are generalisable.
4 Development from one stage to the next occurs through processes that Piaget calls **assimilation**, **accommodation** and **equilibration**.

## Knowledge is constructed by the learner

Piaget would argue that Georgia's knowledge is not necessarily transmitted from someone else to her. Georgia's learning is an *active* process during which she constructs knowledge from her own firsthand experiences. When Georgia asks a question about something she desperately wants to understand, it is not simply a question of her parents responding to her question and transferring their knowledge to her. For example, when Georgia is 2 years 7 months, she watches some rabbits in a hutch outside. It is pouring with rain and she says repeatedly, 'Rabbits get wet?'. Her mum explains that they are inside the hutch and the rain does not go through. It is not until months later, that Georgia displays her understanding of *how* the roof protects the rabbits from the rain. We see how she does this in the next section.

## Learners pass through stages of development

Piaget is famous for his stage theory. Georgia, he would suggest, passes through stages of development and can only function at a higher level when she reaches that particular stage of development. He would say that her intellectual development is taking place in four major periods:

1 **Sensorimotor** (from birth to 2 years).
2 **Preoperational** (2 to 7 years).
3 **Concrete operational** (7 to 11 years).
4 **Formal operational** (11 years and above).

Piaget suggests these as average ages at which transformations in intellectual functioning might take place. Piaget would expect Georgia to be active in constructing ideas through her own actions, which she later internalises as thoughts (Donaldson, 1978). Continuing the story above, at 2 years 7 months Georgia can see heavy rain pouring down and rabbits outside of the building in which she is physically dry. In order to understand the concept of covering in order to protect, Georgia actively explores getting wet and covering, or **enveloping**. Her development plays a role, in that she becomes able to combine more than one idea together at a time. Georgia also becomes interested in cause and effect, so pays attention to *how* the rabbits are protected from the heavy rain.

The ages at which Piaget suggested children pass through the four stages have been strongly challenged (Bruce, 1997). Donaldson's discovery that the problems children are presented with must be embedded in the context of their lives, was a real breakthrough and challenged all early childhood educators to consider children's knowledge in the context of their real lives (Donaldson, 1978).

## Children display schemas that are generalisable

Piaget's theory suggests that Georgia explores the world by trying out patterns of behaviour or schemas on everything she meets in her environment. She generalises new information into her current schemas. Schemas become co-ordinated into increasingly complex combinations. For example, we might consider Georgia's concern that the rabbits are getting wet from the heavy rain. Subsequently Georgia spends several months exploring an envelopment schema, covering objects with various materials in order to see what happens. Finally she understands how covering the rabbits with the roof protects them from the rain. Then Georgia begins to notice how a gap in the covering allows some materials to go through the covering. She is sensitive to and explores ideas about going through and is able to adapt her current schema to include these new ideas (see Chapter Five for a more extensive explanation).

## An aside – schemas

Piaget's research on schemas has been developed by a number of people in the last 30 years (Nicholls, 1986; Athey, 1990; Arnold, 1990; Shaw, 1991; Nutbrown, 1994; Matthews, 1994; Meade with Cubey, 1995; Rice, 1996; Arnold, 1997; Bruce, 1997). Schemas are patterns of behaviour which children try out on everything they come across in their environment. Bruce (1997) says that,

*Schemas are part of human development, from birth to death, but they are not in a constant state. They are always adjusting and changing in the light of experience. This is why they are such powerful learning mechanisms.*

When we are trying to identify children's schemas it is helpful to look at current research findings. In a study of four children over 18 months, the aspects of schemas observed in all four children were ranked from the most to least frequently observed (Arnold, 1997). Each schema is accompanied by a brief explanation:

### Most frequently observed

- **Envelopment** – enveloping, covering or surrounding oneself, an object or a space.
- **Trajectory** – moving in or representing straight lines, arcs or curves.
- **Enclosure** – enclosing oneself, an object or a space.
- **Transporting** – carrying objects or being carried from one place to another.
- **Connection** – an interest in connecting themselves to objects and objects to each other.
- **Rotation** – turning, twisting or rolling oneself or objects in the environment around.
- **Going through a boundary** – causing oneself or material or an object to go through a boundary and emerge at the other side.
- **Oblique trajectory** – moving in, using or drawing oblique lines.
- **Containment** – putting materials inside an object which is capable of containing them.
- **Transformation** – transforming oneself by dressing differently or being interested in changes in state.

### Least frequently observed
Altogether 41 aspects of schemas were observed, but many were combinations and co-ordinations of those listed above.

Schemas are explored in different ways. They can be **dynamic** (moving like a piece of video) or **configurative** (still like a photograph) (Bruce, 1997). They also function at different levels:

- **Sensori motor level** – through the senses, actions and movement.

- **Symbolic level** – making something stand for something else.

- **Cause and effect** – sometimes called **functional dependency** (if I do this, then that will happen).

- **Abstract thought level** – when there is increasing understanding of reversibility and transformations and a co-ordinated understanding of these.

The advantage of using schemas as observation tools is that we do not need to know the theory in great depth to begin spotting patterns of behaviour and extending our provision accordingly. We can begin by reflecting back to children what we have observed. For example, Georgia's Family Worker might say to her, 'I see you are covering your babies to keep them warm and dry'. We could offer her different coverings and watch what she does with them.

## Assimilation, accommodation and equilibration

Piaget's explanation is that, as Georgia tries out her current schemas on objects in the environment, she assimilates new content into her current structures. When she comes across something that will not fit into that structure, she accommodates the new information by changing the structure and, in doing this, reaches a kind of equilibrium. For example, when Georgia becomes 3 years old, she counts 1, 2, 3 and says she is 3. The number '3' is a label. Her age is, to her, synonymous with her name. She assimilates the information that she 'is 3' into her current 'naming of age' structure. Some months later, her friend Stephanie, has her fourth birthday. Georgia is concerned and puzzled that her friend becomes 4 years old before her. Her current 'naming of age' structure does not explain why her friend suddenly has a different age label to hers. She frequently asks why Steph is 4 years old before she is. Her mum explains many times that Steph was born before she was and that Steph has lived longer. Georgia asks the same questions repeatedly over several months. Finally she accommodates the information by changing her structure from a 'naming of age' structure to include a 'lived age' structure and reaches a sort of equilibrium or balance.

The urge to explore the world in this way is a biological one. The content or experiences through which Georgia learns, depends on the culture or community in which she is born and raised. The concern with the influence of culture is Vygotskerian.

# Lev Vygotsky

Vygotsky was the second of eight children born to a Jewish family in Russia in 1896. It is probably not a coincidence that his main concern was with the social context of learning.

## Vygotsky's major theories

1   Children develop by interacting with other people.
2   There is a **zone of proximal** (or **potential**) **development** within which children can function at a higher level with help.
3   Children develop **spontaneous concepts** before learning **scientific concepts**.

## Children develop by interacting with other people

Vygotsky believes that social interaction is the force that drives intellectual development. He sees social interaction as the source of development. He would say that Georgia 'internalises' the conversations she has had with others (Flanagan, 1996). At first Georgia speaks to herself out loud, but eventually, this kind of 'self-talk' becomes her thinking. An example of this is Georgia's early repetition of the sorts of things she has heard her parents say in shops and at the park. During her own play, she repeats these phrases for example, 'Pay the man', 'pay 60' and 'I don't know if I've got 60'. Through using these phrases in her play she converts them into her own language, which she can use to think.

## There is a zone of proximal development

Vygotsky puts a great deal of emphasis on the role of the adult or older child who, by instruction and support, guides children to achieve at a higher level than they would alone. The zone of proximal development (Moll, 1990) is the area of nearest potential development for a child. So, with help and guidance, Georgia can tackle things that are a challenge to her, but that are still connected to her earlier learning. When Georgia is interested in size and fit, her mum helps her to measure a picture for framing. Gradually, over time, Georgia learns to do this accurately without help.

## Spontaneous and scientific concepts

Vygotsky puts forward the idea that concepts develop as a result of children's experience in the world. He refers to these as spontaneous concepts. He emphasises that scientific concepts must be taught. So, only when Georgia has learned through experience and been taught systematically will she gain **true concepts** (Au, 1990). Vygotsky believes that instruction precedes development (Vygotsky, 1962; Daniels, 1996). For example, when Georgia looks at books about pregnancy and her parents explain what will happen when her sibling is born, she is receiving 'instruction'. But Georgia does not grasp the full concept until she has experienced related spontaneous concepts and is developmentally mature enough to understand how a baby is born. (See Chapter Five for a full explanation of Georgia's explorations.)

Piaget and Vygotsky look at different aspects of learning and teaching. The theories they each develop are not necessarily in opposition to each other. Piaget leaves us with the view of Georgia as a **lone explorer** constructing knowledge for herself. He is not explicit about the role of her parents, teachers or care workers. The danger in taking a Piagetian approach is in being too laissez-faire, that is, structuring the environment with resources but paying little attention to the interactions with and between Georgia and other children within that environment.

Vygotsky's emphasis leaves us with the view of Georgia as a **social being** who learns through her interactions with other people. The danger in taking a Vygotskerian approach is that the adult may dominate with ideas and instruction. This is particularly inappropriate during the early years when Georgia needs to initiate her own learning (Bruce, 1997).

Other than the fundamentally different ideas, that 'actions become thoughts' (Piaget) and 'conversations become thoughts' (Vygotsky), we can apply both Piagetian theory and Vygotskerian theory to our work with Georgia. In fact, using aspects of both theories to help her learn creates a balanced approach. We need to remember that both actions and conversations are important to Georgia as she learns. Bruce (1997) supports the idea that 'there are two aspects of a child's development: the **biological path** and the **socio-cultural path**.'

## Current views of early childhood

In this section we shall see how the work of Ferre Laevers, Daniel Goleman, Howard Gardner and recent research by several neuroscientists can help us to make sense of Georgia's learning.

### Ferre Laevers

Laevers has been working at Leuven University in Belgium for more than 20 years on a 'process–oriented child monitoring system' (Laevers, 1995). In carrying out this work, and drawing on the theories of both Piaget and

Vygotsky, Laevers has developed two tools for monitoring how and when children are developing and learning. Laevers says:

> For development to occur, children need to be high on 'emotional well-being' and high on 'involvement'.

## Emotional well-being

Well-being can be characterised by:

- openness and receptivity
- flexibility
- self-confidence and self-esteem
- assertiveness
- vitality
- relaxation and inner peace
- enjoyment
- the child feeling connected and in touch with herself.

## Involvement

Signs of involvement are:

- concentration
- energy
- complexity and creativity
- facial expression and composure
- persistence
- precision
- reaction time
- verbal expression
- satisfaction.

Involvement is about the *quality* of activity not the *contents* (Laevers, 1997). Highly involved human beings 'feel intrinsically motivated to carry on because the activity falls in with what they want to learn and know, i.e. their exploratory drive . . .' Linked with the ability to be highly involved intellectually, is the need for emotional well-being. The idea of emotional well-being as a concern of teachers, nursery nurses, parents or health visitors is not a new one, but has recently been highlighted in the work of Laevers and also of Daniel Goleman in the USA.

## Daniel Goleman

Daniel Goleman emphasises 'emotional intelligence'. He would focus on the all round ability of Georgia, particularly in terms of her knowing 'how to learn'. He says,

> . . . *success in school depends to a surprising extent on emotional characteristics formed in the years before a child enters school.*
> (Goleman, 1996)

Goleman lists seven ingredients that contribute to a child's ability to know how to learn:

- Confidence
- Curiosity
- Intentionality
- Self-control
- Relatedness
- Capacity to communicate
- Co-operativeness.

Georgia's parents intuitively know that it is important for her to become independent and to learn to make friends in her early years. Starting nursery or going into childcare provision is, as it is for many children, her first step on the road to becoming independent.

## Howard Gardner

Gardner has put forward a theory of multiple intelligences. His theory is that there are at least 'seven ways of knowing the world' (Gardner, 1991). People learn in many different ways and may favour one way rather than another. The learning paths he has identified operate through:

- language
- logical, mathematical representation
- spatial representation
- musical thinking
- the use of the body to solve problems or to make things
- an understanding of other individuals
- an understanding of ourselves.

Gardner and his colleagues have devised an educational approach called **Project Spectrum**, which we can use to identify Georgia's talents and abilities and to build on them.

> *In a Spectrum classroom, children are surrounded each day by rich and engaging materials . . . there is a naturalist's corner . . . a storytelling area . . . a building corner . . . Numerous other intelligences, and combinations of intelligences, are tapped in the remaining dozen areas and activities . . .*
> (Gardner, 1991)

The Spectrum team feel it is important for children to be alongside adults or older children. Georgia would benefit from such an environment. It would encourage her to be both a Piagetian 'explorer' and a Vygotskerian 'apprentice'.

### Recent research by neuroscientists

The importance of the early years has recently been confirmed by the findings of a number of neuroscientists. The discovery that the brain develops at an alarming rate shortly after birth, means that this 'sensitive period' is a time when all children, including Georgia, need stimulation (Barnes, 1995). At birth, children's brains have a surplus of neurons and only those that make connections (or synapses) survive.

> *. . . the number of connections (synapses) between neurons . . . are thought to be crucial to the integrity and complexity of information processing in the brain.*
> (Oates, 1994)

Babies are born with great potential for learning and it is the environment in which they are brought up that provides the stimulation for what they learn.

Susan Greenfield (1997) says,

> *In the brain, then, activity and growth go hand in hand: it is not only a question of 'use it or lose it' but 'use it as much as you can'.*

Nash (1997) confirms the need for young children to explore, when she says,

> *Rich experiences really do produce rich brains.*

# ASSESSING WHAT GEORGIA IS LEARNING

*Our nets define what we will catch.*
(Eisner, 1985)

The views of childhood that we have been considering seem to indicate that Georgia is a unique individual, who learns in many different ways. Our way of assessing her learning needs to be equally comprehensive. In fact, Georgia makes this a fairly straightforward task. She does not respond well to experiments, and observation of her actions in the normal course of events seems to be the only option.

## Observing Georgia

We (as workers and parents) could decide to focus on particular aspects of Georgia's learning, for example, her conversation or what she does out of doors. We would make notes whenever conversation or outdoor play occurred and, over time, assess aspects of Georgia's development or learning through her language or how she plays out of doors. However, by restricting our focus, we would miss a great deal of her development and learning. The essence of a **whole child approach** is that we really do not know what, how or where Georgia is going to develop and learn. So, we decide to record *whatever* Georgia does while we are observing, without analysing what we see. This means recording, as *accurately* and *precisely* as possible, without making judgements, the actions and language we observe and hear. There are several tools which we could choose to do this, for example:

- paper and pen
- dictaphone

- camera

- video camera.

Each tool has advantages and disadvantages and may tell us something different.

### Pen and paper

There is often too much happening to record in any detail – we may end up writing down only the essence of what we see. Conversations, in particular, are so fast that it is difficult to record everything said. As an observer, we will notice other things happening which may be significant. It can be an advantage to know what else is happening in the area surrounding the child who is the target of our observation. Events nearby can have an influence on what a target child does. Alternatively, if they have no influence, we can ignore the information.

### Dictaphone

A dictaphone is useful, but if we are physically close to Georgia, she may become interested in the dictaphone. (This may be true of any technological tool.) In one sense this does not matter, as the dictaphone can be regarded as fresh stimulation. Therefore, whatever Georgia does or says in connection with the tool, becomes the focus.

### Camera

A camera takes one or several snapshots, which just capture a moment in time unless we add contextual information.

### Video

A video camera preserves what happens, but all we capture is what is in focus at the time of recording. There is, however, the possibility of using the video material as a stimulus to help Georgia and her parents recall what else happened both on and off camera. A set of video stills can illustrate a process.

Gathering information over time provides the raw data to make a formative assessment of Georgia's development and learning. The data, in all sorts of different forms, can be collected by professionals and by her parents. Georgia's Family Workers are trying to make connections with Georgia's home context, which makes learning at nursery more meaningful for her. Her parents are trying to ensure the best education and care for Georgia and their contribution to recordkeeping will make nursery better for her.

*A set of video stills can illustrate a process*

## Looking back with Georgia's parents

Georgia's parents are the true experts on Georgia (Whalley, 1997). It is, therefore, crucial that professionals working with Georgia listen to her parents. Parents and workers can share information about what she says and does, during informal daily chats. It will also be important for professionals working with Georgia to ask her parents for more detailed feedback about what she does at home. Georgia's parents kept a diary for 18 months of some of her actions and language at home.

### What to record

One difficulty is what to record. Georgia's parents were asked to gather a **time sample** (Webb, 1975), that is, to record whatever happened during a 20 minute period, once a week. They were also asked to record anything they found 'curious' or 'interesting' that Georgia did or said. The information her parents recorded, along with the record of what and who Georgia played with at nursery formed the basis for further discussion and analysis.

### Involving parents

More recently, as part of the *Parents' Involvement in Their Children's Learning* project (funded by the Esmee Fairbairn Trust) parents are being asked to write down or video what their children are doing when they are 'deeply involved' (Laevers, 1995). This project seems to be capturing the essence of what children are interested in and motivated to do at home.

Piaget's early work on schemas was superbly developed during the 1970s by the Froebel team who were working in partnership with parents. Identifying children's schemas and providing content and language to extend each identified 'form' or schema was the main focus of the project (Athey, 1990).

Athey reports.

*A genuine 'open-ended' type of enquiry was encouraged with everyone working together to find patterns of cognition.*

If a truly collaborative approach is fostered, then there will be benefits for Georgia, her parents and the professionals who work with her. Athey believes 'the greatest benefit to teachers in working with parents is the spur towards making their own pedagogy more conscious and explicit'. The process of sharing information about learning, helps professionals to articulate with more clarity their ideas about teaching Georgia.

When we listen to Georgia's parents, we not only gain valuable information about the place, events and the people with whom she spends most of her time, but we also convey hidden messages about valuing each parent's contribution to her education. Acknowledging and being interested in Georgia's experiences at home means being interested in her whole educational experience.

## Gathering narrative observations

There is a long tradition of gathering narrative observations in early childhood education (Bartholomew and Bruce, 1993). Bartholomew and Bruce say that,

*Narrative records keep emphasising strengths, while pre-structured record forms can quickly lead to a focus on weakness, failure and 'can't do'.*

Observations such as those made by Piaget (1951) of his own children give us a glimpse of the rich complexity of what happened in their learning and development.

For example,

*At 3 [years]; 3 [months] J asked her first question about birth in the shape of a query as to where L came from (L was 1 [year]; 8 [months]): 'Daddy where did you find the little baby in a cradle? – Which baby? – Nonette (i.e. L).' My reply was simply that mummy and daddy had given her a little sister. At 3 [years]; 6 [months] she touched her grandmother's eyes, nose, etc., and said to her: 'Is that how grannies are made? Did you make yourself?' And later: 'Did she make herself? What made her?' The same evening, when looking at L: 'Why do they have little hands, little teeth, little eyes, a little mouth?'*

Piaget's concern is to discover what J is thinking about and wanting to discover. He makes links, over time, between her spontaneous enquiries.

Susan Isaacs ran an experimental school in Cambridge for 3 years during the 1920s. Her work continues to influence ideas about early childhood education today. She and her staff kept extensive narrative records of what happened in the Malting House School and some of the parents kept records of what their children did and said at home. This is a sample (1966):

*17.2.25. One of the children stood on a chair, and said, 'I'm taller than you' to the others. They all of them then got on chairs, and Frank and Christopher both said they were taller than Dan. Dan [3 years, 9 months] then said to Frank, 'Yes we are taller than Christopher, aren't we?' (Dan being much the smallest of the three.)*

Susan Isaacs' concern was to encourage the children in her school to develop their own interests in the fullest way.

Gathering observations in this way is like being a reporter who writes down or films whatever happens. The focus is on the *here* and *now*.

# ANALYSING OBSERVATIONS

*But most by numbers judge a poet's song:*
*And smooth or rough with them, is right or wrong:*
(Pope, 1985)

By analysing observations we show the progress that Georgia makes in her learning. At this point, we may want to consider **normative development** or what is considered 'normal' for most children of the same age (Oates, 1994). We must not allow normative goals to limit what Georgia does and what we record about Georgia's learning. There can be a tendency, when considering norms to see them as *outcomes to be achieved* and to judge what Georgia does as right or wrong in this context. Achievement at any given moment must not be confused with *ability*. A full record gathered over time gives us information about Georgia's experience of specific subject areas, as well as information about her particular interests and her 'dispositions', such as curiosity (Katz, 1993). One observation gives us only a limited amount of information about Georgia. It is a sort of snapshot of her. However, even a snapshot can be analysed in more than one way. This section shows how we can analyse one day's observation from home in two different ways.

> *Georgia (3 years 7 months) has a roll of sellotape which she has really enjoyed playing with lately. She has been cutting off different length strips and sticking them, randomly, onto paper.*
>
> *Georgia has been jumping up trying to reach things – still doing things with tiptoes and without. A couple of times, she has also got inside a pillowcase and jumped out.*
>
> *Georgia is still <u>obsessed</u> with time – how long it takes to get places – how long until something happens. It does not seem to matter whether it is a long time or not. She is already picking the watch she wants from Argos and trying to tell the time.*
> (Parent Diary)

## Introducing analysis according to AIRSS

**AIRSS** stands for: **Autonomy**, **Involvement**, **Relationships**, **Schemas** and **Strategies** (Arnold, 1997).

The AIRSS tool has evolved from considering Georgia's learning and examines:

- how Georgia chooses and acts independently, therefore displaying self-government or autonomy (Dweck and Leggett, 1988; Whalley, 1994)

- Georgia's inner state of involvement (Laevers, 1995)

- who she interacts with and the nature of the interactions or relationships (Pollard, 1996)

- Georgia's repeated patterns of behaviour or schema (Piaget, 1951; Athey, 1990)

- how she approaches new situations and people. These are her strategies (Nisbet and Shucksmith, 1986; Pollard, 1996)

## Autonomy
Georgia seems to be *choosing* to do what she does with the sellotape, as well as *choosing* which watch she wants from Argos. She has decided which materials to play with and how she uses the materials.

## Involvement
The tone of the parent observations indicates Georgia's *intrinsic motivation* to use sellotape, jump to reach and ask questions about time.

## Relationships
There is no record of play with peers although the observations indicate a good relationship with her parents. (That is, she is able to explore and practise as well as ask questions.)

## Schemas
All three observations indicate an interest in trajectory behaviour (see page 22). In the first, she is using different *lengths* of sellotape; in the second, she is using her body to reach an increased *height*; in the third she is interested in the *duration* or *length of time* until something happens. Georgia is using her trajectory schema at a sensori-motor level (see page 23) when cutting the sellotape and jumping. She is using her trajectory schema at a cause and effect level when jumping to reach, that is, 'if I jump higher, I will reach a higher point'. She is moving towards Abstract thought level when asking about duration of time (understanding the duration of time involves holding in mind a sort of line from one point in time to another point in time). Like Athey in some of the observations gathered in the Froebel project, in the absence of clues from Georgia, we cannot tell whether or not she is functioning at a symbolic level (making one thing stand for another).

## Strategies
Georgia seems to be using *spontaneous activity* and *asking questions* as her two main strategies.

# Analysis according to the traditional subject areas

### Communication, language and literacy

Georgia is asking questions to gain information about time. She is interested in cracking the code which will enable her to read number symbols and tell the time.

### Mathematical understanding

Georgia is exploring ideas about length, height and duration. Her parents have not included the specific language she uses, although she is involved in practical activities that are mathematical. She is asking questions about time and distance.

### Scientific understanding

Georgia is exploring the properties of matter, in this case the stickiness of the sellotape. She displays scientific curiosity (a disposition which helps her to learn) in relation to understanding time as a concept.

### Personal and social development

Georgia is eager to explore and initiate new ideas. This is indicated by her enjoyment when playing with the sellotape, her pursuit of jumping up and her obsession with time.

# IMPLICATIONS FOR STAFF TRAINING

As professionals and parents, we may find it helpful to discuss what kind of childhood we want for the children in our care. Most adults have had some positive experiences and some less positive to inform their views. The focus for a parents' evening could be a discussion of 'The Education We Want for Our Children'.

## Stating our principles

It is helpful to examine our principles, that is, what we and the parents of the children we work with, see as important. Bruce et al (1995) say that it is 'when theory and educational principles interact' that 'practice makes progress'. It is a question of looking out at the world and considering the theories and practice of others, whilst making explicit our own underlying principles about young children.

There are several ways of finding out about current theories:

- reading education, health and research journals
- visiting other settings in this country and abroad
- going on courses and to conferences
- undertaking education or training which links with the work that we do.

## Sharing ideas

Within a group of staff, it can be quite difficult for any one individual to exert influence on the group to effect changes in practice. The vision needs to be a shared one. Therefore, inviting a trainer to work with the group, might be the most effective way of improving practice.

It is increasingly recognised that some regular non-contact time is central to work in any early years setting if quality is to be maintained. Time in which to analyse and discuss observations and to make home visits is an important part of the work.

Home visiting forms a major part of some professionals' work while others might need training to undertake home visits. For example, health visitors carry out most of their work in family homes, whereas some teachers might find it daunting to visit children at home. Some cross fertilisation of ideas might be productive. Teachers might feel confident to share their ideas about theories and principles of education with health visitors, while health visitors might be able to offer reassurance and support with home visiting. Practitioners, who have undertaken CACHE/NNEB training, usually have a good grounding in writing observations. This is a skill which can be shared with other colleagues and parents.

## Gathering narrative observations

Making good observations is a skill that we can improve by practising. Showing every written observation of Georgia to her parents, not only improves our expressive writing skills, but raises out awareness of how it reads to her parents. Rich descriptions of Georgia's actions and language, recorded in as much detail as possible, gives us raw data to analyse. Adding information about the surrounding context enhances the information. We will become more observant and better at predicting what will help Georgia next in her learning. We can improve our skills further by writing observations as often as we can, taking a number of children, who choose a variety of ways to learn, as subjects. Observations over time can be linked together to show progress or to produce a case study.

### Using a case study approach

Gathering observations of Georgia over a period of time can lead to a case study. It tells the story of her early childhood with information about different aspects of her life from different perspectives. The process of writing a case study of Georgia helps us to get to grips with the progress she makes and some of the challenges she faces. From these we can extract the appropriate information. Presenting a case study to colleagues is a brave thing to do – to invite comments and questions and then to rewrite on the basis of these, makes the analysis much stronger.

Georgia is a unique individual and when we observe we are learning how she learns. This is valuable work but remember that it can never be complete.

---

## SUMMARY

- Piaget's Georgia is a 'lone explorer', who constructs knowledge for herself.

- Vygotsky's Georgia is a 'social being', who learns in the context of her family.

- Current theories emphasise Georgia's well-being, involvement and individual approach to learning.

- Georgia's parents are the true experts on Georgia.

- Narrative observations of Georgia provide raw data for analysis and emphasise what Georgia can do.

- Workers and parents can develop a shared vision of the sort of education that they want for Georgia.

---

We have now been introduced to both the theories underpinning our work with Georgia and her family and to the importance of developing effective observation techniques. In the following chapter we are going to look at how Georgia learns to write and read.

# 3 GEORGIA LEARNS TO WRITE AND READ

*What we make available to the child is a central factor in what the child will and can do.*
(Kress, 1995)

*In school, literacy teaching and learning is largely overt and specific, whereas at home, it often occurs almost invisibly as an integral part of some everyday activities.*
(Weinberger, 1996)

---

This chapter describes:

● Georgia's emergent writing

● Georgia's emergent reading

● ideas for supporting literacy development at home, nursery or in reception classes.

---

From the moment Georgia's parents and Family Worker begin to keep records on her when she is 2 years old, Georgia is motivated to make marks, engage in role play and talk and listen. Her intrinsic motivation and spontaneous desire to engage with writing and reading is sparked off both by the resources available to her and the actions of the people she meets. We can trace the emergence of her writing through examining samples of the marks she makes over a period of time. These marks speak for themselves, offering us a record of Georgia's progress. However, the learning process which will eventually enable Georgia to read and write, begins long before she actually makes marks on paper.

## GEORGIA LEARNS TO WRITE

### Representation

When Georgia is 2 years 3 months old, 5 minutes after being given a present by her grandmother, she plays handing gifts to everyone at home.

*She said 'card', handing a pretend card and 'open it' and 'present', handing each person a bag. Looked very pleased when 'presents' were looked at and commented upon.*
(Parent Diary)

Although she does not make marks, she uses 'paper' and a 'bag' to stand for or **represent** a 'card' and 'gift'. She also uses these objects to communicate with each person in turn. There is an emotional response too, indicating the reciprocal nature of the interactions.

At 2 years 5 months, she is with Uncle Paul and plays with 'tickets' and real money, which she carries in a clutch bag. When her grandmother arrives home, she runs to the couch to get a picture for her.

**Grandmother**: *'She made a mark on it saying "write Mop". She gave me all of the tickets and talked about "paying". She gave me some money and expected me to give her some back.'*

At 2 years 5 months Georgia does some 'writing' for Eloise.

*Writing for Eloise*

The following month the family are on holiday in Cornwall. One day it rains heavily and Georgia becomes interested in watching the rain and the rabbits in a hutch outside. She does some writing and explains to her mum what her writing says. Then she asks her mum to write down the things that she says out loud.

## Writing and drawing

The family visit Georgia's great grandparents and she does a series of pictures for 'Nanny Bonan and Bic' (Nanny Bowman and Vic). She seems to differentiate between drawing and writing and also 'signs' some of her drawings.

At 2 years 7 months Georgia visits her grandmother's house. Her favourite Aunty, Eloise, is still asleep, so Georgia 'writes' her a note.

She explains what she would like to happen.

> **Georgia:** *'Eloise eyes open.'*

Georgia is attempting to communicate her wishes in a written form.

When Georgia is 2 years 8 months, it is her grandmother's birthday. She chooses a card, writes on it and puts it in an envelope. When her dad comes home, Georgia opens it.

> **Mum** (several times): *'It's for Mop's birthday!'*
> **Georgia:** *'Mine. Mine card. Mine birthday.'*

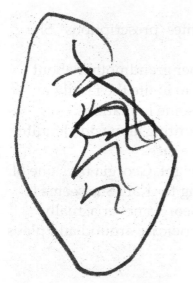

*Georgia drew an enclosure and some crosses. She also 'signed' her drawing 'For Nanny Bonan and Bic'*

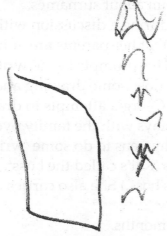

*Here Georgia has done some writing next to the enclosure*

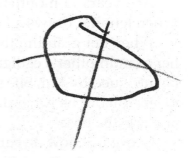

*Cross and enclosure*

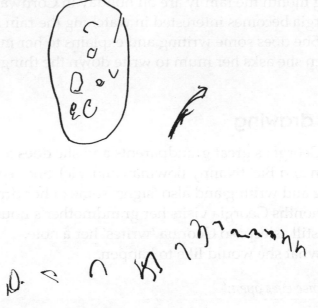

*Georgia's drawing of a Christmas tree, with writing along the bottom*

At this stage Georgia seems to enjoy the action of putting the card in an envelope, giving it to someone and getting some acknowledgement for her gift. She does not seem able to wait for her grandmother's birthday.

At 2 years 9 months, Georgia does some drawing and writing that is clearly differentiated. She drew a Christmas tree and wrote her grandmother's name at the bottom.

The following day, Georgia plays 'doctor's' and writes 'prescriptions'. She has a discussion with her mum about surnames.

A couple of weeks later, during a discussion with her grandmother about parties, Georgia remembers that her parents are going to invite the family to their house on Boxing Day. This prompts her to write some invitations.

At 2 years 11 months she does some drawing and writing alongside Jennifer. When Jennifer draws a face, Georgia attempts to draw a face.

When her grandmother stays with the family overnight, Georgia uses one of her grandmother's calligraphy pens to do some 'writing for Kai'. She seems to be intrigued by Kai. She says 'Kai's called the boss'. (Georgia never actually meets Kai but he is her dad's boss.) She also carries a briefcase around and plays at being the boss.

Georgia is now 3 years 2 months.

**Mum:** *'She accidentally drew an M and yelled at me saying, "Mummy me did Donald's" (meaning McDonald's).'*

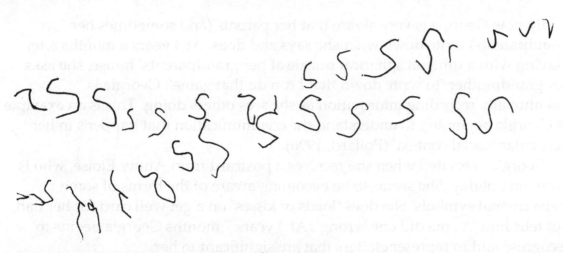

*Georgia's invitation to her Uncle Paul consists just of her writing*

At 3 years 4 months Georgia continues to practise writing curved symbols. Soon after, she copies her mum's writing of 'Harry' and wants to know why 'mum' and 'Colette' (her mum's name) look different. On Father's Day, she asks her mum to write 'daddy' and 'Georgia and Harry' on the card. At 3 years 5 months Georgia writes some 'tickets' and distributes them. At 3 years 6 months she writes a shopping list and pretends to read words from it. Shopping lists or any writing that children see others doing as a routine are, Kress (1995) points out, 'most telling'. He describes them as 'mundane texts'. We have not always recognised the influence of mundane texts in contributing to children's literacy development.

When Georgia and her family are on holiday, she has a turn on a scooter and although it is only early August, she writes a letter to Santa Claus to ask for a scooter.

Here Georgia says she is writing her own name and her grandmother's name.

*Georgia wrote her own name*

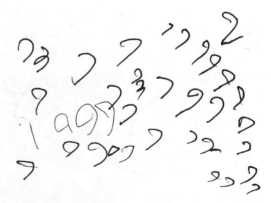

*This is Georgia's grandmother's name*

By now Georgia is very aware that her parents (and sometimes her grandparents) write down what she says and does. At 3 years 6 months after playing with a difficult spherical puzzle at her grandparents' house, she asks her grandmother 'to write down that I can do that game'. Georgia is intentionally recording information as she sees others doing. This is an example of Georgia beginning to understand the communication that happens in her particular 'social context' (Pollard, 1996).

Georgia is excited when she receives a postcard from Aunty Eloise, who is away on holiday. She seems to be becoming aware of the forms of some conventional symbols. She does 'loads of kisses' on a get well card for her dad, but tells him '. . . me did one wrong'. At 3 years 7 months Georgia begins to recognise and to represent letters that are significant to her.

> **Mum:** *'She did some drawing outside and talked about G for Georgia and H for Harry. (She could write H but not G.)'*

At 3 years 8 months, Georgia uses her grandparents' computer to do 'writing'.

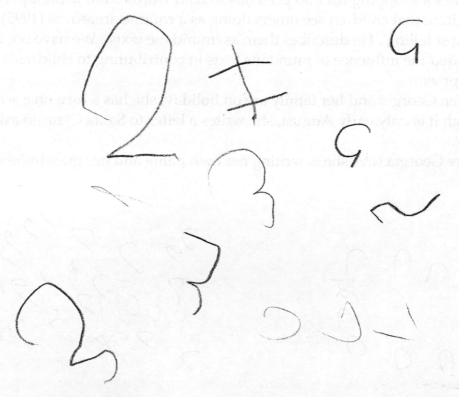

*'G's and 'H's crop up in Georgia's drawings*

**Grandmother:** *'She wanted to do my name and Georgia – talked about G for Georgia, H for Harry and mummy's number.'*

It does not seem a coincidence that while Georgia is struggling to write the letter G, she seeks out and participates in other activities which involve circular movements and enclosures (Athey, 1990). The following extracts from Georgia's parents' diary illustrate this point.

> *Georgia spends a lot of time making friendship bracelets to fit various people. She is deeply involved and when her dad says 'Men don't wear them', she offers, 'Want me to make you a really nice one you don't put on?' and 'Dad, want some to hang down your glasses?' (at 3 years 7 months)*

> *Georgia has been trying to tie shoe laces. (at 3 years 7 months)*

> *Came home today with some embroidery thread and asked me to tie it around her wrist. (at 3 years 7 months)*

> *Has been playing 'Ring-a-roses' and 'Farmer's in the Den'. (at 3 years 7 months and 3 years 8 months)*

> *Asks me to put her broken watch on for her. (at 3 years 8 months)*

> *Says she is going 'to tie something around her waist'. (at 3 years 8 months)*

Georgia begins going to nursery, where her early interests are stories, using the computer and building. At 3 years 8 months, Georgia seems interested in using up all of the maple blocks. She spends time placing them individually, which later may help her to understand that individual letters make words.

Gura (1992 (ed)) describes

> *The kinds of knowledge the child will discover about the physical qualities of unit blocks . . . Blocks occupy spaces that correspond to their shape, form, length, width and volume . . . Blocks can be arranged and rearranged.*

Individual blocks have the potential to be manipulated and placed in various ways, for example, 'next to', 'on top of', 'under'. In her early writing Georgia represents whole lines or vertical lists rather than individual letters. In a similar way, Gura points out that 'a brick in a wall is not necessarily understood as part of a whole by the young child'. Georgia, by manipulating each block, may be

*Georgia uses individual blocks to create a complex whole – this may help her to understand how letters make words and words make sentences*

beginning to understand each block as part of her whole building. This is similar to understanding that individual letters make up words and that words make up sentences or passages of text.

When Georgia is 3 years 8 months, she seems to understand that individual letters make up words. When Georgia is writing on her grandmother's birthday card, her mum spells out 'M o p' and describes how to write the letters – 'M for McDonalds', 'a round shape' and 'a round shape with a line'.

Four days later, Georgia writes her dad's name, 'Ian' in the parent diary.

A couple of months later, when Georgia is 3 years 11 months, she writes her own name conventionally for the first time. Two days later she 'verbally spelt GEORGIA and IAN'. She practises writing her name, frequently incorporating

*Georgia writes Mop, addressing her grandmother's birthday card*

the letters into her drawings. She is very keen to draw a recognisable Christmas tree. After constructing and manipulating a plastic marble run which she is given for Christmas, Georgia manages to draw zig-zags. She makes several attempts before she is satisfied with the form of her tree.

Drawing a tree like this is a complex representation, which involves making a zig-zag (Athey, 1990) into an enclosure, while retaining the zig-zag edge. The Christmas tree is Georgia's co-ordination of zig-zags, previously used to represent writing, and enclosures, previously used for friendship bracelets, round letters and drawings.

## Learning about words

At nursery when Georgia is 4 years old, she and Angela, her current Family Worker, look at a book that has been brailled.

> **Angela:** *'Georgia's query was why was the braille not the same size (length) as the print?'*

When Georgia is 4 years 1 month, she writes that she wants to visit Thomas the Tank Engine.

*Georgia makes several attempts to draw a Christmas tree before she is happy with the result*

*Georgia can write her own name and 'Thomas' for Thomas the Tank Engine*

Georgia is progressing fast. Two weeks after writing about Thomas the Tank Engine, it is her grandad's birthday. She writes her own name and her brother's as well as her grandad's and lots of kisses.

At 4 years 2 months Georgia's concern seems to be the length of each word she writes and the space it occupies. Georgia's mum notes that she is 'writing and fitting words into a space'. Georgia has a discussion with her grandmother who is pointing to words as she reads. Georgia seems surprised.

*Georgia addresses an envelope*

**Georgia:** *'Does that say me?'*
**Grandmother:** *'Yes'.*
**Georgia:** *'Just M and E?'*
**Gran:** *'Yes.'*
**Georgia:** *'Just two letters?'*
**Gran:** *'Yes'.*

**Mum:** *'Later on when she was writing names she wrote Georgia quite small ''so it'll fit''.'*

Lee and Das Gupta (1995), in a discussion about young children learning to read, say that,

*Even very obvious features of words, spoken or written length, for example, may be difficult for children to perceive.*

GEorsiA

HArry

IAn

MUM

CATH

MoP

LaUrA

JANIEL

*Georgia uses a narrow strip of paper and writes a list of names that will fit*

Georgia is sensitive to word length at this time and naturally learns which names are short and which are longer. This will contribute to her general understanding when she learns to write and read more formally.

At 4 years 4 months, Georgia writes her full name.

GeorGIATAIT

*Five months after Georgia writes her name conventionally for the first time, she is able to write her full name*

At nursery Georgia frequently paints. Labelling her work with her name is important to her and seems to be part of the creative process. Georgia announces that she is 'going to do another one and another one and another one until the paper's all finished.'

Georgia leaves nursery in July. In September she starts school and her favourite Aunty Eloise goes to University. Over the first few months Georgia is strongly motivated to draw pictures and to write to Eloise. Eloise always replies and this encourages Georgia to continue to communicate with her by post. One of her first sentences of writing is 'I love Eloise'. There is obviously an emotional dimension to Georgia's desire to communicate with Eloise, to whom she has been closely 'attached' from birth. Meek (1982) says that 'Reading, writing, thinking, knowing and feeling are all bound up in each other'.

## Looking back with Georgia's parents

Georgia's parents acknowledge her early attempts at making marks as important and this undoubtedly encourages her to continue to make marks. Often the marks are made in the context of role play.

> **Dad:** *'There was always role play because of the older children. They used to play buses and they would use tickets.'*

It seems that from when Georgia is about a year old, the older children would include her in some of their games. As she becomes older herself (about 2 years of age), she begins to initiate role play, either alone or with others.

> **Mum:** *'Her role play was about work, school or families. I remember her playing "sisters". She used to play shops or Doctors.'*

Georgia (at 7 years) remembers playing 'sisters' at nursery.

> **Georgia:** *'Stephanie was the mum 'cos she liked it – we would get the dolls from nursery and I would pretend to be five or something and help her.'*

Her dad remembers that there was a sort of pecking order.

> **Dad:** *'Stephanie was in charge – she was the eldest, then Georgia, then Laura.'*

### Using role play
On one occasion, at home, Georgia plays alone at being Kai, her dad's boss, who she has heard about but never actually met. Her mum thinks Kai intrigues

Georgia partly because she does not meet him. He seems a powerful person. Kai can tell her dad what to do.

> **Mum:** *'She seemed to be working out what Kai did, without seeing him for herself.'*

Being Kai involves Georgia in transporting things (papers and briefcase), and in writing, both of which she enjoys. When Georgia becomes a fluent writer she continues to finds ways to practise.

> **Dad:** *'She would plan parties months ahead in order to write lists of names.'*
> **Mum:** *'She always liked lists and names. Even now, she does lists for her party, what she wants for Christmas etc. She looks through the Next Directory, ticks what she likes and makes a list of page number, item, description, price etc. – sometimes asterisks things she really wants.'*

During our discussion this is borne out by Georgia who produces a chart on the spot.

| georgia | cath | georgia | cath |
|---|---|---|---|
| Things I liked at nursery. | Things I wrote. | things I like now | Things I wrote |
| Dressing up. Playing with the blocks. Playing mums and babies. Playing in the home corner. Playing with water. Playing in wood work area. Playing in sand. Playing on the horse. | | Reading Secret seven books Goosebumps and The mystery of.... Writing stories. Playing clapping games and singing songs to it. * listening to music. | |

Georgia has always had writing materials available to her at home. By the time she is 2 years old, her parents place a low coffee table in one corner of the living-room. On this table are Georgia's things, felt pens, scissors, paper and real money.

## Exploring Georgia's motivation to write

In Chapter One, Georgia's mum describes her as a 'people person' and this seems to be the key to understanding her motivation to write. Whitehead (1997) talks about 'the inspiration for early writing'.

> *The inspiration for writing arises partly from children's perceptions of it as a high status activity – something that is done by significant people in their social world.*

Georgia's early experience of

- playing with older children, who are already writers

- visiting her parents' workplaces

- attending a nursery, where records and documentation are part of the daily work of the adults

- being aware that close adults write down what she does and says

all appear to contribute to her place in a world of writers. It is not surprising that, within this context, Georgia makes meaningful marks fairly early.

The emergent nature of writing development has been widely studied (Weinberger, 1996; Whitehead, 1997). Weinberger says that,

> *Even in the early stages, children's writing often takes on visual similarities with the script the child is most familiar with.*

Georgia, like most young writers, has a sense of the joined up nature of writing and this is how she first represents the marks she sees adults and older children make.

### Writing one's own name
The motivation to learn to write one's own name is common to many children. Whitehead attributes more meaning to the writing of one's own name than merely making the right marks.

*Personal names are charged with meaning: they encapsulate our sense of self-worth and our place in the world.*

It certainly seems important to Georgia, as an emergent writer, to be able to write the letters of her name and to place them in the right order.

## Understanding what the marks mean

The marks young children make have been widely studied, but there have been fewer studies of meaning and communication in relation to emergent writing. Some followers of Vygotsky (Moll, 1990; Goodman and Goodman, 1990; Blanck, 1990) believe that children learn language as a complex whole within a social context. Goodman and Goodman say:

> *The whole-language view of literacy development is thus an immersion view. Children growing up in literate societies are surrounded by print. They begin to be aware of the functions of written language and to play at its use long before they come to school.*

This view seems to fit how Georgia spontaneously uses the print and writing practices she comes across and makes them her own, constantly setting herself new challenges. In most cases, from 2 to 5 years Georgia is:

- acting out what she has seen

- imitating the sorts of writing activities she has seen

- communicating something real.

## Whole body movement and manipulation of materials

There are other actions that Georgia is intrinsically motivated to try out, repeatedly and in different ways. Her sustained interest in enclosures when she is struggling to write the letter 'G' is a good example. The evidence indicates that the actual mark (the 'G') is like the tip of an iceberg. The greater part, which is hidden, is all of the related actions, some that involve whole body movement and others that involve the manipulation of materials. It is not a coincidence that while Georgia is making enclosures she becomes sensitive to and able to use related language, for example 'tie around'. Evidence from the Froebel Project (Athey, 1990) supports the idea that 'speech is acquired in synchrony with acquired meanings'. In other words, children learn to use appropriate language at the same time as they gain concepts.

Georgia's 'writing related' activities precede her 'reading related' activities, but only slightly. The records indicate clusters of activity, for example, the records show a month of listening and talking, followed by two weeks of writing. It is as though certain activities come to the fore for a matter of weeks.

# GEORGIA LEARNS TO READ

Stories feature strongly in Georgia's life. She has favourite books, which are stories or rhymes, and also favourite tales about real events. However, she begins 'reading' by imitating the actions of others.

The first record that indicates Georgia's understanding of meaning conveyed by print, is at 2 years 6 months.

> **Mum:** *'Georgia wanted another fromage frais. I said "What flavour was that one?" She went over, picked it up, turned it around and looked closely at each side of the container and then said "30p"!'*

Rueda (1990) says,

> *Clay (1975) and Read (1975) have shown that children know a lot about literacy before they can write and read in an 'adult' conventional sense.*

Often Georgia wants to listen to stories over and over again. When she is 2 years 7 months, something unusual happens, and she is keen to be the 'teller' rather than the 'told'.

> **Grandmother:** *'When they came in today, Georgia was desperate to tell me they had seen a bike lying on the ground. Her mum thought she had seen a person lying beside it, so they went back to have a look. They thought it might have been a car crash. The person seemed to be drunk and got up and rode off on the bike.'*

Georgia is able to tell this story to her grandmother in the right sequence. To relate a story in the order of what happens is very skilled. Georgia relates her very recent firsthand experience, which she has been discussing with her mum. Two things are important. Firstly, the significance of what she has observed has made her 'excited': the neurons in her brain are literally 'firing' away (Carter, 1998) and increasing the intensity of her perception of the dramatic events. Secondly, Georgia may have already developed a 'script' from past experiences which helps her to categorise this new experience (Gardner, 1991).

*Katherine Nelson has named this area 'the use of scripts.'*

*. . . a script entails the identification and ordering of those features that are reliably associated with a recurrent event.*

*These scripts serve as an entry point to storytelling and story understanding.*

We heard at the beginning of this section that Georgia has listened to stories from books and also stories about real events in the family. The stories she has heard provide 'sequences of events against which newly encountered events are judged'.

At 2 years 9 months Georgia makes connections between written words and songs and also adds her own communication.

**Grandmother:** *'Georgia sang me some Christmas carols when we were trying to get Harry to sleep. She brought over a book, went through it and knew which carol was on each page. Suddenly she started singing Baa Baa Black Sheep. She went and fetched her nursery rhyme book and started singing rhymes. (Again as though she was reading them.) She began adding 'at the hotel' at the end of each rhyme. I said, "Where did the hotel come from?" She said "At the wedding." ' (The family were going to a wedding and would be staying overnight in a hotel.)*

It is months later, when Georgia is 3 years 2 months, that she demonstrates her recognition of a conventional symbol when she accidentally drew an M and says, 'Mummy me did Donald's' (meaning McDonalds). Here Georgia links **encoding** (writing using conventional symbols) with **decoding** (reading from conventional symbols).

On the same day, Georgia remarks that a lorry without writing on the side is 'not Safeway lorry'. Later that day, Georgia's mum got out some new books for her. She immediately recognised one of a series and said 'An Alfie book!' (referring to the series of books by Shirley Hughes).

At 3 years 4 months, Georgia is making comparisons between words when she asked why 'mum' looked different to 'Colette'.

Although, at this stage, Georgia is beginning to recognise conventional symbols and to understand that there is a code to crack, she still does pretend writing and pretends to read from her lists. The transition between pretend reading and real reading is interesting. Georgia does not reject her pretend reading just because she now begins to understand that a set of symbols represent sounds (Riley, 1995). The two stages seem to overlap.

When Georgia starts attending nursery, she begins to 'sign' her work with her name. This is a usual convention for the adults at nursery and therefore has a real world value for Georgia.

## Reaching a plateau

For about 4 months, there does not appear to be any progress as far as reading is concerned, Georgia does, however, listen to lots of stories both at home and at nursery, during this period.

When Georgia is 4 years old she is interested in braille and asks 'does it say the same as that?' pointing at the print.

A few days later, Georgia picks up a card from the floor of her grandmother's car, as they are driving along.

> **Grandmother:** *'It's from one of the shops.'*
> **Georgia:** *'It might be from Aldi [pause] it's from Asda, I think, it says A S D A.'*

For about 3 months after her fourth birthday, Georgia frequently asks which letters words begin with.

At nursery when Georgia is 4 years, she listens to familiar stories and when her Family Worker is reading, Georgia completes sentences correctly, indicating that she has learnt parts of stories off by heart.

At home when Georgia is 4 years 3 months, she pretends to read a story and includes Harry as part of the storyline.

> **Mum:** *'Georgia held the book entitled* My Naughty Little Sister at the Fair. *She pretended to read, making up a story which included Harry.'*

A week later, she is less willing to include him. Georgia was reading her school leaflet out loud – Harry sat next to her.

> **Georgia:** *'It's not a story.'*
> **Dad:** *'He just wants to sit next to you.'*
> **Georgia:** *'I'll just read it in my head then, so he can't hear it.' (This indicates an understanding of silent reading, as well as a desire to keep information about school to herself.)*

> **Mum:** *'Georgia still asks me to read her school information pack for her bedtime story. She knows lines of it by heart – referring to the school uniform. She also talks about what colour uniform she wants and what drink she will take in her packed lunch, as "fizzy drinks are unsuitable"! (Georgia repeats the whole phrase from the leaflet.)'*

## Looking back with Georgia's parents

Both parents remember that Georgia 'was always interested in books'.

> **Mum:** *'She always liked books over and over again.'*
> **Dad:** *'Amy and Jennifer used to read to her.'*

Her mum remembers that her favourite stories were *The Tiger Who Came to Tea*, *Papa, Please Get Me the Moon* and a *Christmas Carol Book*. She knew the carol book off by heart and 'you couldn't miss one out 'cos she would know'.

### Learning about real life

Georgia likes to know about real life.

> **Mum:** *'She used to love my pregnancy books when I was expecting Harry. I think she liked anything that related to anything real.'*

Before she was born, her parents were involved in a serious car accident. Her dad remembers that she wanted to hear about the car crash.

> **Dad:** *'We used to tell her over and over and over again.'*

Georgia may be using this 'script' to retell what happens when she and her mum see someone lying on the ground and possibly injured (Gardner, 1991).

### Learning through books

Books are Georgia's favourite medium.

> **Mum:** *'She wasn't bothered about watching videos or telly or anything.'*

Georgia (at 7 years) remembers a story.

> **Georgia:** *'Avocado Baby was about a really strong baby who pushes the car.'*

> **Mum:** *'The school leaflet was her bedtime story for about a month.'*

Georgia seems to have knowledge of a range of stories and, at nursery, could choose either familiar stories or new ones.

## Exploring Georgia's motivation to read

Georgia may have seen reading, as well as writing, as a 'high status activity' (Whitehead, 1997). She is surrounded by people who can read and she is aware of the exciting content of many stories. Georgia is eager to gain information, particularly about real events in her world. Her need to hear stories over and over and over again indicates her sheer pleasure in this activity.

Although, for the purposes of this book, I have separated the accounts of writing and reading, they are, of course, tied very closely together. Riley (1995) describes 'developing literary competence':

> Concepts about print are slowly acquired through the emergent literacy phase; they develop through rich and meaningful encounters with print in the twin processes of early reading and primitive message writing.

When Georgia begins to learn 'the sounds that letters make' (Lee and Das Gupta, 1995), for example how to spell and recognise ASDA, she is aware of her own progress. Simultaneously, she makes progress in her use of language, and again, seems to be aware of her own advances. Georgia often self-corrects and comments on her own correct use of language, for example, at 3 years 6 months she says, 'Me say that right – Laura at our house yesterday'. She is referring, not only to her correct use of language, but to the concept of 'yesterday', which she uses correctly in this instance.

### Georgia learns about reading

Georgia's parents acknowledge her early pretend reading and are also prepared to respond to her queries about sounds and letters. This way of responding in a 'casual rather than didactic way' (Weinberger, 1996) to her queries may be significant. Weinberger describes this way of responding as characteristic of fostering literacy development.

Amy and Jennifer read to Georgia, which may give her a sense of her own future as a reader. She learns the content of the stories they read to her, as well as learning that reading is pleasurable.

The ease with which Georgia is able to choose stories at nursery is also significant and may be the result of her earlier experiences at home. In her longitudinal study, Weinberger (1996) found that,

> Children's familiarity and enjoyment of books at home probably made the children more likely to choose to look at books on their own when they came to nursery.

So, Georgia starts nursery and, subsequently, school with the general idea that books are enjoyable and informative, and also feeling confident about extending her range of knowledge through books.

# IDEAS FOR SUPPORTING LITERACY DEVELOPMENT

Although Georgia's story is presented in chronological order, we know that she does not learn in a simple, linear way. As adults, we need to be open to any opportunities for learning and teaching, as they present themselves. We can draw from this record of Georgia's emergent writing and reading some **principles** and **strategies** that we might apply to other children learning to write and read. Principles are our firm beliefs that underpin what we do. Strategies are the ways through which we stand by our principles.

## Principles in developing Georgia's literacy

1  Start by making close observations of Georgia.
2  Provide open ended materials for making marks and role play.
3  Assess what Georgia knows.
4  Extend from what Georgia knows and wants to know.

### Start by making close observations

All children in the UK have some experiences of literacy. It is up to the adults in Georgia's life to discover what she has noticed in her environment. We can do this by watching her at play, by listening to her parents and by responding to her questions. It is important to treat Georgia as an individual. When we respond to her as an individual we increase her pleasure, competence and self-esteem (Roberts, 1995). We can respond immediately in a variety of ways, from giving her our undivided attention for a couple of seconds to introducing a story we think she will like.

### Provide materials

Georgia needs a range of open-ended materials with which to make marks. The quality of materials provided does make a difference. Georgia was interested in improving the form of what she drew and wrote. Felt pens produce much better marks for beginners than thin crayons. I would argue for quality and range: chalk, pens, pencils, sticks, cotton buds, paint brushes, rollers, knives and so on. Offering a wide range opens up the possibilities for Georgia. Cloaks, hats and shoes often attract her, enticing her to get into role and to reveal what she is thinking about.

### Assess what Georgia knows

The best time to assess what Georgia knows is when she is 'deeply involved' (Laevers, 1997) and using materials spontaneously. Laevers (1993) has shown that, when a learner is 'deeply involved', 'the mind is exactly doing what is favourable to its own development'. (The involvement signals are listed in Chapter Two.) If we provide an environment, rich in the type of materials described and with adults who are interested in discovering her world, Georgia will provide the starting points for discussion through her actions. We must discuss what she is learning with parents and colleagues. Georgia revealed her understanding of writing and communication through writing materials to adults who were prepared to encourage and support her. Telling stories and writing alongside Georgia contributed to her knowledge and helped us to assess what she knew at any one point in time.

### Extend from what Georgia knows and wants to know

When Georgia asks questions, usually it is because she genuinely wants to know something. Therefore, her questions provide a guide to what she is ready to learn. Georgia often asks her parents questions. Nursery practitioners may also be asked. When Georgia wanted to know which letters words begin with, she was actively seeking out the knowledge she was ready to learn. Her parents and workers could simply tell her what she asked each time or tell her in different ways: by singing songs which include letter sounds, by having an alphabet frieze for her to look at or by playing games which include sounds. Providing these different routes, with no pressure to take up the knowledge in any particular way, preserves Georgia's enjoyment of learning.

## Strategies for helping Georgia to develop her literacy

1    Practitioners from nursery or school can visit Georgia and her family at home, discuss writing and reading and try to discover what her parents think about literacy.
2    Good reading material should be available and accessible to Georgia, giving her time to look at books and to make her own marks, with and without an adult present. Set up a lending library and encourage Georgia to bring in her favourite books or videos from home.
3    Extend Georgia's interests through the 'form' or repeated pattern of behaviour (for example, enclosure) as well as through 'content' (Athey, 1990), (eg the bracelet).
4    Encourage Georgia to talk to adults and to other children. Have toy mobile phones available, puppets, role play areas and small world equipment.

5    Capitalise on any special events or on what Georgia plays spontaneously, for example in the home corner or outside.

6    Do some research on current trends – what is currently on TV for this age group? What is the latest toy or street or playground game being played by the older children Georgia knows?

## Visit Georgia at home and discuss literacy

We know that children who are familiar with books, choose books more readily and may extend their knowledge through reading. If we begin by validating the literacy that exists in Georgia's home environment, not by judging her home as better than another but by seeing families as different to each other, we can discover a starting point for Georgia at nursery. Although Georgia did not choose to learn through watching videos, some children access stories through watching videos and learning a favourite script off by heart. We can make links with home by what we provide at nursery or school. I am not suggesting that children at school or nursery watch videos as part of the curriculum, but we can provide props that encourage Georgia and other children to act out stories and we may be able to provide the original story on which a favourite video is based.

We can also ensure that the nursery environment includes similar writing and reading materials to those Georgia would see at home: junk mail, yellow pages, a catalogue, payment card or airmail letters in another language. Whatever is familiar is a starting point.

## Have good reading material available

If we want Georgia to learn to read and to feel confident with books, we must offer her a range of books. Books need to be chosen carefully to ensure that they are not racist, sexist, disablist or tokenist. We also need to consider the cultural messages that we are passing on to Georgia through literature. Reference books are important and are often more popular with boys. Georgia cannot learn to use and take care of books if they are out of her reach. We can display books on low shelves and encourage Georgia to help herself to books whenever she wants to.

Writing and reading materials can be offered to Georgia in various areas of the nursery. For example, notebooks, writing paper and envelopes can be placed in the home corner, and chalk, clipboards and pencils can be used outside.

Setting up a system to lend books to Georgia and other children means that all families can have access to materials at home. Encouraging Georgia to bring her favourite books or videos from home means that we can have access to her family's materials.

Making books using Georgia's role play or the stories she invents as the text enables Georgia to become the author. Graves (1983) describes a wonderful project in which schoolchildren write and review books for each other, making a classroom library of their own works.

## Extend what we offer

We have seen how writing and reading are only the tip of the iceberg. Athey (1990) shows how we can extend Georgia's thinking by closely observing her repeated actions and offering content to 'feed' those patterns or repeated actions. We might suppose that, when Georgia was repeatedly drawing curves and enclosures, we could only extend through offering writing materials and paper. But she was exploring something bigger: going around and enclosure. There are all sorts of materials, games and stories we could offer to help her get to grips with going around.

We noticed that Georgia was sensitive to related language when she was forming concepts. Nutbrown (1994) links the content of various stories with the 'forms' or 'schemas' that children explore. For example, when Georgia is interested in enveloping, Nutbrown suggests that she might enjoy *A Dark, Dark Tale* by Ruth Brown (1992), in which successive coverings are removed to reveal a mouse asleep inside a box.

## Encourage Georgia to talk

Narrative begins with the telling of tales (Whitehead, 1997). Talking, therefore, precedes writing and reading. Some children will only explore talk using a phone or puppets. Providing the right props will encourage Georgia to talk, act and improve her organisational skills necessary for later writing and reading. Listening to Georgia conveys the message that what she is saying is as important as what adults say.

## Capitalise on special events and spontaneous play

We can discover what Georgia is thinking by closely observing her spontaneous play. We can add literacy content to almost any game. We can provide anything from a shopping list to a memo from the boss to genuine instructions for constructing a new piece of equipment. We can allow Georgia to be involved in real writing or reading. Having systems such as registers or records of whose turn it is to take part in particular activities, such as cooking or going on the computer, is a real reason to read and write daily.

Special events such as birthdays, Christmas and Diwali all have the potential for literacy related activities. Writing invitations, decorating cakes and writing place cards can be part of these events. Georgia loves authenticity and will know when she is doing a genuine job. We need to give Georgia enough time to do these real jobs and be prepared to finish off for her if the task proves too difficult.

## Do some research

Anything older children do Georgia perceives as a 'high status activity' (Whitehead, 1997). These activities are, therefore, worthy of our attention. When the 'dispositions' to learn are strong, Georgia will make 'decisions' about getting involved and about taking responsibility for her own learning as far as she can (Carr et al, 1998). So whether the latest craze is a cult toy or TV programme, it is worth finding out what is in it as far as literacy development is concerned.

---

# SUMMARY

- Georgia learns to write through imitating writers, recognising print in the environment, recognising significant words and practising movements in various ways with a range of materials.

- Georgia learns to read through listening to stories, imitating readers, recognising environmental print and asking questions about sounds and letters.

- There are many principles and strategies for supporting Georgia's literacy development.

---

We have now looked at how Georgia approached writing and reading and at how her parents and nursery workers supported her emergent literacy. In the next chapter we will be looking at how Georgia's understanding of Maths develops.

# 4 UNDERSTANDING MATHEMATICAL CONCEPTS

*Mathematics – the abstract science of number, quantity and space studied in its own right.*
(Tulloch (Ed), 1990)

*Certainty is a word that mathematicians often use when they try to describe the appeal of what they do.*
(Hoffman, 1998)

The kind of certainty that Hoffman is talking about involves proving that something is always the same.

> The mathematical concepts that Georgia spends most time exploring from 2 to 5 years are:
>
> - quantity, including counting and dividing
>
> - size and fit
>
> - time, particularly chronology.

Long before Georgia's parents realise that she is exploring mathematical ideas, Georgia spends a lot of her time carrying objects about. Often she gives objects to people, only to take them back from them seconds later and then carry them about some more. She is transporting. While she is doing this, she is proving to herself that although her load looks different depending on whether it is held by five different people, or whether she carries it in a bag or pushes it in a trolley, it is never-the-less exactly the same load. It only changes if another object is added or something is removed.

- As a 1-year-old, she pushes her trolley about – sometimes with wooden bricks in it and sometimes with other objects.

- As a 2-year-old, she pushes her buggy, rides her truck, and carries various bags, purses and buckets. She carries objects in these different containers distributing them and gathering them together over and over again.

This strong transporting behaviour contributes to Georgia's mathematical future (Athey, 1990). Georgia will eventually understand that the number of objects stays the same (or is **invariant**) unless anything is added or taken away (Lee and Das Gupta, 1995).

We observed what Georgia knew about writing from the marks she made and what she knew about reading from what she said. Mathematical and scientific understanding involves abstract concepts. Therefore, in this chapter and the next, we can only speculate about what Georgia might be learning. These speculations usually take the form of questions following direct observations of her actions.

# EXPLORING IDEAS ABOUT QUANTITY AND AMOUNT

Georgia plays with real money and often this is what she manipulates, carries about and distributes. Before she understands conventional counting, at 2 years 5 months she has a sense of what happens when money changes hands.

> **Mum:** *'She took a couple of coins out of a tin and was talking to herself, saying "20, 20". Then she gave me some coins and said "Play moneypops".'*

A few days later, Georgia is playing with tickets and money.

> **Mum:** *'She gave me all of the tickets and talked about paying. She gave me some money and waited for me to give her some back ... She shared the money out giving me all of the copper coins and she kept the silver ones. She referred to the 20p as a "choo choo" ie a ride on a toy train at the supermarket.'*

Georgia seems to be drawing on her experiences of going to the supermarket and paying for goods as well as paying for rides. The tickets may connect with her frequent visits to Wicksteed Park as she often says 'Pay the man' when manipulating tickets and money. She seems to understand that 20p pays for a ride. This is an example of something from the everyday context of her own life which Georgia quickly learns and uses in her play.

Nunes et al (1993) describe 'street mathematics' learnt by children and adults, who have had no schooling but who experience 'everyday practices'. Vygotsky would say that Georgia is learning 'everyday concepts' about money through her experiences (Moll, 1990).

# Using language to describe quantity

Four months later, when Georgia is 2 years 9 months, she demonstrates her ideas about quantity in the language she uses. She talks about running 'really, really, giant fast' to describe great speed.

A few days later, Georgia is playing with money.

> *'Had money in purse, inside box. Talked to herself about 'paying sixty', said 'don't know if I've got sixty.'*
> (Parent Diary)

'Sixty' seems to be a number she likes the sound of. It is not unusual for children to have favourite numbers or words. (Carruthers, 1997)

Georgia at 2 years 9 months continues to try out language which relates to the concept of greater amount or quantity.

> *Giant . . . signifies greatest amount e.g. giant quiet if you want her to be very quiet.*
> (Parent Diary)

She is more specific when she says, 'Daddy been London on six times.'

Georgia tries out a different word to describe amount.

> *'Father' signifies 'very' or greatest amount of something.*
> (Parent Diary)

It is several months later, on her brother's first birthday, when Georgia is 3 years 3 months that she, again, reveals her knowledge of quantity.

> *When everyone but the family had left, Georgia got out some cards with numbers on and played a game for about an hour with Mop, Pop, Uncle Paul, Mum and Dad. She was definitely in charge 'sharing' and telling Paul and Pop 'You only allowed three'. Also 'I need number one 'cos Harry's one'. Several times during the game she said she had 'winned' or someone else or two others had 'winned'. She asked me how old I was. Also said 'I need number four 'cos I gonna be four next year'. Several times she said some of the players were 'in' and some were 'out'. She recognised numbers (1, 2, 3, 4 and 5) and at times said to Paul or Pop, 'You got number five?' or 'You got number three?' If they had and they showed her, she would swap it, usually for a lower number or tell them they were 'allowed' less cards than they had. Mostly she had more cards than anyone else.*
> (Parent Diary)

Clearly Georgia has some experience of older children or adults playing cards. She is imitating or replicating, to some extent, what she has seen or been part of. If she has been part of a game, the rules seemed arbitrary to her. However, in her representation of a card game, Georgia does show that she has a good grasp of the order of numbers, at least from one to five and the values associated with those numbers. There also seems to be a gender aspect, in that she appears to identify with the other females and to pick on Pop and Paul as though they are from an opposing team. (This is implicit rather than explicit. The hidden message seems to be that whatever hand the males are dealt, they will not win as Georgia regularly reviews what they are holding and swaps it for something less or lower.) She may be identifying with the women rather than the men and possibly seeing herself as part of a larger group.

Two months later, when Georgia is 3 years 5 months, she plays dropping a tennis ball and catching it, counting up to 12 catches. (Now she can keep in mind the quantity without being able to see the objects that make up that quantity.)

Georgia continues to play with money, sometimes lining it up and counting it. She also cuts paper 'into tiny bits for Eloise for money for the till'. Georgia may be puzzling over whether it is the same amount of paper when cut up into tiny pieces.

## Dividing and connecting materials

On holiday, at 3 years 6 months, Georgia cuts up mushrooms and cucumber for the salad – as she gets towards the end of the job, she cuts them smaller and smaller. Is it a sign that she is enjoying cutting so much that she wants to prolong the time spent on this job? Does she wonder whether the vegetables increase in amount when cut up? This links closely with something Georgia does early in the morning, at home, when she is 3 years 7 months.

> *This morning Georgia came to me in bed and told me she had some blu-tack and that she was going to do a picture and put it up. A bit later, she asked me to come and see 'cos it looks really good'. She had cut up pictures from a travel brochure into quite small pieces and then blu-tacked them to my bathroom wall.*
> (Parent Diary)

Georgia is able to view what she has divided like pieces of a jigsaw laid out on the floor. Is she looking to see whether the parts can be put back together to form a whole picture? Piaget (1951) offers an example of a child 'breaking up' clay and putting it together again.

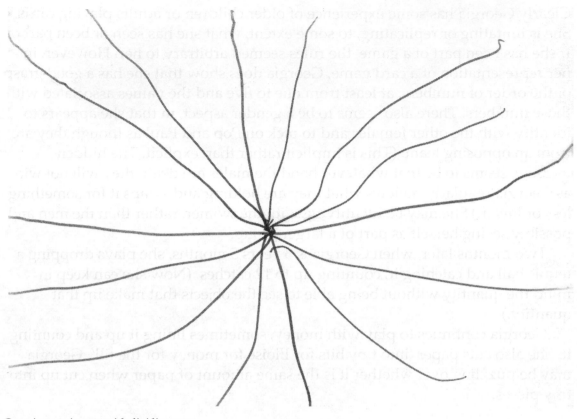

*Georgia experiments with dividing space*

Around the same time, Georgia's interest in division is reflected in her language and in her drawing.

> *Georgia tells her dad she has been a little bit naughty and a little bit good.*
> (Parent Diary)

This is like dividing her day into different parts.

Athey (1990) found that some children in the Froebel project '*divided circles into two halves for various representations*'.

At nursery, at 3 years 5 months, Georgia builds using maple unit blocks. The blocks are mathematically related to one another and this is important to Georgia when she is learning about division and parts of a whole. Gura (1992) says that children have 'an intuitive urge to unite' parts of dissected wholes.

At the same age, when Georgia uses the computer at nursery, she demands five copies of her picture. She explains why to Alison, her Family Worker.

**Georgia:** *'One for mummy, one for daddy, one for Harry, one for me, one for you (Alison).'*

Close people are her first references when deciding 'how many'. Georgia is *multiplying* her one picture by five in order to *share* it between all of her important people.

## An understanding of counting

At 3 years 9 months, Georgia seems to be on the cusp of understanding counting. She can count in a conventional, stable order and knows about making each number correspond with one object being counted. She also knows that the final number is the total amount. Gelman and Gallistel (1978) call these 'how to count' principles. However, at home, Georgia sets herself a difficult counting task.

> *Georgia is playing with eight 2p coins, whilst looking out of the window.*
> **Georgia:** *'I'm going to make a circle.'*
> (Parent Diary)

Is she representing the formation of the houses in the close?

> **Georgia:** *'I'm going to count them now.'*
> *Georgia then counted from one of the coins near the top – and counted nine – she didn't remember where she started!*
> (Parent Diary)

It is much more tricky to count a circle of objects than a line of objects. Georgia has been arranging money in lines for a long time and is trying out a different arrangement.

Ten days later, again at home, Georgia demonstrates her understanding of what a total of three means.

> *Georgia has been doing different '3s' eg holding up her thumb and first two fingers, then just her first three fingers, then her last three fingers – she seems to be getting the idea of the amount rather than 'naming' each item with a number.*
> (Parent Diary)

Georgia continues practising counting and when she is 4 years 2 months she counts to about 60. Georgia also continues to work on division and parts of whole objects. At nursery, at 3 years 9 months, Georgia plays with dough.

*Rolling the dough backwards and forwards, now adding little pieces from the table and rolling them into the larger piece.*
(Observation by Family Worker)

Dividing and combining dough is very different because the shape of the whole lump can change. Is it the same when it is a long sausage as it is when it is a round flat shape?

Georgia continues to fold and cut paper both at nursery and at home.

## Estimating and counting on

At 3 years 10 months, when she is about to travel to London by train, Georgia estimates that there will be ten tunnels between Kettering and London. She spends the journey counting them. Georgia is able to 'keep the meaning of the problem in mind' (Nunes, 1995). She remembers her estimate and 'counts on' as the train goes through each tunnel (McLellan, 1997).

## Understanding the limits

Then at 3 years 11 months, Georgia becomes interested in limits (or what is *finite* and what is *infinite*). She has already experimented with using up all of the maple blocks at nursery. She is using the computer at her grandparents' house and suddenly asks, 'Will the G's run out?' Her grandmother explains what can limit the computer's use and about the printer using up ink.

Months later, at nursery, when she is painting, Georgia (aged 4 years 5 months) says she is going to do 'another one and another one and another one until the paper is all gone'. This may be to prolong enjoyment or to test out whether she is allowed to use up all of the resources on the table.

Georgia shows a well-developed understanding of the use of fuel, when, at 4 years 4 months, she suggests to her mum, 'Park in Danny's drive (nearer the edge of the close) – that would save some petrol!' Georgia is able to link distance travelled with the amount of fuel used.

## Looking back with Georgia's parents

### Money

Both of Georgia's parents remember her playing with real money.

> **Mum:** *'She used to play with it all of the time.'*

I wonder when and why that began, because most parents worry that little children will swallow small coins. Her dad recalls that he had a very large bottle in which he saved any loose change. He says that Georgia was allowed to play with coins from that bottle when they knew she would not put them in her mouth. He thinks she was under 2 years. Georgia did not play with just a few coins. Her uncle remembers her carrying money around in a carrier bag and sometimes it was so heavy that she had to ask an adult to move it from one place to another. Once Georgia had experience of real money, there seemed no point in giving her anything else.

> **Mum:** *'One Christmas she got a till and we thought it was ridiculous to buy plastic money when she could just have real money.'*

Both parents also remember Georgia playing cards with the older children from the close.

> **Dad:** *'She used to play with Jennifer and Amy. They tried to teach her to play.'*

They also played other games which may have contributed to Georgia's ideas about quantity.

> **Mum:** *'When she was older, she used to play cards, schools and shops in the close. They all involved counting, sharing things out, taking things back and making lists.'*

## Dividing and connecting materials

Cutting and dividing was not such a memorable part of her play, although, again, her dad remembers that she had scissors before she was 2 years old. He also remembers that it did not take her long to learn to use them. 'We held the paper stiff for her at first.' He also recalls that she liked cutting veg: 'We couldn't give her a really sharp knife so it was hard work for her – she would get fed up after 5 minutes.'

Both parents remember her displaying the divided travel brochure on the bathroom wall. Blu-tack was one of the things that was always on her low table in the living room.

> **Dad:** *'She used to spend ages in that corner.'*

When I was demonstrating to Georgia's dad how she divided space in her drawing, Georgia (aged 7 years) added a line making my rough sketch symmetrical, showing that the mathematical form is still important to her.

# What Georgia learns about quantity and amount

Georgia's early behaviour in which she carries objects (often money) from one place to another and arranges the individual coins in different ways, is very similar to what Piaget describes (1951).

> *At 3 [years] 6 [months] she put some pebbles in a pail, took them out one by one, put them back, transferred them from one pail to another, etc.*

Piaget describes these sorts of actions as 'sensory motor practice games'. In other words children play them for sheer pleasure. Piaget says that these games develop when 'they become symbolic' or 'become games with rules' or 'lead to real adaptation'. We see Georgia's play become 'symbolic' when she imitates 'paying the man'. In this sort of play, Georgia builds up a story around her use of money and incorporates into her story the sharing of money, which has previously been an end in itself.

## Playing games

The card game is an early example of Georgia developing the expertise to play a game with shared rules. In this case the rules are her own personal ones. Within the game Georgia reveals what she knows about numbers and values. There is the number of actual cards each person holds. Georgia definitely knows what is 'more' and what is 'less'. She manipulates the rules so that she always has more. Then there is the number value or currency of each card. She shows that at this stage she can seriate up to five.

## The importance of learning to count

Piaget did not attach much importance to counting, but more recent research indicates that it is important for children to learn to count (MacLellan, 1997). MacLellan says that 'the emergence of counting in children is complex and a bit messy'. MacLellan is referring not just to the recital of numbers in the conventional order, which can be learnt parrot fashion, but to a real understanding of how to count. We can see that understanding developing in Georgia towards the end of her nursery time. Experiences in all areas of her life contribute to her understanding of number.

Carruthers (1996) argues that young children develop ideas about number in the same way that they develop ideas about literacy. She says,

> *Numbers exist in the child's world from birth and they are gradually building up a meaning for number and how it fits into the whole pattern of life.*

# EXPLORING IDEAS ABOUT SIZE AND FIT

When Georgia explores size, her concern is with filling a space or area and whether one object will fit inside or around another object.

Georgia is completely engrossed, at 2 years 8 months, when she picks up a small perspex container (approximately 5 cm × 4 cm).

> *She tries various things in the container eg photo, fold-up toothbrush, none of which would fit. She spotted a piece of paper, which was already folded in half. She picked it up, unfolded it and looked at it, then folded it in half again, then in half again, then again and put it into the container and closed it. She looked pleased with herself.*
> (Parent Diary)

(At this stage Georgia seems happy with the action of putting something *inside* a container.)

Georgia spends the next 2 months folding and enveloping everything possible. She folds her pictures and paintings and carries a bag full of things, has money in a purse inside a box and sits on her truck, with pram attached, blanket draped over the pram and wearing a hat. (Georgia is happy to cover anything, including her head with a hat.)

Months later, at 3 years 3 months Georgia is more concerned with what can fit through a narrow space, when she says to her dad, 'Better shut the window. The rain's only small, can get in there'. Georgia now understands that rain going through the window depends on the window being open.

That summer, when the family are on holiday, Georgia spends a long time playing with laces and a wristwatch. She is interested in fastening and unfastening, as well as in what will fit. She is 3 years 6 months.

> *Georgia spent the best part of an hour fastening and unfastening my watch. She put the watch on her wrist, round her leg, round her ankle without sock pulled up then with sock pulled up. Talked a lot about watch and parts of it, speculating about whether it would fit.*
> (Parent Diary)

Georgia has refined her earlier enveloping behaviour and is more concerned with fitting.

## Exploring friendship bracelets

The trend in the close is friendship bracelets. Georgia has observed how to make them during social interactions with older children, who have made them for her and each other (Schaffer, 1996). Two weeks later, Georgia has one on each wrist made for her by the older children. In the following observation, Georgia is at home and attempting to make friendship bracelets.

> *Georgia is 'trying' to make friendship bracelets. She has three pieces of embroidery thread knotted together and spends most of her time cutting one piece of thread and then the other two to even it up.*
> (Parent Diary)

Georgia is obviously very involved and talks all the way through, though, her mum says, she expects no reply, as her sentences all run into each other. This is some of her accompanying language.

**Georgia:** *'Want a little one for Harry? How little Harry needs. I need to just cut. This is small enough Mum?'*
**Mum:** *'Very small.'*
**Georgia:** *. . . Mummy want me to cut this for Harry? Want these three colours for Harry? Think it's all right. Dad, you could help me do a bracelet? I can't do it. I can do . . .'*
**Dad:** *'You need it quite long.'*
**Georgia:** *'You can do it that small? That going to be mine. Dad, I'm going to give you some – not that – that's my favourite. You're allowed that for him (piece of thread) . . .'*

Georgia pursues this interest for at least 3 weeks. At the same time as Georgia is exploring wrapping thread or laces *around* objects, she is also interested in *distance* and in extending her own body to reach things 'with tiptoes and without tiptoes'. This may indicate that the unravelled state of the thread is equally important to her investigation as the enclosure she makes when she wraps it around an object. Georgia may be grappling with the idea of the length of the thread being 'equivalent' to the 'breadth of the enclosure' (Athey, 1990). Athey suggests that,

> *Mathematically this schema is extended in the primary school in activities such as measuring around wrist, waist, ankle and various kinds of perimeters.*

## Georgia chooses stories

Georgia chooses stories which relate to ideas about size and listens to them over and over again. Two favourites are:

- *Papa Please Get Me the Moon* (Carle, 1986), a storybook containing a ladder which unfolds to reach the moon and a story in which ideas about the waxing and waning of the moon are explored.

- *Where's My Teddy* (Alborough, 1992) in which a boy loses his teddy and finds a giant teddy, which belongs to a huge bear. The anomaly is resolved when they swap teddies.

## Symbols on clothing

At 3 years 7 months, Georgia knows about the symbols on clothes labels that denote sizes and is clear that she wants to be bigger rather than smaller.

> *Georgia went to show Ian her new vest which, I told her, was aged 5–6. I then asked her to try on some trousers from last year.*
> **Mum:** *'I think these should fit, as the label says they're 3–4.'*
> **Georgia:** *'No, I need 3–5.'*
> (Parent Diary)

## Journeys

Georgia is also interested in larger distances. At 3 years 8 months, when they are visiting her great grandmother, she suggests going 'to Asda as it's nearer'. She also knows that 'Safeway is nearer' if they are at home. (This is accurate.)

At nursery, at 3 years 11 months, Georgia uses collage materials in the workshop area and fits materials into a defined space.

## Measuring and fitting

> *We measured a picture to frame it – I helped Georgia. I then sent her to measure another picture.*
> **Georgia:** *'It measured two threes.'*
> (Parent Diary)

*Georgia fits lolly sticks into a space*

Georgia at 4 years has an idea of what measuring is, at this stage. She knows that it involves a tape measure and numbers. She may also understand why we measure things.

At 4 years 2 months Georgia's concern when writing names is fitting words into a space. (See Chapter Three.) Also at 4 years 4 months, Georgia went to bed with paper, ribbon and scissors in order to wrap something after watching her mum wrap up a gift for a friend. Wrapping objects with paper requires skill in measuring or estimating the size of paper needed and in folding and securing parcels.

When Georgia is 4 years 5 months, Steph brings a Doctor's bag to nursery. Several children play with the instruments. When they are putting everything back into the bag, Georgia picks up a stethoscope, saying 'If I can get it in' and 'I don't think I can get it in'. It did fit in. Georgia is estimating whether she thinks something will fit before trying it.

## Looking back with Georgia's parents

Georgia's interest in size and fit seems to be rooted in her early experience with the large bottle of coins that her dad was collecting.

> **Dad:** *'She was interested in which coins would go into the bottle. 2p coins would not fit, so she could have those.'*

Georgia rarely plays with jigsaws at nursery but her dad says that 'she loved her inset jigsaws' at home. In those, the task is to fit the correct shape in the space, so it is about matching for size and shape.

> **Dad:** *'She had several of that type of puzzle and because I worked for a toy firm, I was able to keep giving her different ones from work.'*

When Georgia is 2 years, she has an inflatable globe and she becomes interested in the comparative size of countries.

> **Dad:** *'She would ask about the countries she had heard of, eg, Is England bigger than America?'*

Georgia has a tape measure, which is usually well extended.

> **Dad:** *'For months she took it everywhere – she liked opening and shutting it.'*

### Looking at size labels

Both parents remember Georgia looking at size labels on clothes. In fact she still does.

> **Dad:** *'She went shopping a lot with her mum and probably saw her doing that . . . also, because of Harry's allergy, we both had to read labels on tins etc, more so than most people.'*

He feels that Georgia 'gives attention to detail' and also that she wants to be grown up.

> **Dad:** *'Georgia can't wait to grow out of shoes so that she can get the next size.'*

## What Georgia learns about size and fit

It appears that when Georgia is enveloping everything in sight, this covering of objects and parts of herself, leads to 'higher order notions such as volume and capacity' (Athey, 1990). Athey suggests that if practitioners are aware of this possibility, then content can be introduced that has 'a *specific capacity*'. Athey suggests 'a picnic basket design to take specific crockery and cutlery'. She says that 'Toddlers *heap* objects but so do older children if more appropriate materials are not available'.

### Using her whole body

There is very little mention in the records of Georgia's spatial awareness in relation to her whole body, except that she practises handstands and enjoys swings at the park. Davies (1995) reminds us that,

> In the movement world of young children size is normally associated with extension . . . 'Near', 'far', 'big' and 'little' feature prominently in the learning of young children and therefore their experience of this area is vitally important.

When Georgia extends her body to reach with tiptoes and without, she is using her own body as a tool to measure. Similarly, trying on a watch with and without her sock pulled up is helping Georgia to measure and compare sizes or fit. It is not surprising that she takes up the idea of making friendship bracelets so enthusiastically. Vygotsky might view the making of friendship bracelets to be in the zone of Georgia's proximal development at that time (Lee and Das Gupta, 1995). Initially, Georgia needs a fair amount of help with making bracelets, but gradually the adult or older child can withdraw and allow Georgia a greater level of control.

## Examining Georgia's progress

One could argue that Georgia's awareness of the possibility of fitting an object inside another object does not progress much from age 2 years 8 months, when she folds paper to fit inside a perspex container, and age 4 years 5 months, when she says that she does not think the stethoscope will fit in the Doctor's bag. However, at 2 years 8 months, she is trying things out, some of which obviously do not fit. At 4 years 5 months, she is thinking and can mentally construct ideas about the available space and the object that is supposed to fit. She is confident enough to express her considered opinion, even though that opinion turns out to be incorrect.

# Exploring ideas about time and chronology

While Georgia is interested in and pursues ideas about quantity, size and fit, she devotes much of her energy towards trying to grasp and understand time concepts. Georgia, like most young children, uses language associated with time concepts long before she understands the full meaning of them. What is most remarkable about Georgia is her persistent quest for meaning.

The records show that she refers to time in role play situations before trying them out in real situations. At 2 years 5 months, Georgia refers to '5 minutes' and at 2 years 8 months when she is making a pretend phonecall to her dad she tells him she will be home in 1 hour.

Harry is 4 months and Georgia is 2 years 8 months when she says that *he wore the jumper that she is wearing when he was a little baby*. (This indicates that she is unclear about the chronological order of events. She may be confusing ideas about now – is he actually wearing something that was hers when she was a baby?)

As a baby and toddler, Georgia is not a good sleeper, frequently waking during the night. This may be the source of her concern with time. Georgia is 2 years 8 months and wakes at 6.15 am.

> *Her dad told her it was too early to get up and gave her a watch to look at and told her when it would be 7 o'clock. She said 'Not see the watch – dark in the way'.*
> (Parent Diary)

Having an advent calendar at 2 years 10 months feeds Georgia's interest in the sequence of events, though, like most young children, she is not ready to wait a whole day for each chocolate.

> *Choc missing from 21st window (tomorrow). Georgia said, when asked where it had gone, 'Not me know me eat it'!*
> (Parent Diary)

At 2 years 11 months, Georgia begins to make her own meaning of time and distance. Her mum tells her that Peterborough (where Thomas the Tank Engine is) is 'only about half an hour in the car, like going to Northampton'.

> **Mum:** *'Georgia nodded and said to herself "Just about 1 minute, near Corby".'*

The important factor for her may be that it is near Corby, where she lives and, therefore, she can go to visit it.

## Linking time and size

Just after her third birthday, Georgia links time and size. She compares her size and Harry's with the size of a new baby. She says, 'Next year me be four – have four candles'. She tells her grandmother that '1 hour is not a long time'.

At 3 years 2 months, Georgia is much more specific about time.

> **Georgia:** *'Last night I stayed up till 8 o'clock. Should go to bed at half past 6. Mummy let me stay up.'*

Georgia knows the number labels of significant times of day.

## Linking time and distance

A few weeks later Georgia and her mum see Nicola, one of the older girls from the close, in Kettering sitting on a wall outside the shopping centre. Georgia wants to know why Nicola is sitting on the wall. Georgia's mum explains that she is probably waiting for her parents to take her home. Georgia is puzzled and says 'She might walk home'. Her mum explains that it is a long way (7 miles) and would take a long time. Georgia hazards a guess 'About half an hour?' Her mum replies 'About 2 hours.' Georgia repeated 'About 2 hours', then said 'about 4 hours'. Initially, Georgia is puzzled about why Nicola who, to Georgia, is grown-up, is waiting for her parents to take her home. Georgia's thinking is challenged and through being challenged, it is possible for 'cognitive change' to occur (Nunes, 1995). The discussion shows Georgia's preoccupation with time. This is the aspect she immediately latches on to and begins thinking about and speculating upon.

## Thinking about future time

After Georgia's third birthday, she frequently refers to 'next year'. When she is 3 years 3 months, she is visiting Alison's family group at nursery. It is James' fourth birthday and the children are having a cake with four candles to celebrate. Georgia says 'I think he's four'. Her mum says 'like you'll be next year'. Georgia says, 'Is it next year already . . . for James?' This gives us an interesting insight into Georgia's thinking. It seems as if she is describing time moving towards individual people, rather than people moving towards points in time.

Georgia is 3 years 4 months.

> **Georgia:** *'Can I go to school?'*
> **Mum:** *'This September you'll go to nursery, then next September you'll go to school with James and little Emma.'*
> **Georgia:** *'Can Harry come to school with me?'*
> **Mum:** *'Harry will be going to playgroup when you go to school. You'll be four and a half and he'll be two.'*

Georgia seems satisfied with the explanation. In this instance Georgia is asking for information that she seems to be ready to understand. Talking about the future indicates some level of understanding about future events (Nunes, 1995).

## Linking age and size

On the same day, Georgia talks about which days her grandmother goes to work and how old her grandmother is. She links age with size. (This time she looks back in time rather than forward.)

> *Pointed to Harry on a photo – said he was 'about 5 months'. And that she was 'about one 'cos that dress doesn't fit her now'.*
> (Parent Diary)

Georgia begins to play with ideas about age when she is 3 years 6 months. It is her great grandmother's birthday.

> **Georgia:** *'I'm four.'*
> **Gran:** *'I thought you were three and a half?'*
> **Georgia:** *'I had my birthday – it's today!'*

Each close person's birthday seems to stimulate Georgia's thinking about time and age.

Georgia is still 3 years 6 months when she uses the word 'yesterday' correctly in context and comments to her dad 'me say that right'. She has an awareness that up to then she has not used 'yesterday' correctly.

In the parent diary, her mum describes Georgia as having 'an obsession with time, distance, dates etc.'

## Making comparisons

Georgia is 3 years 7 months when she has her first of many conversations about why Steph is going to be 4 years old before her.

> **Georgia:** 'Steph is three or four?'
> **Mum:** 'Three – nearly four. I think she'll be four in October or November.'
> **Georgia:** 'When me going to be four?'
> **Mum:** 'January the 26th.'
> **Georgia:** 'Me going to be four first?'
> **Mum:** 'No you're not.'
> **Georgia:** 'Why is Steph going to be four first?'
> **Mum:** 'Because she was in her mummy's tummy before you were in mine.'
> **Georgia:** 'Why?'
> **Mum:** 'Because her mummy was pregnant before me.'

Two weeks later and Georgia is still asking why Steph was born before her.

> *Georgia is still very interested in why Steph is four before her. She wants to be four first. She just keeps asking why Steph is going to be four before her – each answer given is replied to by Georgia with 'Why?'*
> (Parent Diary)

Georgia is not satisfied with the explanations she is given. Nathan Isaacs (1930) collected information about children's 'why' questions and from his data, said that children from about 4 years ask 'why' and that we continue to do so into adulthood. The need to ask 'why' occurs as a result of 'a sudden gap, clash or disparity between our past experience and any present event'. This information about Steph really throws Georgia's current ideas and expectations. She is challenged by the information and continues to ask 'why' until she gains an understanding of why Steph's birthday is before hers.

Georgia begins asking more questions about future time. At 3 years 8 months, just after starting nursery, she asks her mum 'When will I be six or seven?' Her mum replies, 'In 3 or 4 years time.' Georgia comments on each chunk of time: 'That's long or not long.'

## Linking age and height

At nursery Georgia stands on some steps and says 'Look at me – I'm about six'. She is linking age and height.

Four weeks after Georgia's first conversation with her mum about Steph, she is 3 years 8 months and is asking about her mum's lived age.

> **Georgia:** 'You are eleventeen?'
> **Mum:** 'No.'

**Georgia:** *'Six?'*
**Mum:** *'No.'*
**Georgia:** *'20?'*
**Mum:** *'No – I've been 20.'*
**Georgia:** *'When were you 20?'*
**Mum:** *'6 years ago.'*
**Georgia:** *'That was about 1 minute ago.'*
**Mum:** *'No – 6 years ago.'*
**Georgia:** *'6 minutes ago?'*
**Mum:** *'No – 6 years ago.'*
**Georgia:** *'20 years ago?'*
**Mum:** *'No – 6 years ago.'*

Georgia seems to be trying to grasp the quantity and the measures of past time. She is trying to 'generate' more information about the past (Nunes, 1995).

## Extending lengths of time

When Georgia is 3 years 9 months she is still working on understanding real time and how it is measured. She has had a sleep during the day and asks if she can get up for a while after going to bed.

> *I said she could get up for 20 minutes if she went back with no bother when I told her to. She moaned 'That's not long.'*
> **Mum:** *'Well, either 20 minutes or 10 minutes or nothing.'*
> **Georgia:** *'20 is more than 10?'*
> **Mum:** *'Yes.'*
> **Georgia:** *'Okay then, 20 minutes.'*
> (Parent Diary)

This seems to be about staying up as long as possible.

Georgia uses a similar strategy at nursery when it is her turn for the favourite bike. Whatever length of time she is offered, she tries to haggle for longer. When the adult says '10 minutes or 5 minutes?' she says, 'Okay, 10 minutes.' It is not always about prolonging the actual time, as she sometimes offers it to the child whose turn is next, before the 10 minutes is up. It may be about testing the limit – 'What is the longest time I can have?'

When Georgia is just 4 years, she asks 'When is Nanny going to die?' Has Georgia discovered that the limit of life is death?

## Locating events in time

At 4 years 2 months, Georgia has a conversation with her grandmother about birthdays and schools.

> **Georgia:** *'When is your birthday?'*
> **Gran:** *'October.'*
> **Georgia:** *'Will I be at school in October? Is it still April? Will it be May after April? Will it be Harry's birthday the first day of May? Is Craig at Danesholme school? (Craig is a friend who has just left nursery to start school.) How long has he been going there? Will I be at school all day?'*

We can see that Georgia now has much clearer ideas about the order of months and seems to be grasping the idea of events being located in time.

Georgia still incorporates time into her role play. She has been to work with her mum (who is doing telesales) and subsequently represents what her mum does.

> **Georgia:** *'Hello Lindsey, sorry to ring you back in 10 minutes. Eismann Frozen Foods – would you like a catalogue?'*

This is an example of social context leading learning (Moll, 1990).

In May, when Georgia is 4 years 3 months, her uncle comes back from India and describes to Georgia the animals he has seen, including 'monkeys on the street'. Again, Georgia takes up a time theme.

> **Georgia:** *'Which day did you see them?'*
> **Paul:** *'Every day.'*
> **Georgia:** *'Sunday?'*
> **Paul:** *'Yes – Sunday.'*
> **Georgia:** *'Tuesday?'*
> **Paul:** *'Yes – Tuesday.'*
> **Georgia:** *'Your birthday?'*
> **Paul:** *'Yes.'*
> **Georgia:** *'My birthday? How old are you?'*
> **Paul:** *'24.'*
> **Georgia:** *'Are you older than Mop?'* (Mop is his mother.)
> **Paul:** *'No.'*

Paul explained that he is 20 years older than Georgia and that his mum (Mop) is about 20 years older than him. Georgia is still attempting to locate events in time.

At nursery when Georgia is 4 years 4 months, she uses watercolours and is interested in how quickly the paint dries. In this instance, Georgia has a sense of how long paint takes to dry and she is surprised when it dries more quickly than usual. Her sensitivity to issues about time makes her notice and comment on the speed of drying.

Georgia and Steph begin to get a sense of their own history when they look at their Celebrations of Achievement (nursery record book) together.

> **Georgia:** *'Is that a good one? Do you like that one? I haven't got that jumper any more. That was my first day at nursery. I started writing.'*

Georgia is now able to think about and to reflect on her own process of learning and her own past.

## Looking back with Georgia's parents

Georgia's parents were both aware of her interest in time concepts. Neither had really thought about how it started. Her dad says that he is 'a light sleeper' and would be up with Georgia 'six, seven or eight times during the night' when she was a baby. Naturally both parents would discuss in the morning what sort of a night it had been. So there would have been a great deal of conversation *about time* when Georgia was a baby. Alongside this, Georgia's mum liked to have a routine. So naturally Georgia was brought up with a sort of structure to her day. It is difficult to know whether routine suited Georgia as a unique individual, or whether she got used to it because of her early experience. She and Harry are very different and her dad says that 'Georgia really needs routine' even now at 7 years. Whatever the source of her interest, Georgia wanted to know about the sequence of events that were going to happen.

### Giving Georgia a sense of time

> **Mum:** *'I tried to give her a sense of what real time is. I reassured her when I left her in creche. I would say "I'll be one and a half hours – it's not a long time – have good fun".'*

Georgia would want to know when Ian would be home.

> **Mum:** *'I think it is that she's looking forward to seeing him and wants a sense of how long to wait.'*

Georgia became *obsessed* with time, wanting to know how long it would take to get to places and how her mum knew how long it would take. Her mum took her questions seriously and would time journeys, telling Georgia as each minute passed.

> **Mum:** *'I knew she wanted to understand – that's why I used to time things.'*

### Timing events in the close
Georgia explored some time concepts in the close.

> **Mum:** *The children used to play handstands and see who could stay up the longest, counting in seconds. Even if Georgia wasn't doing it, she was watching the older girls.'*

One of her favourite toys was a cart, which she played with in the close.

> **Mum:** *'That was all about experiencing weight, speed – who could pull it fastest – how fast they could go without it being dangerous and tipping over.'*

### Explaining how events are located in time
Georgia's most memorable question for both parents was why Steph was going to be 4 years before her. Her parents tried to explain it in concrete terms to her by making a calendar.

> **Mum:** *'When she was going on and on and on about Steph's birthday being before hers, after explaining lots of times, we made a sort of calendar. It went from January to December with little pictures to signify when it was in the year eg snow in January. Then we wrote on it whose birthday was when. Georgia's is in January so I explained that hers came first in the year – she had already had hers for this year but Steph was just about to have hers. She still wasn't happy.'*
> **Dad:** *'She just thought it wasn't fair! By the following year, it wasn't a problem – she seemed to understand.'*

Georgia (at 7 years) has been reading about Isaac Newton and is interested in when he died and how long he lived. There is a chronological list of events at the end of the book and this interests her. She understands that the events described in the book occurred 300 years ago and that it was around the time of the Great Plague.

# What Georgia learns about time and chronology

Georgia was interested in and intrigued by two separate aspects of time concepts – 'order' and 'duration'. The ability to put things into a logical order is important in all areas of life. Bancroft (1995) says,

> An understanding of the temporal concepts of 'order' and 'duration' is crucial to our ability to plan and organise as well as to our ability to understand things like stories and to solve problems where order is important.

Piaget carried out research into children's understanding of time. When he carried out clinical observations, he found that children have difficulties with the concept of time until they are in their tenth year (Bancroft, 1995). However, there is evidence in his naturalistic observations of his own children, that they were interested in time and using related language from the age of 2 years.

> . . . between 2 [years] and 2 [years]; 6 [months] she understood the length of time indicated by: 'in a minute,' 'just a moment,' etc.
> At 3 [years]; 10 [months] L asked, in reference to that day, which she had been told the day before would be 'to-morrow': 'Is it to-morrow in Pinochet (our district) or is it to-morrow everywhere?'
> J at 5 [years]; 9 [months]: 'Are there times when there aren't any hours, or are there always, always hours?'

This partial understanding of and interest in time has been observed in a more recent study by Bancroft (1985). He says that,

> . . . there was some evidence that these children were talking about time concepts from the beginning of their third year.

Like Georgia's understanding of it being 'next year already . . . for James', it is a sort of time and space problem. Time is such an abstract concept that young children must be struggling with what it is and where it is. It is important for children to ask questions over and over again, as there are several related concepts for them to grapple with.

## Learning language related to time

Georgia learnt time-related language, such as the words for units of time, days and months. Vygotsky would say that the words are important. To him each word is 'a generalisation' and therefore already 'a thought' (Vygotsky, 1962).

In other words, when Georgia expresses ideas using words, she is already thinking and conceiving ideas about what she is expressing.

Georgia's sequencing of days and months became clearer when she was over 4 years and, from what her parents say, her development caught up with what she wanted to know about 'why Steph was four before her' by her fifth birthday!

---

## SUMMARY

Georgia's mathematical explorations and questions related to:

- quantity and amount, division and parts of whole objects
- size and fit
- time and chronology.

She was persistent in her search for understanding, often wanting to achieve or understand to the same extent as the older children she spent time with.

---

We have now looked at how Georgia's mathematical understanding developed. In the next chapter we will be looking at how Georgia develops her understanding of scientific concepts.

# 5 DEVELOPING SCIENTIFIC CONCEPTS

*Our actions in everyday life require that we take into account the physical world.*
(Nunes, 1995)

*Children are born passionately eager to make as much sense as they can of things around them ... Children observe, they wonder, they speculate and they ask themselves questions. They think up possible answers, they make theories, they hypothesise ...*
(Holt, 1989)

---

The scientific concepts that Georgia is most concerned with from the ages of 2 to 5 years are:

- food allergy

- childbirth

- changes in state.

---

Georgia, like any other child in the world, is part of the society in which she has been born. Her quest for knowledge of that world is determined by a number of factors:

- Her particular interests and the circumstances in which she finds herself are important.

- Georgia seeks and gains knowledge about her world that is at times very specialist and at other times more general.

- Georgia is free to discover some properties of materials by experimentation.

- Other information she seeks by asking questions.

- Some information is vitally important for her parents to share with her. Information connected with her younger brother's food allergy comes into this category. Her brother, Harry, has several severe reactions to dairy products and other foods, which are potentially life-threatening.

# Scientific concepts about food allergy

By the time she is 3 years 6 months, Georgia appears to have an understanding of what causes her brother's allergy. She takes it for granted and rarely mentions it unless it is necessary. During a conversation about her grandmother's birthday the subject comes up.

> **Georgia:** *'Have a small cake for Harry, cos he's not allowed eggs or chocolate.'*

She is most interested in checking or in pretending to check the ingredients of products. At 2 years 9 months she seems to know what she is looking for on the side of a carton, but then announces, 'It's from Safeways.' A year later, at 3 years 9 months, she sees her dad looking closely at a pot of fromage frais.

> **Georgia:** *'You are looking to see if Harry's allowed that? You looking at ingredients?'*

At 3 years 5 months she is confident enough to play with and to joke about the information.

> **Mum:** *'If she has something she doesn't want him to have, she'll say "It's got eggs or milk in!" whether it has or not!'*

## Looking back with Georgia's parents

Her parents do not, at the time, see Georgia as having specialist knowledge. However, in retrospect, they realise that what the family discovers about her brother, constitutes knowledge that most adults do not possess. The first signs of the allergy appear when Harry is 6 months and Georgia is 2 years 10 months, although he has always been a sickly baby. Therefore, her interest in reading the carton at 2 years 9 months does not stem from her parents' anxieties about ingredients, but is already an interest of hers. Before Harry's allergy is diagnosed, there is a period of uncertainty. Initially the doctor thinks the swelling around his face might have been caused by a different fabric softener, as the family have been to a friend's wedding and stayed overnight in an hotel. Although they do not directly discuss this with Georgia, she is around when it is mentioned and is aware of her parents' anxieties. Once the diagnosis is made, however, she has to know the rules immediately.

**Dad:** *'It was important that she knew because she loved fromage frais and we had to tell her not to share hers with him.'*

**Mum:** *'We also had to tell the other children in the close. Things like Wotsits and frommes are easy to eat when you are little.'*

Georgia is sometimes in situations where she has to tell adults.

**Dad:** *'She was aware of the symptoms and could relate to an adult what was happening and knew to get help.'*

**Mum:** *'We had been in a lot of situations where other people did not know and would share out food . . . or children would leave drinks on the floor.'*

It seems to me that her parents have high expectations of Georgia at 3 and 4 years, but they are clear that she has to have the information. The alternative is very little freedom for them to even be in a different room for a matter of seconds. Her parents feel it is right to tell her and to expect her to tell others if necessary.

**Mum:** *'I think the more trust you give, the more trustworthy they become. The allergy may have set up a context in which she was given trust and responded positively.'*

Of course it is a gradual process.

**Dad:** *'She had shown in her understanding that she knew.'*

She is able to practise what she knows at home and in the close where the family live. Almost everyone here knows about the allergy. It is an extremely dangerous and serious situation and not one with which they can take risks.

**Mum:** *'She was really doing it, not playing at doing it.'*

At almost 5 years, Harry has outgrown his allergy, but Georgia, at 7 years, can still remember the problems.

**Georgia:** *'He weren't allowed to eat some things like cheese . . . his eyes and mouth would swell up . . . I'd tell you . . . he'd go to hospital.'*

## Georgia's scientific knowledge about allergies

So what is the nature of scientific knowledge that Georgia learns about her brother's allergy? She has enough factual information to know not to explore the situation by giving him different foods. She is not free to solve any part of the problem. Her parents welcome her questions and are happy to explain and repeat the facts as many times as necessary. They want her to link what he eats with the result. Therefore, it is not enough to focus on the different 'states' of her brother's health: 'well' and obviously 'ill' with swollen head and eyes (Das Gupta and Richardson, 1995). She needs to understand the process and the relationship between the products he eats and his resulting reaction.

### Helping Georgia to link cause and effect

Georgia has to know that a negative reaction is *caused* by eating certain foods. She needs to know about the raw products he is allergic to but she also needs to know that it is not always obvious which products contain the problem foods. She needs to know, for example, that chocolate contains milk. So, not only does her brother's appearance change, but, food products that look different can contain some of the same ingredients. These are complex ideas and Georgia seems to cope with the important aspects. The emotions experienced by Georgia and her parents each time Harry shows signs of the allergy may contribute to her ability to remember. Carter (1998) says that 'events that happen in a state of emotional excitement' are likely to be remembered easily and over a long time.

## SCIENTIFIC CONCEPTS ABOUT CHILDBIRTH

The birth of Georgia's younger brother, when she is 2 years 3 months, provides a scientific context in which she is likely to gain some general information about babies and childbirth. Georgia's parents are aware that the birth of her sibling gives them an opportunity to show her books with illustrations about how a baby grows and is born, as well as stories which explore the emotional aspects of a baby being born into a family.

Her brother is 7 weeks and she is 2 years 5 months when her parents notice that she takes a special interest in three books which deal with issues about new babies joining the family.

> *Suddenly wanting three books about expected baby and baby's arrival. Likes saying 'Walter' and repeats the name several times.*
> (Parent Diary)

(Walter is the name of a baby in one of the stories).

## Noticing differences

Georgia is interested in the physical differences between herself and her brother. When Georgia is 2 years 7 months, she jokes about physical features. Her parents connect this with 'the fact that she changed Harry's nappy yesterday'.

A few days later Georgia makes an announcement.

**Georgia:** *For Christmas I want a boy dolly that can wee out of his willy.'*

Around this time Georgia (2 years 8 months) frequently plays mummies and babies. She explores different roles.

*Georgia, Nicola and Samantha were all playing at Samantha's house this week. Georgia got the buggy she wanted and also a doll and said 'I Colette (mum), this Harry (pointing at doll) and Georgia at playgroup.'*
(Parent Diary)

The schemas that Georgia explores extensively during this period seem to link with her later understanding of how babies are born. She puts objects inside other objects which are capable of covering them completely. Athey refers to this action as 'containing' and 'enveloping' objects or oneself (1990). Georgia tries covering or putting objects inside containers using all sorts of different materials. She is 2 years 9 months when her parents record that 'She put a coin inside a tea infuser and shook it'. The infuser is spherical, can open and close, and can contain and conceal small objects. The concealed object rattles when shaken proving that the object is still inside though it cannot be seen. Babies inside wombs are also concealed.

**Mum:** *'She does a lot of wrapping up coins at home, also getting her bag ready (in buggy and wrapped up).'*

Wrapping coins conceals them with flexible covering, just as skin stretches with the baby still inside the womb.

A week later Georgia is still exploring these themes.

*She is well into enveloping. Lots of babies in pram, buggy and truck. Carrying a bag full of things (looked quite big and heavy). When I asked what was in it, she said 'nappies and things'.*

> *Had money in purse, inside box . . . Wore hairband, then a bit later hat . . . then a*
> *different hat. Sat on truck with pram attached and blanket draped over pram*
> *wearing hat.*
> (Parent Diary)

These explorations of envelopment seem to help her to understand one function or purpose of covering or enveloping objects, animals or people, often babies.

## Exploring going through a boundary

Another schema which Georgia investigates is going through a boundary. This exploration helps her to understand how an object inside a container comes through to the outside of the container. This relates to the actual passage of a baby from the womb to the outside world.

At 3 years 1 month Georgia is worried 'About her teeth – "Just bleeds a little bit".' She is concerned with blood coming through her gums. The blood is not apparent until it comes through the gum.

At 3 years 2 months, 'Georgia is very interested in Harry's arm – he has had a blood test.' She is interested in the actual breaking of the skin. One of her ideas is that the tummy is cut open to allow the baby to come out.

> **Mum:** *'She was using the outside tap and watering can. She poured lots of water*
> *into the chimney pot (plant pot).'*

The watering can is a container with a spout, so that when it is tipped up the contents come out. The properties of liquids are suitable for pouring. A less flexible material might not fit through the spout. A baby is not liquid and does not seem very flexible, therefore it is difficult to imagine it coming through a space much smaller than itself.

> **Georgia** (3 years 3 months): *'Better shut the window, the rain's only small, can*
> *get in there.'*

She is differentiating according to size and displaying her understanding of what stops the rain from going through. Again, she is thinking about and estimating what will fit through a space. A baby cannot fit through a small space.

## What a 'dead end' is

At 3 years 4 months Georgia becomes interested in what prevents a clear passage through a boundary. She wants to know what a 'dead end' is. Her mum drives her to the end of a cul-de-sac to show her. On the same day, she makes a representation of a 'dead end' when she is painting.

Later that day at her grandmother's house, Georgia plays with earrings.

> **Grandmother:** *'She liked putting earrings in my ear – gave her a huge sense of satisfaction – did each about 20 times, putting them in, putting the back bit on and taking them out.'*

Georgia is gaining firsthand experience of putting rigid material through a small space. Interestingly, a hole in an ear lobe looks almost invisible when there is no ring through it. The baby goes through a small space – is there a parallel?

A month later Georgia is 3 years 5 months.

> *Georgia is playing at the table with colour pegs . . . Talks about pushing them right down and pressing them right down. Frequently turns pegboard over.*
> (Parent Diary)

She uses force and gravity. Both force and gravity are used in childbirth. She is able to co-ordinate ideas about containing and going through at 3 years 6 months.

> *She played in the sand with sand tray toy placed over a dumper truck. She filled the container, which was on top, with sand, then opened the 'plug' and the sand went through to the truck.*
> (Parent Diary)

One way of containing then releasing an object or some material is to use a plug. Perhaps the human female has a plug or trapdoor, which when removed, releases the baby?

Her earliest interest at nursery at 3 years 7 months, is woodwork, particularly hammering nails through wood. She continues to pursue this interest for several months. Again, she is using force and the weight of the hammer. A powerful force might push the baby out.

## Pushing things through

Georgia (3 years 11 months) at nursery, is playing with dough.

*Georgia starts pushing dough into the dough train (works a bit like a garlic press). She pushes the handle down and, as the dough comes through, she looks at me and says 'Look!'*
(Family Worker Observation)

With this tool she can see and experience a mass which is solid but flexible, pushed through a space smaller than itself. This is similar to what actually happens during the birth of a baby.

A few minutes later, she compares dough with earrings, clearly showing that she is interested in the going through action.

It is 3 months later, after gaining the necessary conceptual knowledge, when visiting the hospital where she and her brother were born, that she begins to show a real understanding about how a baby is born. She is 4 years 2 months.

*... we passed the maternity unit and I told Georgia that the last time I'd been there, it was for Harry to come out of my tummy and that it was where she had come out of my tummy.*
*Georgia asked 'Do they cut your tummy open and get the baby out?'*

(She offers her own theory.)

*(I just assumed she knew how babies came out, as she'd seen all my pregnancy books when I was having Harry.)*
**Mum:** *'No, they come out of your gina.'*
**Georgia:** *'Out your gina? Out your gina?' (in amazement at the top of her voice!)*
*'The baby comes out of your gina?'*
*I then explained about caesareans and Georgia said, 'But why would they cut your tummy if you could just push it out your gina?'*
(Parent Diary)

This statement shows that at this stage she could think about and construct a mental model of the process.

## Looking back with Georgia's parents

Georgia's parents are aware that, although they have told her how babies are born and have shown her several well-illustrated books about the birth, it is a long time before she has an even partial understanding of the process. They assume that going to antenatal clinic with her mum, looking at books together and being prepared to answer her questions around the time of her brother's birth, helps her to understand.

Her dad recalls very little information about her question. Her mum feels that she asks questions mostly about the 'historical' aspects.

> **Mum:** *'She wanted to know what she weighed, where she was weighed and measured – gory details like the blood etc.'*

> **Georgia** (at 7 years): *'Was I 45 centimetres and he was 54 centimetres – cos they're the same numbers the other way around?'*

This is totally accurate showing that the questions she asks at the time are important to her and that she has retained that information.

> **Georgia:** *'Mum – why do some people be born late? Harry was born 13 days late and I was born 1 day late.'*

Again this is accurate. When we discuss these aspects, Georgia also offers more information.

> **Georgia:** *'I don't play mummies and babies anymore. I stopped when I was six.'*

## Georgia's scientific knowledge of childbirth

Before Georgia can understand how a baby is born, it appears that she has to be able to think of the womb as a container with the growing or expanding baby contained inside. The period when she envelops various objects, some flexible and others inflexible, helps her to partially understand. However, it is only after exploring a going through a boundary action schema, that she is able to co-ordinate and 'mentally construct' (Athey, 1990) ideas about a birth. What is not clear is 'how much experience is required for a new form to be constructed'. The other issue is that she is given the factual information much earlier, at a stage when it appears she is unable to understand it. Does the factual information in fact contribute something to her later understanding? Vygotsky would support the idea that instruction and information should be offered ahead of development (1962). This also raises questions about the importance of always having reference books available to children, which may support their own explorations and discoveries with accurate information and illustrations.

# SCIENTIFIC CONCEPTS ABOUT CHANGES IN STATE

Georgia is interested in experimenting with materials, noticing and causing changes, particularly in consistency, as well as noticing when a material or person changes its appearance. She often plays with sand and water in the garden, but a holiday at the seaside when she is 2 years 5 months gives her the chance to experiment further.

> *Visit to beach – Georgia most interested in picking up lumps of very soggy sand on a spade and throwing it into the water.*
> (Parent Diary)

A lump of soggy solid disappears and appears to dissolve in the large mass of liquid.

During the next few weeks, she enjoys 'watering the flowers' in the garden each time she visits her grandparents. Liquid poured on soil disappears.

In November at 2 years 10 months, she notices something new.

> **Mum:** *'She could see her breath outside – she went to the front door, blew and said "smoke", then came into the room and did the same and said "no smoke"!'*

Georgia is observing the transformation from gas to liquid.

Around Christmas, at 2 years 11 months, Georgia paints, using poster paints and water colours.

> *She partially enveloped the paper with paint, starting in one corner and adding different colours, which blended together . . . she used water colours, trying each in turn, making a separate mark on the paper with each . . . she said, 'Look at the colours I've oozed' and spoke about 'navy-blue'.*
> (Parent Diary)

This could be an interest in how colours change when blended with other colours.

She visits nursery at 3 years 3 months and is involved in melting chocolate to make krispie cakes. This explores the transformation from solid to liquid and back to solid.

Later the same day, Georgia pours lots of water into a chimney pot containing plants.

**Georgia:** *'It's okay, it's melting.'*

It is disappearing but making the soil soggy. The liquid appears to be changing to a soggy solid state, which has a similar consistency to melted chocolate.

**Mum:** *'Georgia told me a boy had put water on her hair.'*

She is feeling the effect of liquid on her hair, which absorbs the liquid in a similar way to the soil.

At 3 years 4 months she was most interested when her dad was throwing away a tub of margarine. The bottom of the tub was covered in a sheet of ice.

**Georgia:** *'Why are you throwing it away?'*
**Dad:** *'Because the fridge was up too high and it's frozen.'*
**Georgia:** *'That's why you making glass.'*

Georgia has noticed that water turns to ice, so once again liquid becomes solid. She compares it with glass which is also solid and transparent.

## Watering flowers

She continues to water the flowers and reveals her interest in the quantity of water and its effect when she is 3 years 4 months.

**Georgia:** *'Look how many water. That gonna make it grow quicker.'*

She has an interest in the effect of water on seeds, which will change by becoming bigger.

Georgia (3 years 4 months) continues to explore and to understand the effects of water on other materials.

*Georgia said, 'It's raining – my slide's wet!'*
*I said, 'You'd better slide down to dry it.'*
*Georgia, No – I can't because my bum will get wet!'*
(Parent Diary)

The liquid on the slide will be absorbed by the material of her clothes and it will penetrate the material reaching her skin. The liquid will disappear.

# Wetting and soaking materials and people

Georgia becomes interested in soaking materials, including other people and herself. She is on holiday at the seaside, aged 3 years 6 months.

> *Splashed herself and me as soon as possible. Kept telling me she wouldn't splash me but then did. I said she wasn't allowed to get wet. She sat down in the water in her clothes and then sang, 'We are soaking and we not allowed to get wet!'*
> (Parent Diary)

There was also the aspect of being able to experiment more freely at the seaside because of the space and feeling free to enjoy what was available, because of being on holiday. She has firsthand experience of being dry and becoming wet.
   A month later, at 3 years 7 months, she plays with a water gun at home.

> **Georgia:** *'Can I get my hair wet? [pause] It's soaked already!'*

Again, she is having firsthand experience of being dry and becoming very wet.

# Soaking with paint

Three weeks later, Georgia is painting.

> *Georgia painted some computer paper. She used mostly red paint and rotated the brush to get lots of paint on it. 'It's all wet – it's soaking.'*
> (Parent Diary)

By now she really knows what 'soaking' means. Dry paper is soaked with paint.
   When Georgia starts nursery, she has opportunities to use a wider range of materials. She frequently plays in the workshop area with glue, paint and other materials. She becomes concerned with the opposite of being soaked, that is the process of liquid drying. This may indicate her interest in the *'reversibility'* of operations (Richardson, 1995). She discovers that liquids dry out when spread thinly over certain materials. She is often more involved in picking the dried-out glue off her fingers, than in producing a picture or model. When she is 3 years 9 months, she takes nail varnish from home to nursery, puts it on her own and other children's nails, then picks it off. Again she is exploring liquid to solid.

*At 3 years 10 months, Georgia spends most of her time in the wet area painting and picking paint off her fingers*

## Allowing paint and glue to dry

Two weeks later Georgia enjoys using clay.

> *Georgia manipulated the clay, adding water to it, before putting a candle in it. She slowly filled the clay with sequins and glitter. (She took her candle-holder home when it dried out.)*
> (Family Worker observation)

Georgia is examining the change from damp clay to malleable soggy clay to dried out clay.

She often uses paint, applying it in different ways to different materials.

## Changing her appearance

It may have been pure coincidence or possibly part of her predominant enveloping schema, but Georgia frequently swaps clothes with her friend Stephanie around this period. Sometimes she changes into nursery clothes for no reason. She tends to choose clothes that are too small or particularly old, thereby changing her appearance.

## Cooking to transform ingredients

At her grandparents' house, she enjoys transforming ingredients by cooking. She likes to make things that involve the transformation of liquids to solids.

At nursery, at 4 years 2 months and 4 years 4 months she uses Modroc (discovering the properties first and still exploring its use later on. This is a Plaster of Paris bandage used to set broken limbs which turns from solid to liquid and back to solid.

At 3 years 11 months Georgia is preoccupied with dough. She is particularly interested in dividing dough using a knife, garlic press or dough train. She is combining dry and wet ingredients to make a malleable solid.

At 4 years Georgia's preferred material is peat.

> Georgia became totally involved in mixing peat and water for over an hour this morning. The peat was with the pulleys. She did not bother about the pulleys, but began putting handfuls of peat from the ground into a bucket and asked if she could add water. (The transformation/consistency seemed to be the important part for her.) She said she was making 'pasta'. She was adding liquid to solid particles.
> (Family Worker Observation)

At home, at 3 years 9 months, Georgia is using crayons.

> She did a picture by colouring all over a piece of card with a crayon then wiping it with a damp cloth and then using another crayon. She spent quite a while experimenting – trying to rub off the crayon etc. (She did both sides with different colours).
> (Parent Diary)

Crayon resists water unlike some of the absorbent materials she has used, so in this case the liquid does not disappear.

## Transforming the living-room

At 3 years 11 months Georgia likes being involved in transforming the living room.

> **Mum:** 'Georgia was ill and got up in the evening when we were changing the room around. She offered suggestions about where to put pieces of furniture.'

This does not involve matter changing state but from Georgia's point of view the effect may be similar. It is not surprising that she wants to direct.

Taking the decorations off the Christmas tree at 3 years 11 months also captures her interest.

> **Georgia:** 'We undecorated the tree today!'

Is this an interest in reversing a process? Some transformations are not reversible. Again she is making something physical look different.

At 4 years, she wants to know 'Why are some people black and some white?' Does she think that people change from one to the other?

Also at 4 years, she describes what she thinks is happening when she puts her hand under the tap as the water is warming up.

> **Georgia:** *'This water's getting lumpy!'*

In this case the water feels as though it is changing from liquid to solid.

At 4 years 4 months, she helps make cakes.

> **Georgia:** *'Dad you can have your cake soon – when it's dried out.'*

## Looking back with Georgia's parents

Georgia's parents are less aware of her consistent interest in changes in state. Quite a lot of her investigations are carried out at nursery when she is 3 years 7 months or more and it is only when we view all of the material as a whole that we recognise how often her explorations link with her subsequent knowledge about changes of state.

> **Dad:** *'She was always interested in the cold weather . . . in water turning to ice. She always wanted water in the sand . . . we had the sandpit from when she was two.'*
> **Mum:** *'Did her interest in changes in state link with her brother's allergy?'*
> **Georgia** (7 years): *'I still like picking glue off my fingers . . . Last year there was ice over the sandpit – I thought it was strong, so I stepped on it and it broke.'*

I am interested in what she knows about reversibility. I ask her about whether glue ever becomes liquid again.

> **Georgia:** *'No'*
> **Me:** *'What about ice to water?'*
> **Georgia:** *'Yes.'*

Her mum remembers her liking a book about water. It is a reference book with factual information about how water evaporates, becomes ice and so on.

Georgia at 7 years stands by her theory about more water making plants grow more quickly.

# Georgia's scientific knowledge about changes in state

Georgia's scientific experiments about changes in state are of two main types:

1   Adding water of varying amounts to other materials.
2   Spreading or sprinkling liquids and allowing them to dry out.

Her scientific method consists of:

- Asking herself 'what if I do X?', for example wet my clothes or hair?

- 'Y will happen' – she is developing a hypothesis, that the liquid will disappear.

- Then carrying out experiments to test her hypothesis by varying the variables: adding different amounts of liquid, different types of liquid to different types of material.

Holt (1989) says that 'real learning is a process of discovery' and that children '*make*' knowledge. Georgia initiates the experiments and is also sensitive to events in the environment which relate to her central concern. For example, occasionally she observes the effect of heat or cold being applied to liquids. She shows great interest in these effects. Georgia appears to be exploring change, both external and internal, reversible and irreversible. She is certainly interested in the effect her actions have on materials, as well as on other people. Piaget views very young children as displaying a 'rigidity of thought' (Miller, 1992). This is characterised by their inability to think in a flexible way. For example a very young child might see a coat 'held in a hand', then 'hung up' and be unable to understand or to think about how it stays near the wall. It is not unusual to see young children holding their coats near a coatpeg as though something magical may happen. When children begin to show an interest in the *transformation process* rather than the *beginning state* and *end state*, this is highly significant. At this stage they begin to understand that 'the coat staying against the wall' depends on 'the loop surrounding the hook'. Athey (1990) believes that this interest in cause and effect directly precedes 'conservation', that is, a full understanding that a quantity or number stays the same, even though it is distributed differently, unless anything is added to it or taken away from it. During this period Georgia seems to be systematically exploring,

- what happens to different materials when they become wet
- what happens to different materials when they are soaked with water

- whether glue always dries when spread thinly

- whether other liquids dry when sprinkled or spread thinly.

An important aspect of experimenting with and focusing on the process of change is the discovery of which procedures are reversible and which are not.

## SUMMARY

The main thrust of Georgia's scientific explorations and discoveries from 2 to 5 years relates to:

- understanding and communicating information about her brother's food allergy

- seeking information about childbirth by asking questions about aspects which she is ready to learn about

- exploring and discovering knowledge about changes in state by firsthand experiences and the manipulation of materials

- her strong schematic concerns are often the source and the means by which she generates new ideas

- what happens for her, is firmly rooted in her experience in her family at that time and never to be replicated again.

In this chapter we have looked at the source and development of Georgia's scientific concepts. In the next chapter we will be looking at Georgia's emotional development.

# 6 GEORGIA'S EMOTIONAL DEVELOPMENT

*Our passions, when well exercised, have wisdom; they guide our thinking, our values, our survival.*
(Goleman, 1996)

We will look at Georgia's emotional development through:

- her spontaneous interest in power issues and her use of power

- her actions and reactions during periods of change, uncertainty and transition

We have already seen that Georgia is very much a 'people person'. The relationships she makes, as well as the relationships she observes and hears about, are central to her development and learning. Georgia learns about the world through people. Two of Gardner's 'multiple intelligences' are:

- to understand other individuals

- to understand ourselves (1991).

For Georgia, people seem to be the essential element in any learning environment. Part of what she learns is about relating to others and understanding and expressing her own feelings and thoughts. Like any young child, Georgia begins by struggling to understand and gain control of the world as she sees it (Stern, 1985).

## POWER ISSUES AND GEORGIA'S USE OF POWER

Like other aspects of Georgia's development and learning, her emotional development does not take a simple, linear route. She is influenced by the people she knows and loves and by their actions and experiences. According to Piaget (1951) children have 'general schemas' about people, based on the people they know. They will 'tend to assimilate all other individuals' into this general schema. Given Georgia's early and sustained relationships with older children, it is not surprising that she seems to have a view of older and bigger people as more powerful than her.

## Who has power?

When Georgia is 3 years 3 months, she asks her dad a question about his relationship with his boss, Kai, which puzzles both parents initially.

> **Georgia:** *'You follow Kai about at work?'*

Georgia's query about how people relate to each other at work becomes clearer when she is cross with her mum and says (in a rebellious tone), 'I'm going to follow Steph about!' (Steph is her friend at creche and playgroup.) The inference is that Georgia (in order to punish her mum) is not going to use her power to do something of her own choosing, but will take on the subordinate role of following Steph. Two other related statements add to our understanding:

1   **Georgia:** *'Gemma follows us about.'* (Gemma is new to playgroup and clings to Georgia and Steph.)
2   **Georgia:** *'We been following baby Daniel about!'* (Again at playgroup, Georgia and Steph play with the idea by following someone who is obviously less knowledgeable than them.)

These two statements illustrate Georgia's understanding of the processes of learning as experienced by other children. Georgia knows that it is a silly idea for her to do what a much younger child ('baby Daniel') does, but she does it for fun. Bruce (1991) says that humour 'involves knowing something so well that it is possible to play with your play'. Georgia is in a powerful position when she knows something so well that she can turn it upside down for fun. Her question about Kai seems to be an attempt to discover more about her dad's relationship with Kai. If younger, less experienced children like Gemma at playgroup, follow older children about, then is that what her dad does at work?

### Using power

Georgia (at 3 years 5 months) is 'ill and stroppy' and desperate to use whatever power she has.

> **Georgia** to her mum: *'You not coming to my birthday then!'*

She says this quite often when she's not happy with someone. The situation becomes quite humorous.

> **Georgia:** *'You can come to mine birthday then but you're not going to have any cake!'*
> **Mum:** *'But I'm going to make the cake.'*
> **Georgia:** *'I don't care anyway!'*

Georgia uses a similar threat a month later (at 3 years 6 months) when she falls out with her grandmother. Her grandmother goes along with her decision to choose who is invited to her birthday.

> **Gran:** *'I'll have to send your present then . . . and the postman will bring it.'*

Georgia immediately becomes interested in what the present will be and changes her mind, saying 'You can come to my birthday.'

This acceptance of Georgia's decision defuses the situation completely.

## Dominating others

On two occasions Georgia tries to dominate children who are younger than her. At 3 years 5 months, Georgia is playing with James, who is 3 months younger and lives next door.

> *I told her to ask James' mum if he was allowed some sweets – then she could choose them at Safeway – this was to appease Georgia as she didn't want to come with me. A bit later, Georgia to James: 'You allowed hard or soft?'*
> *James, 'Hard.'*
> *Georgia, 'No, you're not.'*
> *James, 'Soft.'*
> (Parent Diary)

In this instance Georgia has the power and is going to abuse it by giving James no choice. She may be behaving in the same way that she experiences older children or adults behaving towards her at times. Does she always know and understand why she is not allowed something? Is she always given genuine choices that she understands? Or does she just realise that, in this instance, she is more powerful than James? Georgia may be using the situation to 'exercise' her power (Goleman, 1996).

At 3 years 8 months, Georgia is playing upstairs in her bedroom with Laura (who is 6 months younger) when there is an argument.

> **Georgia:** *'I wasn't letting Laura out of my room 'cos I wanted her to play mummies and babies and she didn't want to.'*

In this instance Georgia is trying to force Laura to play her choice of game. Georgia's more usual companions are older rather than younger than her. Georgia may be struggling to negotiate with a younger child. Pollard (1996) describes some of the negotiations which go on at school between teacher and pupils, as well as at home between parents and children or siblings. He says,

> *In general, adults have the power to initiate, assert, maintain and change rules, whilst children must comply, adapt, mediate or resist.*

## Strategies for joining other children at play

When Georgia is 3 years 6 months her parents write down in the Parent Diary her range of strategies for joining other children at play.

> *With Harry or Laura, she takes over or tries to get him or her to do what she wants. She says things like,*
> *'. . . want me to show you . . .'*
> *'. . . want me to do . . .'*
> *'. . . want to do this . . .'*
> *Outside in the close she will just watch until asked to join in (if the older children are playing an actual game) or say, 'Me have a turn?'*
> *If the children in the close are just hanging around or all doing different things she'll just go and join in by doing similar things nearby.*

This shows that Georgia already has a range of adaptable strategies for getting along with other children. She takes the lead with younger children. With older children, she tries to assess what kind of play they are engaging in, before either asking whether she can follow their lead or replicating what they are doing alongside them, in order to make a smooth transition into their play. With younger children, Georgia is the initiator. With older children, she wants to join in and discover what they are playing.

## Power to express feelings

Around the same time, Georgia is confused and seems powerless to express her feelings.

> *She fell over when demonstrating hopping. Immediately her mood changed, she looked down, fiddled with her T-shirt. She looked cross and unhappy and did not want to speak to anyone. (3 years 6 months)*

> *She wanted to sit in the back of the car. The seatbelt is only effective with her carseat in the front. Was very stubborn and kept refusing to go in the front – eventually I told her she had to. (3 years 7 months)*

*(Grandmother) I babysat because Ian was late. Both children were tired and upset. Georgia tore up the writing which she had done for me. Was distraught till she said she wanted dummy and Nancy and I said that was fine. (3 years 9 months)*
(Parent Diary)

Georgia has just started nursery. Her dad has changed jobs and her mum begins working evenings. There is more tension within the family than usual. Things are less predictable than previously. Georgia is able to 'soothe' herself with her dummy and Nancy (Goleman, 1995) and in choosing to do this, seems to restore some of the power she feels is slipping away from her (Winnicott, 1975).

At nursery the staff encourage children to choose where, what and with whom to play. Georgia is happiest when she is near adults or children whom she already knows. Rutter (1992) says 'familiarity tends to be associated with interactions that are better meshed, more complex and which involve more fantasy'. Pollard (1996) observed a child in his study as 'more self-confident and relaxed' when alongside a peer.

At nursery Georgia exercises her power in different ways:

- by participating in family role play (3 years 9 months)

- by choosing a different Family Worker when Alison is off (at 3 years 10 months)

- by choosing what to wear (at 3 years 9 months), particularly enjoying transforming her appearance – she can anticipate her mum's reaction to her altered appearance.

At 3 years 11 months, Georgia throws her dummy in the bin after advice from the dentist.

## Becoming empowered

The nursery staff are proactive in offering the older children small group sessions on:

- friendships and conflict

- bullying

- physical boundaries

- strangers

- good feelings and bad feeling (Mars et al, 1990).

Georgia participates in all five sessions and is happiest discussing these issues when Steph is alongside her.

## Looking back with Georgia's parents

Both parents remember Georgia's dummy and Nancy being really important to her. She always had to have them with her when she was very young. Once, before Georgia was 2 years, she lost Nancy

> **Dad:** *'Losing Nancy was the most traumatic 2 days of her life – and ours, because we knew she wasn't going to sleep without Nancy.'*

Her parents were able to replace Nancy after 2 days by contacting the person who had bought her and finding out where Nancy came from. Georgia ended up with two Nancys – an identical one from the supplier in Germany and a larger one donated by an older child, who had received it as a gift from the same person that gave Georgia hers. Georgia (at 7 years) still has both dolls and sometimes takes one of them to bed with her.

### The power of complex play

Georgia has close attachments to Aunty Eloise and Jennifer, as well as to her parents and brother. However, her parents feel that the balance of power in these early relationships, is not the same as the balance of power in subsequent peer relationships.

> **Dad:** *'She always had Jennifer and Amy.'*

We have seen in Chapter One that the twins liked Georgia to be the baby and also that they might 'give in to her.'

> **Mum:** *'She had to learn to negotiate – even with Steph and Laura – they weren't going to give in to her.'*

Her dad noticed that at nursery 'She tended to stay with Steph – they knew what they were going to do.' This fits with the view of Rutter and others (Tizard, 1986) that 'more complex' play develops when children know each other well.

### The power to destroy

When Georgia destroys her writing, she is using her power destructively. This is something that happens only rarely when Georgia is very distressed. Her parents remember this.

**Dad:** *'She screwed a picture up a couple of weeks ago because we didn't have something she wanted to use on it.'*

Her mum feels that she can 'usually stop her from destroying her work' by talking to her about what she is doing and discussing why.

### The power of humour

Georgia is at her most powerful when she displays her sense of humour. It was in a spirit of humour that she would deliberately change into nursery clothes that were too small or did not suit her. Her mum is aware that 'she purposefully chose clothes she knew I would hate – it really amused her.' This is a little like 'playing with play' (Bruce, 1991). In this instance she is aware of her mum's opinions and attitudes about how she wants Georgia to dress and look. Rather than take these opinions seriously, Georgia is able to poke fun at her mum and is confident that her mum will see the funny side of the joke too.

## Georgia's use of power and her emotional development

It is important for babies and young children to form 'attachments' with the people who care for them (Schaffer, 1995). Georgia formed 'several attachments' with adults and older children who responded sensitively to her. Those attachments form a secure base from which to explore and take risks. Rutter says that 'secure attachments' are the 'key to good relationships' (1992) and 'foster autonomy rather than dependency'. Georgia clearly feels most powerful and able to explore and take risks when she is alongside an adult or child she knows well.

The humour Georgia uses is interactive. It is shared with others she knows well and dependent on 'in-group knowledge and familiarity' (Rutter, 1992). Laughter is beneficial in all sorts of ways. Goleman (1996) says that even 'mild mood changes can sway thinking'. Laughter encourages a positive outlook and creative thinking. It is 'the ratio of positive to negative emotions that determines the sense of well-being'. Although, at times Georgia struggled to express her hurt, this was balanced by her ability to find or create humour, which she shared with close friends and family.

### The power of mastering problems

Dweck and Leggett (1988) have put forward the idea that children generally react in one of two ways when faced with challenging tasks. They either see themselves as inadequate failures and display 'helplessness' or they relish the challenge and display what they call 'mastery-oriented' behaviour. A child who is being helpless will very quickly give up, but a child who relishes a challenge will believe in themselves, persevere and generally be more in control of any situation. Georgia's outlook generally was positive, but her confidence became a little shaky at times. We have already seen that she had some strategies for 'soothing' herself. Those strategies also seemed to involve Georgia in being able to use her power. There were small choices that Georgia could make, for example, when she needed the comfort of dummy and Nancy, who to be near at nursery and so on. We shall see in the next section what happens during periods of uncertainty and change.

# PERIODS OF CHANGE, UNCERTAINTY AND TRANSITION

In Chapter One we saw that Georgia was born into a very stable family:

- two parents who had lived together for some time before her birth
- a father in a steady, well established job
- a close, supportive extended family
- friendly neighbours in a small, intimate close.

Georgia, as an individual, has a sociable temperament and her early environment seems to suit her. We are now going to look at what happens when change occurs within that stable environment.

## The birth of Georgia's brother

The first major change in Georgia's life is the birth of her brother, Harry, when she is 2 years 3 months. We have already heard that Georgia liked looking at reference books about how babies grow and are born (Chapter Five). Her parents spend a lot of time explaining what will happen and how things will change. She seems to take all of this in her stride. Harry is 2 months when her parents notice Georgia *suddenly* exploring stories 'about expected baby and baby's arrival'.

This sudden rekindled interest takes her parents by surprise. However, as human beings we need to 'assimilate' and 'digest' new information (Piaget, 1951). Stories can enable us to express our feelings and to identify with other perspectives (Barnes, 1995). Life has changed for Georgia and maybe, at this point, she is beginning to realise that Harry is here to stay.

Georgia continues to react positively towards Harry but is nasty towards her mum quite often when Harry is a baby. She may be 'displacing' her confused or angry feelings by punishing her mum, who she is certain will always love her, rather than hurting or showing her anger towards Harry (Isaacs, 1933).

## Starting playgroup

At 2 years 7 months Georgia starts playgroup. The transition seems to be smooth but Georgia must be thinking about where Harry and mummy are when she is at playgroup. At 2 years 8 months Georgia explores these issues through role play.

> *Georgia, Nicola and Samantha were all playing at Samantha's house this week. Georgia got the buggy she wanted and also a doll and said 'I Colette, this Harry' (pointing at the doll) 'Georgia at playgroup'.*
> (Parent Diary)

Whitehead (1997) says that 'the experiences children bring to group settings must be re-enacted or tried out in many different symbolic ways'. Role play and stories are two of the ways in which Georgia explores her changing world.

## Harry's allergic reaction to dairy products

The next major change is Harry's allergic reaction to dairy products. This happens, for the first time, when Georgia is 2 years 10 months. Unlike Harry's birth, her parents cannot prepare her for this. They cannot offer an explanation about the cause. All they can do is reassure her that it is not her fault and that Harry will be all right. The records do not show any negative or unusual reactions from Georgia during this period of uncertainty, which lasts several months. It is reasonable to suppose that Georgia was aware of her parents' anxiety. Miller (1992) says that young children 'are sensitive to their parents' state of mind'. There are several factors which may account for the Parent Diary showing no change in her behaviour:

- Her parents are so focussed on Harry that they take less notice of Georgia and write less in the diary?

- She recognises their anxiety and understands that it is about Harry and not about her?

- She trusts her parents' power to make things okay?

- She can see the reaction – it is physical and, therefore, tangible?

- Her parents discuss the allergy in her presence and, therefore, there is no hidden agenda?

- Her attitude to Harry is positive and, therefore, she is less likely to feel she is to blame in any way?

Dunn and Kendrick (1982) found that,

> *If the mother talked to the first-born about the new baby before the birth, relations between the siblings were much friendlier by the time the baby was 14 months than they were in families where this did not happen.*

So maybe the time given to discussing the baby with Georgia before the allergy was discovered, contributes to her understanding and interest in his state of health when he has a reaction.

By the time Georgia is 3 years 5 months the allergy has been diagnosed and the family know what to do in an emergency. When Georgia is 3 years 6 months her mum has written in the Parent Diary that she sees Georgia most involved in 'pretend games – going to the doctor's, doing cholesterol tests and writing prescriptions.' Georgia is almost certainly playing out some of her fears to 'make them bearable' (Piaget, 1951) and to put them behind her.

## Georgia's transition to nursery

Georgia's transition to nursery is not as easy as her parents expect. She displays her ambivalence before she starts nursery by refusing to go to creche. A combination of changes occur around the time that Georgia is starting nursery. Her dad changes his job for a second time and her mum begins evening work. This changes the pattern of care. What actually happens is that sometimes her dad cannot get home in time to take over, so he has to ring their grandmother, who rushes over to care for the children until he arrives home. We have already heard from her dad that Georgia likes to know what is going to happen. So a sudden change of arrangement, at a time when Georgia is already coping with several changes, results in her feeling angry and powerless.

Georgia has also possibly held on to her negative feelings for several months while Harry's allergy was the focus of attention. The resulting behaviour may be a reaction to an accumulation of feelings (Goleman, 1995). It does not seem a coincidence that her favourite stories at this time are *Angry Arthur* which is the

*Georgia and Steph having a story*

story of a child whose anger explodes, and *Avocado Baby* which is about a baby who becomes incredibly strong and powerful through eating avocado each day. She listens to these stories several times both at nursery and at home.

Georgia's reactions, even throughout this period of change, were not extreme. At nursery, she would be clingy and stay near adults rather than becoming involved with other children. Rutter (1992) points out that 'children are most likely to cling when they are frightened and upset'. At home she would sulk or cry if she could not have what she wanted. There was less flexibility than normal. Georgia was not willing to 'make compromises'. If we were to use Laever's indicators of well-being, we might notice that, at times, Georgia's well-being was lower than usual.

Just after Christmas, when Georgia is 3 years 11 months, her dad is made redundant and is out of work for 2 months. Her mum switches to morning work. There is some friction between her parents. Georgia's mum sees this redundancy as an opportunity for her to work full-time. Georgia's dad does not want this solution and is determined to resolve it by finding a new career. During this time the effect on Georgia at nursery does not seem very great. At home, at 4 years, she draws a picture of the whole family.

> **Georgia:** *'Daddy's angry.'* (His features were all scrunched up – like a frown).

## Strategies for settling at nursery

Georgia still finds it difficult to separate from her parents when she arrives at nursery, but has developed some strategies, which help her feel more in control of the situation.

- She chooses a particular adult – Georgia becomes friendly with Angela as well as Alison.

- She brings something from home to use as an object of transition, usually a toy.

- One day, when she feels particularly vulnerable, she wears a sunhat all morning (even though it is February).

Georgia's dad starts work again when she is 4 years 1 month and a period of stability follows.

Georgia begins to be unsettled again about a month before leaving nursery to start school and shows this by behaving differently and unco-operatively. This time, her parents recognise the signs and realise that she needs help to express her feelings of fear and uncertainty about the impending change.

## Looking back with Georgia's parents

Georgia's parents realise that around the time of Harry's birth and the discovery of the allergy, they had very high expectations of Georgia.

> **Mum:** *'I think we expected her to be grown-up when we had Harry. We expected emotional maturity and she was only two.'*

Georgia's parents feel that her close friendships were important to her throughout periods of change and transition.

> **Dad:** *'She's more sociable than Harry. She learnt a lot from the older children – she was never bored when she was with them.'*
> **Mum:** *'She became friendly with James the year before school – then they were in the same class when they started school.'*

Georgia (at 7 years) remembers her friends at nursery.

> **Georgia:** *'Me, Stephanie and Laura played together.'*

I remember Georgia's concern with Steph's age, asking 'Steph's a bit older than you?'

> **Georgia:** *'She's 4 months older than me.'*

(Some things stay the same despite other changes.)
  Both parents remember Georgia participating in role play.

> **Mum:** *'I remember her being the sister.'*
> **Dad:** *'She liked being the baby – she loved being pushed around in a buggy or cart.'*

### Georgia learns to express her fears

Georgia's mum realises that big changes, like leaving nursery to go to school, are difficult for Georgia.

> **Mum:** *'She's grotty if there's any change – I tell her "I used to be scared" – and once she realises that I was scared of starting school, she changes her attitude. She still won't express it verbally, but her behaviour will change after we have explored it.'*

Her parents did not realise that sometimes their worries had an impact on Georgia.

> **Mum:** *'When Ian was out of work for 2 months, we probably did not realise that Georgia would be worried about Ian not having a job.'*

After reading this chapter, Georgia's mum adds that 'when Ian was made redundant, there was a real power struggle going on between us. Georgia would have witnessed those negotiations and experienced some of the friction'. Power was an issue for the parents. Is it a coincidence that Georgia was interested in power?

*Georgia enjoys being pushed around in a cart*

A year after this power struggle, Georgia's parents separated. Her mum moved into her own house a few months later. The way her parents have handled this and have explained to the children what is happening and why, has been crucial in ensuring their well-being. Negotiating what is best for the children has been paramount.

## Learning to negotiate

Georgia seems to find it difficult to back down, when she is negotiating.

> **Mum:** *'The other night I said I'd read a chapter of her book – it was only three pages, so she said she didn't want it at all. She backed down, in this instance, after I explained to her that she could ask for more (nicely), that she was cutting off her nose to spite her face and she would miss out on what she wanted, and that it was okay to back down and have what she really did want.'*

Rather than being prepared to negotiate for the best deal she can get, sometimes Georgia will give up or be inflexible.

> **Mum:** *'She did the classic with her birthday – wanted more children for Dinomites than we were prepared to pay for. She knew we would not give in. I explained why and what she could have. She said she would not have anything. She wanted to have 20 children at £4 per head. We said 10. She said she would contribute her money – £11 – I said we would put £1 to it and have another three children. That still was not good enough. It is as if she cannot back down.'*

Although Georgia's parents live separately, they are only a couple of closes apart and the children spend time each week with each parent. This makes it even more important for the parents to have a consistent approach.

Georgia adds, during the discussion, 'If I asked dad, he would' implying that she thinks her dad might back down.

However she has loyalties to both parents. Although she would like 20 children to her party, she ends up choosing something completely different.

**Mum:** *'She has ended up with a sleepover for two friends.'*

Georgia can choose which house she has her sleepover.

I ask Georgia, 'How do you get ideas for what you want for your party?'

**Georgia:** *'I read a book called* The Sleepover Club *– they sleep over at each other's houses.'*

Towards the end of our discussion, her mum is reflecting.

**Mum:** *'Is her being able to deal with change about me telling her that I understand why she feels like that and that I feel like that sometimes? . . . that only happened after we split up and I was very worried about her.'*

## How Georgia learns to cope

Georgia can cope with small changes, in fact some events she finds exciting and stimulating. It seems that when several things change simultaneously, over which she has no power, that everything becomes confusing and overwhelming. Miller (1992) advises parents that 'giving something a shape and talking it over can be a help'. This is what Georgia's mum has learnt to do over the years.

Georgia herself seems to use role play in a therapeutic way. Faulkner (1995) says that the 'themes of children's play can tell us about their developing social knowledge and also about their emotional fears and anxieties'. Children can control what happens in their play in a way that they cannot do in real life.

### Making small choices

When Georgia is feeling particularly vulnerable even small choices seem to restore her confidence. Roberts (1995) sees 'acceptance' as 'the heart of self-concept'. Maybe if those around you accept your instinct to be near a familiar person, to carry something from home to nursery or to wear something you wore as a younger child, then you truly feel accepted and valued as the person you are on that day.

In her studies Dunn (1984) acknowledges that there is 'pressure on a firstborn to "grow up" and be independent because there is now a baby'.

Parents often do this without realising it. Georgia's parents realise that they had high expectations of her. Her mum also comments that, because of what she has found works with Georgia in relation to impending change, she now tries to offer Harry the opportunity to talk through his fears and anxieties. This shows that as parents and workers, we can learn from the children we get to know, as we go along.

## SUMMARY

1  Georgia explores the use of power over others and shows an interest in hierarchies and relationships at work. Attachments to others, the use of humour and a mastery-oriented approach to learning are investigated.
2  Georgia copes with change and transition by:

- participating in role play

- using stories to explore feelings

- transporting objects of transition from home to nursery.

We have now explored some aspects of Georgia's emotional development. This concludes our exploration of Georgia's learning through four subject areas. In the final chapter we will conclude by making links across the subject areas and paying particular attention to how learning in one subject affects learning in other subject areas.

# 7 GEORGIA'S STORY — MAKING CONNECTIONS

*Everything about the child's development links and enmeshes. Feelings, thoughts, physical movement and spiritual life are all part of the 'whole child'.*
(Bruce et al, 1995)

At the beginning of this book, we were thinking about how Georgia and other young children seek to make connections between their experiences. After introducing Georgia and her family, we considered her progress in different areas. Although we looked at each subject area separately, Georgia often explored the subjects simultaneously. It was important to her that they were connected and not isolated from each other.

> In this final chapter we will look at:
>
> • how we can help Georgia to connect the different things she learns
>
> • Georgia starting school
>
> • Georgia as she is now – her friendships, interests and what she likes to do

## HELPING GEORGIA TO CONNECT

Georgia's world seems to be held together by relationships. Georgia's relationships with other people and her interest in the relationships of others, seems to make up the integrating mechanism which pulls together her feelings, actions, thoughts and everything she learns.

### Georgia's role play

Georgia uses role play to understand a complex world. For example, when Kai intrigues her, Georgia plays at being Kai. Being Kai entails:

- Feeling like Kai. Woodhead et al (1995) say that 'pretend feelings are at the heart of pretend play'.

- Acting like Kai – carrying things in a briefcase and making marks on paper as she thinks Kai does.

- Thinking about Kai in relation to her dad – building concepts about 'work' and 'being a boss'.

Bancroft (1995) says that,

> Once experiences can be organised in terms of their similarity, children have the basic skills to develop concepts.

Practising writing and transporting objects is part of being Kai. Both writing and transporting seem incidental, but at times, they are important aspects of the play. It seems that Georgia learns about writing through imitating Kai, then imitates Kai in order to practise writing.

## Planning to extend what Georgia is doing

At nursery, when Georgia is interested in practising writing, we might offer her genuine tasks that involve writing and communication, for example, putting her own name in the computer book, helping to mark the register or recording in some way who has had snacks. We might introduce her to different alphabets, writing systems and languages. Looking at different languages might lead us to discover where people live, aspects of their different lifestyles and cultures. Pinker (1994) says that 'early childhood' is the 'critical period' for 'language acquisition'. Colin Blakemore (1998) says that currently, our school system is not making use of this information. Starting to learn a second language at secondary school is, in fact, much too late as the sensitive or critical period for acquiring language lasts until the age of seven. People can learn new languages as adults, of course, but may struggle with pronunciation and have to work much harder than young children do.

## Accepting Georgia's feelings

Looking across the areas of the curriculum includes taking into account both emotional and intellectual needs. Roberts (1995) reminds us that 'knowledge and acceptance' are important when we are considering feelings. When Georgia was settling into nursery and feeling emotionally vulnerable, Angela (Family

Worker) used her prior knowledge of what Georgia was currently enjoying at home (making friendship bracelets) to engage her at nursery. There was a hidden message which Georgia recognised: 'this person knows and accepts me'. A less skilled worker might have tried distracting Georgia without first accepting how she was feeling.

## Focussing on processes not products

This idea of knowing and accepting each child's agenda and approach means that, as adults, we focus on processes rather than products. In Chapter Five we saw that Georgia was more interested in how glue changed from liquid to solid, than in producing a picture or collage. If we have ideas about predetermined outcomes, Georgia might miss out on learning about scientific changes. We would miss the opportunity to offer her language to support her learning and other materials to add to her growing knowledge of changes in state and consistency.

## Supporting Georgia's learning

Adults need to take the lead and offer rich materials for Georgia to experience scientifically (a workshop environment is best, so that children can select their own materials). We need to observe whether she can choose, note what she chooses and take it from there. It seems a little like two people creating a dance – one leads, the other follows, then offers a new step. The first responds with a sidestep, the second takes it forward in their own way, and so it goes on. If the adult takes too large a step, then the child cannot keep up. If the adult takes the dance in the wrong direction the child is left behind. It is important to stay close and keep checking out which way your partner wants to go. All too often children are not expected to be the creators, but merely the followers.

Let us take, as an example, a real scenario – Georgia (at 3 years 6 months) is playing with junk mail.

1    Georgia initiates: '. . . *got big scissors and cut up paper . . . in half, in half again progressively until there were lots of very tiny pieces.*'

2    Adult offers a resource to extend what Georgia is doing: '. . . *an envelope to put them in so that she can take them home.*'

3    Georgia extends her ideas: '. . . *she cuts up any big pieces "so they'll fit" into the envelope.*'

4    Adult can assess Georgia's knowledge: Georgia is dividing and is working at a 'functional dependency' level (Athey, 1990). That is, she understands

that fitting the pieces of paper into a 3-dimensional defined space (inside the envelope) depends on making them small enough to fit. She is interested in dividing and in fitting objects inside other objects.

5    Adult can offer further extensions based on knowledge of Georgia's interests: these activities can include words such as, 'fit', 'size', 'inside', 'half', 'quarter', 'eighth', 'fill' and 'seal' (Language). If unit blocks are available, this might be a good time to show Georgia the similarities between the blocks and her divided paper (Maths). Georgia might like to make simple concertina type books, which fold inside a cover (Technology). Stories can be told which include ideas about objects being inside other objects, such as *A Dark, Dark Tale* (Brown, 1992) or *The Very Hungry Caterpillar* (Carle, 1969) (Literature). Georgia might enjoy and learn from chopping up fruit for snacks and sharing it between a small group of children (Personal and Social Development). She might be interested in watching the pet hamster gather large amounts of food in its mouth (Knowledge and Understanding). Any of these offerings may be taken up or rejected by Georgia. Whatever she takes up may lead her and the adult in a new direction. The adult can, at any stage, be thinking about extending across all areas of the curriculum in order to ensure that what Georgia is offered is broad and balanced.

## The environment as the source of development

When Georgia participates in role play she is practising what she sees as the whole behaviour of whoever she is imitating. At other times, for example, when she is cutting out, she is trying out aspects of what she has seen others do. We can make a comparison here with what Vygotsky claims happens in language development (Van der Veer and Valsiner, 1994),

> *The child speaks in one word phrases, but his mother talks to him in language which is already grammatically and syntactically formed and which has a large vocabulary, even though it is being toned down for the child's benefit. All the same, she speaks using the fully perfected form of speech . . .* Something which is only supposed to take shape at the very end of development, somehow influences the very first steps in this development.

Georgia's environment includes people using language, maths and every other skill and concept at a fully developed level. The 'environment', Vygotsky argues therefore, is the 'source of development'. He would say that the fully developed forms used by adults influence Georgia while she is developing and therefore drive the developmental process. The lesson we can learn is to ensure that when we offer materials in nursery, we enable children to play with them using scenarios from the real world of home and nursery. It is infinitely more important at this early stage, for children to enjoy and to understand real purposes of writing than it is for them to form letters correctly. Each child will practise in his or her own way, just as Georgia does, while continuing to be influenced by the real purposes which can be seen in the environment.

We have looked at how Georgia explored all areas of the curriculum at nursery. We are now going to look at how Georgia coped with the transition to school.

# GEORGIA STARTING SCHOOL

## Georgia explores the ideas about school

We heard in Chapter Three that, for about a month, Georgia wants the school leaflet as her bedtime story every night. She seems to be learning about the rules from the leaflet – what is allowed and what is not allowed! We also heard that in the close Georgia plays at 'schools' with a number of older children. She knows for a long time, prior to starting school, that James and Little Emma will be starting the same school at the same time as her. She seems intrigued by the concept of 'school' and wants to understand in much the same way that she tried to understand what Kai does at work. She plays at being at school, listens to stories about school and asks questions about school. The difference is that Georgia knows she will soon become part of the school community. The final stage for her, is expressing her fear of the unknown aspects of going to school.

### Georgia discovers what it is like at school

Once Georgia has expressed her fears of starting school, she begins to look forward to the new experiences. James, who lives next door, is in the same class as her. The teacher is very important to Georgia. Her first teacher, Jean, makes friends with Georgia very quickly. Georgia's mum feels that the relationship with the teacher must be good for Georgia to be happy and to learn.

> **Mum:** *'The most important thing for me is that the teacher likes my child – I know Jean likes her.'*

Georgia fits in very easily with the school routine and is happy. She likes writing, reading and maths and enjoys meeting new people. At playtime she and James play together continuing with the play that goes on at home.

*Georgia just after starting school*

Again it is the 'goodness of fit' between Georgia's temperament and the school context in which she finds herself that matters (Oates, 1994). She is in the position of being alongside James, whom she has known since his birth, and surrounded by other new people. During her year at nursery she has risen to several emotional challenges, as well as exploring, discovering and practising her skills in building, using the computer, listening to stories, painting, gluing, using clay and dough and role play.

## What Georgia does at home after starting school

After Georgia starts school, she continues to do the same things at home, but at a more complex level. She practises drawing and writing at every opportunity, as well as taking her schoolwork in her stride. She continues to combine drawing and writing. At 4 years 10 months she produces the piece below. This is a core with radials in the form of a house, infilled with enclosures.

*Georgia still enjoys writing and drawing*

Georgia is displaying her sense of humour at 5 years when she writes 'Look – mummy is not little'. She reads it aloud and hoots with laughter. The records end there, but Georgia continues to thrive at school and is fortunate to have Jean as her teacher again for her third year at school.

# GEORGIA AS SHE IS NOW

## Her friendships, interests and what she likes to do

Georgia is now 7 years old. She is still close to and identifies with her mum, Aunty Eloise and Jennifer. She continues to be close to her brother, Harry, though this can mean arguing and falling out, or ganging up on their parents, as well as playing together. Equity is an issue for Georgia. Although she might give in to Harry's wishes some of the time, she is now more likely to fight for equality. Georgia and Harry are very important to each other, particularly as they both spend time together each week with each of their parents. They always have each other, even though they might be missing one of their parents.

Georgia has several sets of friends:

- two close friends at school who are both girls

- friends in dad's close – all of the same children who have been there since her birth

- friends near mum's close

- children of her parents' friends.

### Living in two homes

James and Stacey (his older sister) helped in the transition to the children's mum's house, as their Gran lived almost next door to the new house. Their parents allowed James and Stacey to spend time with Georgia and Harry at both houses. They also allowed them to sleep over at both houses and Georgia and Harry to sleep over at their house.

Georgia and her brother see both parents most days each week and, up to now, have spent Christmas days and birthdays together as a family. Her parents have, however, taken them on separate holidays, and although this was quite daunting the first time, Georgia seems to think this is exciting now.

## Georgia's interests

Georgia's interests have not changed. She still enjoys drawing and writing and is an avid reader. She likes adventure stories and can be seen walking around with her nose in a book if the story is exciting enough for her. She often reads to Harry. At Christmas, both children made presents for the rest of the family. Georgia painted glass candle holders and made models with plaster of Paris. One of the favourite presents she received was a personal organiser into which you enter two dates of birth and the organiser tells you how compatible the two people are.

Georgia is less interested in using the computer now, though she dabbles with Harry's Nintendo. She has given up gymnastics but enjoys swimming. She likes to go and watch her mum playing netball and last summer started playing tennis with Harry, when her mum and Aunty Eloise took the children to the tennis courts with them. One of Georgia's favourite trips is to Dinomites, which is a huge softplay area for children.

## Georgia's interest in people

People and their relationships still seem to be the main motivation for Georgia. She likes all of the soap operas on television. She also watches documentaries about people. A particular favourite was 'Children's Hospital', which took viewers through the traumas experienced by real children and included their surgical operations.

Georgia likes playing games like Monopoly and Yahtzee. Naturally her peer group are more important to her now. She likes clothes and pop music and has already been to a school disco.

Recently, she was very excited that there was going to be a residential trip from school. However numbers were limited and her name did not come out of the hat. She was very disappointed until she realised that her two close friends from school could not go either. Georgia likes to be challenged by her schoolwork. At home she often asks for hard sums or difficult spellings in order to practise. Recently her class have been studying natural disasters and she has been motivated to discover more information from reference books. Could it be the consequences for the people involved that interests her?

## GEORGIA – A SUMMARY

- Georgia learns through imitating whole scenarios.

- We extend Georgia's learning by offering content across the curriculum to match her specific concerns.

- When Georgia starts school, social relationships continue to be her primary concern.

- Georgia continues to develop her interests through the people she knows and through her interest in people in the wider world.

# APPENDIX: GEORGIA'S GALLERY

These photographs show Georgia growing in age and in confidence. As you will know from reading the text, relationships with other people are very important to Georgia. Her well-being is high when she is with her favourite people. I have included photos of Georgia with the individuals who have been closest to her during her early years.

*A massage group*

*On holiday*

*Jennifer, Samantha and Georgia*

*Harry and Georgia*

*Aunty Eloise with Georgia*

*Dad, Georgia and Harry*

*Harry and Georgia*

*Georgia and her Mum*

*Georgia age 7 years*

# BIBLIOGRAPHY AND REFERENCES

Alborough, J. (1992), *Where's My Teddy?* Walker Books, Falmouth Cornwall.

Arnold, C. (1990), *Children Who Play Together have Similar Schemas*, Unpublished project submitted as part of a Certificate in Post-Qualifying Studies.

Arnold, C. (1997), *Understanding Young Children and their Contexts for Learning and Development: Building on Early Experience*, Unpublished dissertation, M.Ed., Leicester University.

Athey, C. (1990), *Extending Thought in Young Children. A Parent Teacher Partnership*, Paul Chapman, London.

Au, K.H. (1990), Chapter entitled 'Changes in a teacher's views of interactive comprehension instruction' in Moll, L.M. (Ed), *Vygotsky and Education*, Cambridge University Press.

Bancroft, D. (1985), *The Development of Temporal Reference: a study of children's language*, unpublished PhD thesis, University of Nottingham.

Bancroft, D. and Carr, R. (Eds) (1995), *Influencing Children's Development*, Blackwell, Oxford.

Barnes, P. (Ed) (1995), *Personal, Social and Emotional Development of Children*, Blackwell, Oxford.

Bartholemew, L. and Bruce, T. (1993), *Getting to Know You*, Hodder and Stoughton, London.

Blakemore, C. (1998), Presentation at Pen Green Conference on 'Giving Children a Sure Start', Nov 1998, Corby, Northants.

Blanck, G. (1990), Chapter entitled 'Vygotsky: the man and his cause' in Moll, L.C. (Ed), *Vygotsky and Education*, Cambridge University Press.

Bowlby, J. (1953), *Child Care and the Growth of Love*, Pelican Books, Harmondsworth.

Bowlby, J. (1958), 'The nature of the child's tie to his mother', *International Journal of Psychoanalysis*, 39, 350–73.

Bowlby, J. (1969), *Attachment and loss: Vol. 1. Attachment*, Basic Books, New York.

Bowlby, J. (1973), *Attachment and loss: Vol. 2. Separation: Anxiety and anger*, Basic Books, New York.

Bowlby, J. (1991), *Attachment and Loss: Volume 1*, Penguin, London.

Brown, R. (1992), *A Dark, Dark Tale*, Red Fox, London.

Bruce, T. (1991), *Time to Play in Early Childhood Education*, Hodder and Stoughton, London.

Bruce, T., Findlay, A., Read, J. and Scarborough, (1995), *Recurring Themes in Education*, Paul Chapman, London.

Bruce, T. (1997), *Early Childhood Education*, (Second Edition), Hodder and Stoughton, London.

Bruner, J. (1980), *Under Five in Britain*, Grant McIntyre Ltd., London.

Burningham, J. (1982), *Avocado Baby*, Jonathan Cape, London.

Buss and Plomin (1984), *Early Developing Personality Traits*. Hillside, NJ: Lawrence Erlbaum.

Carle, E. (1969), *The Very Hungry Caterpillar*, Puffin Books, Harmondsworth.

Carle, E. (1986), *Papa please get the moon for me*, Hodder and Stoughton, London.

Carr, M., May, H. and Podmore, V. (1998), Paper entitled 'Learning and Teaching Stories: New approaches to assessment and evaluation in relation to Te Whariki', Symposium for 8th European Conference on Quality in Early Childhood Settings, Santiago de Compostela, Spain, Sept 1998.

Carruthers, E. (1996), 'A young child talks numbers': A developmental link between literacy and numeracy', Paper from unpublished M.Ed. (1996), University of Plymouth.

Carter, R. (1998), *Mapping the Mind*, Weidenfeld and Nicolson, London.

Clay, M.M. (1975), *What Did I Write?* London: Heinemann.

Cohen, J.M. and M.J. (1993), *The New Penguin Dictionary of Quotations*. London: Penguin.

Daniels, H. (Ed) (1996), *An Introduction to Vygotsky*, Routledge, London.

Das Gupta, P. and Richardson, K. 'Theories of cognitive development in Lee, V. and Das Gupta, P. (1995), *Children's Cognitive and Language Development*. Milton Keynes: Open University Press.

Davies, M. (1995), *Helping Children to Learn Through a Movement Perspective*, Hodder and Stoughton, London.

Donaldson, M. (1978, 1987), *Children's Minds*, Fontana Press, London.

Donaldson, M. (1992), *Human Minds*, Penguin, London.

Dunn, J.B. (1977), 'Patterns of early interaction: continuities and consequences' in Schaffer, H.R. (Ed), *Studies of Mother-infant Interaction*, Academic Press, New York.

Dunn, J. and Kendrick, C. (1982a), *Siblings: love, envy and understanding*, Harvard University Press, Cambridge (Mass.).

Dunn, J. and Kendrick, C. (1982b), *Temperamental differences in infants and young children*, Pitman Books Ltd., London.

Dunn, J. (1984), *Brothers and Sisters*, Fontana Books, London.

Dunn, J. (1988), *The Beginnings of Social Understanding*, Blackwell, Oxford.

Dunn, J., Brown, J.R. and Beardsall, L. (1991), 'Family talk about emotions, and children's later understanding of others' emotions', *Developmental Psychology*, 27, pp 448–55.

Dunn, J. (1993), 'Studying Relationships and Social Understanding' in Barnes, P. (Ed), (1995), *Personal, Social and Emotional Development of Children*, Blackwell, Oxford.

Dweck, C. and Leggett, E. (1988), A Social-Cognitive Approach to Motivation and Personality, *Psychological Review*, Vol 95, Pt 2, pp 256–733.

Eisner, E. (1985), *The Art of Educational Evaluation: A Personal View*, Falmer, Lewes.

Faulkner, D. (1995), Chapter entitled 'Play, Self and the Social World' in Barnes, P. (1995), *Personal, Social and Emotional Development of Children*, OU, Milton Keynes.

Flanagan, C. (1996), *Applying Psychology to Early Child Development*, Hodder and Stoughton, London.

Gardner, H. (1991, 1993), *The Unschooled Mind*, Fontana Press, London.

Gelman, R. and Gallistel, C. (1978), *The Child's Understanding of Number*, Harvard University Press, Cambridge, MA.

Goleman, D. (1996), *Emotional Intelligence*, Bloomsbury, London.

Goodman, Y.M. and Goodman K.S. (1990), Chapter entitled 'Vygotsky in a whole language perspective' in Moll, L.C. (Ed) (1990), *Vygotsky and Education*, Cambridge University Press.

Graves, D. (1983), *Writing: Teachers and Children at Work*, Heinemann, London.

Greenfield, S. (1997), *The Human Brain A Guided Tour*, Phoenix, London.

Gura, P. (Ed) (1992), *Exploring Learning: Young Children and Blockplay*, Paul Chapman, London.

Henry, M. (1996), *Young Children, Parents and Professionals*, Routledge, London.

Hoffman, P. (1998), *The Man Who Loved Only Numbers*, Fourth Estate, London.

Holt, J. (1989, 1991), *Learning All the Time*, Education Now, Ticknall.

Isaacs, N. (1930), Appendix A on 'Children's "Why" Questions' in Isaacs, S. (1930), *Intellectual Growth in Young Children*, Routledge and Kegan Paul Ltd., London.

Isaacs, N. (1974), *Children's Ways of Knowing*, Teachers College Press, London.

Isaacs, S. (1930, 1966), *Intellectual Growth in Young Children*, Routledge and Kegan Paul Ltd., London.

Isaacs, S. (1933), *Social Development in Young Children*, Routledge and Sons, London.

Isaacs, S. (1968), *The Nursery Years*, Routledge and Kegan Paul, London.

Katz, L. (1993), Lecture on 'Engaging Children's Minds' at the University of North London.

Katz, L. and Chard, S. (1989), *Engaging Children's Minds – the Project Approach*, Ablex Publishing Corporation.

Kerr, J. (1973), *The Tiger who came to tea*, Harpercollins, London.

Kress, G. (1995), *Making signs and making subjects: the English curriculum and social futures*, Inaugural Lecture, Institute of Education, London.

Laevers, F. (1993), 'Deep Level Learning', *European Early Childhood Research*, Vol 1, No 1, pp 53–68.

Laevers, F. (1994), 'The Innovative Project Experiential Education and the Definition of Quality in Education', *Studia Pedagogica*, 16, pp 159–72.

Laevers, F. (1995), Lecture at Worcester College.

Laevers, F. (1997), *A Process-Oriented Child Follow-up System for Young Children*, Centre for Experiential Education, Leuven.

Lee, V. and Das Gupta, P. (1995), *Children's Cognitive and Language Development*, OU Press, Milton Keynes.

Mairs, K., Stone, R. and Young, E. (1990), *Learning to be Strong: Developing assertiveness with young children*, Pen Green Centre, Changing Perspectives, Northwich.

Malcolm, A. (1993), *Father's Involvement with Their Children and Outside Work Commitments*, Unpublished study submitted as part of a Diploma in Post-Qualifying Studies.

Matthews, J. (1994), *Helping Children to Paint and Draw in Early Childhood*, Hodder and Stoughton, London.

McDougall in Nicholls, B. (1986), *Rumpus Schema Extra*, Cleveland Teachers in Education (LEA).

McLellan, E. (1997), 'The Importance of Counting' in Thompson, I. *Teaching and Learning Early Numbers*, Buckingham: Open University Press.

Meade, A. with Cubey, P. (1995), *Thinking Children*, New Zealand Council for Educational Research, Wellington.

Meek, M. (1982), *Learning to Read*, Bodley Head, London.

Miller, L. (1992), *Understanding Your 4 year old*, Rosendale Press, London.

Miller, P.H. (1989; 2nd Edition), *Theories of Developmental Psychology*, Freeman, New York.

Moll, L.C. (Ed) (1990, reprinted 1994), *Vygotsky and Education*, Cambridge University Press, Cambridge.

Moll, L.C. and Greenberg, J.B. (1990), Chapter entitled 'Creating zones of possibilities: Combining social contexts' in Moll, L.C. (Ed) (1990), *Vygotsky and Education*, Cambridge University Press, Cambridge.

Nash, J.M. (1997), 'Fertile minds' in *Time* Magazine, 3 February 1997.

Nicholls, R. (Ed) (1986), *Rumpus Schema Extra*, Cleveland Teachers in Education (LEA).

Nisbet, J. and Schucksmith, J. (1986), *Learning Strategies*, Routledge and Kegan Paul, London.

Nunes, T., Schliemann, A.D. and Carraher, D.W. (1993), *Street mathematics and school mathematics*, Cambridge University Press.

Nunes, T. (1995), Chapter entitled 'Mathematical and Scientific Thinking' in Lee, V. and Das Gupta, P. (Eds) (1995), *Children's Cognitive and Language Development*, OU Press, Milton Keynes.

Nunes, T. (1998), *Developing children's minds through literacy and numeracy*, Inaugural Lecture, Institute of Education, London.

Nutbrown, C. (1994), *Threads of Thinking*, Paul Chapman, London.

Oates, J. (Ed) (1994), *The Foundation of Child Development*, Blackwell, Oxford.

Oram, H. (1993), *Angry Arthur*, Red Fox, London.

Pascal, C. and Bertram, A.D. (1997), *Effective Early Learning*, Hodder and Stoughton, London.

Piaget, J. (1926, 1959), *The Language and Thought of the Child*, Routledge and Kegan Paul Ltd., London.

Piaget, J. (1936 – translation 1953), *The Origin of Intelligence in the Child*, Routledge and Kegan Paul, Ltd., London.

Piaget, J. (1937 – translation 1955), *The Child's Construction of Reality*, Routledge and Kegan Paul, Ltd., London.

Piaget, J. (1951, 1972), *Play, Dreams and Imitation in Childhood*, William Heinemann Ltd., London.

Piaget, J., Grize, J.B., Szeminska, A. and Vinh-Bang (1968), 'Epistemologie et Psychologie de la Fonction', *Etudes D'Epistemologie Genetique*, xxiii, Press Universitaires de France, cited in Athey, C. (1990), *Extending Thought in Young Children*, Paul Chapman, London.

Pinker, S. (1994), *The Language Instinct*, Penguin, London.

Pollard, A. (1996), *The Social World of Children's Learning*, Cassell, London.

Pope, A. (1985), *Pope*, Penguin, London

Read, C. (1975), 'Children's Categorization of Speech Sounds in English'. Urbana, I.L.: National Council of Teachers in English.

Rice, S. (1996), *An Investigation of Schemas as a Way of Supporting and Extending*

*Young Children's Learning*, unpublished dissertation as part of M.Ed, University of West of England.

Richardson, K. (1995), Chapter entitled 'The Development of Intelligence' in Lee, V. and Das Gupta, P. (1995), *Children's Cognitive and Language Development*, OU Press, Milton Keynes.

Riley, J. (1995), 'The Transition Phase between Emergent Literacy and Conventional Beginning Reading: New Research Findings', *Early Years*, Vol 16 No 1.

Roberts, R. (1995), *Self-Esteem and Successful Early Learning*, Hodder and Stoughton, London.

Rueda, R. (1990), Chapter entitled 'Assisted Performance in Writing' in Moll, L.C. (Ed)(1990), *Vygotsky and Education*, Cambridge University Press, Cambridge.

Rutter, M. and Rutter, M. (1992), *Developing Minds*, Penguin Group, London.

Schaffer, H.R. and Emerson, P.E. (1964b), 'Patterns of response to physical contact in early human development' *J. Child Psychol, Psychiat.*, **5,** 1–13.

Schaffer, H.R. (1998), 'Joint involvement episodes as context for cognitive development' in McGurk, H. (Ed) *Contemporary Issues in Childhood Social Development*, Routledge, London.

Schaffer, R. (1995), *Early Socialization*, British Psychological Society, Leicester.

Schaffer, H.R. (1996), Chapter entitled 'Joint Involvement Episodes' in Daniels. H. (Ed) (1996), *An Introduction to Vygotsky*, Routledge, London.

Schaffer, H.R. (1996), *Social Development*, Blackwell, Oxford.

Shaw, J. (1991), *An Investigation of Parents' Conceptual Development in the Context of Dialogue with a Community Teacher*, Ph.D Thesis, Newcastle University.

Stern, D. (1985), *The Interpersonal World of the Infant*, Basic Books Inc, U.S.

Tizard, B. and Hughes, M. (1984), *Young Children Learning*, Fontana, London.

Tizard, B. (1986), *The Care of Young Children*. Implications of Recent Research, University of London Institute of Education, London.

Tulloch, S. (1990), *Complete Wordfinder*. Oxford: Oxford University Press.

Van der Veer, R. and Valsiner, J. (1994), *The Vygotsky Reader*, Blackwell, Oxford.

Vygotsky, L.S. (1962), *Thoughts and Language*, M.I.T. Press and Wiley and Sons, London.

Webb, L. (1975), *Making a Start on Child Study*, Basil Blackwell, Oxford.

Weinberger, J. (1996), *Literacy goes to School – the parents' role in young children's literacy learning*, Paul Chapman, London.

Whalley, M. (1994), *Learning to be Strong – Setting up a neighbourhood service for under-fives and their families*, Hodder and Stoughton, London.

Whalley, M. (Ed) (1997), *Working with Parents*, Hodder and Stoughton, London.

White in J.M. and M.J. Cohen (1993), *The New Penguin Dictionary of Quotations*, London: Penguin.

Whitehead, M. (1997), *Language and Literacy in the Early Years*, Second Edition, Paul Chapman, London.

Winnicott, D.W. (1975), *Through Pediatrics to Psychoanalysis*, Hogarth Press, London.

Woodhead, M. et al (1995), 'Developmental perspectives on emotion' in Barnes, P. (Ed), *Personal, Social and Emotional Development of Children*, Open University Press, Milton Keynes.

# INDEX

References to authors of research are not included in the index.

# PROBLEMS AND SOLUTIONS

for
GENERAL CHEMISTRY and
COLLEGE CHEMISTRY
Sixth Editions

BY NEBERGALL, HOLTZCLAW, AND ROBINSON

Frederick K. Ault
Ball State University

John H. Meiser
Ball State University

Henry F. Holtzclaw, Jr.
University of Nebraska

William R. Robinson
Purdue University

**D.C. HEATH AND COMPANY**
Lexington, Massachusetts      Toronto

# Preface

Through chemistry we try to describe quantitatively the phenomena we observe in ourselves and our surroundings. Much of the work in chemistry thus involves measurement, and many of its concepts require the use of mathematics.

*Problems and Solutions for General Chemistry and College Chemistry* was developed because of requests by our students to have more problems such as those presented in their textbook worked out in detail. Many of the chapters in *General Chemistry* and *College Chemistry,* Sixth Editions, by Nebergall, Holtzclaw, and Robinson, involve discussion of concepts requiring specific use of mathematics. The problems solved in this manual are taken from the problems and questions included at the ends of those chapters.

A major purpose of this manual is to provide students with helpful step-by-step analysis of solutions to specific types of problems. Each unit, keyed to a specific chapter of the Nebergall et al. texts, begins with a short introduction to the particular subject area. A detailed section on definitions and formulas pertinent to that subject area and the problems and solutions section follow next. A useful feature to note is that the presentation includes the statement of each problem selected, making the manual suitable for use as a supplement for problem-solving in general chemistry level courses. The problems selected are indicated in the textbooks by the symbol Ⓢ. At least one example of each type of problem in the chapter is chosen for a detailed solution. A full explanation is provided in addition to the required mathematical manipulations. The selected problems comprise one-third to one-half the problems in each chapter. Where it seemed appropriate, we have also provided answers to Questions that require mathematical insight.

*Problems and Solutions for General Chemistry and College Chemistry* also contains a self-instructional section (Part Two) that teaches the use of exponential numbers and logarithms. Self-evaluation exercises enable students to check on their progress at appropriate intervals.

We know that many thousands of students have successfully used the textbooks *General Chemistry* and *College Chemistry* through the past five editions in pursuing goals in chemistry and the allied-health sciences. The use of this manual should help students become more independent learners and gain a better understanding of the quantitative aspects of the sciences.

In producing this manual, we are indebted to our colleagues, our students, and our associates from other institutions for many helpful suggestions; our typist for the physical body of the manuscript; and our families, particularly for their understanding during the long hours spent in preparing this work.

F.K. Ault
J.H. Meiser
H.F. Holtzclaw, Jr.
W.R. Robinson

# Contents

# PROBLEMS AND SOLUTIONS

for General Chemistry and College Chemistry

# Part One

## Problems
## and
## Solutions

# Chapter 1: Some Fundamental Concepts

## INTRODUCTION

This chapter of the textbook includes a brief introduction to the nature of matter and energy. It also details the units of measurement essential for quantifying and communicating observations of scientific phenomena.

The almost universally accepted system of measurement, the metric system, originally was adopted in France and has undergone continuous improvement since the early nineteenth century. In 1960, the Eleventh Conference on Weights and Measures, as a result of major revisions of the metric system, renamed the system the "International System of Units." The abbreviation of the original French title "le Système International d'Unites," SI, is now the preferred form for identifying the system.

The seven base units of the SI are listed in Table 1. Units needed for expressing quantities such as volume, density, velocity, energy, and weight are derived from these base units. The discussion of this manual, as well as in the major textbooks, emphasizes SI units, with the exception of several of the older metric units, including the liter, the Celsius or centigrade temperature scale, and mm Hg for pressure, which remain very much a part of the language of science. These units, because of their convenience and because existing laboratory glassware and apparatus are mostly labeled in terms of the non-SI units, will remain part of the working language of scientists for some years to come. (Even some SI units appear to be destined for a distinctively American spelling, such as "meter" rather than the official "metre.")

**Table 1** SI Base Units

| Quantity | Symbol for Quantity | SI Physical Unit | Symbol |
|---|---|---|---|
| Length | $d$ | Meter | m |
| Mass | $M$ | Kilogram | kg |
| Time | $t$ | Second | s |
| Electric current | $I$ | Ampere | A |
| Thermodynamic temperature | $T$ | Kelvin | K |
| Amount of substance | $n$ | Mole | mol |
| Luminous intensity | $I_v$ | Candela | cd |

The problem-solving exercises stress development of skills for treating each of the following examples: expression of numbers in scientific notation; conversion among SI prefixes; expression of mass-to-volume ratios such as density and specific gravity; conversion of measurements expressed in English units to appropriate SI and derived units; conversion of temperatures from one system to another; and the transfer of heat. Although scientific work is communicated in terms of SI language, U.S. industry is only gradually moving away from the English system of measurement. As a consequence, scientific workers in the near future will have to tolerate working with two systems. Exercises are included in this chapter to help you become more adept at both systems.

## FORMULAS AND DEFINITIONS

The SI base units are frequently large with respect to the quantities to be measured. For example, the mass of a dime is approximately 0.0025 kg and the wavelength of red light is 0.0000007 m. To avoid the cumbersome use of decimals, a system of prefixes specifying a multiplication factor to use with the base units has been developed. The most commonly employed prefixes are shown in Table 2. The SI unit is multiplied by the prefix that permits us to keep the numerical value of the measurement as near to 1 as is practicable.

**Table 2** Common Prefixes for Measurement Units

| Prefix | Symbol | | | |
|---|---|---|---|---|
| Kilo | $k$ | 1000 times | = | $10^3$ times |
| Deci | $d$ | 1/10 of | = | $10^{-1}$ times |
| Centi | $c$ | 1/100 of | = | $10^{-2}$ times |
| Milli | $m$ | 1/1000 of | = | $10^{-3}$ times |
| Micro | $\mu$ | 1/1,000,000 of | = | $10^{-6}$ times |
| Nano | $n$ | 1/1,000,000,000 of | = | $10^{-9}$ times |
| Pico | $p$ | | | $10^{-12}$ times |

**Length** (meter, m)  The meter is the standard unit of lineal measure and is used in conjunction with the prefixes for most linear measurements in science. Another commonly employed non-SI unit is the angstrom (1 Å = $10^{-8}$ cm = $10^{-10}$ m), which appears in measurements and calculations in spectrographic work.

**Mass** (kilogram, kg)  The kilogram is the standard unit of mass, and is a measure of the quantity of matter a body possesses. The mass of a body is constant while at rest regardless of geographic position, and always is considered constant for chemical studies. Weighings made in the chemical laboratory are balanced against the mass of an object used as a standard; values obtained in this manner are masses. Because the kilogram is a large unit of mass, the more familiar mass in laboratory practice is the gram (g), defined as 1/1000 kg. Stated differently, 1000 g = 1 kg.

**Volume** (cubic meter, $m^3$)  The cubic meter, the standard unit of volume, is not widely used for measuring laboratory quantities. The volumes of laboratory glassware and other lab ware are more conventionally expressed in cubic centimeters, $cm^3$, or in terms of liters. Although the liter is not SI, its value is defined to be one cubic decimeter ($dm^3$) or 0.001 $m^3$. The milliliter and the cubic centimeter now are defined to be equal: 1 ml = 1 $cm^3$; and 1000 ml = 1000 $cm^3$ = 1.0 ℓ.

**Density** ($D$)  The density of a substance is the ratio of its mass $M$ to its volume $V$. The usual expression for the density of solids and liquids is mass (grams) per cubic centimeter or per milliliter. Based on these units, the densities of elements range from a low of 8.99 × $10^{-5}$ g/cm$^3$ for hydrogen gas to a high of 22.57 g/cm$^3$ for osmium. Among compounds, water has a maximum density of 1.0 g/cm$^3$ at 3.98°C. The densities of gases, such as hydrogen or oxygen, for example, are typically reported in units of grams per liter to avoid the excessive use of decimals.

$$\text{Density} = \frac{\text{mass}}{\text{volume}} = \frac{M}{V} = \frac{\text{g}}{\text{ml or cm}^3}$$

**Specific gravity** (sp gr)  The specific gravity of a substance is the ratio of the density of that substance to the density of a substance used as a reference standard. (Both densities are measured at the same temperature.) Water generally serves as the standard for both solids and liquids; air is the standard for gases. Specific gravity may alternatively be expressed as the ratio of the masses of equal volumes of two substances, where one of the substances is arbitrarily designated as the standard. (Again both substances must be at the same temperature.) Notice from the following expression that specific gravity values are unitless:

$$\text{sp gr} = \frac{\text{density of unknown}}{\text{density of known}} = \frac{\text{g/cm}^3}{\text{g/cm}^3} \quad \begin{array}{l}\text{(Units divide out, leaving a} \\ \text{dimensionless value.)}\end{array}$$

In essence, the specific gravity of a body can be thought of as a measure of "heaviness." For example, when a person says that a cork stopper is much "lighter" than a lead stopper of the same size, what is implied is that lead has a much greater density than cork. Indeed, if the masses of both are compared to the mass of an equal volume of water, the specific gravities of lead and cork will be about 11.4 and 0.2, respectively; that is, lead is 11.4 times as dense as water and cork is 0.2 times as dense as water.

**Heat** ($q$)   Heat is a form of energy arising from the motion of particles composing a substance such as a solid or fluid. Like other forms of energy, heat is measured by using the derived unit for energy called the joule (J). The calorie is an older unit of energy and is still very much a part of our language. It is widely utilized for work in nutrition, physiology, and the health sciences in general. For purposes of conversion, 1 joule equals 0.239 calories or 1 calorie (cal) equals 4.184 J. The calorie is liberally defined as the amount of heat required to raise the temperature of 1.0 g of water 1.0°C. The nutrition calorie (Cal) equals 1.0 kcal or 4184 J (4.184 kJ).

**Specific heat capacity** ($C$)   Energy is intangible in that only *changes* in energy can be measured. While the joule or calorie serves as the standard unit of energy, changes in energy must be determined by measuring temperature changes of specific substances. The specific heat capacity (formally known as the specific heat) of a substance is the amount of heat required to change the temperature of 1 gram of that substance by one degree Celsius; the specific heat capacity for a given substance is unique to that substance. An algebraic interpretation of this definition applied to any substance is

$$\text{Heat} = \text{mass} \times \text{sp ht} \times \text{temp change}$$
$$Q = M \times C \times \Delta t$$

The transfer of heat between two bodies (heat flow) always occurs from the "hotter" body to the "colder" body. In the process of heat flow both bodies eventually reach an equilibrium temperature. Since heat is conserved, the amount of heat lost by the "hotter" body equals the amount of heat gained by the "colder" body.

$$Q_{\text{lost}} = Q_{\text{gained}}$$

**Significant figures**   In making measurements, it is important to recognize the limitations of the measuring instruments. For example, a typical bathroom scale, while possibly accurate, is calibrated to register weights to the nearest pound, and would not be useful for measuring small quantities such as you will use in laboratory experiments; the uncertainty in each measurement is too great.

Laboratory measurements generally require a higher degree of precision or less uncertainty than would be required in weighing yourself on a scale. Common laboratory balances used in general chemistry have a range of uncertainties from 0.01 g to 0.1 g for simple beam balances and from 0.0001 g to 0.001 g for analytical balances.

6

The reporting of measurements should be made in a way that conveys the maximum information about the measurements to the user. Numbers that are actually read from an instrument are considered to be *significant figures*. As a general rule, answers to mathematical operations may not contain more significant figures (less uncertainty) than the operant with the smallest number of significant figures (greatest uncertainty). The solved problems in this manual follow the rules on significant figures as presented in the textbooks. Many of the solved problems have been analyzed into steps, and in these cases, intermediate answers are written with one more significant figure than is justified in the final answer. *Computations have been made with an electronic calculator. Generally, all the numbers that were generated in the calculator resulting from mathematical operations have been carried through to the final answer. The answer is rounded to the proper number of significant figures at the end of the computation.*

**Use of prefixes**  A conversion scheme using some common prefixes and examples is shown below.

$$
\text{Length} \quad \text{km} \underset{1000\div}{\overset{\times 1000}{\rightleftharpoons}} \text{m} \underset{100\div}{\overset{\times 100}{\rightleftharpoons}} \text{cm} \underset{10\div}{\overset{\times 10}{\rightleftharpoons}} \text{mm} \underset{1000\div}{\overset{\times 1000}{\rightleftharpoons}} \mu\text{m} \underset{1000\div}{\overset{\times 1000}{\rightleftharpoons}} \text{nm}
$$

$$
\text{Mass} \quad \text{kg} \underset{1000\div}{\overset{\times 1000}{\rightleftharpoons}} \text{g} \underset{1000\div}{\overset{\times 1000}{\rightleftharpoons}} \text{mg} \underset{1000\div}{\overset{\times 1000}{\rightleftharpoons}} \mu\text{g}
$$

$$
\text{Volume} \quad \text{m}^3 \underset{1000\div}{\overset{\times 1000}{\rightleftharpoons}} \text{dm}^3 = \text{liter (}\ell\text{)} \underset{1000\div}{\overset{\times 1000}{\rightleftharpoons}} \text{ml} \underset{1000\div}{\overset{\times 1000}{\rightleftharpoons}} \mu\ell
$$

## PROBLEMS

1. Express 6.28 meters in centimeters, millimeters, kilometers, and angstrom units. (See Appendix C.)

   **Solution**

   Conversions among units must begin with defining the units as identities or equivalencies relative to each other. The definition can be rearranged into a fraction with the unit of the quantity to be converted in the denominator. Multiplication of this fraction times the quantity yields the desired unit. Prefixes used with SI units are exact definitions, and the number of significant figures included in computations depends only on the number of significant figures in the measurements.

   $$1 \text{ m} = 100 \text{ cm}$$

   $$\text{Length in cm} = 6.28 \text{ m} \times \frac{100 \text{ cm}}{\text{m}} = 628 \text{ cm}$$

$$1 \text{ m} = 1000 \text{ mm}$$

$$\text{Length in mm} = 6.28 \times \frac{1000 \text{ mm}}{\text{m}} = 6.28 \times 10^3 \text{ mm}$$

Three significant figures are allowed.

$$\text{Length in km} = 6.28 \text{ m} \times \frac{1 \text{ km}}{1000 \text{ m}} = 6.28 \times 10^{-3} \text{ km}$$

$$1 \text{ m} = 1 \times 10^{10} \text{ Å}$$

$$\text{Length in Å} = 6.28 \text{ m} \times \frac{1 \times 10^{10} \text{ Å}}{\text{m}} = 6.28 \times 10^{10} \text{ Å}$$

6. Express 1.39 quarts in liters, milliliters, and cubic centimeters. (See Appendix C.)

**Solution**

$$1 \text{ qt} = 0.946 \text{ } \ell \quad \text{(3 significant figures)}$$

$$\text{Vol in } \ell = 1.39 \text{ qt} \times \frac{0.946 \text{ } \ell}{1 \text{ qt}} = 1.31 \text{ } \ell$$

$$1 \text{ qt} = 0.946 \text{ } \ell = 946 \text{ cm}^3 = 946 \text{ ml}$$

$$\text{Vol in ml} = 1.39 \text{ qt} \times \frac{946 \text{ ml}}{1 \text{ qt}} = 1.31 \times 10^3 \text{ ml}$$

$$\text{Vol in cm}^3 = 1.39 \text{ qt} \times \frac{946 \text{ cm}^3}{1 \text{ qt}} = 1.31 \times 10^3 \text{ cm}^3$$

11. Express 90.8 pounds in kilograms, grams, milligrams, and metric tons. (See Appendix C.)

**Solution**

The pound is a unit of weight; the kilogram is a unit of mass. The weight of a body varies slightly with changes in latitude and altitude at the earth's surface due to gravitational changes. The mass of a body is constant and unrelated to gravity. Conversions between weight units (pounds) and mass units (kilograms) can be made, however, by assuming that a mass of 1.00 kg has a weight of 2.20 lb (3 significant figures) uniformly over the surface of the earth.

$$1 \text{ lb} = 0.454 \text{ kg}$$

$$\text{Mass in kg} = 90.8 \text{ lb} \times \frac{0.454 \text{ kg}}{1 \text{ lb}} = 41.2 \text{ kg}$$

$$\text{Mass in g} = 41.2 \text{ kg} \times \frac{1 \times 10^3 \text{ g}}{\text{kg}} = 4.12 \times 10^4 \text{ g}$$

$$\text{Mass in mg} = 4.12 \times 10^4 \text{ g} \times \frac{1 \times 10^6 \text{ mg}}{1 \times 10^3 \text{ kg}} = 4.12 \times 10^7 \text{ mg}$$

$$\text{Mass in m-ton} = 41.2 \text{ kg} \times \frac{1 \text{ m-ton}}{1 \times 10^3 \text{ kg}} = 4.12 \times 10^{-2} \text{ metric-ton}$$

17. A student places 28.70 g of iron, 0.3807 oz of aluminum, and 0.00389 lb of copper in a beaker that weighs 138 g. What is the total mass in grams of the beaker and its contents?

**Solution**

Compute the mass of Al and Cu in grams.

$$1 \text{ lb} = 453.6 \text{ g} = 16 \text{ oz}$$

$$\text{Mass Al} = 0.3807 \text{ oz} \times \frac{453.6 \text{ g}}{16 \text{ oz}} = 10.79 \text{ g}$$

$$\text{Mass Cu} = 0.00389 \text{ lb} \times \frac{453.6 \text{ g}}{1 \text{ lb}} = 1.76 \text{ g}$$

| Total mass | 138 | g |
|---|---|---|
| | 28.70 | g |
| | 10.79 | g |
| | 1.76 | g |
| | 179.25 | g |

The sum of the masses cannot be more precise than that of the mass of the beaker ($\pm 1$ g). The total mass therefore must be recorded as 179 g.

23. What is the mass of each of the following?

(a) 6.00 cm$^3$ of mercury; density = 13.5939 g/cm$^3$

**Solution**

The definition of density, $D = M/V$, can be rearranged to give $M = D \times V$.

$$M = 6.00 \text{ cm}^3 \times 13.5939 \text{ g/cm}^3 = 81.6 \text{ g}$$

(d) 125 ml of gaseous chlorine; density = 3.16 g/ℓ

$$M = 125 \text{ ml} \times \frac{1.00 \, \ell}{1000 \text{ ml}} \times \frac{3.16 \text{ g}}{\ell} = 0.395 \text{ g}$$

27. What is the specific gravity of ethyl alcohol at 20° relative to water with a density of 0.9982 g/cm$^3$ at 20°? (See problem 26.)

**Solution**

The specific gravity of ethyl alcohol is calculated from the definition

$$\text{sp gr} = \frac{\text{density of unknown}}{\text{density of standard}}$$

since both densities are known

$$\text{sp gr ethyl alcohol} = \frac{0.789 \text{ g/cm}^3}{0.9982 \text{ g/cm}^3} = 0.790$$

9

This value must include a temperature reference since the densities of substances vary with temperature. In this case, both densities were measured at 20° and the specific gravity should be written as

$$\text{sp gr ethyl alcohol} = 0.790 \ @ \ 20°C$$

29. Using water as a reference at 15°C (density = 0.9991 g/cm³), what is the specific gravity of acetone at 25°C if 26.0 ml of acetone at 25° has the same mass as 22.5 ml of benzene at the same temperature? The density of benzene is 0.8787 g/cm³.

**Solution**

Calculate the mass of 25.0 ml of acetone given that the mass of 25.0 ml of acetone equals the mass of 22.5 ml of benzene.

$$\text{Mass acetone} = \text{Mass benzene} = 22.5 \ cm^3 \times 0.8787 \ g/cm^3 = 19.8 \ g$$

$$\text{sp gr acetone} = \frac{\text{density of acetone}}{\text{density of } H_2O} = \frac{\dfrac{19.8 \ g}{25.0 \ cm^3}}{0.9991 \ g/cm^3} = 0.793 \ @ \ \frac{25}{15}°C$$

In this case, the calculation of specific gravity involves densities determined at different temperatures. The specific gravity value as written, 0.793 @ $\frac{25}{15}$ °C, means that the density of acetone was measured at 25° and the density of the standard was measured at 15°.

32. What mass in kilograms of concentrated hydrochloric acid is contained in a standard 5.0-pt container? The specific gravity of concentrated hydrochloric acid is 1.21.

**Solution**

The specific gravities of concentrated reagents are listed on the manufacturers' labels to indicate approximate densities of the solutions. In this case, the specific gravity of HCl is listed as 1.21, meaning that its density is 1.21 times that of water. The temperature is not indicated because the density of water to three significant figures is 1.00 g/cm³ at or near ordinary laboratory temperatures. It is safe, therefore, to assume that the density of the concentrated (concd) HCl solution is 1.21 g/cm³ or 1.21 kg/ℓ. Next, convert the volume of the 5.0-pt container to liters and multiply the volume times the density of HCl to obtain the mass.

$$2 \ pt = 1 \ qt = 0.9463 \ \ell$$

$$\text{Vol in } \ell = 5.0 \ pt \times \frac{0.946 \ \ell}{2.0 \ pt} = 2.4 \ \ell$$

$$\text{Mass in kg} = 2.4 \ \ell \times 1.21 \ \frac{kg}{\ell} = 2.9 \ kg$$

33. Copper melts at 1083°C. What is its melting temperature in °F and K?

**Solution**

Use the following identities to make the conversions.

$$°F = \tfrac{9}{5}°C + 32; \quad K = °C + 273$$
$$°F = \tfrac{9}{5}(1083°) + 32 = 1949° + 32 = 1981°F$$
$$K = 1083° + 273 = 1356 \text{ K}$$

37. How many calories would be required to raise the temperature of 235 ml of water from 26.8°C to 39.9°C? How many joules? Assume that the specific heat of water is 4.184 J/g °C.

**Solution**

The amount of heat $Q$ necessary to produce this change is calculated from the relationship

$$\text{Heat} = \text{mass} \times \text{sp ht} \times \text{temp change}$$

and by assuming that 235 ml of water has a mass of 235 g, i.e., the density of water is 1.00 g/ml over this temperature range, we have

$$Q = 235 \text{ g} \times \frac{4.184 \text{ J}}{\text{g} °C} \times (39.9 - 26.8)°C = 1.29 \times 10^4 \text{ J}$$

In calories,

$$Q = 235g \times \frac{1 \text{ cal}}{\text{g} °C} \times (39.9 - 26.8)°C = 3.08 \times 10^3 \text{ cal}$$

40. If 5 g of copper cools from 35.0°C to 22.6°C and loses 23.6 joules, what is the specific heat of copper in J/g °C?

**Solution**

Specific heat $C$ is calculated from the relationship $Q = MC \, \Delta t$. In this case, we are considering the heat lost by the copper sample as it cools, and the heat lost is given in joules.

$$Q = MC \, \Delta t$$
$$C = \frac{Q}{M \, \Delta t} = \frac{23.6 \text{ J}}{5 \text{ g} \cdot 12.4°C} = 0.4 \text{ J/g} °C$$

42. What is the final temperature of the combination when 50.0 g of chromium at 15°C (specific heat = 0.107 cal/g °C) is added to 25 ml of water at 45°C? Assume the specific heat of water is 1.00 cal/g °C

**Solution**

Since the water is at a higher temperature than the chromium, heat will be transferred to the metal; water will lose heat to the metal. Heat is conserved and is defined as

$$Q_{lost}(\text{water}) = Q_{gained}(\text{chromium})$$
$$M_{H_2O} C_{H_2O} \, \Delta t_{H_2O} = M_{Cr} C_{Cr} \, \Delta t_{Cr}$$

Both components of the system reach the same final temperature, but do not undergo equal temperature changes—only equal heat changes. The unknown in this relation is the temperature change for both substances. We do, however, know the initial temperature of the substances. Therefore:

$$\Delta t_{H_2O} = (45° - t_f) : \Delta t_{Cr} = (t_f - 15°)$$

The above expressions as written are intended to show that the temperature of water decreases to $t_f$ and that of chromium increases to $t_f$. Substitution of these values for $\Delta t$ and the other data into the equation gives

$$(25\ g)\left(\frac{1\ cal}{g\,°C}\right)(45°C - t_f) = (50.0\ g)\left(0.107\ \frac{cal}{g\,°C}\right)(t_f - 15°C)$$

Division of common units yields

$$(25)\left(\frac{1}{°C}\right)(45°C - t_f) = (50.0)\left(\frac{0.107}{°C}\right)(t_f - 15°C)$$

Multiplication results in

$$1125 - \frac{25\,t_f}{°C} = \frac{5.35\,t_f}{°C} - 80.25$$

Transposing terms yields

$$\frac{30.35\,t_f}{°C} = 1205 \quad \text{and} \quad t_f = \frac{1205°C}{30.35} = 40°C$$

## RELATED PROBLEMS

1. Recently a sign in front of a fast-food restaurant indicated that 30 billion hamburgers sold. If the buns used for the sandwiches are four inches in diameter, what length (in miles) of a chain of buns could be constructed from this number of buns? in meters? *Answer: 1.9 X 10⁶ miles; 3.0 X 10⁹ m*

2. Assuming you walk on the chain of buns described in problem 1, and you can walk 8 km per hour, how long would it take you to walk the chain? *Answer: 3.8 X 10⁵ hours; 1.6 X 10⁴ days; 44 years*

3. Meteorologists usually indicate the amount of rainfall in inches and centimeters. Let's assume that a square city block, 0.10 mile per edge, is drenched by 3.0 cm of rain. Calculate the volume of water (in gallons) resulting from the rainfall in this area. What is the volume in liters? *Answer: 2.1 X 10⁵ gal; 7.8 X 10⁵ ℓ*

4.  Which one of the following numbers has the greatest number of significant figures?

    (a)  1.0001 g　　　　(b)  2.2000 ml　　　　(c)  0.000001 g
    (d)  4.01010 ml　　　(e)  1.26 × 10⁸ kg

    *Answer: d*

5.  Given the following data, calculate the density of ethanol ($C_2H_5OH$).

    | | |
    |---|---|
    | Weighing bottle plus ethanol | 162.65 g |
    | Weighing bottle | 126.95 g |
    | Volume of ethanol | 45.25 ml |

    *Answer: 0.789 g/ml*

6.  The food energy content of white sugar is 3.85 kcal/g. Given that 1 joule of energy is sufficient to lift a 1.0-kg mass to a height of 4.0 inches, calculate the amount of white sugar that would be required at 50% utilization efficiency for a 160-lb gymnast to climb a 5.0-m rope.

    *Answer: 0.44 g*

# Chapter 2: Symbols, Formulas, and Equations; Elementary Stoichiometry

## INTRODUCTION

The essence of chemistry is understanding the interactions of matter that occur both in nature and in the laboratory. Our ability to describe these interactions is shown in the language of chemistry, which includes symbols, formulas, equations, and the interpretations used to provide qualitative and quantitative information about the substances involved.

Symbols consisting of a single capital letter or a capital letter and a small letter, such as O, N, Cl, Na, and S, are used as shorthand abbreviations for elements. Combinations of symbols are used to write formulas of compounds such as methane, $CH_4$; vitamin C (ascorbic acid), $C_6H_8O_6$; and table sugar (sucrose), $C_{12}H_{22}O_{11}$. Elements and compounds enter into chemical reactions, which are described by symbols and formulas.

Chemical equations are similar to household recipes in that both provide directions for preparing products from particular quantities of reactants. Unlike household recipes, however, chemical equations usually do not detail reaction conditions or laboratory procedures other than noting that energy or a specific catalyst must be used in conjunction with the reactants. The purpose of a chemical equation is to quickly convey to the reader pertinent information about the reaction that includes the substances involved and their quantitative ratio.

Most of the reactions you will study in general chemistry involve substances in solution. The solution phase either facilitates and/or provides the medium for reactions to occur. Using substances in solution as reactants requires us to describe the solution in terms of how much substance (solute) is contained in a specified quantity (volume or mass) of solvent. Although several units of concentration are commonly used in chemistry, molarity, $M$, is presented in Chapter 2 to enable you to begin work with solutions in the laboratory as soon as possible. Other units of concentration are presented in detail in Chapter 13 of the text.

In this chapter you will have the opportunity to study quantitative aspects of reactions and begin to understand that quantities of substances found in nature are finite and that many are quite limited. By working with symbols, formulas, and equations you soon will become comfortable with the basic language tools of chemistry. The problems given here involve using formulas and equations to calculate the amount of substances involved in reactions, determining the formulas of substances from experimental data, and using solutions in the laboratory.

## FORMULAS AND DEFINITIONS

**Atomic weight**  The atomic weight of an element is the average mass of all atoms composing a normal sample of the element. For example, consider a sample of naturally occurring carbon atoms. Most of the carbon atoms (98.89%) would contain six protons and six neutrons, $^{12}C$; some (1.11%) would contain six protons and seven neutrons, $^{13}C$; and a trace (1 atom in $10^{12}$ atoms) would contain six protons and eight neutrons, $^{14}C$. Carbon-12, -13, and -14 are called isotopes of carbon and differ only in the number of neutrons in their nuclei.

Carbon-12 has been arbitrarily assigned a mass of exactly 12.00 and is used as the reference standard for determining the masses of other atoms. Based on this standard the atomic weight of carbon is 12.011 and represents the average mass of the atoms composing a statistical sample of carbon atoms.

**Formula weight (FW)**  The formula weight of a substance is the sum of the atomic weights of all of the atoms appearing in a formula. For example, the formula weight of copper(II) sulfate, $CuSO_4$, is calculated in the following way:

No. atoms:　　1 Cu　　　1 S　　　4 O

$$FW = 1(63.5) + 1(32.1) + 4(16.0) = 159.6$$

Formula weights are conventionally written as unitless entities, with atomic mass units implied or understood.

**Molecular weight (MW)**  The formula weight of a substance that exists as discrete molecules.

**Gram-atomic weight (GAW)**  The atomic weight of an element expressed in grams.

**Gram-formula weight** (GFW)   The formula weight of a substance expressed in grams.

**Gram-molecular weight** (GMW)   The molecular weight of a substance expressed in grams.

**Mole** (mol)   The mole is defined as a number equal to the number of atoms in exactly 12 grams of carbon-12. This number, called Avogadro's number, $6.022 \times 10^{23}$, has wide application in chemistry. For the purposes of this chapter, one mole (mol) can be interpreted in the following ways:

The number of atoms in a gram-atomic weight of an elemental substance. For example, the number of atoms in 23.0 g of sodium (Na) is $6.022 \times 10^{23}$.

The number of formula units in a gram-formula weight of an ionic substance. For example, the number of formula units in 58.8 g of sodium chloride (NaCl) is $6.022 \times 10^{23}$.

The number of molecules in a gram-molecular weight of a molecular substance. For example, the number of molecules in 44.0 g of carbon dioxide ($CO_2$) is $6.022 \times 10^{23}$.

Identities used for computations involving the mole and quantities of substances should be interpreted as equivalencies and not equalities as in mathematics. As cited above, one mole of sodium atoms (GAW) has a mass of 23.0 g, and, because of limited language, we write this equivalence as

$$1 \text{ mole Na} = \text{GAW Na} = 23.0 \text{ g} = 6.022 \times 10^{23} \text{ atoms}$$

This equivalence can be used to calculate the number of moles of a substance contained in a specified amount of that substance in the following ways:

$$\text{No. moles} = \text{mass of substance} \times \frac{1 \text{ mole}}{\text{GAW, GFW, or GMW of substance}}$$

or

$$= \text{no. of particles (atoms, formula units, or molecules)}$$

$$\times \frac{1 \text{ mole}}{6.022 \times 10^{23} \text{ particles}}$$

**Molarity** (*M*)   Molarity is a unit of concentration used to describe a solution in terms of the number of moles of solute present in one liter of solution.

$$\text{Molarity} = \frac{\text{no. moles of solute}}{\text{vol of solution in liters}} = \frac{\text{moles}}{\text{vol in } \ell}$$

This definition can be rearranged to express the amount of solute (in moles) contained in a given volume of solution,

$$\text{No. moles} = \text{molarity} \times \text{vol in } \ell = \left(\frac{\text{moles}}{\text{liter}}\right)(\text{liters}) = \text{moles}$$

and to express the volume of a solution in terms of molarity and the amount of solute:

$$\text{Vol in } \ell = \frac{\text{no. moles of solute}}{\text{molarity}}$$

The definition of molarity is readily extended to calculate the amount of solute required to prepare a specified volume of solution.

$$\text{Molarity} = \frac{\text{no. moles}}{\text{vol in } \ell} = \frac{\text{mass} \times \dfrac{1 \text{ mole}}{\text{GFW}}}{\text{vol in } \ell}$$

or

$$\text{Mass} = \text{molarity} \times \text{vol in } \ell \times \text{GFW}$$

$$= \left(\frac{\text{moles}}{\text{liter}}\right)(\text{liters})\left(\frac{\text{grams}}{\text{mole}}\right) = \text{grams}$$

## PROBLEMS

1. Calculate the molecular weight of each of the following compounds.

    **Solution**

    (a) Hydrogen chloride, HCl. At. wts: H = 1.008, Cl = 35.453. Atomic weight values should be rounded to the nearest tenth except in calculations involving data that require a greater number of significant figures.

    $$\text{MW} = \text{sum of all atomic weights of elements as they appear in the formula}$$

    $$= 1.0 + 35.4 = 36.4$$

    (d) Sulfuric acid, $H_2SO_4$. At. wts: H = 1.0, S = 32.1, O = 16.0.

    $$\text{MW} = 2(1.0) + 32.1 + 4(16.0) = 98.1$$

    (e) Tetraethyl lead, $Pb(C_2H_5)_4$. At. wts: Pb = 207.2, C = 12.0, H = 1.0. Total atoms: Pb = 1, C = 4 × 2 = 8, H = 4 × 5 = 20.

    $$\text{MW} = 207.2 + 8(12.0) + 20(1.0) = 323.2$$

4. A sample of FeO contains 0.777 g of Fe and 0.223 g of O. The atomic weight of O is 16.00. Determine the atomic weight of Fe.

**Solution**

The formula FeO indicates a one-to-one ratio of iron atoms to oxygen atoms. The mass of each element in the compound is proportional to its respective atomic weight and to its mass ratio in the formula. The mass ratio of Fe to O is

$$\frac{Fe}{O} = \frac{0.777 \text{ g}}{0.223 \text{ g}} = \frac{\text{at. wt Fe}}{\text{at. wt O (16.00)}}$$

$$\text{at. wt Fe} = \frac{0.777 \text{ g}}{0.223 \text{ g}} \times 16.00 = 55.7$$

5. Determine the number of

(a) moles of ammonia, $NH_3$, in 8.5 g of $NH_3$.

**Solution**

$$1 \text{ mol } NH_3 = \text{GMW } NH_3 = 17.0 \text{ g}$$

$$\text{No. moles} = 8.5 \text{ g } NH_3 \times \frac{1 \text{ mol}}{17.0 \text{ g}} = 0.50 \text{ mol}$$

(d) moles of caffeine, $C_8 H_{10} N_4 O_2$, in 0.381 g of caffeine.

**Solution**

$$1 \text{ mol caffeine} = 1 \text{ GMW } C_8 H_{10} N_4 O_2$$

$$\text{GMW} = 8(12.0) + 10(1.0) + 4(14.0) + 2(16.0) = 194 \text{ g}$$

$$\text{No. moles} = 0.381 \text{ g} \times \frac{1 \text{ mol}}{194 \text{ g}} = 1.96 \times 10^{-3} \text{ mol}$$

6. What is the mass of each of the following in grams?

(a) 0.178 mol of potassium bromide, KBr.

**Solution**

$$1 \text{ mol KBr} = 1 \text{ GFW KBr} = 119.0 \text{ g}$$

$$\text{Mass} = 0.178 \text{ mol KBr} \left( \frac{119.0 \text{ g}}{\text{mol}} \right) = 21.2 \text{ g}$$

(e) $2.60 \times 10^{-4}$ mol of glycine, $CH_2 (NH_2)CO_2 H$

**Solution**

$$1 \text{ mol glycine} = 1 \text{ GMW glycine} = 75.0 \text{ g}$$

$$\text{Mass} = 2.60 \times 10^{-4} \text{ mol glycine} \times \frac{75.0 \text{ g}}{\text{mol}} = 1.95 \times 10^{-2} \text{ g}$$

(i) 1.378 mol of oxygen molecules, $O_2$.

**Solution**

$$1 \text{ mol } O_2 \text{ molecules} = 1 \text{ GMW } O_2 = 32.00 \text{ g}$$

$$\text{Mass} = 1.378 \text{ mol } O_2 \times \frac{32.00 \text{ g}}{\text{mol}} = 44.10 \text{ g}$$

8. Determine the moles of nickel phosphate, $Ni_3(PO_4)_2$, the moles of nickel atoms, the moles of oxygen atoms, the number of nickel atoms, and the number of oxygen atoms in 9.37 g of $Ni_3(PO_4)_2$.

**Solution**

$$1 \text{ mol } Ni_3(PO_4)_2 = \text{GFW } Ni_3(PO_4)_2$$

$$\text{GFW } Ni_3(PO_4)_2 = 3(58.7) + 2(31.0) + 8(16.0) = 366.1 \text{ g}$$

$$\text{No. moles } Ni_3(PO_4)_2 = 9.37 \text{ g} \times \frac{1 \text{ mol}}{366.1 \text{ g}} = 2.56 \times 10^{-2} \text{ mol}$$

Moles of nickel atoms and of oxygen atoms: One mole of $Ni_3(PO_4)_2$ formula units contains 3 moles of Ni atoms, 2 moles of P atoms, and 8 moles of O atoms. Therefore $2.56 \times 10^{-2}$ moles of $Ni_3(PO_4)_2$ contain

$$\text{No. moles Ni atoms} = 2.56 \times 10^{-2} \text{ mol} \times \frac{3 \text{ mol Ni atoms}}{\text{mol}}$$

$$= 7.68 \times 10^{-2} \text{ mol}$$

$$\text{No. moles O atoms} = 2.56 \times 10^{-2} \text{ mol} \times \frac{8 \text{ mol O atoms}}{\text{mol}}$$

$$= 2.05 \times 10^{-1} \text{ mol}$$

Number of atoms of Ni and O:

$$1 \text{ mol atoms} = 6.02 \times 10^{23} \text{ atoms}$$

$$\text{No. Ni atoms} = 7.68 \times 10^{-2} \text{ mol} \times \frac{6.022 \times 10^{23} \text{ atoms}}{\text{mol}}$$

$$= 4.62 \times 10^{22} \text{ atoms}$$

$$\text{No. O atoms} = 2.05 \times 10^{-1} \text{ mol} \times \frac{6.022 \times 10^{23} \text{ atoms}}{\text{mol}}$$

$$= 1.23 \times 10^{23} \text{ atoms}$$

15. Calculate the number of moles of ethanol, $CH_3CH_2OH$, in 7.55 kg of ethanol.

**Solution**

$$1 \text{ mol ethanol} = 1 \text{ GMW ethanol} = 46.0 \text{ g}$$

$$\text{No. moles ethanol} = 7.55 \text{ kg} \times \frac{1000 \text{ g}}{\text{kg}} \times \frac{1 \text{ mol}}{46.0 \text{ g}} = 164 \text{ mol}$$

16. Calculate the molar concentration of each of the following solutions:

    (a) 98.1 g of sulfuric acid, $H_2SO_4$, in 1.00 ℓ of solution.

**Solution**

To solve a problem of this type, begin by writing the definition of the concept and identifying the known and unknown quantities, and then solve for the unknown. ·

$$\text{Molarity} = \frac{\text{no. moles solute}}{\text{vol soln in } \ell}$$

In this case, calculate the number of moles of $H_2SO_4$ in 98.1 g and substitute the value into the equation along with the volume.

$$M = \frac{98.1 \text{ g } H_2SO_4 \times \dfrac{1 \text{ mol}}{98.1 \text{ g}}}{1.00 \text{ } \ell} = \frac{1.00 \text{ mol}}{\ell} = 1.00 \text{ } M$$

(c) 24.5 g of sodium cyanide, NaCN, in 2.000 ℓ of solution.

**Solution**

$$1 \text{ mol NaCN} = \text{GFW NaCN} = 49.0 \text{ g}$$

$$M = \frac{24.5 \text{ g NaCN} \times \dfrac{1 \text{ mol}}{49.0 \text{ g}}}{2.00 \text{ } \ell} = 0.250 \text{ } M$$

(e) 2.12 g of potassium bromide, KBr, in 458 ml of solution.

**Solution**

$$1 \text{ mol KBr} = 1 \text{ GFW KBr} = 119.0 \text{ g}$$

$$M = \frac{2.12 \text{ g} \times \dfrac{1 \text{ mol}}{119.0 \text{ g}}}{0.458 \text{ } \ell} = \frac{0.0389 \text{ mol}}{\ell} = 3.89 \times 10^{-2} \text{ } M$$

17. Determine the moles of solute present in each of the following solutions:

    (b) 2.0 ℓ of 0.480 $M$ $MgCl_2$ solution

**Solution**

As in problem 16, the data given here involve the definition of molarity. The definition can be rearranged as follows:

$$\text{Molarity} = \frac{\text{no. moles}}{\text{vol in } \ell}$$

No. moles = molarity × vol in $\ell$

No. moles $MgCl_2$ = (0.480 $M$) (2.0 $\ell$) = 0.96 mol

(d) 2.50 ml of 0.1812 $M$ $KMnO_4$ solution.

**Solution**

No. moles $KMnO_4$ = (0.1812 $M$) (0.00250 $\ell$) = 4.53 × $10^{-4}$ mol

To avoid the use of decimals, molarity can be expressed in terms of millimoles and milliliters as

$$\text{Molarity} = \frac{\text{no. millimoles of solute}}{\text{vol in ml}}$$

The number of millimoles of solute equals

No. millimoles (mmol) = molarity × vol in ml

Since

$$\frac{\text{mol}}{\ell} \left( \frac{1 \; \ell}{1000 \; \text{ml}} \right) \text{ml} = \text{mmol}$$

$$= (0.1812) (2.50 \; \text{ml}) = 0.453 \; \text{mmol}$$

$$= 4.53 \times 10^{-4} \; \text{mol } KMnO_4$$

18. Determine the mass of each of the following solutes required to make the indicated amount of solution:

(a) 1.00 $\ell$ of 1.00 $M$ $LiNO_3$ solution.

**Solution**

Problems of this type are further extensions of the definition of molarity. The mass of solute can be calculated from the definition in one operation by rearranging the definition as

$$\text{Molarity} = \frac{\text{no. moles}}{\text{vol in } \ell} = \frac{\text{mass of solute} \times \frac{1 \; \text{mol}}{\text{GFW}}}{\text{vol in } \ell}$$

and

$$\text{Mass} = \text{molarity} \times \text{vol in } \ell \times \text{GFW} = \left( \frac{\text{moles}}{\ell} \right) \times \text{vol in } \ell \times \text{GFW}$$

$$\text{GFW LiNO}_3 = 6.94 + 14.0 + 3(16.0) = 68.9 \text{ g}$$

$$\text{Mass} = (1.00 \, M)(1.00 \, \ell)(68.9 \text{ g}) = 68.9 \text{ g LiNO}_3$$

(d)  275 ml of 0.5151 $M$ KClO$_4$ solution.

**Solution**

$$\text{GFW KClO}_4 = 39.1 + 35.4 + 4(16.0) = 138.5 \text{ g}$$

$$\text{Mass} = \text{molarity} \times \text{vol in } \ell \times \text{GFW}$$

$$= (0.5151 \, M)(0.275 \, \ell)(138.5 \text{ g}) = 19.6 \text{ g KClO}_4$$

20. Calculate the per cent composition of each of the following compounds to three significant figures.

(a)  Lead sulfide, PbS

**Solution**

Per cent composition can be calculated from the formula of a compound based on the atomic weights of the elements present and the mass contribution each element makes to the formula weight of the compound.

$$\% \text{ element} = \frac{\text{total mass of the element in the compound}}{\text{FW or GFW of the compound}} \times 100$$

$$\text{FW PbS} = 207.2 + 32.1 = 239.3$$

$$\% \text{ Pb} = \frac{207.2}{239.3} \times 100 = 86.6\%$$

$$\% \text{ S} = \frac{32.1}{239.3} \times 100 = 13.4\%$$

(c)  Iron(III) nitrate, Fe(NO$_3$)$_3$

**Solution**

$$\text{FW Fe(NO}_3)_3 = 55.8 + 3(14.0) + 9(16.0) = 241.8$$

$$\% \text{ Fe} = \frac{55.8}{241.8} \times 100 = 23.1\%$$

$$\% \text{ N} = \frac{3(14.0)}{241.8} \times 100 = 17.4\%$$

$$\% \text{ O} = \frac{9(16.0)}{241.8} \times 100 = 59.6\%$$

Any deviation from 100% is due to rounding.

23. From the per cent composition data given, work out the empirical formulas of the following compounds:

(a) Potassium bromide: K, 32.85%; Br, 67.15%.

**Solution**

The empirical formula of a compound is the simplest whole number atom ratio of elements as they appear in the formula of the compound. Per cent composition data can be used to determine the atomic ratio of elements in a compound by recognizing that per cent composition represents the mass fraction of each element in a compound. In doing these problems consider a 100-g sample quantity. By using 100 g we effectively eliminate the bother of the per cent sign because percentage is converted directly to grams. In this case, a 100.0-g sample of KBr contains 32.85 g of K and 67.15 g of Br. The next step is to determine the number of moles of each element in the sample.

$$\text{No. moles K} = 32.85 \text{ g} \times \frac{1 \text{ mol}}{39.10 \text{ g}} = 0.8402 \text{ mol}$$

$$\text{No. moles Br} = 67.15 \text{ g} \times \frac{1 \text{ mol}}{79.91 \text{ g}} = 0.8403 \text{ mol}$$

The ratio of atoms of K to atoms of Br is

$$\text{K}_{0.8402} \quad : \quad \text{Br}_{0.8403}$$

and can be converted to a whole number ratio by dividing each term by the smallest value.

$$\text{K:} \quad \frac{0.8402}{0.8402} = 1 \qquad \text{Br:} \quad \frac{0.8403}{0.8402} = 1$$

The empirical formula is therefore KBr.

(d) Aluminum oxide: Al, 52.9%; O, 47.1%.

**Solution**

Assume a 100.0-g sample.

$$\text{Mass Al} = 52.9 \text{ g}, \qquad \text{Mass O} = 47.1 \text{ g}$$

$$\text{No. moles Al} = 52.9 \text{ g} \times \frac{1 \text{ mol}}{27.0 \text{ g}} = 1.96 \text{ mol}$$

$$\text{No. moles O} = 47.1 \text{ g} \times \frac{1 \text{ mol}}{16.0 \text{ g}} = 2.94 \text{ mol}$$

$$\text{Al}_{1.96} \quad : \quad \text{O}_{2.94}$$

Division by the smaller factor yields

$$\text{Al:} \quad \frac{1.96}{1.96} = 1 \qquad \text{O:} \quad \frac{2.94}{1.96} = 1.50$$

$$Al_1 \ : \ O_{1.5}$$

The smallest whole number ratio is obtained by multiplying the subscripts by a factor that converts them to whole numbers; in this case multiply by 2.

$$Al_2O_3$$

24. (a) What is the empirical formula of hydrazine, which contains 87.5% N and 12.5% H?

**Solution**

Assume a 100.0-g sample.

$$\text{Mass N} = 87.5 \text{ g}, \qquad \text{Mass H} = 12.5 \text{ g}$$

$$\text{No. moles N} = 87.5 \text{ g} \times \frac{1 \text{ mol}}{14.0 \text{ g}} = 6.25 \text{ mol}$$

$$\text{No. moles H} = 12.5 \text{ g} \times \frac{1 \text{ mol}}{1.0 \text{ g}} = 12.5 \text{ mol}$$

$$N_{6.25} \ : \ H_{12.5}$$

Divide by the smallest term and obtain $NH_2$.

(b) The molecular weight of hydrazine is 32. What is its molecular formula?

**Solution**

The empirical formula of a compound represents the simplest whole number ratio of atoms in the compound. The molecular formula of a compound represents the ratio of atoms in the compound and the number of times the atoms appear in the formula of the compound. The molecular formula is a whole number multiple of the empirical formula. In many cases, especially involving inorganic compounds, the molecular formula and the empirical formula are the same. The molecular formula can be determined from the empirical formula and the molecular weight of the compound as follows:

$$(\text{Empirical formula})_n \ = \ \text{molecular formula}$$

$$(\text{FW of empirical formula})_n \ = \ \text{molecular formula weight}$$

$$(NH_2)_n \ = \ \text{molecular formula of hydrazine}$$

$$[14.0 + 2(1.0)]_n \ = \ \text{MFW} = 32.0$$

$$(16.0)_n \ = \ 32.0 \ n = 2$$

Therefore hydrazine is $N_2H_4$.

25. A 4.00-g sample of an oxide of cobalt contains 2.937 g of cobalt. What is the empirical formula of this oxide?

**Solution**

The empirical formula of this compound is determined from the data in the same manner as was done with percentages; only the amount of sample is different.

Mass Co = 2.937 g,    Mass O = 4.00 g − 2.937 g = 1.06 g

$$\text{No. moles Co} = 2.937 \text{ g} \times \frac{1 \text{ mol}}{58.93 \text{ g}} = 0.0498 \text{ mol}$$

$$\text{No. moles O} = 1.06 \text{ g} \times \frac{1 \text{ mol}}{16.0 \text{ g}} = 0.0662 \text{ mol}$$

$$Co_{0.0498} \ : \ O_{0.0662}$$

Divide by the smaller of the two numbers:

$$Co_1 \ : \ O_{1.33}$$

Multiply by 3 to obtain the smallest whole number ratio.

$$Co_3O_4$$

32. The mineral gypsum contains 20.91% water and 79.09% $CaSO_4$. What is the empirical formula of gypsum?

**Solution**

Assume a 100.0-g sample of gypsum.

Mass $CaSO_4$ = 79.09 g,    Mass $H_2O$ = 20.91 g

GFW $CaSO_4$ = 40.1 + 32.1 + 4(16.0) = 136.2 g

GFW $H_2O$ = 2(1.0) + 16.0 = 18.0 g

$$\text{No. moles } CaSO_4 = 79.09 \text{ g} \times \frac{1 \text{ mol}}{136.2 \text{ g}} = 0.581 \text{ mol}$$

$$\text{No. moles } H_2O = 20.91 \text{ g} \times \frac{1 \text{ mol}}{18.0 \text{ g}} = 1.16 \text{ mol}$$

$$(CaSO_4)_{0.581} \ : \ (H_2O)_{1.16}$$

Divide by the smaller number to obtain $CaSO_4 \cdot 2H_2O$

35. The reaction of chromium metal with $H_3PO_4$ produces hydrogen, $H_2$, and a green solid containing 35.38% Cr, 21.07% P, and 43.55% O. Identify the product and write the balanced equation for the reaction.

**Solution**

To write the chemical equation we must know the formulas of all the substances involved in the reaction. First, determine the empirical formula of the green solid. Assume a 100.0-g sample.

Mass Cr = 35.38 g,    Mass P = 21.07 g,    Mass O = 43.55 g

No. moles Cr = 35.38 g $\times \dfrac{1\ \text{mol}}{52.0\ \text{g}}$ = 0.680 mol

No. moles P = 21.07 g $\times \dfrac{1\ \text{mol}}{31.0\ \text{g}}$ = 0.680 mol

No. moles O = 43.55 g $\times \dfrac{1\ \text{mol}}{16.0\ \text{g}}$ = 2.72 mol

Divide by the smallest factor to obtain

$$Cr_1 P_1 O_4 \quad \text{or} \quad CrPO_4$$

The balanced chemical equation is

$$2Cr + 2H_3PO_4 \longrightarrow 3H_2 + 2CrPO_4$$

40. What mass of calcium chloride, $CaCl_2$, contains 17.8 g of chlorine?

**Solution**

There are several ways to solve a problem of this type. One logical way is to determine the mass of Cl in a GFW of $CaCl_2$ and then write a relation to solve for the amount of $CaCl_2$ containing 17.8 g of Cl.

$$\text{GFW } CaCl_2 = 40.1 + 2(35.4) = 110.9\ \text{g}$$

That is, 110.9 g $CaCl_2$ contains or can produce 70.8 g Cl. Then what mass of $CaCl_2$ produces 17.8 g Cl? By simple ratio, the mass of $CaCl_2$ is

$$\text{Mass } CaCl_2 = \dfrac{17.8\ \text{g}}{70.8\ \text{g}} \times 110.9\ \text{g} = 27.9\ \text{g}$$

43. How many moles of phosphorus(V) sulfide are produced when 0.50 mol of $S_8$ reacts according to the following equation?

$$4P_4 + 5S_8 \longrightarrow 4P_4S_{10}$$

**Solution**

The relationship between reactants and products is clearly defined by the balanced equation. Write the mole ratio of reactants to products below the balanced equation as shown below.

  0.5 mol                                no. mol?

  $4P_4$   +   $5S_8$   $\longrightarrow$   $4P_4S_{10}$

  4 mol $P_4$ + 5 mol $S_8$ $\longrightarrow$ 4 mol $P_4S_{10}$

Next identify the given quantities and the unknown and write them above the equation in their respective positions. A simple ratio between the known, $S_8$, and the unknown, $P_4S_{10}$, yields

$$\text{No. moles } P_4S_{10} = 0.50 \text{ mol } S_8 \times \frac{4 \text{ mol } P_4S_{10}}{5 \text{ mol } S_8} = 0.40 \text{ mol}$$

45. How many moles of HF are produced by the reaction of $1.5 \times 10^{23}$ $H_2$ molecules in the following reaction?

$$H_2 + F_2 \longrightarrow 2HF$$

**Solution**

According to the balanced equation, one mole of $H_2$ reacts with one mole of $F_2$ to produce two moles of HF.

$$\overset{1.5 \times 10^{23} \text{ molecules}}{H_2} + F_2 \qquad \overset{\text{no. moles?}}{\longrightarrow 2HF}$$

$$1 \text{ mol } H_2 + 1 \text{ mol } F_2 \longrightarrow 2 \text{ mol HF}$$

Since the amount of $H_2$ is given as a number of particles, the relation for calculating the number of moles $H_2$ must be in terms of a number of particles.

$$1 \text{ mol } H_2 = 6.02 \times 10^{23} \text{ molecules of } H_2$$

Identify the known and the unknown and write them over the equation. The relationship between the known and unknown is as follows:

$$\text{No. moles HF} = 1.5 \times 10^{23} \text{ molecules } H_2 \times \frac{1 \text{ mol } H_2}{6.02 \times 10^{23} \text{ molecules}}$$

$$\times \frac{2 \text{ mol HF}}{1 \text{ mol } H_2} = 0.50 \text{ mol}$$

49. How many grams of $O_2$ will be produced by the thermal decomposition of 7.79 mol of potassium nitrate, $KNO_3$?

$$2KNO_3 \overset{\Delta}{\longrightarrow} 2KNO_2 + O_2$$

**Solution**

According to the balanced equation, two moles of $KNO_3$ produce one mole of $O_2$. Write the mole relationship below the equation as

$$\overset{7.79 \text{ mol}}{2 \, KNO_3} \overset{\Delta}{\longrightarrow} \overset{\text{Mass (g)?}}{2KNO_2 + O_2}$$

$$2 \text{ moles} \longrightarrow 2 \text{ moles} + 1 \text{ mole}$$

Identify the known and the unknown and write them over the equation. Write a mole relation statement to solve for the mass of $O_2$ as follows:

$$1 \text{ mol } O_2 = \text{GMW } O_2 = 32.0 \text{ g}$$

$$\text{Mass } O_2 = 7.79 \text{ mol } KNO_3 \times \frac{1 \text{ mol } O_2}{2 \text{ mol } KNO_3} \times \frac{32.0 \text{ g } O_2}{\text{mol } O_2} = 125 \text{ g}$$

52. What mass of ammonia, $NH_3$, is required to react with 1.33 kg of $H_3PO_4$ according to the following equation?

$$2NH_3 + H_3PO_4 \longrightarrow (NH_4)_2 HPO_4$$

**Solution**

According to the balanced equation, two moles of $NH_3$ react with one mole of $H_3PO_4$. The quantities of the known and unknown, however, are expressed in kilograms. The problem can be solved by converting kilograms to grams, solving the mole relation in grams, and converting the answer in grams to kilograms. The balanced equation actually represents a particle-by-particle relationship and the relationship is valid for all units of mass or weight.

| Mass (kg)? | | 1.33 kg |
|---|---|---|

$$2NH_3 \quad + H_3PO_4 \longrightarrow (NH_4)_2 HPO_4$$
$$2 \text{ moles} \quad + 1 \text{ mole} \longrightarrow 1 \text{ mole}$$
$$2(17.0 \text{ kg}) + 98.0 \text{ kg}$$

A mass ratio can be written for the equation in terms of kilograms and the amount of $NH_3$ calculated as follows:

$$\text{Mass } NH_3 = 1.33 \text{ kg } H_3PO_4 \times \frac{34.0 \text{ kg } NH_3}{98.0 \text{ kg } H_3PO_4} = 0.461 \text{ kg}$$

54. How many moles of nitric acid, $HNO_3$, are required to react with the calcium hydroxide, $Ca(OH)_2$, in 250 ml of a 0.1 $M$ $Ca(OH)_2$ solution?

$$2HNO_3 (aq) + Ca(OH)_2 (aq) \longrightarrow Ca(NO_3)_2 (aq) + 2H_2O(\ell)$$

**Solution**

The relationship between $HNO_3$ and $Ca(OH)_2$ in the reaction is 2 moles of $HNO_3$ to 1 mole of $Ca(OH)_2$. The number of moles of $HNO_3$ required for the reaction equals two times the number of moles of $Ca(OH)_2$ available.

$$\text{No. moles } HNO_3 \text{ required} = 2 \text{ [no. moles } Ca(OH)_2 \text{ available]}$$
$$= 2 \text{ (molarity} \times \text{vol in } \ell)$$
$$= 2 \text{ (0.1 } M) \text{ (0.250 } \ell)$$
$$= 0.05 \text{ mol} = 5 \times 10^{-2} \text{ mol}$$

56. What mass of silver nitrate, $AgNO_3$, is required to react exactly with the calcium chloride in 25.00 ml of a 0.5285 $M$ solution of $CaCl_2$?

$$2AgNO_3 (aq) + CaCl_2 (aq) \longrightarrow 2AgCl(s) + Ca(NO_3)_2 (aq)$$

**Solution**

The number of moles of $AgNO_3$ required for the reaction equals two times the amount of $CaCl_2$ available.

No. moles $AgNO_3$ required = 2(no. moles $CaCl_2$ available)

No. moles $AgNO_3$ = 2(0.02500 ℓ) (0.5285 $M$) = 0.026425 mol

GFW $AgNO_3$ = 107.87 + 14.01 + 48.00 = 169.88 g

Mass $AgNO_3$ = (0.026425 mol) (169.88 g/mol) = 4.489 g

59. An excess of barium chloride reacted with 50.0 ml of a dilute solution of sulfuric acid, producing 0.482 g of $BaSO_4$. What is the molarity of the sulfuric acid solution?

$$BaCl_2\,(aq) + H_2\,SO_4\,(aq) \longrightarrow BaSO_4\,(s) + 2HCl(aq)$$

**Solution**

One mole of $H_2\,SO_4$ produces one mole of $BaSO_4$. Therefore the number of moles of $H_2\,SO_4$ in the solution must equal the number of moles of $BaSO_4$ produced.

GFW $BaSO_4$ = 137.3 + 32.1 + 64.0 = 233.4 g

No. moles $H_2\,SO_4$ = no. moles $BaSO_4$ = 0.482 g $\times \dfrac{1\ mol}{233.4\ g}$

$$= 0.002065\ mol$$

The molarity of $H_2\,SO_4$ is based on this number of moles in 50.0 ml of solution.

$$\text{Molarity } H_2\,SO_4 = \frac{0.002065\ mol}{0.0500\ \ell} = 0.0413\ M$$

61. The nitric acid in 125 ml of a 0.600 $M$ solution reacts exactly with the potassium hydroxide in 47.0 ml of KOH solution. What is the molar concentration of the KOH solution?

$$KOH(aq) + HNO_3\,(aq) \longrightarrow KNO_3\,(aq) + H_2\,O(\ell)$$

**Solution**

Both reactants are in solution, and they react on a one mole to one mole basis. In other words,

No. moles $HNO_3$ reacted = no. moles KOH reacted

No. moles KOH = (0.125 ℓ $HNO_3$) (0.600 $M$) = 0.0750 mol

$$\text{Molarity KOH} = \frac{0.0750\ mol}{0.047\ \ell} = 1.60\ M$$

## RELATED PROBLEMS

1. Calculate the formula weight of each of the following compounds.

    (a) A common soap, sodium stearate, $C_{17}H_{35}COONa$.
    (b) MSG, monosodium glutamate, $HOOCCH_2 CH_2 CHNH_2 COONa$
    (c) The acid responsible for the odor in rancid butter, butyric acid or butanoic acid, $CH_3 CH_2 CH_2 COOH$.
    (d) A food preservative, sodium benzoate, $C_6 H_5 COONa$

    *Answer: (a) 306; (b) 169; (c) 88; (d) 144*

2. The composition of regular gasoline is approximately 70% heptane, $C_7 H_{16}$, and 30% octane, $C_8 H_{18}$, by volume. The densities of heptane and octane are 683.76 g/ℓ and 702.5 g/ℓ, respectively at 20°C. Calculate the mass of water that would be produced by the combustion of 1.00 gallon of gasoline according to the following equation.

$$C_7 H_{16} + 11O_2 \longrightarrow 7CO_2 + 8H_2 O$$

$$2C_8 H_{18} + 25O_2 \longrightarrow 16CO_2 + 18H_2 O$$

*Answer: 3740 g*

3. The analysis of a sample of brass shows the composition to be 72.0% Cu and 28.0% Zn by weight. Calculate the mass of brass that can be made from 5.5 kg of copper assuming adequate zinc is available. What mass of zinc would be required? *Answer: 7.64 kg of brass; 2.14 kg of zinc*

4. Much of the world reserve of mercury is located in Spain and Italy in the form of cinnabar, HgS. Assuming that ore is pure HgS, how much ore would be required to produce 8.0 million kg of mercury, equal to about a one-year supply? *Answer: 9.3 X 10⁶ kg HgS*

5. Calculate the mass of oxalic acid dihydrate, $H_2 C_2 O_4 \cdot 2H_2 O$, required to prepare 5.00 ℓ of 0.250 M solution. *Answer: 158 g*

6. Which one of the following solutions has the greatest molarity?

    (a) 60.0 mg of NaOH in 250 ml of solution
    (b) 200. g of glucose, $C_6 H_{12} O_6$, in 5.0 ℓ of solution
    (c) 5.00 mg of $Al_2 (SO_4)_3$ in 200 ml of solution    *Answer (b) 0.22 M*

7. Calculate the volume of 0.125 M $HNO_3$ required to neutralize 550. ml of 2.0 M NaOH.

$$HNO_3 (aq) + NaOH(aq) \longrightarrow NaNO_3 (aq) + H_2 O(\ell)$$

*Answer: 8.8 X 10³ ml*

# Chapter 3: Applications of Chemical Stoichiometry

## INTRODUCTION

This chapter extends the presentation of Chapter 2 to include broader classes of reactions and equations and to bring out their utility in the study of chemistry. Various examples are used to emphasize systematic procedures for analyzing a problem into its essential components.

Although the simplicity of most chemical equations tends to convey the idea that reactions occur in a single step, most reactions require completion of several steps before the desired product is formed. For example, some complex biochemical compounds may require a hundred individual steps in which intermediate products result, yet the equation representing the formation of such a compound may be a simple one-line expression.

To illustrate the complexity of what appears to be a simple reaction, consider the production of table salt, $NaCl(s)$, from its elements according to the equation

$$Na(s) + \frac{1}{2}Cl_2\,(g) \longrightarrow NaCl(s)$$

The production of $NaCl(s)$ is exothermic (that is, it proceeds with the liberation of heat) and occurs spontaneously in the presence of sunlight or heat. Without going into great detail, the overall reaction process can be broken down into the following five reaction steps:

1. $Na(s) + 108.8 \text{ kJ} \rightarrow Na(g)$    (endothermic, requires heat to proceed)

2. $Na(g) + 496.0 \text{ kJ} \rightarrow Na^+ + e^-$  (endothermic)
3. $\frac{1}{2} Cl_2(g) + 119.7 \text{ kJ} \rightarrow Cl(g)$  (endothermic)
4. $Cl(g) + e^- \rightarrow Cl^-(g) + 364.8 \text{ kJ}$  (exothermic)
5. $Na^+(g) + Cl^-(g) \rightarrow NaCl(g) \rightarrow NaCl(s) + 770.7 \text{ kJ}$  (exothermic)

The total heat released in producing one mole of NaCl(s) is 411.0 kJ, obtained by subtracting the sum of the endothermic values from the sum of the exo- thermic values. Much of the work in chemical research lies in the elucidation of similar reaction processes and their attendant energy changes.

A variety of problems that have industrial and/or physiological importance appear in this chapter. The solutions to many of these problems involve several steps that can generally be categorized into a format for a systematic solution. To develop a format, read each problem carefully in order to iden- tify the knowns and unknowns. Then write the equation for the reaction and balance it as necessary. The next step is to develop expressions relating the knowns and unknowns, and solve for the unknowns accordingly. After studying examples and solving a few problems, you will begin to develop a personal method for organizing data and solving problems. After all, solv- ing problems is a human endeavor, and probably no two people solve prob- lems in exactly the same way.

There are many possible methods for solving problems in chemistry involv- ing reactants and products. The problem-solving format used in the texts is basically the same as that used in this manual, but you will notice slightly different organizational practices that should enable you to see other ways of approaching problems.


## FORMULAS AND DEFINITIONS


**Limiting reagent**  The reagent (or reagents) completely consumed by a reac- tion is called the limiting reagent(s). In a balanced chemical equation, which represents a reaction, the proper mole ratio for reactants is given. If, however, the reaction mixture contains one reactant in excess of the proper mole ratio, the other reactant(s) will be completely consumed and the excess amount of the reactant in excess will remain unreacted. The amount of product produced by the reaction, therefore, is limited by the amount of reagent available for reaction. As an analogy, we may liken a chemical reaction to the assembly of bicycles in which we begin with three bicycle frames and eight tires. Three complete bicycles can obviously be built, with two tires in excess. The available bicycle frames *limit* (like the limiting reagent) the number of bicycles that can be built when tires are in excess.

**Theoretical yield**  The potential amount of product that can be produced in a reaction determined by the mole ratio in the balanced equation and calculated from the amounts of available reactant(s).

**Actual yield** The actual amount of product produced in a chemical reaction.

**Per cent yield** The per cent yield for a reaction is the yield fraction, actual yield divided by theoretical yield, times 100.

$$\% \text{ yield} = \frac{\text{actual yield}}{\text{theoretical yield}} \times 100$$

## PROBLEMS

1. How many moles of calcium sulfate, $CaSO_4$, will be required to prepare 50.0 g of plaster of paris? Plaster of paris contains 93.8% $CaSO_4$ by mass.

**Solution**

To calculate the number of moles of $CaSO_4$ needed, the mass of $CaSO_4$ in the product must be known. Since plaster of paris is 93.8% $CaSO_4$ by mass, the mass of $CaSO_4$ in 50.0 g of plaster of paris is

$$\text{Mass } CaSO_4 = \frac{93.8\%}{100\%} \times 50.0 \text{ g} = 46.9 \text{ g}$$

$$\text{GFW } CaSO_4 = 40.1 + 32.1 + 4(16.0) = 136.2 \text{ g}$$

$$\text{No. moles } CaSO_4 = 46.9 \text{ g} \times \frac{1 \text{ mol}}{136.2 \text{ g}} = 0.344 \text{ mol}$$

4. What volume of a solution of 37.0% HCl in water with a density of 1.181 g/ml (concentrated hydrochloric acid) can be prepared from 2.744 mol of HCl?

**Solution**

Each milliliter of HCl solution weighs 1.181 g and is 37.0% HCl by weight:

$$\text{Mass HCl per ml} = \frac{37.0\%}{100\%} \times 1.181 \text{ g} = 0.437 \text{ g}$$

Calculate the mass of available HCl:

$$\text{GFW HCl} = 1.01 + 35.45 = 36.46 \text{ g}$$

$$\text{Mass HCl} = 2.744 \text{ mol} \times \frac{36.46 \text{ g}}{\text{mol}} = 100.05 \text{ g}$$

The volume of solution that can be prepared from 100.05 g of HCl at 0.437 g HCl per milliliter is

$$1.00 \text{ ml solution} = 0.437 \text{ g HCl}$$

$$\text{Vol HCl} = 100.05 \text{ g} \times \frac{1 \text{ ml}}{0.437 \text{ g}} = 229 \text{ ml}$$

7. How many grams of CaO are required for reaction with the HCl in 275 ml of a 0.523 $M$ HCl solution? The equation for the reaction is

$$CaO + 2HCl \longrightarrow CaCl_2 + H_2O$$

**Solution**

According to the balanced equation, two moles of HCl react with one mole of CaO. To compute the mass of CaO required, calculate the number of moles of available HCl. From this value, the number of moles of CaO required is found from the reaction equation and then converted to grams of CaO.

$$\text{No. moles CaO required} = \frac{\text{no. moles HCl}}{2} = \frac{0.1438}{2} = 0.0719 \text{ mol}$$

GFW CaO = 56.1 g

$$\text{Mass CaO} = 0.0719 \text{ mol} \times \frac{56.1}{\text{mol}} g = 4.03 \text{ g}$$

9. Elemental phosphorus, $P_4$, is prepared by the following reaction:

$$2Ca_3(PO_4)_2 + 6SiO_2 + 10C \longrightarrow 6CaSiO_3 + 10CO + P_4$$

How much phosphorus can be prepared from a 374-g sample of an ore that is 75.9% $Ca_3(PO_4)_2$?

**Solution**

The amount of phosphorus produced by the reaction is dependent on the amount of $Ca_3(PO_4)_2$ available. The 374-g sample of phosphate ore is 75.9% $Ca_3(PO_4)_2$, and the amount of $Ca_3(PO_4)_2$ is

$$\text{Mass } Ca_3(PO_4)_2 = \frac{75.9\%}{100\%} \times 374 \text{ g} = 283.9 \text{ g}$$

Calculate the GFW of $Ca_3(PO_4)_2$ and $P_4$:

GFW $Ca_3(PO_4)_2 = 3(40.1) + 2(31.0) + 8(16.0) = 310.3$ g

GFW $P_4 = 4(31.0) = 124.0$ g

The mole ratio between $Ca_3(PO_4)_2$ and $P_4$ is

$$2 \text{ moles } Ca_3(PO_4)_2 : 1 \text{ mole } P_4$$

$$\text{No. moles } P_4 \text{ produced} = \tfrac{1}{2} \text{ no. moles } Ca_2(PO_4)_2 \text{ available}$$

$$\text{No. moles } Ca_3(PO_4)_2 = 283.9 \text{ g} \times \frac{1 \text{ mol}}{310.3 \text{ g}} = 0.9149 \text{ mol}$$

$$\text{No. moles } P_4 \text{ produced} = \frac{0.9149 \text{ mol}}{2} = 0.4575 \text{ mol}$$

$$\text{Mass } P_4 = 0.4575 \text{ mol} \times \frac{124.0 \text{ g}}{\text{mol}} = 56.7 \text{ g}$$

Starting with the balanced equation, these steps can be combined into a single statement relating the known, $Ca_3(PO_4)_2$, to the unknown, $P_4$.

283.9 g                                                                                        *M?*

$$2Ca_3(PO_4)_2 + 6SiO_2 + 10C \longrightarrow 6CaSiO_3 + 10CO + \quad P_4$$

2 moles ——————————————————————→ 1 mole

$$\text{Mass } P_4 = \left(283.9 \text{ g } Ca_3(PO_4)_2 \times \frac{1 \text{ mol}}{310.3 \text{ g}}\right)\left(\frac{1 \text{ mol } P_4}{2 \text{ mol } Ca_3(PO_4)_2}\right)$$

$$= \left(\frac{124.0 \text{ g } P_4}{\text{mol}}\right) = 56.7 \text{ g}$$

11. Calculate the mass of sodium nitrate required to produce 5.00 ℓ of $O_2$ (density = 1.43 g/ℓ) according to the reaction

$$2NaNO_3 \xrightarrow{\Delta} 2NaNO_2 + O_2$$

if the per cent yield of the reaction is 78.4%.

**Solution**

The balanced equation indicates that 2 moles of $NaNO_3$ produce 1 mole of $O_2$, but the yield is 78.4%. That is, only 78.4% of the $NaNO_3$ reacted is converted to the desired product and, therefore, more $NaNO_3$ will be required for the reaction than implied by the balanced equation and the mole ratio. This type of calculation is required for virtually all chemical processes since a yield of 100% is all but impossible. To solve the problem, simply calculate the amount of $NaNO_3$ that would be needed if the yield were 100%; then use the per cent factor to calculate the final amount required.

$$\text{Mass } O_2 = 5.00 \text{ ℓ} \times 1.43 \frac{g}{\text{ℓ}} = 7.150 \text{ g}$$

$$\text{GFW's: } NaNO_3 = 84.99 \text{ g}, O_2 = 32.00 \text{ g}$$

At 100% yield,

No. moles $NaNO_3$ required = 2(no. moles $O_2$ produced)

$$\text{No. moles } NaNO_3 = 2\left(7.150 \text{ g } O_2 \times \frac{1 \text{ mol}}{32.00 \text{ g}}\right) = 0.4469 \text{ mol}$$

$$\text{Mass } NaNO_3 = 0.4469 \text{ mol} \times \frac{84.99 \text{ g}}{\text{mol}} = 37.98 \text{ g}$$

At 78.4% yield,

35

$$\text{Mass NaNO}_3 = \frac{37.98 \text{ g}}{0.784} = 48.4 \text{ g}$$

Four significant figures were carried in each step to avoid rounding errors. Final answer then was rounded to the justified three significant figures.

13. Benzene, $C_6H_6 (l)$, combines with oxygen (burns) giving $CO_2 (g)$ and $H_2O(g)$. How many liters of $CO_2 (g)$, with a density of 1.428 g/ℓ, will be produced by burning 1.00 ℓ of benzene (density 0.88 g/ml)?

**Solution**

Write and balance the equation for the reaction. Calculate the mass of benzene available, and use the mole ratio in the balanced equation to calculate the theoretical yield of $CO_2$.

$$\begin{array}{cc} 880 \text{ g} & V? \end{array}$$

$$2C_6H_6 (l) + 15O_2 (g) \longrightarrow 12CO_2 (g) + 6H_2O(g)$$

$$2 \text{ moles} \longrightarrow 12 \text{ moles}$$

$$\text{Mass } C_6H_6 = 1.00 \text{ ℓ} \times 1000 \frac{\text{ml}}{\text{ℓ}} \times 0.88 \frac{\text{g}}{\text{ml}} = 880 \text{ g}$$

$$\text{No. moles } CO_2 \text{ produced} = \frac{12}{2} (\text{no. moles } C_6H_6 \text{ available})$$

GFW's: $C_6H_6 = 78.0$ g, $CO_2 = 44.0$ g

$$\text{No. moles } CO_2 = 6 \left( 880 \text{ g } C_6H_6 \times \frac{1 \text{ mol}}{78.0 \text{ g}} \right) = 67.7 \text{ mol}$$

$$\text{Mass } CO_2 = 67.7 \text{ mol} \times \frac{44.0 \text{ g}}{\text{mol}} = 2978 \text{ g}$$

The volume of $CO_2$ can be calculated from the mass of $CO_2$ by use of the density relation.

$$1.000 \text{ ℓ } CO_2 = 1.428 \text{ g}$$

$$\text{Vol } CO_2 = 2978 \text{ g} \times \frac{1.000 \text{ ℓ}}{1.428 \text{ g}} = 2.1 \times 10^3 \text{ ℓ}$$

The mass of $CO_2$ calculated from a single statement is

$$\text{Mass } CO_2 = \left( 880 \text{ g } C_6H_6 \times \frac{1 \text{ mol}}{78.0 \text{ g}} \right) \left( \frac{12 \text{ mol } CO_2}{2 \text{ mol } C_6H_6} \right) \left( \frac{44.0 \text{ g}}{\text{mol}} \right) = 2978 \text{ g}$$

14. A sample of a compound containing oxygen, boron, and fluorine decomposed, giving 152 ml of $BF_3$ (density = 2.99 g/ℓ), 150 ml of $O_2$ (density = 1.43 g/ℓ, and 76.2 ml of $F_2$ (density = 1.69 g/ℓ). What is the empirical formula of the compound?

**Solution**

Calculate the masses of each element produced by the decomposition of the sample, and then determine the empirical formula according to the method used in Unit 2. The mass of an element in a sample of a compound can easily be computed by determining its mass fraction from the formula weight of the compound as follows:

$$\text{Mass BF}_3 = 0.152 \text{ } \ell \times 2.99 \frac{g}{\ell} = 0.4545 \text{ g}$$

$$\text{GFW BF}_3 = 10.8 + 3(19.0) = 67.8 \text{ g}$$

$$\text{Mass B in BF}_3 = 0.4545 \text{ g BF}_3 \times \frac{10.8 \text{ g B}}{67.8 \text{ g BF}_3} = 0.0724 \text{ g}$$

$$\text{Mass F in BF}_3 = 0.4545 \text{ g BF}_3 \times \frac{57.0 \text{ g F}}{67.8 \text{ g BF}_3} = 0.3821 \text{ g}$$

or

$$\text{Mass F} = 0.4545 \text{ g} - 0.0724 \text{ g} = 0.3821 \text{ g}$$

$$\text{Mass F as F}_2 = 0.0762 \text{ } \ell \times 1.69 \text{ g}/\ell = 0.1288 \text{ g}$$

$$\text{Total mass F} = 0.1288 \text{ g} + 0.3821 \text{ g} = 0.5109 \text{ g}$$

$$\text{Mass O} = 0.150 \text{ } \ell \times 1.43 \frac{g}{\ell} = 0.2145 \text{ g}$$

Determine the mole ratio of O:B:F

$$\text{No. moles O} = 0.2145 \text{ g} \times \frac{1 \text{ mol}}{16.0 \text{ g}} = 0.0134$$

$$\text{No. moles B} = 0.07240 \text{ g} \times \frac{1 \text{ mol}}{10.8 \text{ g}} = 0.00670$$

$$\text{No. moles F} = 0.5109 \text{ g} \times \frac{1 \text{ mol}}{19.0 \text{ g}} = 0.02689$$

Determine the smallest ratio:

$$\text{O:} \frac{0.0134}{0.00670} = 2 \qquad \text{B:} \frac{0.00670}{0.00670} = 1 \qquad \text{F:} \frac{0.02689}{0.00670} = 4$$

The simplest ratio is $O_2 BF_4$ or $BO_2 F_4$.

17. Reaction of rhenium metal with $Re_2 O_7$ gives a solid of metallic appearance which conducts electricity almost as well as copper. A 0.788-g sample of this material, which contains only rhenium and oxygen, was oxidized in an acidic solution of hydrogen peroxide. Addition of an excess of KOH gave 0.973 g of $KReO_4$. What is the equation for the reaction of Re with $Re_2 O_7$?

The formula of the unknown solid must be known before the equation for the reaction can be written.  The empirical formula of the unknown compound containing only Re and O can be determined after calculating the total amount of Re in 0.973 g of $KReO_4$; the Re in $KReO_4$ originated from the oxide of rhenium.

$$GFW\ KReO_4 = 39.1 + 186.2 + (4 \times 16.0) = 289.3\ g$$

$$Mass\ Re\ in\ KReO_4 = \frac{186.2\ g\ Re}{289.3\ g\ KReO_2} \times 0.973\ g\ KReO_4 = 0.626\ g$$

$$Mass\ O\ in\ unknown\ sample = 0.788\ g - 0.626\ g = 0.162\ g$$

The empirical formula of the unknown is found next.

$$No.\ moles\ Re = 0.626\ g \times \frac{1\ mol}{186.2\ g} = 0.00336$$

$$No.\ moles\ O = 0.162\ g \times \frac{1\ mol}{16.0\ g} = 0.0101$$

Determine the smallest ratio:

$$Re: \frac{0.00336}{0.00336} = 1 \qquad O: \frac{0.0101}{0.00336} = 3 \qquad or\ ReO_3$$

The equation for the reaction of Re with $Re_2O_7$ is

$$Re + 3Re_2O_7 \longrightarrow 7ReO_3$$

18. Bronzes used in bearings are often alloys (solid solutions) of copper and aluminum.  A 2.053-g sample of one such bronze was analyzed for its copper content by the sequence of reactions given below.  The aluminum also dissolves, but we do not need to consider it because aluminum sulfate, $Al_2(SO_4)_3$, does not react with KI.

$$Cu + 2H_2SO_4 \longrightarrow CuSO_4 + 2H_2O + SO_2\ (1)$$

$$2CuSO_4 + 4KI \longrightarrow 2CuI + I_2 + 2K_2SO_4 \quad (2)$$

$$I_2 + 2Na_2S_2O_3 \longrightarrow Na_2S_4O_6 + 2NaI$$

If 35.11 ml of 0.8375 $M$ $Na_2S_2O_3$ is required to react with the $I_2$ formed, what is the per cent Cu in the sample?

**Solution**

From equations (1) and (3) observe that two moles of Cu are required to produce one mole of $I_2$.  The $I_2$ produced in equation (2) reacts with two moles of $Na_2S_2O_3$.  In essence, 2 moles of Cu produce 1 mole of $I_2$, which requires 2 moles of $Na_2S_2O_3$ for reaction.  Stated differently,

$$No.\ moles\ Cu\ consumed = no.\ moles\ Na_2S_2O_3\ consumed$$

The moles of $Na_2S_2O_3$ are found from the expression

$$\ell \times M = \ell \times \frac{mol}{\ell} = mol$$

Since 35.11 ml = 0.03511 $\ell$,

$$\ell \times M = 0.03511 \, \ell \times \frac{0.8375 \, mol}{\ell} = 0.029405 \, mol$$

Mass of Cu in the bronze sample = $0.029405 \, mol \times \frac{63.546 \, g}{mol} = 1.8686 \, g$

$$\% \, Cu = \frac{1.8686 \, g}{2.053 \, g} \times 100\% = 91.02\%$$

20. What mass of a sample that is 98.0% sulfur would be required in the production of 75.0 kg of $H_2SO_4$ by the following reaction sequence?

$$S_8 + 8O_2 \longrightarrow 8SO_2$$
$$2SO_2 + O_2 \longrightarrow 2SO_2$$
$$SO_3 + H_2O \longrightarrow H_2SO_4$$

**Solution**

Although the production of sulfuric acid requires three reactions, these reactions can be summarized as follows: one mole of S atoms combines with two moles of H atoms and 4 moles of O atoms to produce 1 mole of $H_2SO_4$. Calculate the mass of S needed to produce 75.0 kg of $H_2SO_4$ at 100% reaction efficiency, then account for the 98.0% purity factor.

$$GFW \, H_2SO_4 = 2(1.0) + 32.1 + 4(16.0) = 98.1 \, g$$

In kilograms, 98.1 kg of $H_2SO_4$ contains 32.1 kg of S. To prepare 75.0 kg of $H_2SO_4$ at 100% efficiency, the mass of S needed is

$$32.1 \, kg \, S \longrightarrow 98.1 \, kg \, H_2SO_4$$

$$Mass \, S = \frac{32.1 \, kg \, S}{98.1 \, kg \, H_2SO_4} \times 75.0 \, kg = 24.5 \, kg$$

At 98.0% S purity, the mass of the sample needed is calculated as follows:

$$98.0\% \, (sample \, mass) = 24.5 \, kg$$

$$Sample \, mass = \frac{24.5 \, kg}{0.980} = 25.0 \, kg$$

22. Zinc reacts with nitric acid according to the equation

$$Zn + 4HNO_3 \longrightarrow Zn(NO_3)_2 + 2H_2O + 2NO_2$$

If 1.05 g of Zn reacts with 2.50 ml of nitric acid (density $= 1.503$ g/cm$^3$), which reagent is the limiting reagent? What mass of $Zn(NO_3)_2$ is produced?

**Solution**

From the data calculate the number of moles of Zn and $HNO_3$ available.

$$\text{No. moles Zn} = 1.05 \text{ g} \times \frac{1 \text{ mol}}{65.37 \text{ g}} = 0.01606 \text{ mol}$$

$$\text{Mass } HNO_3 = 2.50 \text{ ml} \times 1.503 \frac{g}{ml} = 3.758 \text{ g}$$

$$\text{No. moles } HNO_3 = 3.758 \text{ g} \times \frac{1 \text{ mol}}{63.02 \text{ g}} = 0.05962 \text{ mol}$$

Since the mole ratio of Zn to $HNO_3$ is 1 mole Zn:4 moles $HNO_3$, the available Zn, 0.01606 mol, would require 4(0.01606) = 0.06424 mol of $HNO_3$. But only 0.05962 mol of $HNO_3$ is available; therefore all the $HNO_3$ would be consumed by the reaction, leaving some of the Zn unreacted. The $HNO_3$ is the limiting reagent, and the mass of $Zn(NO_3)_2$ produced is determined from the available $HNO_3$.

$$4 \text{ moles } HNO_3 \text{ produce } 1 \text{ mole } Zn(NO_3)_2$$

$$\text{GFW } Zn(NO_3)_2 = 65.37 + 2(14.01) + 6(16.00) = 189.4 \text{ g}$$

$$\text{Mass } Zn(NO_3)_2 = 0.0596 \text{ mol } HNO_3 \times \frac{1 \text{ mol } Zn(NO_3)_2}{4 \text{ mol } HNO_3}$$

$$\times \frac{189.4 \text{ g}}{\text{mol } Zn(NO_3)_2} = 2.82 \text{ g}$$

24. Calculate the molarity of each of the following solutions:

(c) 50.0 mg of $HNO_3$ in 15.1 ml of solution
(d) 7.0 mmol of $I_2$ in 100 ml of solution

**Solution**

(c) $\text{Molarity} = \dfrac{\text{no. moles solute}}{\text{vol of solution in } \ell} = \dfrac{\text{no. mmoles solute}}{\text{vol of solution in ml}}$

The data are given in *mg* of solute and *ml* of solution. Rather than changing these quantities to terms involving g and $\ell$, respectively, compute molarity in terms of millimoles and milliliters.

$$\text{GFW } HNO_3 = 63.0 \text{ g/mol} = 63.0 \frac{mg}{mmol}$$

$$M = \frac{50.0 \text{ mg} \times \dfrac{1 \text{ mmol}}{63.0 \text{ mg}}}{15.1 \text{ ml}} = 5.26 \times 10^{-2} \text{ M}$$

40

(d) As in part (c) above, the molarity is

$$M = \frac{7.0 \text{ mmol}}{100 \text{ ml}} = 7.0 \times 10^{-2} \text{ } M$$

26. What mass of solid NaOH of 97.0% purity would be required to prepare 250.0 ml of 0.350 $M$ NaOH solution?

**Solution**

Calculate the mass of NaOH at 100% purity required to prepare the solution, then account for the impure solid.

$$\text{Mass NaOH 100\%} = \text{molarity} \times \text{vol in } \ell \times \text{GFW}$$

$$= (0.350 \text{ } M) (0.2500 \text{ } \ell) (40.0 \text{ g})$$

$$= 3.50 \text{ g}$$

The mass of the impure solid required is

$$97.0\% \text{ (mass of solid)} = 3.50 \text{ g}$$

$$\text{Mass solid NaOH} = \frac{3.50 \text{ g}}{0.970} = 3.61 \text{ g}$$

29. Crystalline potassium hydrogen phthalate, $KHC_8 H_4 O_4$, is often used as a "standard" acid because it is easy to purity and to weigh. If 1.5428 g of this salt reacts with a solution of $Ca(OH)_2$, the reaction is complete when 42.37 ml of the solution has been added. What is the concentration of the $Ca(OH)_2$ solution?

$$2KHC_8 H_4 O_4 + Ca(OH)_2 \longrightarrow CaK_2 (C_8 H_4 O_4)_2 + 2H_2 O$$

**Solution**

According to the equation, one mole of $Ca(OH)_2$ reacts with two moles of $KHC_8 H_4 O_4$; therefore the number of moles of $Ca(OH)_2$ contained in the 42.37 ml sample equals one-half the number of moles of $KHC_8 H_4 O_4$ in the reaction sample.

GFW's: $Ca(OH)_2 = 40.08 + 2(16.00) + 2(1.01) = 74.09$ g

$KHC_8 H_4 O_4 = 39.10 + 1.01 + 8(12.01) + 4(1.01) + 4(16.00) = 204.23$ g

$$\text{No. moles } KHC_8 H_4 O_4 = 1.5428 \text{ g} \times \frac{1 \text{ mol}}{204.23 \text{ g}} = 0.007554 \text{ mol}$$

$$\text{No. moles } Ca(OH)_2 \text{ reacted} = \frac{0.007554 \text{ mol}}{2} = 0.003777 \text{ mol}$$

Use the definition of molarity to obtain the value $M$:

$$\text{Molarity Ca(OH)}_2 = \frac{\text{no. moles Ca(OH)}_2}{\text{vol in } \ell} = \frac{0.003777 \text{ mol}}{0.04237 \ell} = 8.914 \times 10^{-2} M$$

31. How many milliliters of concentrated sulfuric acid (a solution of $H_2SO_4$ with a density of 1.841 $g/cm^3$ and which contains 98.0% $H_2SO_4$ by mass) is required to produce 1.000 $\ell$ of a 0.500 $M$ $H_2SO_4$ solution?

**Solution**

Calculate the mass of $H_2SO_4$ needed to prepare 1.000 $\ell$ of 0.500 $M$ solution. Then, from the data on the concentrated solution, calculate the mass of $H_2SO_4$ per milliliter of the solution. Use this value to calculate the volume of the concentrated solution needed.

$$\text{GFW } H_2SO_4 = 2(1.01) + 32.06 + 4(16.00) = 98.08 \text{ g}$$

$$\text{Mass } H_2SO_4 \text{ needed} = (0.500 \text{ mol}) (1.000 \text{ } \ell) \left( \frac{98.08 \text{ g}}{\text{mol}} \right) = 49.04 \text{ g}$$

$$\text{Mass } H_2SO_4 \text{ per ml concd sol} = \left( \frac{98.0\%}{100.0\%} \right) \left( 1.841 \frac{g}{ml} \right) = 1.804 \frac{g}{ml}$$

$$\text{Vol concd } H_2SO_4 = 49.04 \text{ g} \times \frac{1 \text{ ml}}{1.804 \text{ g}} = 27.2 \text{ ml}$$

35. If 1.00 g of sodium carbonate, $Na_2CO_3$, reacts with sulfuric acid according to the following equation and produces 1.301 g of sodium sulfate, $Na_2SO_4$, what is the per cent yield?

$$Na_2CO_3 + H_2SO_4 \longrightarrow Na_2SO_4 + CO_2 + H_2O$$

**Solution**

Calculate the theoretical yield of $Na_2SO_4$ based on the total reaction of 1.00 g of $Na_2CO_3$. The per cent yield can be calculated from this value and the actual yield of 1.301 g of $Na_2SO_4$.

$$\begin{array}{cc} 1.00 \text{ g} & M? \\ Na_2CO_3 + H_2SO_4 \longrightarrow & Na_2SO_4 + CO_2 + H_2O \\ 1 \text{ mole} \longrightarrow & 1 \text{ mole} \end{array}$$

GFW's: $Na_2CO_3 = 106.01$, $Na_2SO_4 = 142.06$

$$\text{Mass } Na_2SO_4 = \left( 1.00 \text{ g } Na_2CO_3 \times \frac{1 \text{ mol}}{106.01 \text{ g}} \right) \left( \frac{1 \text{ mol } Na_2SO_4}{1 \text{ mol } Na_2CO_3} \right)$$

$$\times \left( \frac{142.06 \text{ g}}{\text{mol } Na_2SO_4} \right) = 1.34 \text{ g}$$

$$\% \text{ yield} = \frac{1.301 \text{ g}}{1.34 \text{ g}} \times 100\% = 97.1\%$$

## RELATED PROBLEMS

1. Glass containers, such as beverage bottles and pickle jars, are made from soda-lime glass. This glass, often called "soft glass," is prepared by melting a mixture of sodium carbonate ($Na_2CO_3$), limestone ($CaCO_3$), and sand ($SiO_2$). The composition of the glass varies, but one accepted reaction is

$$Na_2CO_3 + CaCO_3 + 6SiO_2 \longrightarrow Na_2O \cdot CaO \cdot 6SiO_2 + 2CO_2$$

By using this equation calculate the amount of sodium carbonate required to produce enough glass to make one million pickle jars, each weighing 0.200 kg.　　　　　　　　*Answer: 4.43 × 10$^7$ g; 4.43 × 10$^4$ kg*

2. The United States is fortunate to have tremendous reserves of coal. Much of the coal, unfortunately, contains a significant amount of sulfur that volatilizes and burns during the combustion of coal. Midwestern and some Western coal may contain as much as 5% by weight volatile sulfur. If this sulfur burns according to the equation

$$S + O_2 \longrightarrow SO_2$$

how much $SO_2$ would be produced by an electric power generating plant that burns 24,000 tons of coal per 24-hour period? for a year at this burning rate?　　　　*Answer: 2400 tons/day; 8.8 × 10$^5$ tons/year*

3. Much of the $SO_2$ produced by combustion is converted to either sulfurous acid, $H_2SO_3$, or sulfuric acid, $H_2SO_4$, by reaction in the environment. Assume that 50% of the $SO_2$ produced by the reaction in problem 2 is converted to $H_2SO_3$ according to the equation

$$SO_2 + H_2O \longrightarrow H_2SO_3$$

Calculate the amount (in kilograms) of $H_2SO_3$ that would be produced per year of plant operation.　　　　　　　*Answer: 5.1 × 10$^8$ kg*

4. One method proposed for removing $SO_2$ from smokestack gases is to "scrub" the gas by reacting the $SO_2$ with limestone in the presence of water according to the equation

$$SO_2 + CaCO_3 \xrightarrow{H_2O} CaSO_3 + CO_2$$

(a) Calculate the amount (in kilograms and tons) of limestone that would be required in the reaction to remove the $SO_2$ produced per year in problem 2. (b) How many trucks carrying 30-ton loads would be required to haul this amount of limestone?
　　　*Answer: (a) 1.4 × 10$^6$ tons, 1.3 × 10$^9$ kg: (b) 47,000 trucks*

5. A combination of cream of tartar and baking soda can be used instead of baking powder in recipes. The reaction responsible for the action of baking powder is

$$KHC_4H_4O_6 + NaHCO_3 \longrightarrow KNaC_4H_4O_6 + H_2O + CO_2$$

Cream of      Baking
tartar        soda

(a) Calculate the mass of $NaHCO_3$ required for complete reaction with two teaspoons (8.0 g) of cream of tartar. (b) Calculate the volume of $CO_2$ released by the reaction given that the density of $CO_2$ is 0.85 g per liter at baking temperature.

*Answer: (a) 3.6 g $NaHCO_3$; (b) 2.2 liters*

# Chapter 4: Structure of the Atom and the Periodic Law

## INTRODUCTION

Ancient records point to the fact that human beings have pondered the basic structure of matter for a long time in the hope of better understanding themselves and their surroundings. The early writings of the physician and philosopher Empedocles of Agrigentum in Sicily (ca. 490-435 B.C.) suggested that all visible objects are composed of four unchanging elements— air, earth, water, and fire. The Greek philosophers Leucippos and his pupil, Demokritos of Abdera (ca. 460-370 B.C.) postulated that matter is composed of small particles of these four elements and that these particles are in motion; this was the first evidence of an atomic and kinetic theory. Building upon these ideas, Aristotle moved away from the atomistic concept and popularized a theory to explain the transformation of one "element" to another. His ideas, including that of the void or "ether," dominated Western scientific thought for centuries. Unfortunately, since Aristotle's theory did not require experimental verification, very little in the way of experimental evidence was found to support the existence of small particles until about 1800.

Most recently, the development of sophisticated instruments has enabled scientists who study atoms to probe into the atoms' structure. We know now that the nature and composition of atoms depend on the interaction of the many smaller particles that provide the building blocks of all atoms. Several theoretical atomic models were proposed during the early 1900s to explain atomic phenomena and predict atomic and molecular behavior.

This chapter treats the discovery of atomic particles, the unparalleled experimentation during the evolution of modern atomic theory, the particulars of the quantum mechanical model of the atom, and the relationship of atomic structure to the Periodic Table. Part of the chapter explains the nature of electromagnetic radiation and its relationship to electronic transition within atoms, and hence, to the entire field of modern chemistry.

Questions and problems are directed to the various atomic models and especially to the current quantum mechanical model. We have selected both questions and problems so that their solution will provide a useful framework to help you organize the important information of this chapter. Remember as you proceed that the development of the models and theories represents the attempt by scientists to advance our knowledge of matter and that these models generally will require further refinement in the future.

## FORMULAS AND DEFINITIONS

**Valence electrons**   Valence electrons are the electrons that occupy the highest energy level of an atom. The electrons in the outermost sublevel when that sublevel is not in the highest energy level (for example, $3d$ electrons when the $4s$ level is occupied) are also valence electrons. The valence electrons are largely responsible for the chemical behavior of the atom. Since all elements within a periodic group or family have the same outer electronic configuration, they also have the same number of valence electrons. For the representative elements, the number of valence electrons in an atom equals its periodic group number.

**Representative elements**   The representative elements are the A-group elements, IA through VIIA and Group IIB, as listed in the Periodic Table. These elements have valence electrons either in $s$ or $s$ and $p$ sublevels. Their valence electrons are in the same primary level ($n$ level) as their period location. For example, the three valence electrons in gallium, $Z = 31$, are in the fourth $n$ level, that is, $4s^2$ and $4p^1$ electrons.

**Transition elements**   The transition elements are metals and are located in the B groups of the Periodic Table (except Group IIB). These elements have outer electrons that include the $(n - 1)d$ sublevels, where $n$ is the period location of the elements. For example, titanium, Ti, $Z = 22$, is in period 4, but its outermost electrons are in the $3d$ orbitals. The period 4 transition metals are relatively abundant and are extremely important to the world steel industry. With a few exceptions, the transition elements in Periods 5 and 6 are in limited supply as far as commercially exploitable deposits are concerned. Several are highly valued for use in jewelry, coinage, and electronic systems.

**Pauli Exclusion Principle**   The rigorous solution of the wave equation representing electrons orbiting an atomic nucleus involves four components. Four quantum numbers describe the behavior of these components, and represent the effective volume of space in which an electron moves, the shape of the orbital in space, the orientation of the electronic charge cloud in space, and the direction of the spin of each electron on its own axis. The Pauli Exclusion Principle states that each electron has a unique set of four quantum numbers; that is, no two electrons in the same atom can have the same four quantum numbers.

**Hund's Rule** Atomic energy levels are filled by electrons in such a way as to achieve the lowest possible total energy state for the atom. Hund's Rule states that each orbital in a subshell or sublevel must be singly filled before any one orbital is completely (doubly) filled. In addition, all electrons in singly filled orbitals within a sublevel must have parallel spins; that is, their spin orientations are the same (aligned).

**Aufbau process** The Aufbau Process refers to the way in which electronic structures of complex atoms are formed by assigning one electron at a time to a sublevel based on Hund's Rule and the Pauli Exclusion Principle.

**Ionization potential** The ionization potential (IP) of an atom, frequently called ionization energy, is the amount of energy required to completely remove the most loosely bound electron from a gaseous atom in its ground state. Values for ionization potentials are usually listed in terms of mole quantities; some examples are

$$\text{General case: } X(g) + \text{energy} \longrightarrow X^+(g) + e^-$$

$$Li(g) \longrightarrow Li^+(g) + e^- \qquad IP = 124 \text{ kcal/mol} = 5.19 \times 10^5 \text{ J/mol}$$

$$N(g) \longrightarrow N^+(g) + e^- \qquad IP = 335 \text{ kcal/mol} = 1.40 \times 10^6 \text{ J/mol}$$

$$He(g) \longrightarrow He^+(g) + e^- \qquad IP = 567 \text{ kcal/mol} = 2.37 \times 10^6 \text{ J/mol}$$

**Electron affinity** The electron affinity (EA) of an atom is a measure of the attraction a neutral gaseous atom in its ground state has for an additional electron. In general, atoms that have half-filled orbitals or incomplete valence levels will attract additional electrons and release energy upon the ionization. Some examples defining the electron affinity for several elements along with their numerical values are

$$\text{General case: } X(g) + e^- \longrightarrow X^-(g) + \text{energy}$$

$$Cl(g) + e^- \longrightarrow Cl^-(g) + 3.48 \times 10^5 \text{ J/mol} \qquad EA = 3.48 \times 10^5 \text{ J/mol}$$

$$O(g) + e^- \longrightarrow O^-(g) + 2.25 \times 10^5 \text{ J/mol} \qquad EA = 2.25 \times 10^5 \text{ J/mol}$$

$$Mg(g) + e^- + (2.89 \times 10^4 \text{ J/mol}) \longrightarrow Mg^-(g) \qquad EA = -2.89 \times 10^4 \text{ J/mol}$$

**Constants and equations**

$$\text{Planck's constant} \quad (h) = 6.626 \times 10^{-34} \text{ J sec}$$
$$= 6.626 \times 10^{-27} \text{ erg sec}$$
$$= 1.584 \times 10^{-37} \text{ kcal sec}$$

$$\text{Speed of light} \quad (c) = 2.998 \times 10^8 \text{ m/sec} \quad (\text{vacuum})$$
$$= 2.998 \times 10^{10} \text{ cm/sec}$$

$$\text{Rydberg equation} \quad E = 2.179 \times 10^{-18}\left(\frac{1}{n_1^2} - \frac{1}{n_2^2}\right) \text{ J,}$$

where $n_1 < n_2$

The Rydberg equation is empirically dervied from spectral data resulting from studies on hydrogen. The energy value calculated from the equation is the energy associated with a photon produced by an electron transition from a higher energy level ($n_2$) to a lower energy level ($n_1$) in a hydrogen atom.

### Bohr model energies

$$E_n = -2.179 \times 10^{-18} \frac{Z^2}{n^2} \text{ J} \qquad \text{or} \qquad -2.179 \times 10^{-18}/n^2 \text{ J}$$

where $Z$ is the atomic number        for a hydrogen atom.

The energy calculated from this equation is the energy associated with a specific energy level in a hydrogenlike atom or ion. By convention, all the values calculated using this equation have a negative sign, and when $n = 1$ the value is $-2.179 \times 10^{-18}$ J. As $n$ increases (higher energy levels) the values of $E$ increase and approach zero at $n = \infty$. The energy required to raise an electron from $n = 1$ to $n = \infty$ is the ionization energy for a hydrogenlike atom or ion in its ground state.

**Electromagnetic wave characteristics**   Visible light and other types of radiant energy described in this chapter are propagated as waves in the form of electromagnetic radiation consisting of two components, one with an electric field, the other with a magnetic field. These components are coupled at right angles to each other and travel as a sine wave as shown in the figure, where $E$ is the electric field and $H$ is the magnetic field.

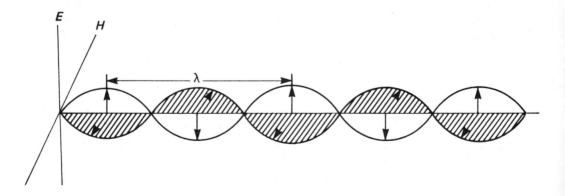

**Wavelength** ($\lambda$, lambda)   Wavelength is the distance between equivalent positions on adjacent waves, for example, from one peak to the next.

**Frequency ($\nu$, nu)** Frequency is the number of wavelengths passing a reference point in unit time. The unit for frequency is waves or cycles per second, but values are usually written as 1/sec or $sec^{-1}$ with the word cycle implied and not written.

**Velocity ($c$)** The velocity of a wave is the distance traveled by the wave per unit time. For electromagnetic radiation in a vacuum, $c = 2.998 \times 10^8$ m $sec^{-1}$.

**Energy-wavelength-frequency relations** Velocity, frequency, and wavelength are related through the equation $c = \lambda\nu$. The velocity of all electromagnetic radiation passing through a continuous medium (air, water, etc.) is the same and varies only with the medium. For our purposes, we shall assume that the velocity of radiation is constant and that the medium of transmission is a vacuum in which the velocity $= 2.998 \times 10^8$ m/sec. Since the value of $c$ is constant, $\lambda$ and $\nu$ are inversely related to each other, that is,

$$\text{constant} = \lambda(\text{short}) \ \nu(\text{high})$$

$$\text{constant} = \lambda(\text{long}) \ \nu(\text{low})$$

The energy of a photon is related to frequency as

$$E = h\nu \qquad (h = \text{Planck's constant})$$

in which energy is directly proportional to frequency.

$$\text{High energy} \longleftrightarrow \text{high frequency}$$

$$\text{Low energy} \longleftrightarrow \text{low frequency,}$$

where $\longleftrightarrow$ may be read as "is associated with." The relationship between energy and wavelength is derived by solving for $\nu$ in the equation $c = \lambda\nu$ and substituting $E = h\nu$:

$$c = \lambda\nu \qquad \text{and} \qquad \nu = c/\lambda$$
$$E = h\nu = hc/\lambda$$

This is an inverse relationship of energy to wavelength. That is,

$$\text{High energy} \longleftrightarrow \text{short wavelength}$$

$$\text{Low energy} \longleftrightarrow \text{long wavelength}$$

These relationships can be extended to the frequency of light in the following way:

$$\text{High energy} \longleftrightarrow \text{high frequency} \longleftrightarrow \text{short wavelength}$$

$$\text{Low energy} \longleftrightarrow \text{low frequency} \longleftrightarrow \text{long wavelength}$$

The proper units for use with energy relationships are

$$E \text{ in joules} = h\nu = (6.626 \times 10^{-34} \text{ J sec}) \ (\nu \text{ as 1/sec or } sec^{-1})$$

$$E \text{ in joules} = hc/\lambda = \frac{(6.626 \times 10^{-34} \text{ J sec}) \ (c \text{ in m/sec})}{\lambda \text{ in m}}$$

## QUESTIONS

13. What is the general relationship between atomic weight and atomic number of an element? Why are there occasional exceptions to this relationship?

**Answer**

The atomic number of an element is defined as the number of protons in the nucleus of the atom. The stable isotopes of elements have a neutron to proton ratio (n/p) that ranges from about 1 in the first 20 elements to about 1.5 for heavier elements. The mass of a single atom largely depends on the number of protons and neutrons in the nucleus, but the atomic weight is the average mass of the naturally occuring isotopes in a normal sample. Observing the Periodic Table, you will see that the elements are arranged according to increasing atomic numbers. Atomic weights also generally increase as the atomic number increases. Very few exceptions exist to this general rule, one exception being that of tellurium ($Z = 52$, atomic weight $= 127.60$) and iodine ($Z = 53$, atomic weight $= 126.90$).

29. Consider the atomic orbitals (a), (b), and (c) shown below in outline.

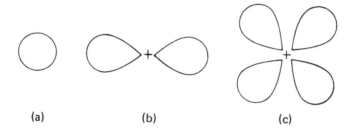

    (a)              (b)              (c)

  (a) What is the maximum number of electrons that can be contained in atomic orbital (c)?

  (b) How many orbitals with the same value of $\ell$ as orbital (a) can be found in the shell with $n = 4$? How many as orbital (b)? How many as orbital (c)?

  (c) What is the smallest $n$ value possible for an electron in an orbital of type (c)? of type (b)? of type (a)?

  (d) What are the $\ell$ values that characterize each of these three orbitals?

  (e) Arrange these orbitals in order of increasing energy in the M shell. Is this order different in other shells?

**Answer**

  (a) The maximum number of electrons that can occupy an orbital is two, regardless of its shape or volume. Hence the orbitals represented in (a), (b), and (c) above can contain a maximum of two electrons.

50

(b) The orbital represented in (a) is an $s$ or $\ell = 0$ type. Each primary level, $n$ level, has a corresponding $s$ or $\ell = 0$ type orbital; only the volume of the $s$ orbital space varies. The orbital represented in (b) is a $p$ or $\ell = 1$ type, and as a requirement of the quantum model, all $n$ levels except $n = 1$ contain three $p$ orbitals. The orbital represented in (c) is a $d$ or $\ell = 2$ type. According to the model, all $n$ levels of 3 and greater have five $d$ or $\ell = 2$ type orbitals.

(c) Type c, $n = 3$; type b, $n = 2$; type a, $n = 1$.

(d) Type c, $\ell = 2$; type b, $\ell = 1$; type a, $\ell = 0$.

(c) The M shell is the $n = 3$ energy level and it has three possible $\ell$ values: 0, 1, and 2. These $\ell$ levels are the $3s$, $3p$, and $3d$ orbitals with the orbital energies increasing as written. Note, however, that conclusions derived from experimental evidence indicate that the $n = 4$, $\ell = 0$ level ($4s$) has a lower energy than the $n = 3$, $\ell = 2$ level ($3d$) and is filled before the $3d$ level. The $s$ and $p$ orbitals for all values of $n$ fill in order, but the $d$ orbitals fill after the $\ell = 0$ level of the next higher $n$ level.

30. Identify the subshell in which electrons with the following quantum numbers are found:

(a) $n = 3, \ell = 0$  (b) $n = 3, \ell = 2$  (c) $n = 2, \ell = 1$
(d) $n = 7, \ell = 4$  (e) $n = 4, \ell = 3$

**Answer**

The $s$ orbital is always associated with an $\ell = 0$ value, $p$ orbital with $\ell = 1$, $d$ orbital with $\ell = 2$, $f$ orbital with $\ell = 3$, and $g$ orbital with $\ell = 4$. Therefore

(a) $3s$;  (b) $3d$;  (c) $2p$;  (d) $7g$;  (e) $4f$

32. Write the quantum numbers for each electron found in a nitrogen atom. For example, the quantum numbers for one of the $2s$ electrons will be $n = 2, \ell = 0, m = 0, s = +1/2$

**Answer**

Nitrogen ($Z = 7$) has seven electrons and its electronic configuration is $1s^2\, 2s^2\, 2p^3$. The quantum numbers for the seven electrons in nitrogen are

| $\bar{e}$ | $n$ | $\ell$ | $m$ | $s$ |
|---|---|---|---|---|
| 1 | 1 | 0 | 0 | $-\frac{1}{2}$ |
| 2 | 1 | 0 | 0 | $+\frac{1}{2}$ |
| 3 | 2 | 0 | 0 | $-\frac{1}{2}$ |
| 4 | 2 | 0 | 0 | $+\frac{1}{2}$ |
| 5 | 2 | 1 | $-1$ | $-\frac{1}{2}$ |
| 6 | 2 | 1 | 0 | $-\frac{1}{2}$ |
| 7 | 2 | 1 | $+1$ | $-\frac{1}{2}$ |

To avoid confusion when assigning quantum numbers, it is important to adopt and consistently use a convention for assigning $m$ and $s$ quantum numbers. The convention used here is to begin by assigning negative values and proceed through positive values, that is, $-\ell$ through $+\ell$ for $m$ and $-\frac{1}{2}$ and then $+\frac{1}{2}$ for $s$.

33. The quantum numbers that describe the electron in the lowest energy level of a hydrogen atom (the ground state) are $n = 1$, $\ell = 0$, $m = 0$, $s = +\frac{1}{2}$. Excitation of the electron can promote it to energy levels described by other sets of quantum numbers. Which of the following sets of quantum numbers *cannot* exist in a hydrogen atom (or any other atom)?

(a) $n = 2$, $\ell = 1$, $m = -1$, $s = +\frac{1}{2}$
(b) $n = 2$, $\ell = 0$, $m = 1$, $s = +\frac{1}{2}$
(c) $n = 7$, $\ell = 3$, $m = 0$, $s = -\frac{1}{2}$
(d) $n = 3$, $\ell = 3$, $m = -2$, $s = -\frac{1}{2}$
(e) $n = 4$, $\ell = 2$, $m = 3$, $s = +\frac{1}{2}$
(f) $n = 3$, $\ell = 2$, $m = -1$, $s = +\frac{3}{2}$

**Answer**

In theory there are an infinite number of possible quantum levels in an atom. But, for all levels, a unique set of four numbers exists to describe an electron occupying a specific level, and the quantum numbers must be allowable as dictated by the model. The hydrogen electron may occupy any one of the $n$ levels cited in (a) through (f) above. In the case of (d), however, where $n = 3$, $\ell$ may not have a value of 3. Values of $\ell$ include all values of 0 through $n - 1$ for a specified atom. Hence the set of quantum numbers in (d) is not possible for hydrogen or any other atom.

The value of $\ell$ limits the values that $m$ may have. The integer values $m$ may have range from $-\ell$ through 0 to $+\ell$. In (b) the value of $m$ (1) exceeds the value of $\ell$ (0) and therefore cannot be an acceptable quantum number. The same is true of (e).

The only values permitted the $s$ quantum number are $+\frac{1}{2}$ and $-\frac{1}{2}$. The set (f) contains the value $\frac{3}{2}$ for $s$ and thus is not permitted.

45. Identify the groups that have the following electronic structures in their valence shells ($n$ represents the principal quantum number).

(a) $ns^2$  (b) $ns^2 np^2$  (c) $ns^2 np^6$  (d) $ns^2 (n-1)d^2$  (e) $ns^2 (n-1)d^5$

**Answer**

The elements represented by (a), (b), and (c) are representative elements, the A-group classification. Elements with electronic configurations ending in $ns$ or $np$ are located in A groups whose numbers equal the sum of the electrons occupying the $s$ and $p$ orbitals in a specific $n$ level.

(a) $ns^2$ –Group IIA

(b) $ns^2 np^2$ –Group IVA

(c) $ns^2 np^6$ –(8 electrons, noble gas)

Group numbers for the transition elements cannot be assigned on the basis of the total number of electrons in the $ns(n-1)d$ levels without knowledge of the order of placement of electrons in the orbitals. To identify the periodic location of the elements in (d) and (e), sum the electrons in the $s$ and $d$ levels, and count from left to right in a given period $(n)$ the number of groups equaling the number of $ns(n-1)d$ electrons.

(d) $ns^2(n-1)d^2 = 4e^-$ –Group IVB

(e) $ns^2(n-1)d^5 = 7e^-$ –Group VIIB

46. Why is the radius of a positive ion smaller than the radius of its parent atom?

**Answer**

The formation of a positive ion from a neutral atom involves the removal of one or more electrons from the valence level of the atom. Consider the formation of a $Mg^{2+}$ ion from a Mg atom:

$$Mg(g) + energy \longrightarrow Mg^{2+}(g) + 2e^-$$

$$\underset{n\text{ level}}{\underline{12\ p^+}} \left. \begin{matrix} 2\ e^- \\ 1 \end{matrix} \right) \left. \begin{matrix} 8\ e^- \\ 2 \end{matrix} \right) \begin{matrix} 2\ e^- \\ 3 \end{matrix} \longrightarrow \underline{12\ p^+} \left. \begin{matrix} 2\ e^- \\ 1 \end{matrix} \right) \left. \begin{matrix} 8\ e^- \\ 2 \end{matrix} \right) \begin{matrix} +2\ e^- \\ \end{matrix}$$

neutral atom                               ion

The ionization of the neutral atom leaves the $n = 3$ level empty. As a consequence, the outer electrons in the ion are in a filled energy level that is one level closer to the nucleus than in the neutral atom. With the electrons closer to the nucleus, the nuclear-charge-to-electronic-charge ratio is increased, which further decreases the radius of the ion from that of the neutral atom.

52. Which of the following sets of quantum numbers describes the most easily removed electron in an unexcited aluminum atom? Which of the electrons described is most difficult to remove?

(a) $n = 1, \ell = 0, m = 0, s = -\frac{1}{2}$

(b) $n = 2, \ell = 1, m = 0, s = -\frac{1}{2}$

(c) $n = 3, \ell = 0, m = 0, s = \frac{1}{2}$

(d) $n = 3, \ell = 1, m = 1, s = -\frac{1}{2}$

(e) $n = 4, \ell = 1, m = 1, s = \frac{1}{2}$

**Answer**

The most easily removed electron in any atom is the one occupying the highest energy level. We are to consider an electron in an unexcited aluminum atom. The quantum numbers for the outermost electron $(3p^1)$ in aluminum are

| $n$ | $\ell$ | $m$ | $s$ | | $n$ | $\ell$ | $m$ | $s$ | | $n$ | $\ell$ | $m$ | $s$ |
|---|---|---|---|---|---|---|---|---|---|---|---|---|---|
| 3 | 1 | $-1$ | $-\frac{1}{2}$ | or | 3 | 1 | 1 | $-\frac{1}{2}$ | or | 3 | 1 | 0 | $-\frac{1}{2}$ |

These three sets are all equivalent since they have the same energy and cannot be distinguished except in a magnetic field. This corresponds to selection in answer (d). The most difficult electron to remove from any atom is the one occupying the lowest energy level.

| $n$ | $\ell$ | $m$ | $s$ |
|---|---|---|---|
| 1 | 0 | 0 | $-\frac{1}{2}$ |

This is given in answer (a).

## PROBLEMS

1. From the per cent abundances and masses given in Table 4-1, calculate the atomic weight of naturally occurring boron.

**Solution**

The composition of naturally occurring boron is $^{10}_{5}$B, mass = 10.0129 daltons (amu), % = 19.6, and $^{11}_{5}$B, mass = 11.0042 daltons, % = 80.4. The atomic weight of an element is the average mass of all atoms composing a normal sample of the element. For boron, 19.6% of the atomic weight is attributable to $^{10}$B and 80.4% to $^{11}$B. The atomic weight is calculated as follows:

$$\text{At. wt} = \frac{19.6\%}{100\%}(10.0129) + \frac{80.4\%}{100\%}(11.0093)$$

$$= 10.81$$

2. Light that looks green has a frequency of $5 \times 10^{14}$ per second. What is the wavelength of green light in centimeters and in angstroms? What is the energy of a quantum of green light in joules?

**Solution**

The equation that relates frequency to wavelength and velocity is $c = \lambda\nu$. Solve the equation for wavelength, substitute values for $c$ and $\nu$, and compute the wavelength.

$$c = 3.0 \times 10^{10} \ \frac{\text{cm}}{\text{sec}}$$

$$\nu = \frac{5 \times 10^{14}}{\text{sec}} \quad \text{or} \quad 5 \times 10^{14} \text{ sec}^{-1}$$

$$\lambda = \frac{c}{\nu} = \frac{3 \times 10^{10} \frac{\text{cm}}{\text{sec}}}{5 \times 10^{14} \text{ sec}^{-1}} = 6 \times 10^{-5} \text{ cm}$$

$\lambda$ in Å: $1$ Å $= 1 \times 10^{-8}$ cm.

$$\lambda \text{ in Å} = 6 \times 10^{-5} \text{ cm} \times \frac{1 \text{ Å}}{1 \times 10^{-8} \text{ cm}} = 6000 \text{ Å}$$

The energy of a photon of green light is given by $E = h\nu$.

$$E = h\nu = (6.627 \times 10^{-34} \text{ J sec}) (5 \times 10^{14} \text{ sec}^{-1})$$

$$= 3 \times 10^{-19} \text{ J}$$

3. Does a photon of the green light described in Problem 2 have enough energy to excite the electron in a hydrogen atom from the K shell to the L shell?

**Solution**

The required energy for the transition can be calculated by applying the Rydberg equation for $n = 1$ and $n = 2$ or by using the data in Table 4-2 and converting the values in electron volts to ergs. We have chosen to calculate the energy difference through the Rydberg equation to provide an example for your reference. The K and L shells correspond to $n = 1$ and $n = 2$, respectively.

$$E_{K \to L} = 2.179 \times 10^{-18} \left( \frac{1}{n_1^2} - \frac{1}{n_2^2} \right) \text{ J}$$

$$= 2.179 \times 10^{-18} \left( \frac{1}{1^2} - \frac{1}{2^2} \right) = 2.179 \times 10^{-18} \left( \frac{3}{4} \right) \text{ J}$$

$$= 1.634 \times 10^{-18} \text{ J}$$

The required energy is greater than that of a photon of green light; hence the photon will not excite the electron from the K shell to the L shell.

5. Consider a collection of hydrogen atoms with electrons randomly distributed in either the $n = 1, 2, 3, 4,$ or $5$ shells. How many different wavelengths of light will be emitted by these atoms as the electrons fall into the lower energy states?

**Solution**

Imagine an electron being placed in each of the five $n$ levels. Each possible transition from a higher level to a lower level releases energy

in the form of radiation. The number of possible transitions beginning
with level 5 through level 2 is

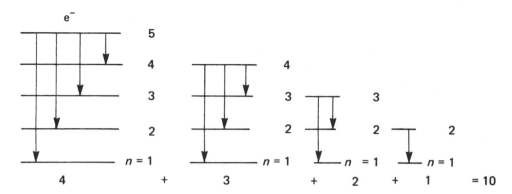

$$4 \quad + \quad 3 \quad + \quad 2 \quad + \quad 1 \quad = 10$$

13. X rays are produced when the electron stream in an x-ray tube knocks
an electron out of a low-lying shell of an atom in the target, and an
electron in a higher shell falls into the lower lying shell. The x ray is
the energy given off as the electron jumps into the lower shell. The
most intense x rays produced by an x-ray tube with a copper target
have wavelengths of 1.542 Å and 1.392 Å. These x rays are produced by an electron from the L or M shell falling into the K shell
of a copper atom. Calculate the energy separation of the K, L, and
M shells in copper.

### Solution

The two x rays are produced from electron shifts between the K and L
shells and the K and M shells. The transition from M to K emits the
x ray with the greatest energy and the shortest wavelength. The energy
difference between the L and M shell is the difference between the
energies of the two x rays.

$$1.392\ \text{Å} \left| \begin{array}{c} \text{M} \\ \text{L} \\ \text{K} \end{array} \right| 1.542\ \text{Å} \qquad E_{M \to L} = E_{M \to K} - E_{L \to K}$$

$$E_{M \to K} = \frac{hc}{\lambda} = \frac{(6.626 \times 10^{-34}\ \text{J sec})\,(2.998 \times 10^{10}\ \text{cm/sec})}{1.392 \times 10^{-8}\ \text{cm}}$$

$$= 1.427 \times 10^{-15}\ \text{J}$$

$$E_{L \to K} = \frac{hc}{\lambda} = \frac{(6.626 \times 10^{-34}\ \text{J sec})\,(2.998 \times 10^{10}\ \text{cm/sec})}{1.542 \times 10^{-8}\ \text{cm}}$$

$$= 1.288 \times 10^{-15}\ \text{J}$$

$$E_{M \to L} = E_{M \to K} - E_{L \to K}$$

$$= (1.427 \times 10^{-15} - 1.288 \times 10^{-15})\text{erg} = 1.39 \times 10^{-16} \text{ J}$$

These values in electron volts are calculated from the relation

$$1 \text{ eV} = 1.602 \times 10^{-19} \text{ J}$$

$$E_{M \to K} = 1.427 \times 10^{-15} \text{ J} \times \frac{1 \text{ eV}}{1.602 \times 10^{-19} \text{ J}} = 8.908 \times 10^3 \text{ eV}$$

$$E_{L \to K} = 1.288 \times 10^{-15} \text{ J} \times \frac{1 \text{ eV}}{1.602 \times 10^{-19} \text{ J}} = 8.040 \times 10^3 \text{ eV}$$

$$E_{M \to L} = 1.39 \times 10^{-16} \text{ J} \times \frac{1 \text{ eV}}{1.602 \times 10^{-19} \text{ J}} = 8.68 \times 10^2 \text{ eV}$$

## RELATED PROBLEMS

1. If nuclear physicists are successful in synthesizing element 114, what would be the predicted $n$ and $\ell$ values for its outermost electron?
   
   *Answer: $n = 7$, $\ell = 1$*

2. An accelerated particle, mass $2 \times 10^{-24}$ g, possessing a kinetic energy of $2.9 \times 10^{-18}$ J interacts with a hydrogen atom in its ground state. The electron in the hydrogen atom is promoted to level 5 and the particle escapes to the surroundings. Calculate the energy of the escaping particle.
   
   *Answer: $8.1 \times 10^{-19}$ J*

3. Given that kinetic energy is defined as $KE = \frac{1}{2} mv^2$, calculate the velocity of the escaping particle as described in problem 2 (in cm/sec, miles/sec, miles/hour).   *Answers: $2.8 \times 10^6$ cm/sec; 18 miles/sec; 64,000 miles/hour*

4. Fog lights are effective for driving under foggy conditions primarily because reflection is minimized since the wavelength of the yellow light is nearly equal to the diameter of a fog particle. A particular filament arrangement in fog lights generates a photon having an energy of $3.4 \times 10^{-19}$ J. Estimate the diameter of a fog particle (in centimeters).
   
   *Answer: $5.8 \times 10^{-5}$ cm*

5. Louis de Broglie, in 1924, reasoned that electromagnetic radiation possesses both wave and particle properties, and suggested that moving particles may exhibit wave characteristics. This concept has been experimentally verified and has led to the development of the electron microscope and more recently the discovery and use of radiation generated by moving particles in nuclear accelerators. The equation derived by de Broglie from equating $E = h\nu$ and $E = mc^2$ relates the wavelength $(\lambda)$ to the momentum $(mv)$ of the moving particle.

$$\lambda = \frac{h}{mv}$$

By using this equation, calculate the wavelength and frequency of a wave generated by a tennis ball, mass 60.0 g, moving at 90 mi/hr. (60 mi/hr = 88 ft/s = 2700 cm/sec). *Answer:* $\lambda = 2.7 \times 10^{-32}$ *cm;* $v = 1.1 \times 10^{42}$ *sec$^{-1}$*

6. The ionization potential of lithium is $5.2 \times 10^5$ J per mole. Atoms are readily ionized through interaction with high-energy radiation. Calculate the wavelength of a photon having sufficient energy just to ionize a lithium atom. *Answer: 2000 Å*

# Chapter 5: Chemical Bonding–General Concepts

## INTRODUCTION

With few exceptions, elements in the earth's crust and atmosphere are found combined with other elements. The forces holding these elements together in compounds are electrical in nature. How the bonding of atoms is accomplished in particular cases is responsible for the great variety of substances making up our universe, thus providing the basis for life itself.

Chemical bonding almost seems to defy definition and description because of the variety and character of the bonds formed by the interactive forces involved. Scientists have developed several models to represent chemical bonds that range from a simple model likening a bond to an interconnective spring between atoms to sophisticated computer simulations generated for mathematical constructs called wave functions. Models are used to help visualize theoretical explanations for the observed characteristics of elements and compounds. Theories and models, however, are not absolutes; they are subject to modification and refinement as our capacity to critically examine matter improves.

The discussion of bonding in this chapter specifically treats the types of bonds formed when atoms interact to form molecules or ion pairs. These bonds are interatomic or intramolecular (bonding within the same molecule), as would exist between hydrogen and oxygen in a water molecule or between sodium and chlorine in a sodium chloride ion pair. Discussed later in the text are the types of bonds formed between neighboring molecules or ion pairs (intermolecular bonds) that provide the basis for the properties and structures of liquids and solids.

The chemical bonds between atoms in molecules vary greatly in terms of their strength, bond length or distance between the atoms, and directional character. Some bonds are relatively weak. For example, the intermolecular bonds in mothballs (napthalene) holding napthalene molecules together are very weak. The mere vibrational motion of the molecules is sufficient to rupture the bonds and allow the napthalene molecules to escape the structure. Other bonds such as those holding calcium, oxygen, and silicon in cement are very strong by comparison. These atoms rarely escape the cement structure by their vibrational motion alone.

The structure of solids primarily results from the directional nature of the bonds. Bonds are directed in ways that produce geometries that provide for the lowest or most stable energy states of the substance. Ions in aqueous solution, however, form bonds that are almost completely nondirectional, with as many water molecules as can gather about them. Furthermore, the distances between the nuclei of bonding atoms varies considerably due to the size and nature of the bonded atoms. Although these characteristics of bonds are introduced in this chapter, virtually all the remainder of the text deals with concepts that are directly related to chemical bonding.

In this chapter the discussion of bonding is limited to ionic or electrovalent bonding and covalent bonding. The characteristics of elements leading to these types of bonds and compounds produced through these bonds are emphasized. Methods used for naming compounds are also discussed.

## FORMULAS AND DEFINITIONS

**Valence electrons**   The electrons involved in the formation of bonds between atoms are those in the highest energy levels. For the representative elements, Group A elements, these electrons are in the outermost $s$ or $s$ and $p$ subshells, and the number of valence electrons in a representative element equals its group number. The number of valence electrons in transition elements is not clearly defined. Bonds involving atoms of transition elements include the electrons in the outermost $s$ sublevel and electrons in the $d$ sublevel one quantum level below the $s$ sublevel. For example, manganese, with atomic number 25 and electronic configuration Ar $4s^2 3d^5$, has seven valence electrons. However, data from experiments with manganese show that manganese may use as few as one electron or as many as seven electrons in bonding with other elements.

**Lewis formula**   The Lewis formula of an element is a means of showing the valence electrons available for bonding. The valence electrons are designated by symbols, such as $\cdot$, $\circ$, or $\times$, as shown in the following:

$$\circ \, Mg \, \circ \qquad \times \overset{\times}{Al} \times \qquad : \overset{..}{S} : \qquad : \overset{..}{I} \cdot$$

Compound formation is shown through the use of the Lewis formula of individual atoms by bringing the symbols next to each other and arranging the valence electrons so that eight electrons (where possible) occur about each symbol. For example.

$$\text{Na} \times \cdot \ddot{\text{B}}\ddot{\text{r}}: \quad \text{or} \quad :\ddot{\text{C}}\text{l} \cdot \times \overset{\times}{\underset{\ddots}{\text{Al}}} \times \cdot \ddot{\text{C}}\text{l}:$$

with $:\overset{\cdot\cdot}{\underset{}{\text{Cl}}}:$ above the Al.

Note that although different symbols may be used for convenience to designate electrons, all electrons are the same regardless of origin.

**Ionic bond**  Ionic bonds result from electrostatic attractions between two oppositely charged particles called ions. These mutual attractions produce bonds between ions to form ionic substances, which include sodium chloride, magnesium fluoride, and molten salts. The formation of ionic bonds when two elements react involves the transfer to electrons from one element to the other. For example, in the formation of sodium chloride, NaCl, the one sodium valence electron is removed and transferred to complete the valence level of chlorine. This transfer creates the ion pair as shown:

$$\text{Na} \times + :\ddot{\text{C}}\text{l} \cdot \longrightarrow \text{Na}^+ + :\ddot{\text{C}}\text{l}_x^-$$

**Anion**  An atom or group of atoms that possesses a greater number of electrons than protons is called an anion. The anion has a negative charge equal to the charge difference. Elemental anions are usually nonmetals; metallic elements rarely form negative ions. The dissociation of compounds, however, often produces ion pairs—one anion and one cation.

**Cation**  An atom or group of atoms that possesses fewer electrons than protons is called a cation. The cation has a positive charge that equals the charge difference. Metallic elements tend to form cations in chemical reactions.

**Representative elements**  The representative elements are those elements found in the A groups of the Periodic Table. Reactions involving these elements utilize electrons in their outermost $s$ or $s$ and $p$ sublevels.

**Noble gas electronic configuration**  The great majority of known chemical reactions produce compounds in which elements are bonded together by transferring or sharing electrons in such a way that each element achieves the same electronic configuration as that of its closest noble gas neighbor. As an example, in the formation of the ionic bond between lithium and chlorine in lithium chloride, lithium loses an electron to chlorine. Both elements achieve electronic configurations like the noble gases, Li like that of helium and Cl like that of argon.

$$\begin{array}{llll} \text{Li} \cdot & \longrightarrow & \text{Li}^+ + e^- & (\text{He } 1s^2) \\ 1s^2 2s^1 & & 1s^2 & \end{array}$$

$$\begin{array}{llll} \text{Cl} & + e^- \longrightarrow & \text{Cl}^- & (\text{Ar} \quad 1s^2 2s^2 2p^6 3s^2 3p^6) \\ 1s^2 2s^2 2p^6 3s^2 3p^5 & & 1s^2 2s^2 2p^6 3s^2 3p^6 & \end{array}$$

61

**Covalent bond**   Two atoms may bond together to form a stable electronic structure in which the bonding electrons are shared between the two atoms. In general, these bonds form between atoms of elements that have little tendency to give up electrons. Indeed, covalent bonds may form between atoms of the same element to form diatomic molecules, including $H_2$, $N_2$, $O_2$ and $F_2$. Reactions involving different nonmetallic elements form compounds through covalent bonding; these compounds include $SO_2$, $N_2O_4$, $HCl$, and $CH_4$. Carbon is particularly noteworthy because it can readily form bonds with itself and with other elements in the same compound. This property gives rise to the field of organic chemistry, in which millions of possible combinations of elements involving carbon can be assembled. Generally speaking, covalent bonds form between non-metallic elements close to each other in the Periodic Table. These elements will generally have electronegativity differences less than 1.7.

**Electronegativity**   Electronegativity is based on a numerical scale repre-senting the tendencies of neutral atoms to attract one additional electron. These values range from a low of 0.7 for cesium, representing little attrac-tion for electrons, to a high of 4.0 for fluorine. In general, metallic ele-ments have lower electronegativities than nonmetallic elements. Stated differently, metallic elements tend to give up electrons in chemical reac-tions while nonmetallic elements tend to gain electrons. Metallic elements show almost no tendency to attract another electron; this behavior is not uncommon for nonmetallic elements.

Electronegativities can be used to predict the nature of bonding between two elements. Elements that form primarily ionic bonds have electro-negativities that differ by more than 1.7, while predominantly covalent bonds are formed between elements having differences less than 1.7. In real chemical bonds, regardless of electronegativity differences, both ionic and covalent characters occur to some extent. For example, the bond between sodium and chlorine in NaCl is mostly ionic, but some sharing of electrons does exist; while in $H_2$, although the hydrogen atoms have little tendency to give up electrons, the bond is still about 5% ionic. Our definitions of ionic and covalent bonding are inadequate because real bonds show some character of both types of bonding.

**Polar bonds**   Atoms do not usually share electrons equally in covalent bonds. This is quite evident for covalently bonded compounds where the electronegativity difference is rather large; the more electronegative element has the strongest attraction for the shared electrons. This unequal attraction causes a shift of the shared electrons toward the more elec-tronegative element, resulting in the electrons being nearer the more electronegative element most of the time. Covalent bonds in which the electrons are shared unequally are called polar bonds. For example, in hydrogen chloride, HCl, chlorine is more electronegative than hydrogen, 3.0 vs 2.1. The electron pair in the bond is shifted toward chlorine, making the electron cloud region about chlorine relatively negative in charge with respect to the region about hydrogen. The partial charges are indicated by the symbol $\delta$ with the appropriate charge written to the upper right. Thus,

$$\overset{\delta^+}{H} \overset{x}{\underset{\cdot}{\longrightarrow}} \overset{\delta^-}{\underset{xx}{\overset{xx}{Cl}}} {x}$$

## QUESTIONS

1.  Why does a cation have a positive charge?

**Answer**

Atoms or groups of atoms that have fewer electrons than protons have a net positive charge. Monatomic cations are mostly formed from metallic elements; some examples indicating the ion charges are

$$Na - 1e^- \longrightarrow Na^+ \qquad 11p^+ + 10e^- = 1+$$
$$Ca - 2e^- \longrightarrow Ca^{2+} \qquad 20p^+ + 18e^- = 2+$$
$$Al - 3e^- \longrightarrow Al^{3+} \qquad 13p^+ + 10e^- = 3+$$
$$Pb - 2e^- \longrightarrow Pb^{2+} \qquad 82p^+ + 80e^- = 2+$$

Polyatomic cations, such as $NH_4^+$, $CH_3NH_2^+$, $CH_3CH_2^+$, and $CaOH^+$, result from neutral species by the breaking or formation of bonds in which the more electronegative component acquires additional electrons and becomes negative, while the cation remains as an electron deficient, and therefore positive, species. As an example,

$$NH_3 + H_2O \longrightarrow NH_4^+ + OH^-$$

2.  Why does an anion have a negative charge?

**Answer**

Atoms or groups of atoms that have more electrons than protons have a net negative charge. Monatomic anions are mostly formed from non-metallic elements; some examples indicating the charge on each ion are:

$$Cl + 1e^- \longrightarrow Cl^- \qquad 17p^+ + 18e^- = -1$$
$$O + 2e^- \longrightarrow O^{2-} \qquad 8p^+ + 10e^- = -2$$
$$N + 3e^- \longrightarrow N^{3-} \qquad 7p^+ + 10e^- = -3$$

Polyatomic anions, such as $SO_4^{2-}$, $PO_4^{3-}$, $CHOO^-$, and $NO_2^-$, result from ionization processes in which the anion portion of the species acquires an excess electrical charge and becomes negative.

$$CH_3COOH + H_2O \longrightarrow CH_3COO^- + H_3O^+$$

6.  Predict the charge on the monatomic ions formed from the following elements in ionic compounds containing these elements: Ag, Al, Ba, Br, K, Zn, N, O, P, Se.

**Answer**

The charge on monatomic ions can be predicted from the oxidation number rules. In the formation of ionic compounds, metallic elements lose electrons and become positive ions, while nonmetallic elements gain electrons and become negative ions. Furthermore, elements tend to gain or lose sufficient electrons to achieve a noble gas electronic configuration. The electrons gained or lost by the above elements in the formation of ionic compounds are

$$\text{Ag (Kr } 5s^1 4d^{10}) \longrightarrow \text{Ag}^+ \text{ (Kr } 4d^{10}) + e^-$$

$$\text{Al (Ne } 3s^2 3p^1) \longrightarrow \text{Al}^{3+}\text{(Ne)} + 3e^-$$

$$\text{Ba (Xe } 6s^2) \longrightarrow \text{Ba}^{2+} \text{ (Xe)} + 2e^-$$

$$\text{Br (Ar } 4s^2 3d^{10} 4p^5) + e^- \longrightarrow \text{Br}^- \text{ (Kr)}$$

$$\text{K (Ar } 4s^1) \longrightarrow \text{K}^+ \text{ (Ar)} + e^-$$

$$\text{Zn (Ar } 4s^2 3d^{10}) \longrightarrow \text{Zn}^{2+} \text{ (Ar } 3d^{10}) + 2e^-$$

$$\text{N (He } 2s^2 2p^3) + 3e^- \longrightarrow \text{N}^{3-} \text{ (Ne)}$$

$$\text{O (He } 2s^2 2p^4) + 2e^- \longrightarrow \text{O}^{2-} \text{ (Ne)}$$

$$\text{P (Ne } 3s^2 3p^3) + 3e^- \longrightarrow \text{P}^{3-} \text{ (Ar)}$$

$$\text{Se (Ar } 4s^2 3d^{10} 4p^4) + 2e^- \longrightarrow \text{Se}^{2-} \text{ (Kr)}$$

10. What are the characteristics of two atoms which will form a covalent bond?

**Answer**

In general, the type of bond formed between two atoms depends on the ability of the two atoms to give up electrons. Since electrons are shared in a covalent bond, the two bonding atoms must have similar electronegativities and similar, high ionization potentials. Relative to the Periodic Table, atoms having these characteristics are mostly nonmetals.

12. How do single, double, and triple bonds differ? How are they similar?

**Answer**

When possible, the formation of bonds between atoms results in completing the valence levels of the elements involved to achieve noble gas electronic structures. Single, double, and triple bonds refer to atoms that are covalently bonded. In ionic bonds one atom has lost one electron to another atom to form an ion pair. In contrast, both bonding atoms in a single covalent bond share a pair of electrons. Furthermore, single bonds can form between two atoms through direct atomic orbital overlap without rearrangement (hybridization) of orbitals.

Double and triple bonds are covalent bonds in which elements must share four and six electrons, respectively. In contrast to single bonds, the formation of these bonds requires that some or all of the atomic orbitals of the bonding atoms be rearranged, that is, hybridized, to create orbitals having compatible geometries for bonding.

Note that there is a gradual increase in the bond energy and decrease in the bond distance. For example, consider the carbon-carbon bonds in the organic molecules shown:

| Ethane | $H_3C-CH_3$ | distance = 1.50 Å, | $E$ = 368 kJ/mol |
|--------|-------------|--------------------|--------------------|
| Ethane | $H_2C=CH_2$ | distance = 1.34 Å, | $E$ = 682 kJ/mol |
| Ethane | $HC\equiv CH$ | distance = 1.20 Å, | $E$ = 828 kJ/mol |

Also note that singly bonded atoms as in ethane, C–C, are free to rotate about each other to form different conformational geometries. On the other hand, doubly or triply bonded atoms as in ethene, $-C=C-$, or ethyne, $-C\equiv C-$, are fixed in a planar geometry that does not permit free rotation but does allow a degree of twisting.

17. Many molecules that contain polar bonds are nonpolar. How can this happen?

**Answer**

A polar bond involves the unequal sharing of electrons by the bonding atoms. The bonding electrons shift toward the more electronegative atom, resulting in a net imbalance in electronic charge, measured by the dipole moment, in that direction. Molecules may contain several polar bonds and as a whole may be nonpolar if there are other bonds in the molecule that offset or balance the imbalance in electronic distribution. For example, in carbon dioxide both carbon-oxygen double bonds are polar and both dipole moments are in the direction of oxygen. The molecule is linear and the two dipole moments are equal but opposite in direction, and hence cancel.

$$:\ddot{O}: \longleftarrow :C: \longrightarrow :\ddot{O}:$$

21. From the location in the Periodic Table of the elements in the following compounds, predict which compounds are ionic and which are covalent:

| | |
|--------|--------|
| $CaF_2$ | $COCl_2$ |
| $CO_2$ | $ClF_3$ |
| $CuS$ | $MgI_2$ |
| $SiCl_4$ | $Cs_2S$ |
| $C_2H_4$ | $MnO$ |
| $SF_6$ | $Al_2O_3$ |

**Answer**

| | | | |
|---|---|---|---|
| $CaF_2$ | ionic | $COCl_2$ | ionic |
| $CO_2$ | covalent | $ClF_3$ | covalent |
| $CuS$ | ionic | $MgI_2$ | ionic |
| $SiCl_4$ | covalent | $Cs_2S$ | ionic |
| $C_2H_4$ | covalent | $MnO$ | ionic |
| $SF_6$ | covalent | $Al_2O_3$ | ionic |

23. Name the following compounds: $CaF_2$, $CO_2$, $CuS$, $SiCl_4$, $SF_6$, $ClF_3$, $MgI_2$, $Cs_2S$, $MnO$, $AgCl$, $HF$, $ZnO$, $Tl_2O$, $Tl_2O_3$, $Fe(NO_3)_2$, $Ca(OH)_2$, $NH_4CN$, $Na_2SO_4$, $Na_2SO_3$, $AgNO_2$, $Cu(NO_3)_2$.

**Answer**

| | | | |
|---|---|---|---|
| $CaF_2$ | calcium fluoride | $ZnO$ | zinc oxide |
| $CO_2$ | carbon dioxide | $Tl_2O$ | thallium(I) oxide |
| $CuS$ | copper(II) sulfide | $Tl_2O_3$ | thallium(III) oxide |
| $SiCl_4$ | silicon tetrachloride | $Fe(NO_3)_2$ | iron(II) nitrate or ferrous nitrate |
| $SF_6$ | sulfur hexafluoride or sulfur VI fluoride | $Ca(OH)_2$ | calcium hydroxide |
| $ClF_3$ | chlorine trifluoride or chlorine(III) fluoride | $NH_4CN$ | ammonium cyanide |
| $MgI_2$ | magnesium iodide | $Na_2SO_4$ | sodium sulfate |
| $Cs_2S$ | cesium sulfide | $Na_2SO_3$ | sodium sulfite |
| $MnO$ | manganese(II) oxide | $AgNO_2$ | silver nitrite |
| $AgCl$ | silver chloride | $Cu(NO_3)_2$ | copper(II) nitrate |
| $HF$ | hydrogen fluoride | | |

Roman numerals are used to designate the oxidation state of an element in a compound in which the element is known to exhibit variable oxidation states. The rules for assigning oxidation numbers delineate these elements.

24. Determine the oxidation number of N in each of the following compounds: $Na_3N$, $NH_4Cl$, $N_2O$, $N_2H_4$, $KNO_2$, $Ca(NO_3)_2$.

**Answer**

The oxidation number of nitrogen in each of the compounds has been calculated from the rules described in Sections 5.11 and 5.12.

$Na_3N$     $3(Na = +1) = +3; + 3 + N = 0; N = -3$

$NH_4^+$     $4(H = +1) = +4; +4 + (N) = +1; N = -3$

$N_2O$     $O = -2; -2 + 2N = 0; N = +1$

66

$N_2 H_4$      $4(H = +1) = +4; +4 + 2N = 0; N = -2$

$KNO_2$      $K = +1; 2(O = -2) = -4; +1 + (-4) + N = 0; N = +3$

$Ca(NO_3)_2$    $Ca = +2; 6(O = -2) = -12; +2 + (-12) + 2N = 0; N = +5$

26. With the aid of oxidation numbers, write chemical formulas for the following compounds: sodium phosphide, potassium oxide, magnesium hydroxide, hydrogen chloride, tin(II) nitrate, lead(IV) acetate, ammonium sulfate, aluminum carbonate, manganese(III) fluoride, silicon hydride, strontium phosphate, lithium perchlorate, nitrogen dioxide, osmium tetraoxide.

**Answer**

| | |
|---|---|
| sodium phosphide | $Na_3 P$ |
| potassium oxide | $K_2 O$ |
| magnesium hydroxide | $Mg(OH)_2$ |
| hydrogen chloride | $HCl$ |
| tin(II) nitrate | $Sn(NO_3)_2$ |
| lead(IV) acetate | $Pb(C_2 H_3 O_2)_4$ |
| ammonium sulfate | $(NH_4)_2 SO_4$ |
| aluminum carbonate | $Al_2 (CO_3)_3$ |
| manganese(III) fluoride | $MnF_3$ |
| silicon hydride | $SiH_4$ |
| strontium phosphate | $Sr_3 (PO_4)_2$ |
| lithium perchlorate | $LiClO_4$ |
| nitrogen dioxide | $NO_2$ |
| osmium tetraoxide | $OsO_4$ |

27. Write Lewis formulas for the following: $BrCl$, $H_2 S$, $ClO_4^-$, $NO^+$, $PCl_3$.

**Answer**

30. How does the electronic structure of an isolated nitrogen atom differ from that of a nitrogen atom in a molecule of nitrogen, $N_2$?

**Answer**

An isolated nitrogen atom, atomic nitrogen, has three unpaired electrons in its $2p$ sublevel and all electrons are associated with the nitrogen nucleus. In a nitrogen molecule, $N_2$, $N\equiv N$, the valence electrons interact to form a molecular electronic system that enables both atoms to achieve a noble gas configuration through the triple covalent bond. Atoms effectively lose their identity once they are bonded as molecules.

32. Draw the resonance structures of the following: nitric acid, $HONO_2$; selenium dioxide, $OSeO$; the nitrate ion, $O\ NO_2^-$; the acetate ion,

$$\begin{matrix} H \\ H\ C\ CO_2^-. \\ H \end{matrix}$$

**Answer**

33. X may indicate a different representative element in each of the following Lewis formulas. To which group does X belong in each case?

**Answer**

Count the number of valence electrons associated with X in each formula; the group number equals the number of valence electrons.

(a) $\overset{\displaystyle :\ddot{F}:}{\underset{\displaystyle :\ddot{F}:}{:X-\ddot{F}:}}$  No. valence e⁻ = 3 shared with $F$ plus lone pair = 5

(b) $:\ddot{X}-\ddot{Br}:$  No. valence e⁻ = 1 shared with Br plus 3 lone pairs = 7

(c) $\overset{\displaystyle :\ddot{Cl}:}{\underset{\displaystyle :\ddot{Cl}:}{:\ddot{Cl}-X-\ddot{Cl}:}}$  No. valence e⁻ = 4 shared with Cl = 4

(d) $\overset{\displaystyle :\ddot{O}:}{\underset{\displaystyle :\ddot{O}:}{:\ddot{O}-X-\ddot{O}:}}$  No. valence e⁻ = 7

(e) 6  (f) 5  (g) 2  (h) 3  (i) 2  (j) 7

## RELATED QUESTIONS

1. Write the Lewis structures for $BCl_3$, $SF_4$, $IF_7$, and $PCl_5$.

   **Answers**

$$|\overline{\underline{Cl}}|$$
$$\overset{\times\,\cdot}{|\underline{Cl} \times B \times \overline{\underline{Cl}}|} \; ; \; |\overline{F} \overset{\times\,\cdot}{\times} S \overset{\times}{\times} \overline{F}| \; ;$$
$$|\overline{F}|$$

(Lewis structures for $IF_7$ and $PCl_5$ shown)

2. Indicate the direction of the dipole moment between the atoms in $CH_4$, $CHCl_3$, and $CH_2Cl_2$.

   **Answer**

3. Calculate the oxidation state of chlorine in each of the following compounds containing chlorine: $NaClO$, $NaClO_2$, $NaClO_3$, $NaClO_4$

   **Answer**

   $NaClO$, $+1$; $NaClO_2$, $+3$; $NaClO_3$, $+5$; $NaClO_4$, $+7$

4. For each of the following pairs of compounds indicate the more polar compound: $CuCl$ or $CuI$; $PbS$ or $FeS$; and $BiCl_3$ or $BiI_3$.

   **Answer**

   $CuCl$; Electronegativities of Pb and Fe are equal and polarities are about equal; $BiCl_3$

5. Draw an outline of the Periodic Table and indicate the direction of trends in atomic size, ionization potential, and electronegativity.

# Chapter 10: The Gaseous State and the Kinetic-Molecular Theory

## INTRODUCTION

As we begin our study of gases we find that gases have occupied a very important position in human thought and imagination from the very earliest recorded times. For example, the Greek Anaximenes (died ca. 528 B.C.) thought that air constituted the primary matter from which all other substances came into being. In this context, water could be formed by the condensation of air. Although we have a different perspective today, the concept then was one of different states of matter, the gaseous state being the most important.

Although the Greeks did not develop the scientific method, experimentation with gases did occur before the seventeenth century. Hero of Alexandria (ca. A.D. 62-150) described many mechanisms operated by steam, even describing a steam engine; the pressure of gases was the motive power in all these systems. Hero therefore had a very clear idea of the nature of gases, and in many respects anticipated the kinetic theory of gases. His ideas on combustion were very close to those of Lavoisier, who lived at the beginning of modern chemistry. However, scientists such as Hero did not anticipate the discoveries of the eighteenth century because they tended to employ experiments only to demonstrate preconceived hypotheses.

The ability to *scientifically* study gases became possible when the Italian physicist Evangelista Torricelli invented the mercury barometer in 1643. Thus a means was finally available to measure pressure. Generally the unit of measurement of pressure is the millimeter of mercury (mm Hg) or *torr* named after Torricelli.

The British chemist Robert Boyle was quick to exploit this advance, and in 1662 showed that the pressure of a gas and its volume were inversely related.

A French physicist named Amontons discovered the relation between the temperature and volume of gas almost immediately after Boyle's work, but it was a century later before Charles, and still later and independently the French chemist Joseph Gay-Lussac, showed the same temperature-volume dependence.

The development of a theoretical explanation of the behavior of gases was developed in 1738 by the Swiss mathematician Daniel Bernoulli, who laid the foundation for the kinetic-molecular theory of gases. The developments from this point are well covered in the text and no attempt to duplicate them will be made here. It might be pointed out, however, that from the early 1800s, the development of chemical science proceeded very rapidly.

## FORMULAS AND DEFINITIONS

**Pressure**   Gas pressure provides the most easily measured gas property. Pressure is the force exerted upon a unit area of surface. Common units for pressure are dynes per $cm^2$, millimeters of mercury (mm Hg) or torr (= 1 mm Hg). Pressure is also expressed in terms of the standard atmosphere (atm) which equals 760 mm Hg. The SI pressure unit which will gain more recognition with time is the pascal (Pa). The pascal is expressed in terms of kg $sec^{-2}$ meter$^{-1}$. The relations necessary for interconversion from one unit to another are

$$1 \text{ atm} = 760 \text{ mm Hg} = 760 \text{ torr} = 101,325 \text{ Pa}$$

**Boyle's Law**   The volume of a given mass of gas held at constant temperature is inversely proportional to its pressure. Mathematically this can be expressed as

$$V = \text{constant} \times \frac{1}{P} = k \times \frac{1}{P}$$

or

$$PV = \text{constant} = k$$

**Charles' Law**   The volume of a given mass of gas is directly proportional to its Kelvin temperature when holding its pressure constant. This may be stated in equation form:

$$V = \text{constant} \times T = k \times T$$

or

$$\frac{V}{T} = \text{constant} = k$$

where $k$ is a constant different from the one in Boyle's Law.

**Kelvin temperature**  A more fundamental temperature scale than the Celsius or Fahrenheit scale.  The Kelvin scale (K) is independent of the working fluid.  Its relation to the Celsius scale is

$$K = °C + 273.15$$

The interval between degrees is the same on the Kelvin and Celsius scales. All temperatures involving the gas laws should be expressed on the Kelvin scale before attempting to work numerical problems involving multiplication and division.

**Gay-Lussac's Law of Combining Volumes**  After studying a large number of reactions, Gay-Lussac generalized that in reactions involving gases at constant temperature and pressure, the volumes of the gases can be expressed as a ratio of small whole numbers.

**Avogadro's Law**  Equal volumes of all gases, measured under the same conditions of temperature and pressure, contain the same number of molecules.  Although this law was proposed in 1811, it was not until 1858 that this idea was generally accepted by chemists. The utility of this law is obvious once the volume of one mole of gas is determined at a particular temperature and pressure.  For 0°C and 1.00 atm (STP, known as *standard temperature and pressure*), the volume of one mole of an ideal gas is 22.4 liters.

**Ideal Gas Law**  This law is an equation that relates the variables $P$, $V$, $T$, of a gas to the number of moles, $n$, of gas present.  The equation is

$$PV = nRT$$

where $R$ is the universal gas constant and can be expressed in several different units.  Expressions showing common units are

$$P(\text{atm}) \times V(\ell) = n(\text{mol}) \times R \left( \frac{\ell \text{ atm}}{\text{mol K}} \right) \times T(\text{K})$$

$$P(\text{Pa}) \times V(\ell) = n(\text{mol}) \times R \left( \frac{\ell \text{ Pa}}{\text{mol K}} \right) \times T(\text{K})$$

where $R$ has the values

$$0.08205 \; \ell \text{ atm/mol K} \quad \text{or} \quad 8314 \; \ell \text{ Pa/mol K}$$

**Dalton's Law of Partial Pressure**  The total pressure of a mixture of gases equals the sum of the partial pressures of the component gases.  If the pressures of the individual gases $A$, $B$, $C$, and so forth are designated $P_A$, $P_B$, $P_C$ and so forth, then the total pressure $P_T$ may be written as

$$P_T = P_A + P_B + P_C + \cdots$$

This law is useful in calculating the pressure of a gas collected over water. The vapor pressure of the water is fixed for a particular temperature.

Consequently, if the vapor pressure of water at the temperature of the vessel is subtracted from the total pressure, the pressure of the gas is determined.

**Graham's Law, diffusion of gases**  This law states that the rates of diffusion of different gases are inversely proportional to the square roots of their densities or molecular weights.  Mathematically,

$$\frac{\text{Rate of diffusion of gas A}}{\text{rate of diffusion of gas B}} = \frac{\sqrt{\text{density B}}}{\sqrt{\text{density A}}} = \frac{\sqrt{\text{mol wt B}}}{\sqrt{\text{mol wt A}}}$$

Note that the time required for the diffusion of a gas is inversely proportional to its rate.  We can write, assuming equal moles,

$$\frac{\text{Time for diffusion of A}}{\text{time for diffusion of B}} = \frac{\sqrt{\text{density A}}}{\sqrt{\text{density B}}} = \frac{\sqrt{\text{mol wt A}}}{\sqrt{\text{mol wt B}}}$$

**Kinetic-molecular theory**  As already mentioned in the introduction, ideas concerning the nature of gases arose early in the development of science. Those that stood the test of time have allowed us to develop the concept of an ideal gas (one that does not actually exist but has the generalized qualities of all gases).

The ideal gas consists of separate particles, either atoms or molecules. The volume occupied by the individual particles is small compared to the total volume of the gas.  As a result, the particles in the gaseous state are relatively far apart and have no attraction for one another.

A second premise concerning the ideal gas is that the gas particles are in continuous motion and traveling in straight lines with varying speeds. As particles collide with each other, no net loss in average kinetic energy occurs; that is, collisions among particles occur as though the particles are perfectly elastic bodies.

Finally, the average kinetic energy ($\frac{1}{2}mu^2$) of all molecules, even of different gases, is the same at the same temperature.

These premises explain the gas laws in a qualitative way, and can be shown to predict the Ideal Gas Law, $PV = nRT$, a mathematical interpretation of the behavior or characteristics of gases.

**The van der Waals equation**  An attempt to explain deviations from ideal gas behavior by real gases led van der Waals to formulate an equation that introduced the term $a/V^2$ to account for the forces of attraction in real gases and the term $b$ to account for the finite volume real gases have.  His equation is

$$\left(P + \frac{n^2 a}{V^2}\right)(V - nb) = nRT$$

73

## PROBLEMS

1. Weather reports in the United States often give barometric pressures in inches of mercury rather than mm Hg or torr; 29.92 in. = 760 mm. Convert a pressure of 29.20 inches of mercury to torr, atm, and Pa.

**Solution**

Conversions between different units may be accomplished by use of the unit method described earlier.

For conversion to torr, use the relation 1 torr = 1 mm Hg.

$$29.20 \text{ in. Hg} \left(\frac{760 \text{ mm Hg}}{29.92 \text{ in. Hg}}\right) \left(\frac{1 \text{ torr}}{1 \text{ mm Hg}}\right) = 742 \text{ torr}$$

For conversion to atmospheres, use the relation 1 atm = 760 mm Hg.

$$29.20 \text{ in Hg} \left(\frac{760 \text{ mm Hg}}{29.92 \text{ in. Hg}}\right) \left(\frac{1 \text{ atm}}{760 \text{ mm Hg}}\right) = 0.976 \text{ atm}$$

For conversion to pascals, use the relation 1 atm = 101,325 Pa.

$$29.20 \text{ in. Hg} \left(\frac{760 \text{ mm Hg}}{29.92 \text{ in. Hg}}\right) \left(\frac{1 \text{ atm}}{760 \text{ mm Hg}}\right) \left(\frac{101,325 \text{ Pa}}{1 \text{ atm}}\right) = 9.90 \times 10^4 \text{ Pa}$$

2. The volume of a sample of ethane is 3.24 ℓ at 477 torr and 27°c.

(b) What volume will it occupy at 27°C if the pressure is 831 torr?

**Solution**

Problems involving gases usually can be solved in a logical fashion by analyzing the problem in terms of the variables. A change in any one of the variables $V$, $T$, $P$, or $n$ (moles of gas) for a confined gas will cause a change in the gas system. Perhaps the best way to visualize these changes is to make a table like the following, including all the factors on which a gas system depends:

| $V_1 =$ | $T_1 =$ | $P_1 =$ | $n_1 =$ |
|---------|---------|---------|---------|
| $V_2 =$ | $T_2 =$ | $P_2 =$ | $n_2 =$ |

where the subscript 1 is used to denote the initial condition of the gas and the subscript 2 indicates the new or final condition of the gas. For this problem, the known values are inserted as shown.

| $V_1 = 3.24$ liters | $T_1 = 27°C$ or 300 K | $P_1 = 477$ torr | $n_1$ |
|---------------------|-----------------------|------------------|-------|
| $V_2 = ? \ell$ | $T_2 = 27°C$ or 300 K | $P_2 = 831$ torr | $n_2$ |

In a closed system, that is, one in which there is no gain or loss in the number of moles of substance, the values $n_1$ and $n_2$ are equal. Since $T$ is held constant, $P$ and $V$ are free to vary. The pressure on the gas is being increased from 477 torr to 831 torr. The volume will change by the same proportion as the change in pressure but in inverse relation, as given by Boyle's Law. In other words, an increase in pressure will cause a decrease in volume; that is, volume is inversely proportional to pressure. Since the volume must decrease, the solution of the problem is accomplished mathematically by multiplication of the original volume by a fraction less than 1 which yields the necessary decrease in volume.

$$V_2 = 3.24 \; \ell \times \frac{477 \text{ torr}}{831 \text{ torr}} = 1.86 \; \ell$$

3. The volume of a sample of carbon monoxide is 405 ml at 10.0 atm and 467 K.

(b) What volume will it occupy at 1873 torr and 467 K?

### Solution

The same principle may be applied here as was applied in the last problem, but first the units must be made consistent.

$$\text{Pressure of CO} = 10 \text{ atm} \times \frac{760 \text{ torr}}{1 \text{ atm}} = 7600 \text{ torr}$$

Now set up the table as in Problem 2.

| | | | |
|---|---|---|---|
| $V_1 = 405$ ml | $T_1 = 467$ K | $P_1 = 7600$ torr | $n_1$ |
| $V_2 = ?$ ml | $T_2 = 467$ K | $P_2 = 1873$ torr | $n_2$ |

Both $T$ and $n$ are constant, so a decrease in pressure will result in an increase in volume. Multiplication of a fraction greater than 1 yields the increase in the volume.

$$405 \text{ ml} \times \frac{7600 \text{ torr}}{1873 \text{ torr}} = 1.64 \times 10^3 \text{ ml}$$

4. A 2.50-$\ell$ volume of hydrogen measured at the normal boiling point of nitrogen, $-210.0°C$, is warmed to the normal boiling point of water, $100°C$. Calculate the new volume of the gas, assuming ideal behavior and no change in pressure.

### Solution

| | | | |
|---|---|---|---|
| $V_1 = 250 \; \ell$ | $T_1 = -210.0°C$ | $P_1$ | $n_1$ |
| $V_2 = ? \; \ell$ | $T_2 = 100°C$ | $P_2$ | $n_2$ |

Both $P$ and $n$ are held constant. According to Charles' or Gay-Lussac's law, the volume is directly proportional to a change in $T$. The temperature is increasing from 63.1 K ($-210.0°C$) to 373.1 K ($100°C$). The volume will increase by the same proportion as the temperature. Thus the temperature is increased by the ratio 373.1/63.1. Mathematically,

$$\text{Vol } H_2 = 2.50 \; \ell \times \frac{373.1}{63.1} = 14.8 \; \ell$$

5. A sample of oxygen occupies 38.9 $\ell$ at STP.

   (a) What volume will it occupy at 456 K and 1 atm?
   (b) What volume will it occupy at 0°C and 917 torr?
   (d) The density of oxygen is 1.429 g/$\ell$ at STP. What is the mass of of oxygen in the sample?

**Solution**

(a) STP conditions are 0°C and 1 atm pressure.

| | | | |
|---|---|---|---|
| $V_1 = 38.9 \; \ell$ | $T_1 = 0°C$ (273 K) | $P_1 = 1$ atm | $n_1$ |
| $V_2 = $ ? | $T_2 = 456$ K | $P_2 = 1$ atm | $n_2$ |

The procedure is the same as in Problem 4. The volume increases with an increase in temperature. Therefore the volume must be multiplied by a ratio of the temperature which is greater than 1, namely 456/273.

$$\text{Vol } O_2 = 38.9 \; \ell \times \frac{456 \text{ K}}{273 \text{ K}} = 65.0 \; \ell$$

| | | | |
|---|---|---|---|
| (b) $V_1 = 38.9 \; \ell$ | $T_1 = 273$ K | $P_1 = 1$ atm (760 torr) | $n_1$ |
| $V_2 = $ ? | $T_2 = 273$ K | $P_2 = 917$ torr | $n_2$ |

Increase in pressure decreases volume. The decrease is achieved by multiplying the volume by the proper ratio of the pressures.

$$\text{Vol } O_2 = 38.9 \; \ell \times \frac{760 \text{ torr}}{917 \text{ torr}} = 32.2 \; \ell$$

(d) The mass of 1 $\ell$ of oxygen gas is 1.429 g. Multiplication of the mass per liter (density) times the number of liters gives the total mass.

$$\text{Mass } O_2 = 38.9 \; \ell \times 1.429 \text{ g/}\ell = 55.6 \text{ g}$$

6. A sample of gas occupies 60.0 ml at $-10°C$ and 720 mm. What pressure will the gas exert in a 101-ml sealed bulb at 25°C?

**Solution**

This problem has two changes occurring simultaneously. The pressure will decrease (Boyle's Law) with an increase in volume and will increase with an increase in temperature.

| | | | |
|---|---|---|---|
| $V_1 = 60.0$ ml | $T_1 = -10°C$ (263 K) | $P_1 = 720$ mm | $n_1$ |
| $V_2 = 101$ ml | $T_2 = 25°C$ (298 K) | $P_2 = ?$ | $n_2$ |

$$P = 720 \text{ mm} \times \frac{60.00 \text{ ml}}{101 \text{ ml}} \times \frac{298 \text{ K}}{263 \text{ K}} = 485 \text{ mm Hg}$$

7. What volume of $O_2$ at STP is required to oxidize 14.0 ℓ of CO at STP to $CO_2$? What volume of $CO_2$ is produced at STP?

**Solution**

First set up the balanced chemical equation.

$$2CO + O_2 \longrightarrow 2CO_2$$

Since all gases are at STP, no conversions are necessary. Furthermore, since one volume of any gas contains the same number of molecules as one volume of any other gas, under the same conditions, the coefficients of the balanced equation also can refer to the volume of substance used. Thus 2.0 ℓ of CO require half as many volumes of $O_2$ for oxidation, thereby producing 2.0 ℓ of $CO_2$. Consequently, 14.0 ℓ of CO requires 7.0 ℓ of $O_2$ and produces 14.0 ℓ of $CO_2$.

9. A 2.50-ℓ sample of a colorless gas at STP decomposed to give 2.50 ℓ of $N_2$ and 1.25 ℓ of $O_2$ at STP. What is the colorless gas?

**Solution**

We again use the principle that, under the same conditions, 1 ℓ of any gas will contain the same number of moles as 1 ℓ of any other gas. Therefore we may write the number of liters as the coefficients in the balanced equation. Thus

$$2.5(N_xO_y) \longrightarrow 2.5N_2 + 1.25O_2$$

where $x$ and $y$ are to be determined. By inspection it is seen that $x = 2$ and $y = 1$. The starting compound must be $N_2O$.

10. How many moles of hydrogen sulfide, $H_2S$, are contained in a 327.3-ml bulb at 48.1°C if the pressure is $1.493 \times 10^5$ Pa?

**Solution**

The variables, $P$, $V$, $n$, and $T$ are related through the Ideal Gas Law, $PV = nRT$, where $R$ is given in units of 8314 ℓ Pa/mol K. Rearranging to solve for $n$ followed by substitution (48.1°C = 321.2 K), yields

$$n = \frac{PV}{RT} = \frac{(1.493 \times 10^5 \text{ Pa}) \left(\dfrac{327.3 \text{ ml}}{1000 \text{ ml/\textit{l}}}\right)}{(8314 \text{ \textit{l} Pa/mol K}) (321.2 \text{ K})}$$

$$= 1.830 \times 10^{-2} \text{ mol}$$

11. What is the volume of a bulb that contains 8.17 g of neon at 13°C with a pressure of 8.73 atm?

**Solution**

To solve this, set up the ideal gas equation to solve for volume, remembering that $n = $ (Mass, g)/GAW. Since $P$ is in atmospheres, $R$ has units of 0.08205 $l$ atm/mol:

$$V = \frac{nRT}{P} = \frac{\left(8.17 \text{ g} \times \dfrac{1 \text{ mol}}{20.18 \text{ g}}\right)\left(0.08205 \dfrac{l \text{ atm}}{\text{K mol}}\right)(286.1 \text{ K})}{8.73 \text{ atm}}$$

$$= 1.09 \text{ } l$$

14. What volume of oxygen at 15°C and 745 torr is produced by the decomposition of 23.6 g of HgO to Hg and $O_2$?

**Solution**

The mass of $O_2$ first must be determined from the balanced chemical equation. The number of moles of $O_2$ may be calculated from the mass and the desired volume calculated from the Ideal Gas Law. Thus

$$2HgO \longrightarrow 2Hg + O_2$$

$$\text{Mass } O_2 = 23.6 \text{ g HgO} \times \frac{1 \text{ mol HgO}}{216.6 \text{ g HgO}} \times \frac{1 \text{ mol } O_2}{2 \text{ mol HgO}} \times \frac{32.0 \text{ g } O_2}{1 \text{ mol } O_2}$$

$$= 1.74 \text{ g}$$

Then, $PV = nRT$ and

$$V = \frac{nRT}{P} = \frac{\left(\dfrac{1.74}{32.0}\right)(0.08205)(288.1)}{745/760} = 1.31 \text{ } l$$

15. The density of a certain phosphorus fluoride gas is 3.93 g/$l$ at STP.

   (a) Calculate the molecular weight of this phosphorus fluoride, given that the density of oxygen is 1.429 g/$l$ at STP.
   (b) Calculate the molecular weight of this phosphorus fluoride using the Ideal Gas Law equation.
   (c) What is the formula of this phosphorus fluoride?

78

**Solution**

(a) This problem may be solved using Graham's Law in the form

$$\frac{\sqrt{\text{density A}}}{\sqrt{\text{density B}}} = \frac{\sqrt{\text{mol wt A}}}{\sqrt{\text{mol wt B}}} \quad \text{or} \quad \frac{\sqrt{\text{mol wt}}}{\sqrt{32 \text{ g mol O}_2}} = \frac{\sqrt{3.93 \text{ g}/\ell}}{\sqrt{1.429 \text{ g}/\ell}}$$

Squaring both sides and solving for the molecular weight,

$$\text{mol wt of gas} = 32.0 \left(\frac{3.93}{1.429}\right) = 88.0$$

(b) The Ideal Gas Law may be written as

$$P = \frac{nRT}{V} = \frac{\left(\frac{\text{mass}}{\text{MW}}\right)RT}{V} = \frac{\left(\frac{\text{no. g}}{\text{MW}}\right)RT}{V}$$

or

$$\text{MW} = \frac{(\text{no. g})RT}{VP}$$

but $g/V$ is a density; therefore

$$\text{MW} = (3.93 \text{ g}/\ell)\,\frac{(0.082 \text{ } \ell \text{ atm/K mol}) (273.1 \text{ K})}{1 \text{ atm}}$$

$$= 88.0 \text{ g/mol}$$

(c) The simplest group of atoms to satisfy the molecular weight of 88 g/mol is

$$\text{1P} \quad 31.0 = 31.0$$
$$\text{3F} \quad 19.0 = 57.0$$
$$\text{MW} \quad \text{PF}_3 = 88.0$$

16. Calculate the density of $C_6H_6$ (g) at 100°C and a pressure of $1.012 \times 10^4$ Pa.

**Solution**

Write the Ideal Gas Law as

$$P = \frac{n}{V}RT = \frac{g}{V}\frac{RT}{\text{MW}}$$

Solving for $g/V$, a density, we have, since MW = 78.11 g/mol,

$$d = \frac{P(MW)}{RT} = \frac{(1.012 \times 10^4 \text{ Pa}) (78.11 \text{ g/mol})}{(8314 \, \ell \text{ Pa/mol K}) (373.1 \text{ K})}$$

$$= 2.55 \times 10^{-1} = 0.255 \text{ g/}\ell$$

19. What mass of $KClO_3$ must be decomposed to KCl and $O_2$ to give 638 ml of $O_2$ at a temperature of 18°C and a pressure of 752 torr?

**Solution**

The number of moles of oxygen is computed first; then the mass of $KClO_3$ determined from the balanced equation for the decomposition:

$$2KClO_3 \longrightarrow 2KCl + 3O_2$$

$$PV = nRT, \quad n = \frac{PV}{RT} = \frac{\left(\frac{752}{760}\right)(0.638 \, \ell)}{(0.082)(291.1)} = 0.0264 \text{ mol}$$

2 moles $KClO_3$ produce 3 moles $O_2$; therefore

$$\text{Moles } KClO_3 = 2 \times \frac{0.026}{3} = 0.0176$$

The formula weight of $KClO_3$ is 122.6 g/mol. Mass $KClO_3$ = 122.6 g/mol $\times$ 0.0176 mol = 2.16 g.

20. Calculate the relative rates of diffusion of the gases CO and $CO_2$.

**Solution**

Use Graham's Law,

$$\frac{\text{Rate CO}}{\text{rate CO}_2} = \sqrt{\frac{\text{MW CO}_2}{\text{MW CO}}} = \sqrt{\frac{44}{28}} = 1.25$$

23. The average velocity of $H_2$ molecules at 25°C is about 1.6 km/sec. What is the average speed of a $CH_4$ molecule at 25°C?

**Solution**

Speed or velocity is inversely proportional to the square root of the molecular weight. Therefore

$$\frac{\text{Velocity CH}_4}{\text{velocity H}_2} = \frac{\text{velocity CH}_4}{1.6 \text{ km/sec}} = \frac{\sqrt{2(H_2)}}{\sqrt{16(CH_4)}}$$

$$\text{Velocity CH}_4 = 1.6 \text{ km/sec} \left(\frac{1.414}{4}\right) = 0.57 \text{ km/sec}$$

25. The volume of a sample of a gas collected over water at 32.0°C and 752 torr is 627 ml. What will the volume of the gas be when dried and measured at STP?

**Solution**

The vapor pressure of water at 32°C is 35.7 torr. Using Dalton's law of partial pressures, the pressure due to the gas sample alone is 752 torr − 36 torr = 716 torr. The rest of the problem is a standard problem:

| | | | |
|---|---|---|---|
| $V_1 = 627$ ml | $T_1 = 32°C(305.1$ K$)$ | $P_1 = 716$ torr | $n_1$ |
| $V_2 = ?$ | $T_2 = 273.1$ K | $P_2 = 760$ torr | $n_2$ |

$$V_2 = 627 \text{ ml} \times \frac{273.1}{305.1} \times \frac{716}{760} = 529 \text{ ml}$$

29. What volume of $SO_2$ at 343°C and 1.21 atm is produced by the combustion of 1.83 kg of sulfur?

**Solution**

$$\begin{array}{ccc} 1830 \text{ g} & & x \text{ g} \\ S & + \ O_2 \ \longrightarrow & SO_2 \\ 32 \text{ g/mole} & & 64 \text{ g/mole} \end{array}$$

First determine the moles of $SO_2$ produced:

$$\text{Moles } SO_2 = 1830 \text{ g S} \times \frac{1 \text{ mol}}{32.1 \text{ g}} \times \frac{1 \text{ mol } SO_2}{1 \text{ mol } S} = 57.0 \text{ mol}$$

Then, from $PV = nRT$, $V = nRT/P$:

$$V = \frac{(57.0)\,(0.08205)\,(616.1)}{1.21} = 2.38 \times 10^3 \text{ } \ell$$

35. (a) What is the total volume of $CO_2\,(g)$ and $H_2O(g)$ at 600°C and 735 torr produced by the combustion of 1.00 $\ell$ of $C_3H_8\,(g)$ measured at STP?

(b) What is the partial pressure of $CO_2$ in the product gases?

**Solution**

(a) First write the balanced equation.

$$C_3H_8\,(g) + 5O_2\,(g) \longrightarrow 3CO_2\,(g) + 4H_2O(g)$$

One liter of $C_3H_8$ will produce 7.00 liters of gas measured at STP. Under the conditions given,

| | | |
|---|---|---|
| $V_1 = 7.00 \text{ } \ell$ | $T_1 = 273$ K | $P_1 = 760$ torr |
| $V_2 = ?$ | $T_2 = 873$ K | $P_2 = 735$ torr |

81

$$V_2 = 7.00 \; \ell \times \frac{873}{273} \times \frac{760}{735} = 23.1 \; \ell$$

(b) The pressure of the two gases is proportioned in direct ratio to the mole ratio of gases present as determined from the coefficients; therefore,

$$\text{Pressure of } CO_2 = 735 \text{ torr} \left(\frac{3}{3+4}\right) = 315 \text{ torr}$$

37. How many grams of gas are present in each of the following?

(a) $0.100 \; \ell$ of NO at 703 torr and 62°C.

**Solution**

Use the Ideal Gas Law with MW NO = 30.0

$$PV = \frac{g}{MW} RT; \qquad \text{no. g} = \frac{(MW)PV}{RT}$$

$$\text{Mass NO} = \frac{\left(30 \dfrac{g}{mol}\right)\left(\dfrac{703}{760} \text{ atm}\right)(0.100 \; \ell)}{(0.08205 \; \ell \text{ atm/mol K}) (335 \text{ K})} = 0.101 \text{ g}$$

38. (a) What is the concentration of the atmosphere in molecules per milliliter at STP?

**Solution**

Using 3 significant figures, the number of moles of gas present in 1 ml at STP can be found from the Ideal Gas Law.

$$0.00100 \; \ell = 1.00 \text{ ml.}$$

$$PV = nRT; \qquad n = \frac{PV}{RT} = \frac{(1.00 \text{ atm}) (0.00100 \; \ell)}{(0.08205) (273)}$$

$$n = 4.47 \times 10^{-5} \text{ mol/ml}$$

$$\text{No.}\left(\frac{\text{molecules}}{\text{ml}}\right) = 4.47 \times 10^{-5} \frac{\text{mol}}{\text{ml}} \times 6.022 \times 10^{23} \frac{\text{molecules}}{\text{mol}} = 2.69 \times 10^{19}$$

41. (a) When two cotton plugs, one moistened with ammonia and the other with hydrochloric acid, are simultaneously inserted into opposite ends of a glass tube 87.0 cm long, a white ring of $NH_4Cl$ forms where gaseous $NH_3$ and gaseous HCl first come into contact $[NH_3(g) + HCl(g) \longrightarrow NH_4Cl(s)]$. At what distance from the ammonia-moistened plug does this occur?

**Solution**

The ring forms when an equal number of molecules of the two gases meet as controlled by the rate of diffusion. Since the rate of gas diffusion is inversely proportional to $\sqrt{MW}$, we write

$$\frac{\text{Rate NH}_3}{\text{rate HCl}} = \frac{\sqrt{\text{MW HCl}}}{\sqrt{\text{MW NH}_3}} = \frac{\sqrt{36.5}}{\sqrt{17.0}} = 1.465$$

The ammonia diffuses 1.465 times as fast as the hydrogen chloride. Therefore equal amounts meet in the tube at the fraction of distance, 1.465/2.465, covered by the ammonia. Thus

$$\text{Distance} = \frac{1.465}{2.465} \times 87.0 \text{ cm} = 51.7 \text{ cm}$$

Interestingly, after the initial formation of the white ring, additional rings will form on both sides of the original ring. This is one example of Liesegang phenomena; similar behavior is known in hundreds of other systems.

46. What is the molecular weight of methylamine if 0.157 g of methylamine occupies 125 ml with a pressure of 99,500 Pa at 22°C?

**Solution**

$$PV = nRT \qquad PV = \frac{g}{MW} RT$$

$$MW = \frac{g\,RT}{PV} = \frac{(0.157 \text{ g}) (8314 \text{ } \ell \text{ Pa/mol K}) (295 \text{ K})}{(99,500 \text{ Pa}) (0.125 \text{ } \ell)}$$

$$= 31.0 \text{ g/mol}$$

47. The density of a gaseous compound containing 45.4% bromine and 54.5% fluorine is 6.13 g/$\ell$ at 75°C and 1.00 atm. What is the molecular formula of the compound?

**Solution**

The mass per mole of bromine and of fluorine in the compound can be found by calculating the density of the unknown at STP and multiplying by 22.4 $\ell$/mol. The simplest formula of the compound is determined in the usual way. In this system, the pressure is standard but the temperature decreases from 348° to 273°. The density of the gas increases with a decrease in temperature. At STP,

$$D = 6.13 \text{ g/}\ell \times \frac{348}{273} = 7.81 \text{ g/}\ell$$

One mole is 7.81 g/ℓ × 22.4 = 174.9 g. Of this, 174.9 g × 45.4% = 79.4 g Br and 174.9 g × 54.5% = 95.3 g F.

$$\text{Br}: \quad \frac{79.4}{79.9} = 0.994 \qquad \text{F}: \quad \frac{95.3}{19.0} = 5.02$$

Therefore the molecular formula is $BrF_5$.

49. Thin films of amorphous silicon for electronic applications are prepared by decomposing silane gas, $SiH_4$, on a hot surface at low pressures.

$$SiH_4\,(g) \xrightarrow{\Delta} Si(s) + 2H_2\,(g)$$

What volume of $SiH_4$ at 130 Pa and 800 K is required to produce a 10.0 cm by 10.0 cm film which is 200 Å thick (1 Å = $10^{-8}$ cm)? The density of amorphous silicon is 1.9 g/cm³.

**Solution**

First find the number of grams of Si needed. The volume is given by

$$\text{Vol Si} = 10 \text{ cm} \times 10 \text{ cm} \times 200 \times 10^{-8} \text{ cm} = 2 \times 10^{-4} \text{ cm}^3$$

The number of grams of Si needed is

$$\text{Mass Si} = 2 \times 10^{-4} \text{ cm}^3 \times 1.9 \text{ g/cm}^3 = 3.8 \times 10^{-4} \text{ g}$$

The mass of $SiH_4$ required to produce this mass of Si is

$$\text{Mass SiH}_4 = 3.8 \times 10^{-4} \text{ g} \times \frac{32.09 \text{ g/mol SiH}_4}{28.09 \text{ g/mol Si}}$$

$$= 4.34 \times 10^{-4} \text{ g}$$

The volume needed is determined from the Ideal Gas Law.

$$V = \frac{nRT}{P} = \frac{(4.34 \times 10^{-4} \text{ g}) (8314 \text{ ℓ Pa/mol K}) (800 \text{ K})}{(32.9 \text{ g/mol}) (130 \text{ Pa})}$$

$$= 0.69 \text{ ℓ}$$

55. Ethanol, $C_2H_5OH$, is often produced by the fermentation of sugars. For example, the preparation of ethanol from the sugar, glucose, is represented by the equation

$$C_6H_{12}O_6\,(aq) \xrightarrow{\text{yeast}} 2C_2H_5OH(aq) + 2CO_2\,(g).$$

What volume of $CO_2$ at STP is produced by the fermentation of 125 g of glucose if the fermentation has a yield of 97.5%?

**Solution**

One mole of glucose produces two moles of $CO_2$. The number of moles of glucose is 125 g/(180 g/mol) = 0.694 mol.

$$\text{No. moles } CO_2 \text{ produced} = 2(0.694 \text{ mol}) = 1.388 \text{ mol}$$

$$\text{Vol } CO_2 \text{ at STP} = 1.388 \text{ mol} \times \frac{22.4 \; \ell}{\text{mol}} \times \frac{97.5\%}{100\%} = 30.3 \; \ell$$

57. One method for the determination of amino acids is the van Slyke method. The characteristic amino groups $(-NH_2)$ in protein material are allowed to react with nitrous acid $(HNO_2)$ to form $N_2$ gas. From the volume of the gas, the amount of amino acid can be determined. A 0.0604-g sample of a biological material containing glycine, $CH_2(NH_2)COOH$, was analyzed by the van Slyke method, giving 3.70 ml of $N_2$ collected over water at a pressure of 735 torr and 29°C. What was the percentage of glycine in the sample?

$$CH_2(NH_2)COOH + HNO_2 \longrightarrow CH_2(OH)COOH + H_2O + N_2$$

**Solution**

$$\text{Pressure of } N_2 = 735 \text{ torr} - 30.0 \text{ torr} (H_2O)$$

$$= 705 \text{ torr}$$

From the Ideal Gas Law the amount of $N_2$ present is

$$n = \frac{PV}{RT} = \frac{\left(\frac{705}{760}\right)(0.00370)}{(0.08205)(302)} = 0.0001385 \text{ mol}$$

From the balanced equation, one mole of glycine produces one mole of $N_2$. Therefore 0.0001385 mol of glycine is present. The molecular weight of glycine is 75.0 g/mol. Thus

$$\text{Mass glycine} = 75.0 \text{ g/mol} \times 0.0001385 \text{ mol}$$

$$= 0.01039 \text{ g}$$

$$\% \text{ glycine} = \frac{0.01039 \text{ g}}{0.0604 \text{ g}} \times 100 = 17.2\%$$

60. A sample of a compound of xenon and fluorine was confined in a bulb with a pressure of 24 torr. Hydrogen was added to the bulb until the pressure was 96 torr. Passage of an electric spark through the mixture produced Xe and HF. After the HF was removed by reaction with solid KOH, the final pressure of xenon and unreacted hydrogen in the bulb was 48 torr. What is the molecular formula of the xenon fluoride in the original sample? *Note:* Xenon fluorides contain only one xenon atom per molecule.

**Solution**

The reaction of hydrogen with the unknown xenon compound, assuming constant temperature, is

$$XeF_y + \frac{y}{2}H_2 \longrightarrow Xe + yHF$$

where

$$H_2 + 2F \longrightarrow 2HF$$

The pressure in the vessel due to the gaseous $XeF_y$ is 24 torr. After the addition of hydrogen, the pressure in the vessel rises to 96 torr.

$$P_{Total} = 96 \text{ torr} = P_{XeF_y} + P_{H_2}$$

$$P_{H_2} = 96 \text{ torr} - 24 \text{ torr} = 72 \text{ torr}$$

After the reaction the vessel contained a mixture of xenon and hydrogen at a total pressure of 48 torr. But the pressure due to xenon must equal 24 torr since each mole of $XeF_y$ contains one mole of Xe. The hydrogen consumed by the production of HF is 72 torr − 24 torr = 48 torr. Since the pressure exerted by a gas is proportional to the number of moles of gas, the mole ratio between reacting substances is equivalent to the ratio of pressures. In this case, the reaction of $XeF_y$ with $H_2$ can be interpreted as

$$XeF_y : H_2$$
24 torr : 48 torr

or

1 mole : 2 moles

A molecule of $XeF_y$, therefore, must contain four atoms of fluorine, $y = 4$, to react with two molecules of hydrogen, hence $XeF_4$.

## RELATED PROBLEMS

1. The van der Waals equation is just one of many equations that describes the nonideal behavior of gases. Compare the pressure of one mole of $SO_2$ contained in a 5.0-ℓ flask maintained at 500 K as given by the Ideal Gas Law and by the van der Waals equation. For $SO_2$, the constant $a$ is 6.71 $ℓ^2$ atm/mol$^2$ and the constant $b$ is 0.0564 ℓ.

*Answer: From ideal gas: 8.20 atm;*
*from van der Waal's equation: 8.02 atm*

2. Water vapor behaves as a gas, and its volume can be calculated from the Ideal Gas Law. Compare the value obtained for the molar volume of water using the Ideal Gas Law with that obtained from the experimental density of 0.0005970 g ml$^{-1}$ both under the condition of 100°C and 1 atm.

*Answer: V (observed) = 30.18 ℓ*
*V (ideal) = 30.60 ℓ*

3. In the early study of air composition, Ramsey in 1894 separated water vapor, nitrogen, oxygen and carbon dioxide from air by absorption processes. Lord Rayleigh separated these gases by a different process.

Both men were left with a small amount of gas with a density of 1.63 g/ℓ at 25°C and 1 atm. What element had they discovered?

*Answer: Argon*

4. A popular method for preparing oxygen is the decomposition of $KClO_3$ and collection of the gas over water. If 36.5 ml of $O_2$ is collected over water at 25°C at a barometric pressure of 751 torr, what volume would the dry oxygen occupy at 0°C at the same pressure?

*Answer: 32.4 ml*

5. Calculate the volume of a balloon necessary to lift 100 kg at 25°C and 1 atm if the balloon is filled with helium. Assume that the composition of air is 80% nitrogen and 20% oxygen at the temperature and pressure given.

*Answer: 84,750 ℓ*

# Chapter II: The Liquid and Solid States

## INTRODUCTION

The subject of this chapter includes various aspects of the liquid and solid states of matter. In our daily experience we encounter three states: solid, liquid, and gas. We see solids in many forms such as salts, metals, ice, and stones. Similarly we see liquids of various types in the form of greases, syrups, water, alcohol, and even the metal mercury. We also experience the effect of gases, although most, like air, are invisible. (Smokestack and other exhaust plumes are often visible, but this is because the plumes consist of dispersions of particulate matter in air rather than gas.) However, some gases are colored, such as chlorine, and are visible if they are present in sufficient concentration.

Different states of aggregation are possible for a substance; these states are called *phases* (from a Greek word meaning *appearance*). The term phase is used in chemistry to indicate a homogeneous region, all parts of which are the same. Water is probably the most familiar example of a substance that may exist in several different forms, existing under certain conditions as solid ice, liquid water, or gaseous water vapor. Ice is the solid phase, liquid water is the liquid phase, and water vapor is the gas phase.

Further variation in forms or phases characterizes certain solids, depending upon the controlled condition imposed on them. For example, carbon appears as two different phases, diamond and graphite.

Typically, a change in temperature will cause a change in phase or state. A familiar example is provided by adding heat to solid ice: The temperature rises and ice experiences a phase change as it is converted to liquid water.

Liquids have properties that are intermediate between those of the solids and gases; they are the molten or fluid form of substances. As a substance is transformed from a solid to a liquid, the rigid lattice structure of the solid is lost. Some structure does exist in liquids, but the structure becomes fluid in the sense that structures are continually forming and dispersing, whereas in the gaseous state all structure is lost. All liquids have an ability to flow because of the continual shifting of internal structure, although some, such as glass, molten polymers, long-chain hydrocarbons, and proteins, tend to flow very slowly or not at all.

The purpose of this chapter is to examine some of the regular structural forms exhibited in solids, some of the reasons why these forms exist, and the energies associated with transformations among liquids, solids, and gases.

## FORMULAS AND DEFINITIONS

**Energy and change of state** The transformation of a substance from one phase or state to another involves a change in the total energy of the substance. Depending on the direction of the phase change, energy is either absorbed or released by the substance during the change. The diagram represents the possible types of transformations a substance may undergo.

$$\text{Solid} \underset{\text{energy} -}{\overset{+\ \text{energy}}{\rightleftarrows}} \text{Liquid} \underset{\text{energy} -}{\overset{+\ \text{energy}}{\rightleftarrows}} \text{Gas}$$

The processes indicated in the diagram are reversible, that is, the energy absorbed in each forward process equals the energy released in the reverse process. The temperature of the substance remains constant during a phase change. The energies associated with these changes at the melting point and boiling point are heat of fusion and heat of vaporization.

**Heat of fusion** The quantity of heat required to transform a substance, at its melting point, from a solid to a liquid. The heat of fusion of water is 333.5 joules per gram, or about 80 calories per gram.

**Heat of vaporization** The quantity of heat required to transform a substance, at its boiling point, from a liquid to a gas. The heat of vaporization of water, at $100°C$, is 2259 joules per gram, or about 540 calories per gram.

**Born-Haber cycle** A thermodynamic cycle that allows the calculation of the heat of a process otherwise difficult to measure. Only rarely can the energy associated with the lattice structure of a crystalline substance be measured directly. Instead we must rely on a basic thermochemical law, which, stated simply, means that the energy associated with the final state of a substance is the same regardless of the pathway or steps used to reach that state. The Born-Haber cycle is an application of this principle in that the formation of a crystalline substance can be analyzed into several independent steps. Because of the vast amount of thermochemical data available in the literature, the necessary steps for completion of the cycle can frequently be written even though data are not available for each step. Thus the otherwise unknown thermochemical step may be resolved.

**Radius ratio ($r^+/r^-$)**  The radius ratio is computed for a compound by dividing the radius of the cation (positive ion) by the radius of the anion (negative ion). Based on empirical data, the ratio is useful for predicting the structural geometry of a crystalline substance.

**Bragg equation**  X-ray techniques are used to determine crystal patterns caused by the location of atoms in crystalline substances. The equation $\lambda = 2d \sin \theta$, developed by Bragg, relates the wavelength $\lambda$ of reflected x rays to the product of the distance between atomic planes $d$ in a crystal times the sine of the angle $\theta$ of the reflected x rays.

**Pythagorean theorem**  This theorem relates the hypotenuse of a right triangle to the other two sides; the square of the hypotenuse equals the sum of the squares of the other two sides.

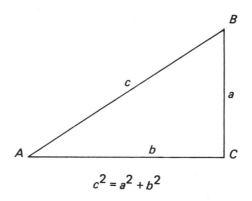

$$c^2 = a^2 + b^2$$

## PROBLEMS

*Note:*  In problems 1-11, the following data for water will be useful.

| | |
|---|---|
| Heat of vaporization of water (100°C) | 2259 J/g |
| Heat of vaporization of water (25°C) | 2443 J/g |
| Heat of fusion of water (0°C) | 333.5 J/g |
| Specific heat of water (solid) | 2.0 J/g °C |
| Specific heat of water (liquid) | 4.18 J/g °C |
| Specific heat of water (gas) | 2.00 J/g °C |

1.  In hot, dry climates water is cooled by allowing some of it to evaporate slowly.  How much water must be evaporated from a system to cool

1.00 kg of water from 37°C to 21°C? Assume that the heat of vaporization of water is constant between 21° and 37° and is equal to the value at 25°C.

### Solution

Cooling 1.00 kg of water from 37°C to 21°C requires the removal of heat as calculated from the relationship

Heat = mass × sp ht × temp change

$$= M \times C \times \Delta t$$

$$= \left(1.00 \text{ kg} \times \frac{1000 \text{ g}}{\text{kg}}\right) \left(\frac{4.18 \text{ J}}{\text{g} \,^\circ \text{C}}\right) (37^\circ - 21^\circ) = 6.7 \times 10^4 \text{ J}$$

Cooling systems of this type involve the loss of water to the surroundings. They are commonly used for large cooling systems needed for electrical generating plants, hospitals, hotels, etc. The amount of heat lost from the system during the evaporation process is given by the equation

Heat = mass × heat of vaporization

Substituting for the amount of heat found above, the mass of water to be evaporated equals

$$\text{Mass H}_2\text{O} = \frac{6.7 \times 10^4 \text{ J}}{2443 \text{ J/g}} = 27 \text{ g}$$

3. How much heat is produced when 75 g of steam at 135°C is converted to ice at −40°C?

### Solution

The transformation of water from steam (135°C) to ice (−40°C) involves phase changes and temperature changes within the phases as shown in the following sequence:

$$\text{H}_2\text{O}(g) \, (135^\circ) \xrightarrow{1} \text{H}_2\text{O}(g) \, (100^\circ) \xrightarrow{2} \text{H}_2\text{O}(l) \, (100^\circ) \xrightarrow{3} \text{H}_2\text{O}(l) \, (0^\circ)$$

$$\xrightarrow{4} \text{H}_2\text{O}(s) \, (0^\circ) \xrightarrow{5} \text{H}_2\text{O}(s) \, (-40^\circ)$$

The amount of heat associated with each step is calculated through application of an expression that relates heat to the specific heat of a substance (heat = $MC \, \Delta t$) or to the heat required for a phase change [heat = (mass) (heat of either fusion or vaporization)].

$$\text{H}_2\text{O}(g) \, (135^\circ) \longrightarrow \text{H}_2\text{O}(g) \, (100^\circ)$$

$$\text{heat} = (75 \text{ g}) \left(\frac{2.00 \text{ J}}{\text{g} \,^\circ \text{C}}\right) (35^\circ \text{C}) = 5250 \text{ J}$$

$$H_2O(g)\,(100°) \longrightarrow H_2O(l)\,(100°)$$

$$\text{heat} = (75\text{ g})\left(2259\,\frac{J}{g}\right) = 169{,}425\text{ J}$$

$$H_2O(l)\,(100°) \longrightarrow H_2O(l)\,(0°)$$

$$\text{heat} = (75\text{ g})\left(\frac{4.18\text{ J}}{g\,°C}\right)(100°) = 31{,}350\text{ J}$$

$$H_2O(l)\,(0°) \longrightarrow H_2O(s)\,(0°)$$

$$\text{heat} = (75\text{ g})\left(333.5\,\frac{J}{g}\right) = 25{,}013\text{ J}$$

$$H_2O(s)\,(0°) \longrightarrow H_2O(s)\,(-40°)$$

$$\text{heat} = (75\text{ g})\left(\frac{2.0\text{ J}}{g\,°C}\right)(40°C) = 6000\text{ J}$$

$$\text{Total } 237{,}038\text{ J}$$

The heat released to the surroundings during the transformation is the sum of the individual steps. Since two significant figures are allowed, the total heat is 240,000 J or 240 kJ.

It is important to recognize that the temperature of a substance does not change during a phase change; for example, water boiling at 100°C continues to boil at 100°C throughout the evaporation process. But temperature changes do accompany either the addition or the removal of heat from a substance remaining in a particular phase.

5. The specific heat of copper is 0.0931 cal/g K. What mass of steam at 100°C must be converted to water at 100°C to raise the temperature of a 1.00 × 10² g copper block from 20°C to 100°C?

**Solution**

During the process the heat released by the transformation of $H_2O(g)$ (100°) to $H_2O(l)$ (100°) is transferred to the copper.

$$\text{Heat lost from steam} = \text{heat gained by copper}$$

The heat needed to raise the temperature of the copper block is

$$\text{Heat} = MC\,\Delta t$$

Convert $C$ in cal/g °C to J/g °C:

$$C = 0.0931\,\frac{\text{cal}}{g\,°C} \times \frac{4.18\text{ J}}{\text{cal}} = 0.389\text{ J/g}\,°C$$

$$\text{Heat} = 1.00 \times 10^2\text{ g} \times \frac{0.389\text{ J}}{g\,°C} \times 80°C = 3.11 \times 10^3\text{ J}$$

The mass of steam required to produce this amount of heat is

$$\text{Heat} = \text{mass} \times 2259 \text{ J/g}$$

$$\text{Mass steam} = 3.11 \times 10^3 \text{ J} \times \frac{1 \text{ g}}{2259 \text{ J}} = 1.38 \text{ g}$$

8. During the fermentation step in the production of beer, $4.5 \times 10^6$ kcal of heat are evolved per 1000 gal of beer produced. How many liters of cooling water are required to maintain the optimum fermentation temperature of $58°F$ for 1000 gal of beer? The cooling water enters with a temperature of $5°C$ and is discharged with a temperature of $13°C$.

**Solution**

The heat produced by the fermentation process is transferred to the cooling water. We must determine how much cooling water is required to absorb the heat from the $8°C$ temperature rise. Since the heat to be removed is expressed in kcal and the constants are expressed in joules, convert to joules:

$$\text{Heat in J} = 4.5 \times 10^6 \text{ kcal} \times \frac{4.184 \times 10^3 \text{ J}}{\text{kcal}} = 1.88 \times 10^{10} \text{ J}$$

$$= 1.88 \times 10^7 \text{ kJ}$$

$$C = \frac{4.184 \text{ J}}{\text{g} °C} = \frac{4.184 \text{ kJ}}{\text{kg} °C}$$

The mass of cooling water required may be determined from

$$\text{Heat} = MC \, \Delta t$$

$$\text{Mass H}_2\text{O} = \frac{\text{heat}}{C \, \Delta t} = \frac{1.88 \times 10^7 \text{ kJ}}{\dfrac{4.184 \text{ kJ}}{\text{kg} °C} \times 8°C} = 6 \times 10^5 \text{ kg}$$

By assuming that the density of water is 1.0 kg/liter, the volume of water required is calculated from $V = M/D$, or

$$V = 6 \times 10^5 \text{ kg} \times \frac{1.0 \text{ } \ell}{1.0 \text{ kg}} = 6 \times 10^5 \text{ } \ell$$

and

$$V = 6 \times 10^5 \text{ } \ell \times \frac{1 \text{ gal}}{3.785 \text{ } \ell} = 2 \times 10^5 \text{ gal} \quad \text{(1 significant figure)}$$

9. A river is 30 ft wide and has an average depth of 5 ft and a current of 2 mi/hr. A power plant dissipates $2.1 \times 10^5$ kJ of waste heat into the river every second. What is the temperature difference between the water upstream and downstream from the plant?

**Solution**

The amount of heat transferred to the river is known, $2.1 \times 10^5$ kJ, but the amount of water that is to absorb this heat must be calculated from the data. To calculate the volume of water flowing past the point of discharge, assume that the volume equals that of a rectangular container having dimensions of

$$\text{Width} = 30 \text{ ft} \times \frac{12 \text{ in.}}{\text{ft}} \times 2.54 \frac{\text{cm}}{\text{in.}} = 914.4 \text{ cm}$$

$$\text{Depth} = 5 \text{ ft} \times \frac{12 \text{ in.}}{\text{ft}} \times 2.54 \frac{\text{cm}}{\text{in.}} = 152.4 \text{ cm}$$

Length = distance traveled at 2 mi/hr in 1 sec

$$= 2 \frac{\text{mi}}{\text{hr}} \times 5280 \frac{\text{ft}}{\text{mi}} \times 12 \frac{\text{in.}}{\text{ft}} \times 2.54 \frac{\text{cm}}{\text{in.}} \times \frac{1 \text{ hr}}{3600 \text{ sec}} = 89.5 \text{ cm}$$

$$\text{Vol } H_2O = (914.4 \text{ cm})(152.4 \text{ cm})(89.4 \text{ cm}) = 1.2 \times 10^7 \text{ cm}^3$$

Assume that the density of river water is $1.0 \text{ g/cm}^3$.

$$\text{Mass } H_2O = 1.2 \times 10^7 \text{ g} = 1.2 \times 10^4 \text{ kg}$$

Express the heat released in terms of the mass of water, the specific heat, and the temperature change. From

$$\text{Heat} = MC \, \Delta t$$

$$\Delta t = \frac{\text{heat}}{MC} = \frac{2.1 \times 10^5 \text{ kJ}}{1.2 \times 10^4 \text{ kg} \times 4.184 \text{ kJ/kg}} = 4°C \quad \text{(1 significant figure)}$$

12. Silver crystallizes in a face-centered cubic unit cell with a silver atom on each lattice point. (a) If the unit cell dimension is 4.0862 Å, what is the radius of silver? (b) Calculate the density of silver.

**Solution**

(a) A face-centered cubic unit cell has the metal atoms in contact across the diagonal of the face.

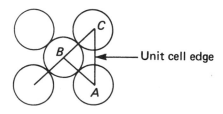

The unit cell edge length is the distance across the face along the edge,

4.0862 Å. The angle $ABC$ is a right angle with $\overline{AB} = \overline{BC} = 2$ (silver radius). Use the Pythagorean theorem to calculate the length of $\overline{AB}$. In a right triangle the square of the hypotenuse equals the sum of squares of the other two sides:

$$c^2 = a^2 + b^2$$

In the case of the line in question;

$$(\overline{AB})^2 + (\overline{BC})^2 = (4.0862)^2$$

or

$$2(\overline{AB})^2 = 16.697$$
$$(\overline{AB})^2 = 8.3485$$
$$\overline{AB} = 2.8894$$
$$\text{Radius Ag atom} = 2.8894/2 = 1.4447 \text{ Å}$$

(b) The density of silver is calculated from its atomic weight and the volume occupied by a mole of silver atoms. The volume of one mole of atoms may be found from the unit cell dimensions. A face-centered unit cell contains four atoms and has a volume of

$$\text{Vol unit cell} = (4.0862 \text{ Å})^3 = (4.0862 \times 10^{-8} \text{ cm})^3$$
$$= 6.8227 \times 10^{-23} \text{ cm}^3$$

$$\text{Vol mole of Ag atoms} = \frac{6.022 \times 10^{23} \text{ atoms}}{\text{mole}} \times \frac{6.8227 \times 10^{-23} \text{ cm}^3}{4 \text{ atoms}}$$

$$= 10.272 \frac{\text{cm}^3}{\text{mole}}$$

$$\text{Density Ag} = \frac{107.87 \text{ g}}{10.272 \text{ cm}^3} = 10.50 \text{ g/cm}^3$$

13. One form of tungsten crystallizes in a body-centered cubic unit cell with one tungsten atom on each lattice point. If the unit cell edge is 3.165 Å , what is the atomic radius of tungsten in this structure?

**Solution**

In a body-centered cubic unit cell, the metal atoms are in contact along the diagonal of the cube. The diagonal of the cube forms a right triangle with the unit cell edge and the diagonal of a face.

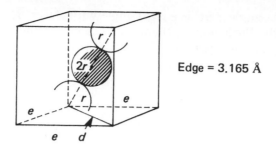

Edge = 3.165 Å

Use the Pythagorean theorem to determine the length of the diagonal, $d$, on the face of the cube in terms of $e$.

$$d^2 = e^2 + e^2 = 2e^2$$

$$d = \sqrt{2}\,e$$

The diagonal of the cube is the length of four atomic radii and can be calculated by again using the Pythagorean theorem.

$$(\text{diagonal})^2 = (4r)^2 = \left(\sqrt{2}\,e\right)^2 + e^2$$

$$= 16r^2 = 3e^2$$

$$\text{diagonal} = 4r = \sqrt{3}\,e \longrightarrow r = \frac{\sqrt{3}}{4}\,e = \frac{\sqrt{3}}{4}(3.165\ \text{Å})$$

$$r = 1.370\ \text{Å}$$

14. The atomic radius of lead is 1.75 Å . If lead crystallizes in a face-centered cubic unit cell with the nearest neighbors in contact, what is the length of the unit cell edge?

**Solution**

In a face-centered cubic cell, the nearest neighbors are in contact across the diagonal $d$ of the face. The length of the diagonal, four radii, is the hypotenuse of the right triangle formed by the edges of the unit cell as shown in the figure.

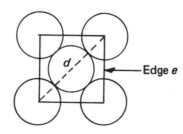

Edge $e$

Calculate the edge length by using the Pythagorean theorem as follows:

$$\text{diagonal}^2 = [4(\text{atomic radius})]^2 = e^2 + e^2$$
$$= [4(1.75 \text{ Å})]^2 = 2e^2$$
$$= (49.0 \text{ Å}) = 2e^2 \qquad (24.5 \text{ Å}) = e^2$$
$$e = \sqrt{24.5 \text{ Å}} = 4.95 \text{ Å}$$

16. LiH crystallizes with the same crystal structure as NaCl. The cubic unit cell dimension of LiH is 4.08 Å. Assuming anion-anion contact, calculate the ionic radius of $H^-$.

**Solution**

The structure is a face-centered cubic with the anions in contact across the diagonal $d$ of the face as shown in the figure.

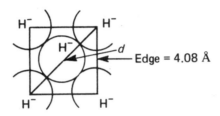

Use the Pythagorean theorem to calculate the length of the diagonal given an edge length of 4.08 Å.

$$d = \left(4r_{H^-}\right)^2 = (4.08 \text{ Å})^2 + (4.08 \text{ Å})^2$$
$$r_{H^-} = 1.44 \text{ Å}$$

21. The following compounds crystallize with either a NaCl, CsCl, ZnS, $CaF_2$, or $TiO_2$ type structure. From their radius ratios, predict the structure formed by each

(a) $CoF_2$      (c) $BaF_2$      (e) AlP
(b) ZnTe      (d) KBr      (f) CaS

**Solution**

The type of crystal structure formed by a compound depends on several factors, including radius ratio, type of close packing, atomic ratio, and lattice energies. Those structures listed here for comparison are common and have cations in either tetrahedral, octahedral, or cubic holes. To predict the structure of a compound, begin by calculating the radius ratio of the compound and identifying the type of close packing for the compound on the basis of data in Table 11-4. The structure of the compound will most likely be the same as that of the common structure, having similar radius and atomic ratios. For $CaF_2$, its radius ratio, 0.73, suggests either octahedral or cubic closest packing, but experimental evidence shows the $Ca^{2+}$ ions to be in cubic holes.

| Compound | $r^+/r^-$ | Type of hole | Structure |
|---|---|---|---|
| NaCl | $0.95/1.81 = 0.52$ | octahedral | NaCl |
| $C_3Cl$ | $1.69/1.81 = 0.93$ | cubic | CsCl |
| ZnS | $0.74/1.84 = 0.40$ | tetrahedral | ZnS |
| $CaF_2$ | $0.99/1.36 = 0.73$ | cubic | $CaF_2$ |
| $TiO_2$ | $0.64/1.40 = 0.46$ | octahedral | $TiO_2$ |
| (a) $*CoF_2$ | $0.72/1.36 = 0.53$ | octahedral | $TiO_2$ |
| (b) ZnTe | $0.74/2.21 = 0.33$ | tetrahedral | ZnS |
| (c) $BaF_2$ | $1.35/1.36 = 0.99$ | cubic | $CaF_2$ |
| (d) KBr | $1.33/1.95 = 0.68$ | octahedral | NaCl |
| (e) AlP | $0.50/2.12 = 0.24$ | tetrahedral | ZnS |
| (f) CaS | $0.99/1.84 = 0.54$ | octahedral | NaCl |

*Based on radius ratio only, the structure of $CoF_2$ could be either that of NaCl or $TiO_2$. The $TiO_2$ structure is chosen because of its equivalent coordination numbers and similar ionic sizes.

22. What x-ray wavelength would be diffracted at a first-order $\theta$ angle of $10.40°$ by planes with a spacing of 2.00 Å.

**Solution**

The Bragg equation is used to calculate the wavelength of the reflected x rays:

$$\lambda = 2d \sin \theta$$

given that $d$ is the distance between atomic planes, 2.00 Å, and the angle of reflection, $\theta$, is $10.40°$.

$$\lambda = 2(2.00 \text{ Å}) \sin 10.40°$$

$$= 4 \text{ Å} (0.1805) = 0.722 \text{ Å}$$

25. When an electron in an excited Mo atom falls from the L to the K shell, an x ray is emitted. These x rays are diffracted at an angle of $7.75°$ by planes with a separation of 2.64 Å. What is the difference in energy between the K and the L shell in molybdenum?

**Solution**

The energy of the x-ray photon can be calculated from its wavelength by using the equation $E = hc/\lambda$. Use the Bragg equation to calculate the wavelength.

$$\lambda = 2d \sin \theta = 2(2.64 \text{ Å}) \sin 7.75°$$

$$= 2(2.64 \text{ Å}) (0.1348) = 0.712 \text{ Å}$$

$$\lambda \text{ in cm} = 0.712 \text{ Å} \times \frac{10^{-8} \text{ cm}}{\text{Å}} = 7.12 \times 10^{-9} \text{ cm}$$

$$E_{L \to K} = \frac{hc}{\lambda} = \frac{(6.627 \times 10^{-34} \text{ J sec}) (2.998 \times 10^{10} \text{ cm/sec})}{7.12 \times 10^{-9} \text{ cm}}$$

$$= 2.79 \times 10^{-15} \text{ J}$$

$$= 1.74 \times 10^4 \text{ eV}$$

## RELATED PROBLEMS

1. Calculate the amount of ice at $0°C$ that could be melted by a 50.0-g block of iron that is at a temperature of $500.0°C$, assuming that the final temperature of the iron is $0°C$. The specific heat of iron is 0.448 J/g $°C$.
   *Answer: 0.672 g*

2. The waste heat from electric power generators could be used for home heating. Let's assume that the heat required for a three-bedroom home, depending on outdoor temperature, is 50,000 Btu per hour. The power generator discussed in Problem 9 must dissipate $2.1 \times 10^5$ kJ per second. By using the 50,000 Btu per hour as an average, calculate the number of homes that could be heated from the waste heat. (1 Btu = 252 cal.)
   *Answer: $1.4 \times 10^4$ homes*

3. Given that the atomic radius of chromium is 1.25 Å and it exists as a body-centered cubic lattice, calculate the length of its unit cell edge.
   *Answer: 2.88 Å*

4. Based on the information in Problem 3, calculate the density of chromium.
   *Answer: $7.2 \text{ g/cm}^3$*

5. Refer to the data in Problem 21 and predict the type of crystal structure for KCl.

# Chapter 13: Solutions; Colloids

## INTRODUCTION

Thus far in our treatment of chemistry we have discussed the nature of pure substances, and to some extent their interactions. The combination of two or more pure substances forms a *mixture*. Mixtures are very common in our surroundings and play very important roles in life processes.

In this chapter we consider a special kind of mixture called a *solution*. A solution is a mixture that has two or more components; one component, the *solvent*, serves to dissolve the other component, the *solute*. Usually the solvent is considered to be the substance in greater amount. Many solutions are quite familiar to us. A few of these are listed as specific cases and then generalized:

1. The juice of sorghum cane: solid (sugar) dissolved in liquid (water)
2. Stainless steel: solid (chromium) dissolved in solid (iron)
3. Air: gas (oxygen, carbon dioxide, and other gases) dissolved in gas (nitrogen)
4. Antifreeze solution: liquid (ethylene glycol) dissolved in liquid (water)

Since matter exists in the solid, liquid, and gaseous states, it is possible for substances to form nine different types of solutions, with each state serving as a solute or as a solvent.

Solutions are homogeneous mixtures; that is, the solute is distributed evenly throughout the solvent. Some substances mix with solvents and form suspensions but do not form solutions; examples include vinegar and oil as in salad dressings, butterfat in water as in homogenized milk, and dust particles in air. Whether or not a solute will form a solution with a solvent depends primarily on three factors. These are (1) the size of solute particles; (2) the capacity of the solvent to form strong bonds with the solute, thereby lowering the energy of the system; and (3) the tendency of the solute particles to form a more random distribution within the solvent, further lowering the energy of the system.

Several types of interactions among solute particles and solvent particles are possible in solution. For example, solvents composed of dipolar molecules dissolve ionic substances and other dipolar substances. Thus water, a dipolar substance, dissolves ionic compounds such as NaCl and KI as well as dipolar substances such as HCl and $HNO_3$. Conversely, solvents composed of nonpolar molecules dissolve nonpolar substances in which the intermolecular bonding in both solvent and solute is primarily van der Waals type. Examples of nonpolar solvent-nonpolar solute solutions include oil in gasoline and grease in dry-cleaning fluid. In general, solvents tend to dissolve solutes that share bonding types. This fact gives rise to an often quoted phrase, "like dissolves like."

The nature of solutions and their special properties, the way they are prepared, methods for describing solutions in terms of composition, and ways for separating solutions into their component parts are all treated in this chapter. In Chapters 2 and 3, we treated the use of solutions in reactions and, specifically, molarity as a unit of concentration. The problems in this chapter include a review of molarity and the use of other common units of concentration to show their utility in chemical processes.

## FORMULAS AND DEFINITIONS

**Solute and solvent**  A solution consists of two parts, a solute and the solvent it is dissolved in. The solute generally is the substance in smallest concentration in a solution. The solvent is the substance in the greatest amount in the solution. The solute may be solid, liquid, or gas; the solvent may be solid, liquid, or gas. Although a solid dissolved in a liquid usually comes to mind when we think of a solution, there are other possibilities; for example, solution combinations include sugar and water, iodine and alcohol, chromium and iron (stainless steel), water vapor and air, and grease and dry-cleaning solvent.

**Solution**  A solution is a special kind of mixture in which all of the particles are of ionic or molecular dimensions not exceeding about 10 Å. In addition, the solute particles are uniformly distributed throughout the solvent. This mixture is referred to as a *homogeneous* mixture, a solution. Solutions are distinguished from other types of mixtures primarily by properties arising from the small size of solute particles in a solution. The particles may be molecular, ionic, or atomic; they may form small clusters in solution, but usually will not exceed diameters of more than a few angstroms.

**Electrolytes**  Substances known as electrolytes dissolve in solvents to produce solutions that conduct electric current. Acids, bases, and salts that form ions in solutions are electrolytes. Other substances are considered electrolytes when, in either a molten or supercooled state, they conduct electricity. The conduction of electric current in aqueous solutions depends on the existence of ions. In molten or supercooled systems it depends on "free" electrons. Strong electrolytes are substances that form solutions that are good electrical conductors. Strong electrolytes are extensively ionized in solution. Some, like sodium chloride dissolved in water, are nearly 100% ionized:

$$NaCl(s) + H_2O(l) \xrightarrow{\sim 100\%} Na^+(aq) + Cl^-(aq)$$

Weak electrolytes are substances that form solutions that are poor electrical conductors. Only a small fraction of a weak electrolyte's particles are ionized in solution. Acetic acid in water is such a case:

$$CH_3COOH(l) + H_2O(l) \xrightarrow{1 \text{ to } 5\%} CH_3COO^-(aq) + H^+(aq)$$

**Per cent composition**  Concentration is often expressed in terms of a percentage because percentage depends only on the easily measured quantities mass and/or volume of the components of the solution. Per cent composition is commonly expressed in two ways.

1. The biological, medical, and allied health professions mostly use percentage in terms of mass or volume of solute to volume of solution. In the first instance, if the mass of the solute is used, we have
    *Mass—volume percent*

$$\% = \frac{\text{mass of solute in grams}}{100 \text{ ml solution}} \times 100\%$$

*Example*: A 5% solution of sodium chloride contains 5 g of NaCl in 100 ml of solution, or, 1000 ml contains 50 g of NaCl.

*Volume—volume percent*  If the volume of the solute is to be compared to the volume of the solution, we have

$$\% = \frac{\text{volume solute in milliliters}}{100 \text{ ml solution}} \times 100\%$$

*Example*: A 5% ethanol solution contains 5 ml of ethanol in 100 ml of solution; or, 1000 ml of this solution contains 50 ml of ethanol.

These percentage units are not readily adaptable to other units normally used in chemistry. They are therefore not commonly used in chemical calculations.

2. In some areas of chemistry, percentage is expressed as a ratio of the mass of solute to the mass of the solvent. Sometimes referred to as weight-weight percentage, this unit can be related to other concentration units including mole fraction and molality.

$$\% = \frac{\text{mass solute}}{\text{mass solution}} \times 100\%$$

*Example*: A 5% solution of sodium chloride in water contains 5 g of NaCl in 95 g $H_2O$. The ratio of NaCl to solution is 5 g : 100 g.

**Molarity**, $M$  A unit that expresses concentration as a ratio of moles of solute to the volume of solution expressed in liters.

$$\text{Molarity} = \frac{\text{no. moles solute}}{\text{volume of solution in liters}}$$

**Molality**, $m$  A unit that expresses the concentration of the solute as a ratio of moles of solute to the mass of solvent expressed in kilograms.

$$\text{Molality} = \frac{\text{no. moles of solute}}{\text{mass of solvent in kilograms}}$$

At first glance molarity and molality appear to be quite similar. A major difference in the two units is that molarity is defined in terms of the volume of solution while molality is defined in terms of the mass of solvent. The volume of a fixed quantity of a solution is temperature dependent, but the mass of solution is not. Molarity therefore varies with temperature, but molality does not.

**Mole fraction**  A unit that expresses the concentration of a component in a solution as a ratio of the number of its moles to the total number of moles of all components in that solution. The mole fraction of component A, $X_A$, in a solution containing components A through D, is

$$X_A = \frac{\text{no. moles of A}}{\text{total number of moles}} = \frac{n_A}{n_A + n_B + n_C + n_D}$$

Most solutions used in laboratories are composed of two or more components, with the mole fractions of their components calculated from the masses of the components used. Mole fractions can also be calculated from molalities and mass percentage.

**Raoult's Law**  The vapor pressure of a solution consisting of a nonvolatile solute in a volatile solvent is always lower than that of its pure solvent. Raoult's Law states that the vapor pressure of the solvent, $P_{solvent}$, in a dilute solution equals the mole fraction of the solvent, $X_{solvent}$, times the vapor pressure of the pure solvent, $P^\circ_{solvent}$.

$$P_{solvent} = X_{solvent} \, P^\circ_{solvent}$$

The implications of this expression are very great. Applied to the phenomenon of boiling, we find that the boiling point of a solution is always higher than that of its solvent. Furthermore, it is found that the elevation of the boiling point is proportional to the mole fraction of solute particles in solution.

**Boiling-point elevation–freezing-point depression**   The addition of a nonvolatile solute to a solvent to form a solution affects the boiling point and also the freezing point of the solvent. These values are changed by amounts proportional to the number of solute particles dissolved in solution. This proportionality is usually expressed in terms of the solution molality and the boiling-point elevation constant, $K_b$, or the freezing-point depression constant, $K_f$. Both $K_b$ and $K_f$ have specific values for each different solvent but are independent of the particular solute. The boiling-point elevation of a solvent is given by

$$\Delta bp = K_b m$$

and the freezing-point depression of a solvent is given by

$$\Delta fp = K_f m$$

For water, $K_b$ and $K_f$ are 0.512°C per molal and 1.86°C per molal, respectively. An aqueous solution containing a nonvolatile, nonelectrolyte solute at a one-molal concentration (a solute-to-water ratio of one mole of solute to 1 kg of water) would have its boiling point increased by

$$\Delta bp = \left(\frac{0.512°C}{m}\right)(1\ m) = 0.512°C$$

The new boiling point of the solution would be

$$bp = 100.000°C + 0.512°C = 100.512°C$$

This solution would have its freezing point lowered by

$$\Delta fp = \left(\frac{1.86°C}{m}\right)(1\ m) = 1.86°C$$

and its final freezing point would then be

$$fp = 0.00°C - 1.86°C = -1.86°C$$

**Molecular weight from boiling-point or freezing-point data**   Since the change in boiling point or freezing point is a function of the molality of the solution, the molecular weight of the solute can be determined by observing its effect on the boiling point or the freezing point of a solvent. The calculation using the freezing-point depression is as follows:

$$\Delta fp = K_f m = K_f \left(\frac{\text{no. moles solute}}{\text{mass of solvent in kg}}\right)$$

Since

$$\text{no. moles solute} = \frac{\text{mass solute}}{\text{MW}}$$

then

$$\Delta\text{fp} = K_f \left( \frac{\dfrac{\text{mass solute}}{\text{MW}}}{\text{mass solvent in kg}} \right)$$

Solving for MW gives

$$\text{MW} = \frac{(K_f)\,(\text{mass solute})}{(\Delta\text{fp})\,(\text{mass solvent in kg})}$$

A similar calculation using the change in boiling point leads to

$$\text{MW} = \frac{(K_b)\,(\text{mass solute})}{(\Delta\text{bp})\,(\text{mass solvent in kg})}$$

We suggest that you work through these derivations until you are comfortable with the equations rather than memorizing the formulas; the factors are easily misplaced in the formula.

**Ion activities**  When an electrolyte is the solute in a solution, the changes in boiling point and freezing point are related to the number of species in the solution. For solutions containing strong electrolytes, we find that the boiling points and freezing points are slightly different from the values calculated on the basis of the number of ions in the formula unit. These discrepancies occur mainly because of solute particle-particle interactions in solution. The actual change in boiling point or freezing point is a measure of the effective molality of the solution. We call this effective molality the activity of the ions. For example, the change in freezing point is given by

$$\Delta\text{fp(actual)} = K_f m_{\text{effective}} = K_f (\text{activity})$$

Simple rearranging of this equation gives

$$\text{Activity} = \frac{\Delta\text{fp(actual)}}{K_f}$$

The activities of ions in solution are related to their actual concentrations through an activity coefficient $f$:

$$\text{Activity} = f \times \text{molality}$$

Although in practice the situation is much more complicated than presented here, we may generalize that in solutions containing very weak electrolytes or nonelectrolytes, the activity coefficient is approximately 1.

## PROBLEMS

1. Calculate the number of moles and the mass of solute in each of the following solutions.

   (a)  1.20 $\ell$ of 1.30 $M$ $HClO_4$.
   (c)  15.0 ml of 0.1600 $M$ $MgCl_2$.

**Solution**

(a)  The definition for molarity

$$\text{Molarity} = \frac{\text{no. moles solute}}{\text{vol in } \ell}$$

leads to

$$\text{No. moles} = \text{molarity} \times \text{vol in } \ell$$

Substitution gives

$$\text{No. moles } HClO_4 = 1.30 \frac{\text{mol}}{\ell} \times 1.20 \ \ell = 1.56 \text{ mol}$$

$$\text{GFW } HClO_4 = 1.01 + 35.45 + 4(16.00) = 100.46 \text{ g}$$

$$\text{Mass } HClO_4 = 1.56 \text{ mol} \times 100.46 \frac{\text{g}}{\text{mol}} = 157 \text{ g}$$

(c)   $\text{No. moles } MgCl_2 = 0.1600 \frac{\text{mol}}{\ell} \times 15.0 \text{ ml} \times \frac{1 \ \ell}{1000 \text{ ml}}$

$$= 2.40 \times 10^{-3} \text{ mol}$$

$$\text{GFW } MgCl_2 = 24.31 + 2(35.45) = 95.21 \text{ g}$$

$$\text{Mass } MgCl_2 = (2.40 \times 10^{-3} \text{ mol}) \left( 95.21 \frac{\text{g}}{\text{mol}} \right) = 0.229 \text{ g}$$

2. Calculate the molarity of each of the following solutions:

   (a)  13.0 g of potassium hydroxide, KOH, in 5.0 $\ell$ of solution.
   (c)  0.0500 g of nitric acid, $HNO_3$, in 10.0 ml of solution.

**Solution**

(a)   $$\text{Molarity} = \frac{\text{no. moles solute}}{\text{vol in } \ell}$$

and

$$\text{No. moles} = \frac{\text{mass solute}}{\text{GFW}}$$

$$\text{GFW KOH} = 39.10 + 16.00 + 1.01 = 56.11 \text{ g}$$

Substitution of the right-hand equation above into the one on the left followed by substitution of numerical values yields

$$M = \frac{13.0 \text{ g KOH} \times \dfrac{1 \text{ mol}}{56.11 \text{ g}}}{5.0 \text{ } \ell} = 0.046 \text{ } M$$

(c)  Molarity $= \dfrac{\text{no. moles}}{\text{vol in } \ell}$

GFW $HNO_3 = 1.01 + 14.01 + 3(16.00) = 63.02$ g

$$\text{Molarity } HNO_3 = \frac{0.0500 \text{ g } HNO_3 \times \dfrac{1 \text{ mol}}{63.02 \text{ g}}}{0.0100 \text{ } \ell} = 0.0793 \text{ } M$$

3.  What mass of solute is present in each of the following solutions? The per cent concentration is by mass.

(a)  1.34 $\ell$ of 19.00% acetic acid, $CH_3 CO_2 H$ (density 1.0267 $g/cm^3$).
(d)  50.0 ml of 8.75% lactose, $C_{12} H_{22} O_{11}$ (specific gravity 1.0355).

**Solution**

(a)  % solution by mass $= \dfrac{\text{mass of solute}}{\text{mass of solution}} \times 100\%$

Calculate the mass of the solution using its volume and density as follows:

$$\text{Mass solution} = 1.34 \text{ } \ell \times 1000 \frac{\text{ml}}{\ell} \times 1.0267 \frac{\text{g}}{\text{ml}} = 1376 \text{ g}$$

Since the mass of solute is 19.00% of the solution mass, the mass of solute is

$$\text{Mass } CH_3 CO_2 H = \frac{19.00\%}{100\%} \times 1376 \text{ g} = 261 \text{ g}$$

(d)  As in (a) above, the mass of the solution is found as

$$\text{Mass solution} = 50.0 \text{ ml} \times 1.0355 \frac{\text{g}}{\text{ml}} = 51.78 \text{ g}$$

$$\text{Mass } C_{12} H_{22} O_{11} = \frac{8.75\%}{100\%} \times 51.78 \text{ g} = 4.53 \text{ g}$$

4.  Calculate the molality of each of the following solutions:

(a)  97.58 g of lead acetate, $Pb(CH_3 CO_2)_2$ in 1.000 kg of water.
(c)  0.372 g of histamine, $C_5 H_9 N$, in 125 g of chloroform, $CHCl_3$.

**Solution**

Molality is defined as

$$\text{Molality} = \frac{\text{no. moles solute}}{\text{no. kilograms solvent}}$$

(a) GFW $Pb(CH_3CO_2)_2 = 207.19 + 4(12.01) + 6(1.01) + 4(16.00)$

$$= 325.29 \text{ g}$$

$$\text{Molality } Pb(CH_3CO_2)_2 = \frac{97.58 \text{ g} \times \dfrac{1 \text{ mol}}{325.29 \text{ g}}}{1.000 \text{ kg } H_2O} = 0.3000 \, m$$

(c)   GFW $C_5H_9N = 5(12.01) + 9(1.01) + 14.01 = 83.15 \text{ g}$

$$\text{Molality } C_5H_9N = \frac{0.372 \text{ g} \times \dfrac{1 \text{ mol}}{83.15 \text{ g}}}{125 \text{ g} \times \dfrac{1 \text{ kg}}{1000 \text{ g}} \quad CHCl_3} = 0.0358 \, m$$

5. Calculate the mole fraction of solute and solvent in each of the solutions in Problem 4.

(a)  97.58 g of lead acetate, $Pb(CH_3CO_2)_2$ in 1.000 kg of water.
(b)  46.85 g of codeine, $C_{18}H_{21}NO_3$, in 125.5 g of ethanol, $C_2H_5OH$.

**Solution**

The mole fraction of substance $a$, $X_a$, in a solution system containing $i$ components is the number of moles of substance $a$, $n_a$, divided by the total number of moles of all substances in the solution.

$$X_a = \frac{n_a}{n_a + n_b + \cdots + n_i}$$

(a)  97.58 g of $Pb(CH_3CO_2)_2$ in 1.000 kg of water.

$$\text{No. moles } Pb(CH_3CO_2)_2 = 97.58 \text{ g} \times \frac{1 \text{ mol}}{325.29 \text{ g}} = 0.3000 \text{ mol}$$

$$\text{No. moles } H_2O = 1000 \text{ g} \times \frac{1 \text{ mol}}{18.015 \text{ g}} = 55.51 \text{ mol}$$

No. moles total = $(55.51 + 0.3000) \text{ mol} = 55.81 \text{ mol}$

$$X_{Pb(CH_3CO_2)_2} = \frac{0.3000 \text{ mol}}{55.81 \text{ mol}} = 5.375 \times 10^{-3}$$

$$X_{H_2O} = \frac{55.51 \text{ mol}}{55.81 \text{ mol}} = 0.9946$$

(b) 46.85 g of codeine, $C_{18}H_{21}NO_3$, in 125.5 g of ethanol, $C_2H_5OH$.

GFW $C_2H_5OH = 2(12.01) + 5(1.01) + 16.00 + 1.01 = 46.08$ g

GFW $C_{18}H_{21}NO_3 = 18(12.01) + 21(1.01) + 14.01 + 3(16.00)$
$$= 299.4 \text{ g}$$

$$n_{C_2H_5OH} = 125.5 \text{ g} \times \frac{1 \text{ mol}}{46.08 \text{ g}} = 2.724 \text{ mol}$$

$$n_{C_{18}H_{21}NO_3} = 46.85 \text{ g} \times \frac{1 \text{ mol}}{299.4 \text{ g}} = 0.1565 \text{ mol}$$

$$n_{total} = 2.8805 \text{ mol}$$

$$X_{C_2H_5OH} = \frac{n_{C_2H_5OH}}{n_{total}} = \frac{2.724 \text{ mol}}{2.8805 \text{ mol}} = 0.9457$$

$$X_{C_{18}H_{21}NO_3} = \frac{n_{C_{18}H_{21}NO_3}}{n_{total}} = \frac{0.1565 \text{ mol}}{2.8805 \text{ mol}} = 0.05433$$

6.  What mass of sulfuric acid (95% by mass) is needed to prepare 200.0 g of a 20.0% solution of the acid by mass?

**Solution**

The amount of sulfuric acid required for the solution is

$$\text{Mass } H_2SO_4 = \frac{20.0\%}{100\%} \times 200.0 \text{ g} = 40.0 \text{ g}$$

The concentrated solution contains 95% $H_2SO_4$ by mass; therefore, the amount of 95% $H_2SO_4$ required is

$$95\% \text{ (mass } H_2SO_4) = 0.95 \text{ (mass } H_2SO_4) = 40.0 \text{ g}$$

$$\text{mass } H_2SO_4 = \frac{40.0 \text{ g}}{0.95} = 42 \text{ g}$$

10. The hardness of water (hardness count) is usually expressed as parts per million (by mass) of $CaCO_3$, which is equivalent to milligrams of $CaCO_3$ per liter of water. What is the molar concentration of $Ca^{2+}$ ions in a water sample with a hardness count of 175?

**Solution**

The amount of $CaCO_3$ in this solution is 175 mg per liter of water. The molarity is

GFW $CaCO_3 = 100.1$ g

$$\text{Molarity } CaCO_3 = \frac{175 \text{ mg} \times \dfrac{1 \text{ g}}{1000 \text{ mg}} \times \dfrac{1 \text{ mol}}{100.1 \text{ g}}}{1.00 \text{ } \ell} = 1.75 \times 10^{-3} \text{ } M$$

14. How many liters of $NH_3$ (g) at 25°C and 1.46 atm is required to prepare 3.00 $\ell$ of a 2.50 $M$ solution of $NH_3$?

**Solution**

Calculate the number of moles of $NH_3$ required for the solution. Then calculate, by using the ideal gas equation, the number of moles of $NH_3$ per liter of gas at the stated conditions.

$$\text{No. moles } NH_3 = (3.00 \text{ } \ell)(2.50 \text{ } M) = 7.50 \text{ mol}$$

$$PV = nRT \quad \text{and} \quad \frac{n}{V} = \frac{P}{RT}$$

$$\frac{n_{NH_3}}{1.00 \text{ } \ell} = \frac{1.46 \text{ atm}}{0.0821 \dfrac{\ell \text{ atm}}{\text{mol °K}} \times 298\text{°K}} = 0.0597 \frac{\text{mol}}{\ell}$$

The volume of $NH_3$ required is

$$\text{Vol } NH_3 = 7.50 \text{ mol} \times \frac{1.00 \text{ } \ell}{0.0597 \text{ mol}} = 126 \text{ } \ell$$

17. Calculate the volume of sulfuric acid solution (specific gravity 1.070, and containing 10.00% $H_2SO_4$ by mass) that would contain 18.50 g of pure $H_2SO_4$, at a temperature of 25°.

**Solution**

Calculate the mass of $H_2SO_4$ per milliliter of solution.

$$\text{Mass } H_2SO_4 = \frac{10.00\%}{100\%} \times 1.070 \text{ g/ml} = 0.1070 \text{ g/ml}$$

The volume of solution that contains 18.50 g of $H_2SO_4$ is

$$\text{Vol } H_2SO_4 \text{ solution} = 18.50 \text{ g} \times \frac{1 \text{ ml}}{0.1070 \text{ g}} = 172.9 \text{ ml}$$

23. It is desired to produce 1.000 $\ell$ of 0.050 $M$ nitric acid by diluting 10.00 $M$ nitric acid. Calculate the volume of the concentrated acid and the volume of water required in the dilution.

**Solution**

This type of dilution is commonly practiced in the laboratory and is accomplished by recognizing that as an amount of concentrated solution (solute) is diluted with solvent to a new volume, the amount of solute is not changed by the dilution. The relationship between the concentrated solution and the diluted solution is given by

$$M_{conc} V_{conc} = M_{dil} V_{dil}$$

Other units of concentration can be used in the expression, but the units must be used consistently on both sides of the equation. Solve the equation for the unknown, substitute values into the equation, and solve.

$$V_{conc} = \frac{M_{dil} V_{dil}}{M_{conc}} = \frac{(0.050\ M)\ (1.000\ \ell)}{(10.00\ M)} = 0.0050\ \ell$$

This solution would be prepared by adding 5.0 ml of concd $HNO_3$ to a flask and diluting it to 1.000 $\ell$ by adding 995 ml of $H_2O$.

27. The sulfate in 50.0 ml of dilute sulfuric acid was precipitated using an excess of barium chloride. The mass of $BaSO_4$ formed was 0.482 g. Calculate the molarity of the sulfuric acid solution.

**Solution**

The equation for this reaction is

No. moles?           0.482 g

$$H_2 SO_4\ (aq) + BaCl_2\ (aq) \longrightarrow BaSO_4\ (s) + HCl(aq)$$

1 mol            1 mol

Calculate the number of moles of $H_2 SO_4$ required to produce 0.482 g of $BaSO_4$. This amount of $H_2 SO_4$ is contained in 50.0 ml of solution, hence, can be equated to molarity through the expression

No. moles = molarity $\times$ volume in $\ell$

The number of moles of $H_2 SO_4$ required is

GFW $BaSO_4$ = 137.3 + 32.1 + 4(16.0) = 233.4 g

$$\text{No. moles } H_2 SO_4 = \left(0.482 \text{ g } BaSO_4 \times \frac{1 \text{ mol}}{233.4 \text{ g}}\right)\left(\frac{1 \text{ mol } H_2 SO_4}{1 \text{ mol } BaSO_4}\right)$$

$$= 2.065 \times 10^{-3} \text{ mol}$$

Then

$$2.065 \times 10^{-3} \text{ mol} = (\text{molarity } H_2 SO_4) \left(50.0 \text{ ml} \times \frac{1\ \ell}{1000 \text{ ml}}\right)$$

$$\text{Molarity } H_2 SO_4 = \frac{2.065 \times 10^{-3} \text{ mol}}{0.050\ \ell} = 0.0413\ M$$

32. What volume of 0.100 $M$ HCl would be required to precipitate the silver in 0.634 g of 98.0% purity $AgNO_3$?

The reaction of $AgNO_3$ with HCl produces AgCl according to the equation

$$\underset{\text{1 mole}}{\underset{(0.98)\,(0.634\text{ g})}{AgNO_3\,(aq)}} + \underset{\text{1 mole}}{\underset{\text{No. moles?}}{HCl(aq)}} \longrightarrow AgCl(s) + HNO_3\,(aq)$$

Calculate the amount of $AgNO_3$ in the impure sample and then calculate the number of moles of HCl required for the reaction.

Mass $AgNO_3$ = 0.980 × 0.634 g = 0.6213 g

GFW $AgNO_3$ = 107.87 + 14.01 + 3(16.00) = 169.88 g

$$\text{No. moles HCl} = \left(0.6213 \text{ g} \times \frac{1 \text{ mol}}{169.88 \text{ g}}\right)\left(\frac{1 \text{ mol HCl}}{1 \text{ mol AgNO}_3}\right)$$

$$= 0.003657 \text{ mol}$$

The volume of HCl required is calculated from

No. moles HCl = molarity × volume in ℓ

$$V = \frac{\text{no. moles HCl}}{M} = \frac{0.003657 \text{ mol}}{0.100} = 0.0366 \,\ell = 36.6 \text{ ml}$$

34. A gaseous solution was found to contain 15% $H_2$, 10.0% CO, and 75% $CO_2$ by mass. What is the mole fraction of each component?

**Solution**

The mole fraction of each component is calculated from the definition of mole fraction as

$$X_{H_2} = \frac{n_{H_2}}{n_{total}}; \quad X_{CO} = \frac{n_{CO}}{n_{total}}; \quad X_{CO_2} = \frac{n_{CO_2}}{n_{total}}$$

For convenience, assume a sample mass of 1 gram and calculate the mass of each component in the sample—then the number of moles of each.

Mass $H_2$ = 0.15 × 1.00 g = 0.15 g

Mass CO = (0.100) (1.00 g) = 0.100 g

Mass $(CO_2)$ = (0.75) (1.00 g) = 0.75 g

$$n_{H_2} = 0.15 \text{ g} \times \frac{1 \text{ mol}}{2.016} = 0.0744$$

$$n_{CO} = 0.100 \text{ g} \times \frac{1 \text{ mol}}{28.01 \text{ g}} = 0.00357 \text{ mol}$$

$$n_{CO_2} = 0.75 \text{ g} \times \frac{1 \text{ mol}}{44.0 \text{ g}} = 0.0170 \text{ mol}$$

$$n_{total} = 0.0950 \text{ mol}$$

$$X_{H_2} = \frac{0.0744 \text{ mol}}{0.0950 \text{ mol}} = 0.78$$

$$X_{CO} = \frac{0.00357 \text{ mol}}{0.0950 \text{ mol}} = 0.038$$

$$X_{CO_2} = \frac{0.017 \text{ mol}}{0.0950 \text{ mol}} = 0.18$$

39. A 1.80-g sample of an acid, $H_2 X$, required 14.00 ml of KOH solution for neutralization of all the hydrogen ion. Exactly 14.2 ml of this same KOH solution was found to neutralize 10.0 ml of 0.750 $M$ $H_2 SO_4$. Calculate the molecular weight of $H_2 X$.

**Solution**

The concentration of the KOH solution must be determined before the reaction with $H_2 X$ can be considered. In essence, the reaction of KOH with $H_2 SO_4$ is a step to standardize the base before it is used in the determination with $H_2 X$. The reaction with $H_2 SO_4$ is

$$2KOH + H_2 SO_4 \longrightarrow K_2 SO_4 + 2H_2 O$$
2 moles + 1 mole

No. moles KOH reacted = 2 (no. moles $H_2 SO_4$ reacted)

No. moles $H_2 SO_4$ = $(0.750 \, M) (0.0100 \, \ell)$ = 0.00750 mol

No. moles KOH = 2(0.00750 mol) = $(M) (\ell)$

Molarity KOH = $\frac{0.0150 \text{ mol}}{0.0142 \, \ell}$ = 1.056 $M$

The reaction of KOH with $H_2 X$ is

$$2KOH + H_2 X \longrightarrow K_2 X + 2H_2 O$$
2 moles + 1 mole

No. moles $H_2 X$ in sample = $\frac{1}{2}$(no. moles KOH reacted)

No. moles $H_2 X = \frac{1}{2}(M) (\ell) = \frac{1}{2}(1.056 \, M) (0.01400 \, \ell)$ = 0.00739 mol

Recognize that this number of moles of $H_2 X$ is contained in the sample, 1.80 g. Therefore

$$0.00739 \text{ mol} = 1.80 \text{ g}$$

$$1 \text{ mol} = \frac{1.80 \text{ g}}{0.00739} = 243 \text{ g}$$

40. A solution of 5.00 g of an organic compound in 25.00 g of carbon tetrachloride (bp, 76.8°; $K_b$, 5.02) boils at 8.15°C at 760 torr. What is the molecular weight of the compound?

The boiling-point elevation of a solvent is proportional to the number of solute particles dissolved in the solvent. Specifically for $CCl_4$, one mole of solute dissolved in 1.00 kg of $CCl_4$ changes the boiling point by 5.02°C, $K_b$. The change in boiling point is expressed as

$$\Delta bp = K_b = \text{molality} = K_b \left( \frac{\text{no. moles solute}}{\text{no. kg solvent}} \right)$$

$$\text{No. moles solute} = \frac{\text{mass solute}}{\text{MW or GFW}}$$

and

$$\Delta bp = K_b \frac{(\text{mass solute/MW})}{\text{no. kg solvent}}$$

Solving this equation for MW yields

$$MW = \frac{K_b \times \text{mass solute}}{\Delta bp \times \text{no. kg solvent}}$$

In this case;

$$\Delta bp = 81.5° - 76.8° = 4.7°C$$

Mass of solute = 5.00 g    No. kg of solvent = 0.02500 kg.

$$MW(\text{unknown}) = \frac{(5.02°C/m) \times 5.00\ g}{4.7°C \times 0.02500\ kg} = 2.1 \times 10^2\ g/mol$$

41. A solution contains 5.00 g of urea, $CO(NH_2)_2$, per 0.100 kg of water. If the vapor pressure of pure water at 25° is 23.7 torr, what is the vapor pressure of the solution?

**Solution**

The vapor pressure of a solution is proportional to the mole fraction of the substance used as the solvent in the solution. This relationship is expressed as Raoult's Law, where the vapor pressure of the solution, $P_{\text{solution}}$,

$$P_{\text{solution}} = P_{\text{solvent}}\, X_{\text{solvent}}$$

equals the vapor pressure of the pure solvent, $P_{\text{solvent}}$, times the mole fraction of the solvent, $X_{\text{solvent}}$,

$$X_{H_2O} = \frac{n_{H_2O}}{n_{\text{total}}}$$

$$\text{GFW's:} \quad CO(NH_2)_2 = 60.06 \text{ g}; \quad H_2O = 18.02 \text{ g}$$

$$n_{urea} = 5.00 \text{ g} \times \frac{1 \text{ mol}}{60.06 \text{ g}} = 0.08325 \text{ mol}$$

$$n_{H_2O} = 100. \text{ g} \times \frac{1 \text{ mol}}{18.02 \text{ g}} = 5.549 \text{ mol}$$

$$n_{total} = 5.6322 \text{ mol}$$

$$X_{H_2O} = \frac{5.549}{0.08325 + 5.549} = 0.9852$$

Vapor pressure of solution = 23.7 torr $\times$ 0.9852 = 23.3 torr

44. Calculate the boiling-point elevation of 0.100 kg of water containing 0.010 mol of NaCl, 0.020 mol of $Na_2SO_4$, and 0.030 mol of $MgCl_2$, assuming complete dissociation of these electrolytes.

**Solution**

The boiling point of any solution is dependent on the number of moles of solute particles in solution. In this example all solutes are ionic and assumed to be completely dissociated in solution. The boiling-point elevation, however, will actually be less than that calculated for 100% dissociation due to ion-ion interactions in solution. Dissociation near 100% occurs only in extremely dilute solutions, <0.001 molal. The total number of moles of particles in this solution is

| | |
|---|---|
| 0.010 mol NaCl | 0.010 mol Na$^+$ + 0.010 mol Cl$^-$ |
| 0.020 mol Na$_2$SO$_4$ | 0.040 mol Na$^+$ + 0.020 mol SO$_4$$^{2-}$ |
| 0.030 mol MgCl$_2$ | 0.030 mol Mg$^{2+}$ + 0.060 mol Cl$^-$ |
| Total = 0.080 mol | + 0.090 mol = 0.17 mol |

$$\Delta bp = K_b(m) = \frac{0.512°C}{m} \times \frac{0.17 \text{ mol}}{0.100 \text{ kg}} = 0.87°C$$

46. How would you prepare a 3.08 $m$ aqueous solution of glycerin $(C_3H_8O_3)$? What would be the freezing point of this solution?

**Solution**

Since a quantity of solution is not stated here, assume that 1.0 kg is to be used. The amount of glycerin required is found as follows. A 3.08-$m$ solution contains 3.08 moles of solute per 1.0 kg of water.

$$\text{GFW } C_3H_8O_3 = 92.0 \text{ g}$$

$$\text{Molality } (C_3H_8O_3) = 3.08 \text{ mol} \times 92.0 \frac{g}{mol} = 284 \text{ g}$$

and

$$\Delta fp = K_f(m) = 1.86\,\frac{°C}{m}\times 3.08\,m = 5.73°, \quad 0°C - 5.73°C = -5.73°C$$

48. A sample of sulfur weighing 0.210 g was dissolved in 17.8 g of carbon disulfide, $CS_2$ ($K_b$, 2.34). If the boiling point elevation was 0.107°, what is the formula of a sulfur molecule in carbon disulfide?

**Solution**

The formula of molecular sulfur can be determined from its molecular weight calculated by using the boiling point data.

$$bp = K_b\left(\frac{\text{mass S/MW}}{\text{no. kg } CS_2}\right)$$

and

$$MW = \frac{K_b \times \text{mass S}}{\text{No. kg } CS_2 \times \Delta bp} = \frac{2.34\,\frac{°C}{m}\times 0.210\,g}{0.0178\,kg \times 0.107°C} = 258\,\frac{g}{mol}$$

Since the atomic weight of S is 32.1, the number of atoms per molecule is

$$32.1\,(\text{no. atoms per molecule}) = 258$$

$$\text{No. atoms} = \frac{258}{32.1} = 8 \quad \text{or} \quad S_8$$

52. A solution of 0.045 g of an unknown organic compound in 0.550 g of camphor melts at 158.4°C. The melting point of pure camphor is 178.4°C. $K_f$ for camphor is 37.7. The solute contains 93.46% C and 6.54% H by mass. What is the molecular formula of the solute? Show your calculation.

**Solution**

The molecular formula is determined from the freezing point and the elemental analysis data. The molecular weight of the unknown is calculated from the change in freezing point as

$$MW = \frac{K_f \times \text{mass solute}}{\text{no. kg camphor} \times \Delta fp} = \frac{37.7\,\frac{°C}{m}\times 0.045\,g}{0.000550\,kg \times 20.0°C} = 154\,\frac{g}{mol}$$

Next, determine the empirical formula of the unknown.

$$C: \quad 93.46\,g \times \frac{1\,mol}{12.01\,g} = 7.78\,mol$$

$$\text{H:} \quad 6.54 \text{ g} \times \frac{1 \text{ mol}}{1.01 \text{ g}} = 6.48 \text{ mol}$$

$$C_{7.78} H_{6.48} = C_{1.2} H_1 \quad \text{or} \quad C_{12} H_{10}$$

The empirical formula has a formula weight of 154, which equals the molecular weight calculated from the freezing-point data, and is the molecular formula of the unknown.

53. The activity of the ions in a 0.20 $m$ solution of $LiNO_3$ at 25.0°C is 0.15 $m$. Calculate the activity coefficient for the ions.

**Solution**

The activity of ions in solution is less than the concentration of the ions in solution, indicating that considerable ion-ion interaction is taking place. The activity of an ion in solution is a function of its concentration and activity coefficient, $f$.

$$\text{activity} = f \times \text{concentration}$$

$$f = \frac{\text{activity}}{\text{concentration}} = \frac{0.15 \, m}{0.20 \, m} = 0.75$$

55. A solution is made by dissolving 0.0745 g of potassium chloride in 100.0 g of water. The solution is observed to freeze at $-0.0358°C$. If one assumes that the activity coefficient of the potassium ion is equal to that of the chloride ion, what is the activity coefficient of the potassium ion under these conditions?

**Solution**

Due to the interaction of ions in solution, the change in freezing point will be less than that calculated on the basis of total dissociation of the solute. The activity of the ions in solution is a measure of the effective molality of the solution, that is, the molality calculated from the actual freezing-point change.

$$\Delta fp = K_f \, m_{eff}$$

$$m_{eff} = \frac{\Delta fp}{K_f} = \frac{0.0358°}{1.86°C/m} = 0.0192 \, m$$

$$\text{GFW KCl} = 74.5 \text{ g}$$

If we assume total dissociation of KCl in solution, the molality of the solution is two times the molality of KCl, and is calculated as

$$m = \frac{0.0745 \text{ g} \times \dfrac{1 \text{ mol}}{74.5 \text{ g}}}{0.100 \text{ kg}} \times \frac{2 \text{ ions}}{\text{formula}} = 0.0200$$

$$\text{Activity} = f \times \text{concentration}$$

$$f = \frac{\text{activity}}{\text{concentration}} = \frac{0.0192}{0.0200} = 0.960$$

## RELATED PROBLEMS

1. Which one of the following methanol-water solutions will have the lowest freezing point? What is the freezing point of this solution?

   (a)  1.00 mol of $CH_3OH$ in 500.0 g of water
   (b)  0.50 mol of $CH_3OH$ in 500.0 g of water
   (c)  0.25 mol of $CH_3OH$ in 125.0 g of water
   (d)  0.75 mol of $CH_3OH$ in 125.0 of water

   *Answer: (d); fp = -11°C*

2. Calculate the volume of 0.200 $M$ $H_2SO_4$ required to completely react with 10.0 g of zinc according to the following reaction.

$$H_2SO_4\,(aq) + Zn(s) \longrightarrow ZnSO_4\,(aq) + H_2\,(g)$$

   *Answer: 764 ml*

3. The assay printed on the manufacturer's label of a bottle of concentrated, reagent grade hydrochloric acid indicates a purity of 36.7% HCl and a specific gravity of 1.186. Calculate the molarity of this solution. Calculate the volume of this solution required to prepare 5.00 liters of 0.250 $M$ solution.       *Answer: 11.9 M; 0.105 ℓ or 105 ml*

4. Diffusion by osmosis can occur when two solutions of different concentrations are separated by a semipermeable membrane that selectively allows water molecules to pass in both directions but prevents the solute molecules or ions from doing so. A net transport of water will occur from the solution of lesser concentration (lower mole fraction) to the solution of greater concentration tending to "level" the concentrations of the two solutions. Given the following two solutions separated by such a membrane, which one will show a net gain in volume? solution A, 4.000 g KCl in 500.0 g $H_2O$ and solution B, 3.000 g NaCl in 350.0 g $H_2O$       *Answer: B*

5. The volume of a given mass of water varies according to the equation

$$V_t = V_o\,(1 - 6.427 \times 10^{-5}\,t + 8.5053 \times 10^{6}\,t^2 - 6.7900 \times 10^{-8}\,t^3)$$

   between temperatures of 0°C and 30°C. Assuming that the molarity of a solution is 1.000 mol/liter at 0°C, calculate the molarity of the solution at 4°C, 10°C, 20°C, 25°C, and 30°C. Show the variation in molarity with temperature by plotting $M$ vs $t$.
   *Answer: M(4°) = 1.0001; M(10°) = 0.9999; M(20°) = 0.9984*

# Chapter 14: Acids, Bases, and Salts

## INTRODUCTION

The chemical literature indicates that scientists have speculated on the nature of acids and bases for some 200 years. Still earlier attempts to define acids were based on easily discernible properties. Thus acids were classified as substances that tasted sour, caused vegetable dyes to change color, and reacted with metals to produce hydrogen. Bases were defined, in essence, as opposites of acids: Bases tasted bitter, felt slippery, and caused vegetable dyes to change to different colors than those produced by acids.

The first classification of acids and bases according to their chemical properties was done by Svanté Arrhenius, who said that acids caused the increase of hydrogen ion in aqueous solution and bases caused the increase of hydroxide ion in solution. This was a rather limited view, since substances that reacted like hydrogen ion or hydroxide ion were not allowed in the classification scheme.

A useful but also somewhat limited definition was proposed independently by Johannes Brönsted and Thomas Lowry. This theory defined acids as proton donors and bases as proton acceptors. According to this theory, acids contain ionizable protons that can be transferred to bases. This definition is broader than the previous one, since now a base can be anything that accepts a hydrogen ion rather than just a hydroxide ion.

Three industrially and physiologically important classes of compounds fit into the Brönsted-Lowry classification scheme:

1. Mineral acids-bases. These compounds include acids such as hydro-chloric ($HCl$), sulfuric ($H_2SO_4$), and nitric ($HNO_3$), and bases such as sodium hydroxide ($NaOH$) and sodium carbonate ($Na_2CO_3$).
2. Organic acids-bases. These compounds include fatty acids such as acetic ($CH_3COOH$) and stearic ($C_{17}H_{35}COOH$), and bases such as methylamine ($CH_3-NH_2$).
3. Amino acids. These acids contain an acid and a base functional group, giving them potential to react with either acids or bases. Examples include glycine ($CHNH_2COOH$) and glutamic acid ($HOOCCH_2CH_2CHNH_2COOH$).

In 1923, G. N. Lewis proposed a definition of acids and bases that was much more comprehensive and encompassing than the two based upon the protonic concept. According to this definition, an acid is *any species that can accept a pair of electrons* from a donor, the base. The Lewis classi-fication scheme includes all ionizable protonic substances and all the donors in the Brönsted-Lowry scheme. The Lewis theory has the advantage of explaining acid versus base characteristics of compounds not containing protons, including metal and nonmetal oxides. Many reactions in organic chemistry also can be explained in terms of the Lewis concept.

A more recent definition of acids and bases involves classifying substances as either acids or bases in terms of their capacity to form cations or anions characteristic of the solvent. This definition is particularly appropriate for work in nonaqueous solvents.

The problems in this chapter mainly deal with acid-base reactions involving protonic substances. Most of the problems illustrate the principle that protons lost from an acid during a reaction are consumed by the base. The concept of equivalent weight is introduced and used in several examples.

## FORMULAS AND DEFINITIONS

**Gram-equivalent weight** (GEW)  The gram-equivalent weight of an acid or base is the amount of substance that donates or accepts one mole ($6.02 \times 10^{23}$) of electrons, $e^-$, or protons, $H^+$, or neutralizes one mole of negative or positive charges. The gram-equivalent weight, or one equivalent (one equiv), of a substance used in a protonic acid-base reaction is the gram-formula weight of the substance divided by the number of protons donated or consumed per molecule of acid or base used, respectively:

$$GEW = \frac{GFW \text{ of acid or base}}{\text{no. of } H^+ \text{donated or consumed}}$$

The GEW of a substance only can be deduced by examination of the chemical equation representing a specific reaction—not merely from the formula of the acid or base. The need to know the balanced chemical equation for the reaction is illustrated in the variability of the GEW's of the acids and bases in the following examples:

1.  $HCl(aq) + NaOH(aq) \longrightarrow NaCl(aq) + H_2O(l)$

In this reaction one mole of protons is donated by one mole of HCl and is accepted by one mole of NaOH. The GEW both of HCl and of NaOH equals their GFW's.

$$\text{GEW HCl} = \frac{36.5 \text{ g}}{1} = 36.5 \text{ g}; \quad \text{GEW NaOH} = \frac{40.0 \text{ g}}{1}$$

2.  $H_2SO_4(aq) + 2NaOH(aq) \longrightarrow Na_2SO_4(aq) + 2H_2O(l)$

In this reaction, one mole of $H_2SO_4$ donates two moles of protons, which are accepted by two moles of NaOH. The equivalent weights of the acid and base are

$$\text{GEW } H_2SO_4 = \text{one equiv} = \frac{\text{GFW}}{2} = \frac{98.08 \text{ g}}{2} = 49.0 \text{ g}$$

$$\text{GEW NaOH} = \text{one equiv} = \frac{\text{GFW}}{1} = \frac{40.01 \text{ g}}{1} = 40.0 \text{ g}$$

3.  $2H_2SO_4(aq) + Ca(OH)_2(aq) \longrightarrow Ca(HSO_4)_2(aq) + H_2O(l)$

In this reaction, only one of the protons from $H_2SO_4$ is reacted, while both hydroxide ions from $Ca(OH)_2$ are reacted. Their equivalent weights are

$$\text{GEW } H_2SO_4 = \frac{\text{GFW}}{1} = 98.1 \text{ g}$$

$$\text{GEW Ca(OH)}_2 = \frac{\text{GFW}}{2} = \frac{74.1 \text{ g}}{2} = 37.0 \text{ g}$$

**Normality** ($N$)  The normality of a solution is the number of equivalents of solute dissolved per liter of solution.

$$\text{Normality} = \frac{\text{no. equiv solute}}{\text{vol of solution in } \ell}$$

Related equations (units only)

$$\text{No. equiv} = \text{Normality} \times \text{vol in } \ell = \frac{\text{equiv}}{\ell} \times \ell = \text{equiv}$$

$$\text{Vol of soln.} = \frac{\text{no. equiv}}{\text{no. equiv}/\ell} = \text{liters}$$

Since the equivalent weight of a substance is specific to a reaction, the normality of a solution must be determined from a known reaction.

A useful relationship involving normality and equivalent weight follows from the definition of gram-equivalent weight. The number of equivalents of all reactants and products in a reaction is equal:

No. GEW reactant 1 = no. GEW reactant 2 = $\cdots$ = no. GEW reactant $n$

= no. GEW product 1 = $\cdots$ = no. GEW product $n$

If the reactants and/or products are in solution, their quantities are related through their normalities as

$$N_{R_1} V_{R_1} = N_{R_1} V_{R_2} = \cdots = N_{R_n} V_{R_n} = N_{P_1} V_{P_1}$$
$$= N_{P_2} V_{P_2} = \cdots = N_{P_n} V_{P_n}$$

**Dilution formulas**   A volume of concentrated solution can be diluted to form a solution of lesser concentration. A larger volume of solution is formed thereby in which the number of moles or equivalents of solute has remained constant; only the volume of solution has changed. The following two relations involving molarity and normality are extremely useful for preparing solutions.

*Molarity* No. moles solute in $soln_1$ = no. moles solute in $soln_2$

$$(M_{soln_1})(V_{soln_1}) = (M_{soln_2})(V_{soln_2})$$

$$\left(\frac{mol\ 1}{\ell}\right)(no.\ \ell_1) = \left(\frac{mol\ 2}{\ell}\right)(no.\ \ell_2)$$

*Example involving molarity*:  Calculate the volume of 0.15 $M$ $H_2SO_4$ solution that can be prepared by diluting 20.0 ml of 6.00 $M$ $H_2SO_4$.

$$(M_1)(V_1) = (M_2)(V_2)$$

$$V_2 = \frac{(M_1)(V_1)}{M_2} = \frac{(6.00\ mol/\ell)(0.0200\ \ell)}{0.15\ mol/\ell}$$

$$= 0.80\ \ell$$

*Normality*

No. equiv solute in $soln_1$ = no. equiv solute in $soln_2$

$$(N_{soln_1})(V_{soln_1}) = (N_{soln_2})(V_{soln_2})$$

$$\left(\frac{equiv_1}{\ell}\right)(no.\ \ell_1) = \left(\frac{equiv_2}{\ell}\right)(no.\ \ell_2)$$

*Example involving normality*:  Calculate the volume of 6.0 $N$ $H_2SO_4$ required to prepare 4.00 $\ell$ of 0.10 $N$ $H_2SO_4$ solution.

$$N_1 V_1 = N_2 V_2$$

$$V_1 = \frac{N_2 V_2}{N_1} = \frac{(0.10\ equiv/\ell)(4.00\ \ell)}{6.0\ equiv/\ell} = 0.067\ \ell = 67\ ml$$

**Neutralization reaction**   Any reaction of an acid and a base in which equal equivalents of acid and base are reacted is known as a neutralization reaction. The resulting solution may be neutral, acidic, or basic depending on the $H^+$ and $OH^-$ concentrations (or their counterparts in nonaqueous systems) that remain. These concentrations, in turn, depend on the relative strengths of the reacting substances.

**End point** This term, normally used with reactions taking place in aqueous solution, defines the point in a reaction at which an equal number of equivalents of the reactants have been consumed. Some type of indicator, either chemical or electronic, is used to monitor the reaction and to determine the end point.

## PROBLEMS

1. Calculate the equivalent weight of each of the reactants in the following equations:

(a) $Ba(OH)_2 + 2HClO_4 \longrightarrow Ba(ClO_4)_2 + 2H_2O$
(c) $Ni(OH)_2 + NaH_2PO_4 \longrightarrow NaNiPO_4 + 2H_2O$
(e) $KOH + H_2SO_4 \longrightarrow KHSO_4 + H_2O$

### Solution

The gram-equivalent weight, GEW, of a protonic acid equals its gram formula weight divided by the number of hydrogen ions transferred in the reaction.

The gram-equivalent weight, GEW, of a base equals its gram formula weight divided by the number of hydroxide ions or the equivalent transferred in the reaction.

(a) $Ba(OH)_2 + 2HClO_4 \longrightarrow Ba(ClO_4)_2 + 2H_2O$

Both hydroxide ions from one mole of $Ba(OH)_2$ are reacted with two moles of hydrogen ion from two moles of $HClO_4$ in the reaction.

$$\text{GEW } Ba(OH)_2 = \frac{GFW}{2} = \frac{137.3 + 2(16.0) + 2(1.0)}{2} = \frac{171.3}{2} = 85.7 \text{ g}$$

$$\text{GEW } HClO_4 = \frac{GFW}{1} = 1.0 + 35.5 + 4(16.0) = 100.5 \text{ g}$$

(c) $Ni(OH)_2 + NaH_2PO_4 \longrightarrow NaNiPO_4 + 2H_2O$

Both hydroxide ions and both hydrogen ions are transferred from the reactants.

$$\text{GEW } Ni(OH)_2 = \frac{GFW}{2} = \frac{58.7 + 2(16.0) + 2(1.0)}{2} = 46.4 \text{ g}$$

$$\text{GEW } NaH_2PO_4 = \frac{GFW}{2} = \frac{23.0 + 2(1.0) + 31.0 + 4(16.0)}{2} = 60.0 \text{ g}$$

(e) $KOH + H_2SO_4 \longrightarrow KHSO_4 + H_2O$

The one hydroxide ion from KOH reacts with one of the two available hydrogen ions from $H_2 SO_4$.

$$GEW\ KOH = \frac{GFW}{1} = 39.1 + 16.0 + 1.0 = 56.1\ g$$

$$GEW\ H_2 SO_4 = \frac{GFW}{1} = 2(1.0) + 32.1 + 4(16.0) = 98.1\ g$$

2. Calculate the normality of each of the following solutions.

   (a) 5.0 equivalents of LiOH in 2.5 $\ell$ of solution
   (c) 0.0015 equivalents of $Ca(OH)_2$ in 100.0 ml of solution

**Solution**

The normality of a solution equals the number of equivalents of solute per liter of solution.

(a) Normality LiOH = $\dfrac{5.0\ equiv\ LiOH}{2.5\ \ell} = 2.0\ N$

(c) Normality $Ca(OH)_2 = \dfrac{0.0015\ equiv\ Ca(OH)_2}{0.1000\ \ell} = 0.015\ N$

3. A 0.144 $N$ solution of KOH is titrated with $H_2 SO_4$ to give $K_2 SO_4$. If a 47.0-ml sample of the KOH solution is used, what volume of 0.144 $M\ H_2 SO_4$ is required to reach the end point? What volume of 0.144 $N\ H_2 SO_4$?

**Solution**

The end point is defined as the point in a reaction at which an equal number of equivalents of both reactants have been reacted. In this case,

$$No.\ equiv\ KOH\ reacted = no.\ equiv\ H_2 SO_4\ reacted$$

The number of equivalents of KOH reacted is

$$KOH = \frac{0.144\ equiv}{\ell} \times 0.0470\ \ell = 0.00677\ equiv$$

This number of equivalents must be equal to the number of equivalents of $H_2 SO_4$ reacted. The volume required is calculated as follows:

$$GEW\ H_2 SO_4 = \frac{GFW}{2} = \frac{98.1\ g}{2} = 49.0\ g$$

Since one mole of $H_2 SO_4$ equals two equivalents,

$$0.144\ M\ H_2 SO_4 = 0.288\ N\ H_2 SO_4$$

The 0.00677 equiv $H_2 SO_4$ must have come from a 0.288 $N$ solution.
Thus

$$0.00677 \text{ equiv } H_2 SO_4 = \left(\frac{0.288 \text{ equiv}}{\ell}\right)(\text{vol in } \ell)$$

$$V = \frac{0.00677}{0.288} \ell = 0.0235 \ell = 23.5 \text{ ml}$$

For the volume of 0.144 $N$ $H_2 SO_4$, follow the same procedure as above.

$$0.00677 \text{ equiv } H_2 SO_4 = \left(\frac{0.144 \text{ equiv}}{\ell}\right)(\text{vol in } \ell)$$

$$V = \frac{0.00677}{0.144} = 0.0470 \ell = 47.0 \text{ ml}$$

5. A particular standard acid solution is 0.800 $N$. What volume of 0.300 $N$ base would be required to neutralize 47.0 ml of the acid?

**Solution**

Neutralization is the point in an acid-base reaction when equal equivalents of a protonic acid and a hydroxyl base have reacted. In most cases, the resulting salt solutions are not neutral; the concentration of hydronium ion and hydroxide ion in solution are unequal because of the relative strengths of the acid and base. In this case, we assume that the acid and base strengths are approximately the same.

$$(N_{acid})(V_{acid}) = (N_{base})(V_{base})$$

$$\left(\frac{0.800 \text{ equiv}}{\ell}\right)(0.0470 \ell) = \left(\frac{0.300 \text{ equiv}}{\ell}\right)(V_{base})$$

$$V_{base} = \frac{(0.800)(0.0470)}{0.300} = 0.125 \ell = 125 \text{ ml}$$

6. A titration of 0.1500 g of an acid requires 47.00 ml of 0.0120 $N$ NaOH to reach the end point. What is the equivalent weight of the acid?

**Solution**

At the end point an equal number of equivalents of acid (in 0.1500 g) has reacted with the same number of equivalents of base.

$$\text{No. equiv acid} = \text{No. equiv base} = \left(\frac{0.0120 \text{ equiv}}{\ell}\right)(0.04700 \ell)$$

$$= 0.000564 \text{ equiv}$$

Since 0.1500 g = 0.000564 equiv,

$$\text{one equiv} = \frac{0.1500 \text{ g}}{0.000564} = 266 \text{ g}$$

9. The reaction of 0.871 g of sodium with an excess of liquid ammonia containing a trace of $FeCl_3$ as a catalyst produced 0.473 $\ell$ of pure $H_2$ measured at 25°C and 745 torr. What is the equation for the reaction of sodium with liquid ammonia? Show your calculations.

### Solution

In the reaction with liquid ammonia, sodium functions as a Lewis base by donating electrons to hydrogen ions formed through the ionization of ammonia:

$$NH_3 \longrightarrow NH_2^- + H^+$$

To write the equation for the overall reaction, first determine the mole ratio of sodium used to hydrogen produced.

$$\text{No. moles Na} = 0.871 \text{ g} \times \frac{1 \text{ mol}}{23.0 \text{ g}} = 0.0379 \text{ mol}$$

From the ideal gas equation, the number of moles of hydrogen produced equals

$$PV = nRT, \qquad n = \frac{PV}{RT}$$

$$n_{H_2} = \frac{\left(\dfrac{745}{760} \text{ atm}\right)(0.473 \text{ }\ell)}{\left(\dfrac{0.08205 \text{ }\ell \text{ atm}}{\text{mol K}}\right)(298 \text{ K})} = 0.0190 \text{ mol}$$

Thus 0.0379 mol of Na reacts with 0.0190 mol of $H_2$. The ratio of Na to $H_2$ is

$$0.0379 : 0.0190 \quad \text{or} \quad 2Na : 1H_2$$

Therefore the balanced equation must be

$$2Na + 2NH_3 \longrightarrow 2NaNH_2 + H_2$$

## RELATED PROBLEMS

1. The molarity of a vinegar solution is found to be 0.90 $M$. Calculate the mass of acetic acid ($CH_3COOH$) per 100 ml of vinegar.

    *Answer: 5.4 g per 100 ml vinegar*

2. Calculate the volume of water that must be added to 10.1 ml of 12.0 $N$ $H_2SO_4$ to prepare a 0.10 $N$ solution. *Answer: 1190 ml*

3. (a) The hydrogen ion concentration in urine from a healthy person is about $1 \times 10^{-6}$ $M$. If a person eliminates 1300 ml of urine per day, calculate the number of equivalents of hydrogen ion eliminated per day. (b). What volume of 1.00 $M$ HCl would contain the same amount of hydrogen ion as 1300 ml of urine?

*Answer: (a) $1.3 \times 10^{-6}$ equiv; (b) $1.3 \times 10^{-6}$ ℓ or 1.3 μℓ*

4. A 0.2500 $M$ sulfuric acid solution is used to standardize a sodium hydroxide solution. The titration of 55.00 ml of the NaOH solution required 11.00 ml of the $H_2 SO_4$ solution. Calculate the molarity of the NaOH solution. *Answer: 0.100 M*

5. Citric acid, found in the juices of oranges and lemons, is commonly used in the first-aid treatment of a victim having swallowed a quantity of alkaline substance. Given that a 2.00 g sample of citric acid neutralizes 313 ml of 0.100 $M$ NaOH, calculate the gram equivalent weight of citric acid. *Answer: 63.9 g*

# Chapter 15: Chemical Kinetics and Chemical Equilibrium

## INTRODUCTION

The concept of speed, velocity, or rate is so familiar that it may come as a surprise that the idea is relatively modern and can be traced to Sir Isaac Newton (1642-1727). So too, the study of the rate of a chemical reaction did not have its origin until recently. In the 1850s the Norwegian scientists Guldberg and Waage were the first to write rate equations; these equations led them to develop the equilibrium expression for a chemical reaction. This early work was quickly followed by studies of the factors on which rates depend, such as temperature and concentration of reactants.

Today, the measurement of the rates of chemical reactions plays a key role in understanding reaction mechanisms (that is, the detailed way in which the reactants come together to form the products). Indeed, the object of most of the work in kinetics today is to elucidate mechanisms.

The importance of mechanisms is easy to understand. Most reactions proceed in several steps and are said to be *complex*; *elementary* reactions, on the other hand, occur in only one step. Complex reactions often occur by free-radical mechanisms. (A free radical is a reactive, neutral species that contains an odd number of electrons. The hydroxyl radical, $H:\overset{..}{\underset{..}{O}}\cdot$, is an example.) Industry as well as science is acutely aware of the study of complex reactions, because the industrial procedures that produce the wide variety of chemical intermediates and final products involve, for the most part, such complex processes. Examples are numerous, and include such diverse ones as the cracking of heavy oil fractions to usable chemicals, the process of explosion, and even the effect on chemicals by enzymes. Indeed, the interest in biochemicals is so great now that a whole area of study, enzyme kinetics, has developed.

Knowledge of the equilibrium constant expression as developed by Guldberg and Waage is equally important to chemists, since the amount of any substance in a chemical reaction at equilibrium may be determined from it. Through a modification of how we view it, we may apply the expression to solubility problems (Unit 11) and to acid-base problems (Unit 9). A knowledge of equilibrium is essential as a theoretical base for studying most areas of chemistry, especially analytical chemistry, which is discussed at a qualitative level in the Qualitative Analysis section of *College Chemistry*, by Nebergall et al.

The problems in this chapter primarily deal with the determination of rates, rate constants, or concentrations using rate laws or the equilibrium constant expression.

## FORMULAS AND DEFINITIONS

**Activated complex-activation energy** Whether or not a product forms as a result of an interaction of reacting particles in a chemical reaction depends on several factors. The collision theory of reactions suggests that reacting species collide, and if conditions are suitable, form an unstable intermediate species called an *activated complex*. The particles composing the complex may further interact and form the desired product or simply dissociate and return to their initial states. The energy required to give reactants sufficient energy to form activated complexes is called the *activation energy*. Most chemical reactions require activation energy. Some examples of different forms of energy used to activate a chemical reaction include a spark or high temperature to ignite motor fuels, a sudden jar to detonate nitroglycerin, or a fire to start charcoal.

**Arrhenius' Law** One of the most important relationships in chemical kinetics is the Arrhenius equation, which connects the rate constant, $k$, of a reaction with the temperature. Its form, as developed by Svante Arrhenius, is $k = A \times 10^{(-E_a/2.303\,RT)}$ where $A$ is the frequency factor, $E_a$ is the activation energy, $R$ is the gas constant, $8.314$ J mol$^{-1}$ K$^{-1}$, and $T$ is the Kelvin temperature. Many natural processes, even though they are complex, obey this law because they are controlled by chemical reactions. For example, the law is obeyed by the chirring of crickets and the flashing of fireflies.

**Catalyst** A catalyst is a substance that changes the rate of a chemical reaction but which is itself unchanged and, in theory, can be recovered at the end of the process. If a substance increases the rate of a catalyzed reaction, it is called an *accelerator*, and if it slows the rate of the reaction, it is called an *inhibitor*.

**Chain reaction**  This refers to a reaction that, once started, occurs in a series of steps in which one or more reactions are repeated in order to provide additional reagent to keep the overall reaction continuing. Such a reaction is characterized by an *initiation* step, a *propagation* step, and a *termination* step. The propagation step generates the species (reactive intermediate) necessary for the initiation step and thus the reaction continues until the termination step finally consumes all of the reactive intermediate.

**Elementary reaction**  Reactions that occur in one step are termed elementary. We speak of the *molecularity of the reaction* in terms of the number of molecules that participate in the single reaction. Thus *unimolecular* refers to a reaction in which only one molecule is needed. Similarly, *bimolecular* means two molecules participate and *termolecular* refers to a simultaneous reaction of three molecules. This latter type of reaction is comparatively rare.

**Equilibrium**  This is a condition in a reacting system when the two opposing (forward and reverse) reactions occur simultaneously at the same rate. Chemical systems at equilibrium are dynamic, but no net change in the amounts of reactants or products occurs.

**Law of Mass Action**  For a general equation of a chemical reaction written as $a\mathrm{A} + b\mathrm{B} + \cdots \rightleftharpoons c\mathrm{C} + d\mathrm{D} + \cdots$, the Law of Mass Action is, at equilibrium,

$$\frac{[\mathrm{C}]^c [\mathrm{D}]^d \cdots}{[\mathrm{A}]^a [\mathrm{B}]^b \cdots} = K_e$$

This law of chemical equilibrium or mass action applies at a particular temperature, where the brackets indicate the molar concentrations of the different chemical species raised to a power equal to their stoichiometric coefficients. Since pressure is proportional to concentration, an equilibrium constant expressed in terms of pressure $K_p$ is defined as

$$K_p = \frac{(p\mathrm{C})^c (p\mathrm{D})^d}{(p\mathrm{A})^a (p\mathrm{B})^b}$$

**Le Châtelier's principle**  If an action causes a change in concentration, pressure, or temperature to occur in a chemical system at equilibrium, the equilibrium shifts in a way that tends to undo the effect of the stress.

**Heat of chemical reaction**  The number of moles of a substance that disappears or is formed by a reaction in a unit of time is the rate of reaction. In a reaction in which the stoichiometric coefficients are all 1 for the products and reactants, the rate $R$ is directly proportional to the concentrations of the reacting substances. For the reaction $\mathrm{A} + \mathrm{B} \rightleftharpoons \mathrm{C} + \mathrm{D}$, the rate equation is written as $R_1 = k_1[A][B]$, where the brackets indicate molar concentrations and $k_1$ is the rate constant for the formation of product. The opposing reaction is the formation of reactants; its rate is $R_2 = k_2[C][D]$. At equilibrium, the opposing rates are equal. Setting the rates equal gives

$$k_1[A][B] = k_2[C][D] \quad \text{or} \quad \frac{k_1}{k_2} = \frac{[C][D]}{[A][B]}$$

Since the ratio of the two constants is a constant, we may write $K_e = k_1/k_2$, where $K_e$ is the equilibrium constant.

**Order of a reaction**  In the general reaction $aA + bB \rightleftharpoons cC + dD$, if the rate of the reaction is $R = k[C]^c[D]^d$ then the order of the reaction is the sum of the exponents, $c + d$. Several common cases occur: If the value of the sum is 1, the reaction is first-order and the rate depends on the concentration of only one species. If the value is 2, the reaction is second order. If the sum is zero (that is, if the rate is independent of the concentration), the reaction is zeroth order.

**Half-life of a reaction**  The half-life, $t_{1/2}$ (time required for one-half of the original amount of limiting reactant to be converted to product), can be expressed in simple terms only for first-order reactions, where

$$t_{1/2} = \frac{0.693}{k}$$

The radioactive decay of elements should be mentioned as one class of substances that decompose via first-order kinetics.

**Van't Hoff's Law**  This law is a special case of Le Châtelier's principle, which states that when the temperature of a system in equilibrium is raised, the equilibrium is displaced in such a way that heat is absorbed.

## PROBLEMS

1.  The rate constant at 45° for the decomposition of dinitrogen pentoxide, $N_2O_5$, dissolved in chloroform, $CHCl_3$, is $6.2 \times 10^{-4}$ min$^{-1}$ ($2N_2O_5 \longrightarrow 4NO_2 + O_2$). The decomposition is first order in $N_2O_5$.

    (a) What is the rate of the reaction when $[N_2O_5] = 0.40\ M$?
    (b) What is the concentration of $N_2O_5$ remaining at the end of one hour if the initial concentration of $N_2O_5$ was 0.40 $M$?

    Solution

    (a) The rate of reaction for a first-order reaction in $N_2O_5$ may be written as

    $$\text{Rate} = k[N_2O_5]$$

where $k$, the rate constant at $45°$, is $6.2 \times 10^{-4}$ min$^{-1}$. When $[N_2O_5] = 0.40\ M$,

$$\text{Rate} = 6.2 \times 10^{-4}\ \text{min}^{-1}\left(0.40\ \frac{\text{mol}}{\ell}\right) = 2.48 \times 10^{-4}$$

$$= 2.5 \times 10^{-4}\ \text{mol}\ \ell^{-1}\ \text{min}^{-1}$$

(b) In 60 min (1 hr), the amount of $N_2O_5$ decomposing is

$$2.5 \times 10^{-4}\ \text{mol}\ \ell^{-1}\ \text{min}^{-1}\ (60\ \text{min}) = 1.5 \times 10^{-2}\ \text{mol}\ \ell^{-1}$$

The amount remaining is

$$0.40\ M - 0.015\ M = 0.38\ M$$

3. Most of the 15.7 billion pounds of $HNO_3$ produced in the United States during 1977 was prepared by the following sequence of reactions:

$$4NH_3\,(g) + 5O_2\,(g) \longrightarrow 4NO(g) + 6H_2O(g) \tag{1}$$

$$2NO(g) + O_2\,(g) \longrightarrow 2NO_2\,(g) \tag{2}$$

$$3NO_2\,(g) + H_2O(\ell) \longrightarrow 2HNO_3\,(aq) + NO(g) \tag{3}$$

The first reaction is run by burning ammonia in air over a platinum catalyst. This reaction is fast. Reaction (3) is also fast. The second reaction limits the rate at which nitric acid can be prepared from ammonia. If Reaction (2) is second order in NO and first order in $O_2$, what is the rate of formation of $NO_2$ when the oxygen concentration is $0.50\ M$ and the nitric oxide concentration is $0.75\ M$? The rate constant for the reaction is $5.8 \times 10^{-6}\ \ell^2\ \text{mol}^{-2}\ \text{sec}^{-1}$.

**Solution**

The rate law governing the formation of $HNO_3$ is Rate $= k\,[NO]^2\,[O_2]$. From the data given,

$$\text{Rate} = 5.8 \times 10^{-6}\ \ell^2\ \text{mol}^{-2}\ \text{sec}^{-1}\left[0.75\ \frac{\text{mol}}{\ell}\right]^2\left[0.50\ \frac{\text{mol}}{\ell}\right]$$

$$= 1.6 \times 10^{-6}\ \text{mol}\ \ell^{-1}\ \text{sec}^{-1}$$

5. Hydrogen reacts with nitric oxide to form nitrous oxide, laughing gas, according to the equation $H_2\,(g) + NO(g) \longrightarrow N_2O(g) + H_2O(g)$. Determine the rate equation and the rate constant for the reaction from the following data:

| Experiment | 1 | 2 | 3 |
|---|---|---|---|
| [NO] ($M$) | 0.30 | 0.60 | 0.60 |
| [H$_2$] ($M$) | 0.35 | 0.35 | 0.70 |
| Rate (mol $\ell^{-1}$ sec$^{-1}$) | $2.835 \times 10^{-3}$ | $1.134 \times 10^{-2}$ | $2.268 \times 10^{-2}$ |

**Solution**

It is intended that the data for each separate experiment given in this problem be substituted into the general rate equation (Rate $= k[NO]^m [H_2]^n$) to determine how $n$ and $m$, the order of the reaction with respect to each component, varies. For the three reactions, after substituting the data, we have

Exp. 1:  $2.835 \times 10^{-3}$ mol $\ell^{-1}$ sec$^{-1}$
$$= k[0.30 \text{ mol } \ell^{-1}]^m [0.35 \text{ mol } \ell^{-1}]^n$$

Exp. 2:  $1.134 \times 10^{-2}$ mol $\ell^{-1}$ sec$^{-1}$
$$= k[0.60 \text{ mol } \ell^{-1}]^m [0.35 \text{ mol } \ell^{-1}]^n$$

Exp. 3:  $2.268 \times 10^{-2}$ mol $\ell^{-1}$ sec$^{-1}$
$$= k[0.60 \text{ mol } \ell^{-1}]^m [0.70 \text{ mol } \ell^{-1}]^n$$

Since $k$, $m$, and $n$ refer to the same reaction, they must retain the same values throughout the three experiments. In going from Experiment 1 to Experiment 2, holding $[H_2]$ constant we find that doubling the concentration of NO causes a fourfold increase in the rate. This can only occur if the value of $m$ is 2 since $[2]^2 = 4$. In a similar manner, holding the concentration of NO constant in Experiment 2 and Experiment 3 with subsequent doubling of the concentrations of $H_2$ doubles the rate. The rate equation holds for this latter group of two experiments only if $n$ equals 1. Therefore the overall rate is second order in NO and first order in $H_2$.

To determine the value of the rate constants, we use the data of Experiment 1 in the rate law.

$$\text{Rate} = k[NO]^2 [H_2]^1$$

$$2.835 \times 10^{-3} \text{ mol } \ell^{-1} \text{ sec}^{-1} = k[0.30 \text{ mol } \ell^{-1}]^2 [0.35 \text{ mol } \ell^{-1}]$$

$$k = \frac{2.835 \times 10^{-3} \text{ mol } \ell^{-1} \text{ sec}^{-1}}{(0.09 \text{ mol}^2 \ell^{-2})(0.35 \text{ mol } \ell^{-1})}$$

$$= 9.0 \times 10^{-2} \text{ mol}^{-2} \ell^2 \text{ sec}^{-1}$$

7.  The rate constant at 325° for the reaction $C_4 H_8 \longrightarrow 2C_2 H_4$ (Section 15.11) is $6.1 \times 10^{-8}$ sec$^{-1}$, and the activation energy is 261 kJ per mole of $C_4 H_8$. Determine the frequency factor for the reaction.

**Solution**

The rate constant, $k$, is related to the activation energy, $E_a$, by a relationship known as the Arrhenius Law. Its form is

$$k = A \times 10^{-(E_a/2.303\,RT)}$$

where $A$ is the frequency factor. Using the above data, and converting kJ to joules, we have

$$6.1 \times 10^{-8}\ sec^{-1} = A \times 10^{-[+261,000\ J/(2.303(8.314\ J\ K^{-1})(325 + 273)K)]}$$

$$= A \times 10^{-22.8}$$

$$A = \frac{6.1 \times 10^{-8}\ sec^{-1}}{1.58 \times 10^{-23}} = 3.8 \times 10^{15}\ sec^{-1}$$

9. The hydrolysis of the sugar sucrose to the sugars glucose and fructose $(C_{12}H_{22}O_{11} + H_2O \longrightarrow C_6H_{12}O_6 + C_6H_{12}O_6)$ follows a first-order rate equation

$$Rate = k[C_{12}H_{22}O_{11}]$$

(The products of the reaction have the same molecular formulas but differ in the arrangement of the atoms in their molecules). In neutral solution, $k = 2.1 \times 10^{-11}\ sec^{-1}$ at $27°$ and $8.5 \times 10^{-11}\ sec^{-1}$ at $37°$. Determine the activation energy, the frequency factor, and the rate constant for this equation at $47°$.

**Solution**

The text demonstrates that the value of $E_a$ may be determined from a plot of $\log k$ against $1/T$ that gives a straight line whose slope is $-E_a/2.303\ R$. This is based on the equation

$$\log k = \log A - \frac{E_a}{2.303\ RT}$$

Only two data points are given and these must determine a straight line when $\log k$ is plotted against $1/T$. The values needed are

$$k_1 = 2.1 \times 10^{-11} \qquad \log k_1 = -10.6778$$

$$k_2 = 8.5 \times 10^{-11} \qquad \log k_2 = -10.0706$$

$$t_1 = 27°C = 300\ K \qquad 1/T_1 = 3.3333 \times 10^{-3}$$

$$t_2 = 37°C = 310\ K \qquad 1/T_2 = 3.2258 \times 10^{-3}$$

The slope of the line determined by these points is given by

$$Slope = \frac{\Delta(\log k)}{\Delta(1/T)} = \frac{(-10.0706) - (-10.6778)}{(3.2258 \times 10^{-3}) - (3.3333 \times 10^{-3})}$$

$$= \frac{0.6072}{-0.1075 \times 10^{-3}} = -5648$$

$$E_a = 2.303(8.314\ J\ mol^{-1})(-5648) = 108,100\ J = 108\ kJ$$

Whenever we take differences of very small numbers, such as the reciprocals of $T$ above, an inherent problem occurs. In order to get accurate differences, a larger number of significant figures than justified by the data must be used. Thus we used five figures to obtain the value $E_a = 108$ kJ. This difficulty may be alleviated by the approach shown below.

For only two data points we may use the Arrhenius Law

$$k = A \times 10^{-E_a/2.303\,RT}$$

in an equally accurate, analytical solution for $E_a$. This is possible because the value of $A$ will be the same throughout the course of the reaction. Once the value of $E_a$ is determined, the value of $A$ may be determined from either of the equations (1) or (2) shown below. Then $k$ at 47°C may be determined using the value of $E_A$ and $A$ so determined. We proceed as follows:

$$k = A \times 10^{-E_a/2.303\,RT}$$

$$2.1 \times 10^{-11} \text{ sec}^{-1} = A \times 10^{-E_a/2.303(8.314 \text{ J K}^{-1})\,(300 \text{ K})} \tag{1}$$

$$8.5 \times 10^{-11} \text{ sec}^{-1} = A \times 10^{-E_a/2.303(8.314 \text{ J K}^{-1})\,(310 \text{ K})} \tag{2}$$

Equating the values of $A$ as solved from (1) and (2) we have

$$2.1 \times 10^{-11} \text{ sec}^{-1} \times 10^{+\,E_a/2.303(8.314 \text{ J K}^{-1})\,(310\,K)}$$

$$= 8.5 \times 10^{-11} \text{ sec}^{-1} \times 10^{+\,E_a/2.303(8.314 \text{ J K}^{-1})\,(310\,K)}$$

or

$$2.1 \times 10^{-11} \times 10^{+E_a/5744} = 8.5 \times 10^{-11} \times 10^{+E_a/5936}$$

Taking common logs of both sides gives

$$(\log 2.1 \times 10^{-11}) + \frac{E_a}{5744} = (\log 8.5 \times 10^{-11}) + \frac{E_a}{5936}$$

$$-10.68 + \frac{E_a}{5744} = -10.07 + \frac{E_a}{5936}$$

$$E_a \left( \frac{1}{5744} - \frac{1}{5936} \right) = -10.07 + 10.68$$

$$E_a (1.741 \times 10^{-4} - 1.685 \times 10^{-4}) = 0.61$$

$$E_a = \frac{0.61}{0.056 \times 10^{-4}}$$

$$= 109 \text{ kJ}$$

The value of $A$ may be found from either Equation (1) or (2). Using (1) we have

$$2.1 \times 10^{-11} \text{ sec}^{-1} = A \times 10^{-109,000/2.303(8.314)(300)} = A \times 10^{-18.98}$$

$A = 2.1 \times 10^{-11} \ sec^{-1} \times 10^{+18.98} = 2.1 \times 10^{-11} \ (9.55 \times 10^{18} \ sec^{-1})$

$= 2.0 \times 10^8 \ sec^{-1}$

The value of $k$ at $47°$ may be determined from the Arrhenius law now that the value of $E_a$ and $A$ have been calculated.

$k = A \times 10^{-E_a/2.303 \, RT}$

$= 2.0 \times 10^8 \ sec^{-1} \times 10^{-109 \, 000 \, J/2.303(8.314 \, J \, K^{-1})(320 \, K)}$

$= 2.0 \times 10^8 \ sec^{-1} \times 10^{-17.79} = 2.0 \times 10^8 \ sec^{-1} \ (1.62 \times 10^{-18})$

$= 3.2 \times 10^{-10} \ sec^{-1}$

10. If the rate of a reaction doubles for every $10°$ rise in temperature, how much faster would the reaction proceed at $55°$ than at $25°$? at $100°$ than at $25°$?

**Solution**

The rate doubles for each $10°C$ rise in temperature. Fifty-five degrees is a $30°$ increase over $25°$. Thus the rate doubles three times, or $2^3$ (rate at $25°$) = 8 times faster. One hundred degrees is a $75°$ increase over $25°$. Thus the rate doubles 7.5 times, or $2^{7.5}$ (rate at $25°$) = 180 times faster. This procedure gives a rough approximation!

13. The decomposition of $SO_2Cl_2$ to $SO_2$ and $Cl_2$ is a first-order reaction with the rate constant $k = 2.2 \times 10^{-5} \ sec^{-1}$ at $320°$. Determine the half-life of this reaction. At $320°$, how much $SO_2Cl_2(g)$ would remain in a 1.00-ℓ flask 90.0 min after the introduction of 0.0238 mol of $SO_2Cl_2$ into the flask? Assume the rate of the reverse reaction is so slow that it can be ignored.

**Solution**

The half-life of a first-order reaction is determined from the expression

$$t_{1/2} = \frac{0.693}{k} = \frac{0.693}{2.2 \times 10^{-5} \ sec^{-1}}$$

$$= 3.2 \times 10^4 \ sec$$

For a first-order reaction,

$$\log \frac{[A_0]}{[A]} = \frac{kt}{2.303}$$

The concentration of $A_0$ is $0.0238 \, M$, and substitution gives

$$\log \frac{[0.0238]}{[A]} = \frac{2.2 \times 10^{-5} \ sec^{-1} \left(90.0 \ min \times \dfrac{60 \ sec}{min}\right)}{2.303}$$

$$\log 0.0238 - \log A = 0.0516$$
$$- \log A = 0.0516 + 1.623$$
$$\log A = -1.675$$
$$A = 0.0211 \, M = 2.11 \times 10^{-2} \text{ mol in the } 1.00\text{-}\ell \text{ flask}$$

14. Assume that the rate equations given below apply to each reaction at equilibrium. Determine the rate equation of each of the reverse reactions.

(a) $NO(g) + O_3(g) \longrightarrow NO_2(g) + O_2(g)$

$\text{Rate}_1 = k_1 [NO][O_3]$

(d) $2NO(g) + 2H_2(g) \longrightarrow N_2(g) + 2H_2O(g)$

$\text{Rate}_1 = k_1 [NO][H_2]$

**Solution**

(a) The overall equilibrium constant is

$$K_e = \frac{[NO_2][O_2]}{[NO][O_3]} = \frac{k_1}{k_2}$$

From the rate expression,

$$k_1 = \frac{\text{Rate}_1}{[NO][O_3]}$$

At equilibrium, $\text{Rate}_1 = \text{Rate}_2$, and therefore, substituting for $k_1$,

$$\frac{k_1}{k_2} = \frac{\dfrac{\text{Rate}_1}{[NO][O_3]}}{k_2} = \frac{\dfrac{\text{Rate}_2}{[NO][O_3]}}{k_2} = \frac{[NO_2][O_2]}{[NO][O_3]}$$

Using the last two terms, we have

$$\frac{\text{Rate}_2}{k_2} = [NO_2][O_2]$$

or

$$\text{Rate}_2 = k_2 [NO_2][O_2]$$

(d)

$$K_e = \frac{[N_2][H_2O]^2}{[NO]^2[H_2]^2} = \frac{k_1}{k_2}$$

Using the same procedure as in part (a), we have

$$\text{Rate}_1 = \text{Rate}_2$$
$$\text{Rate}_1 = k_1 [NO][H_2]$$

$$k_1 = \frac{\text{Rate}_1}{[NO][H_2]} = \frac{\text{Rate}_2}{[NO][H_2]}$$

Substitution into the value for $K_e$ gives

$$\frac{k_1}{k_2} = \frac{\frac{\text{Rate}_2}{[\text{NO}][\text{H}_2]}}{k_2} = \frac{[\text{N}_2][\text{H}_2\text{O}]^2}{[\text{NO}]^2[\text{H}_2]^2}$$

$$\text{Rate}_2 = k_2 \frac{[\text{N}_2][\text{H}_2\text{O}]^2}{[\text{NO}][\text{H}_2]}$$

15. The rate of the reaction $H_2(g) + I_2(g) \longrightarrow 2HI(g)$ at 25° is given by Rate = $1.7 \times 10^{-18}$ $[H_2][I_2]$. The rate of decomposition of gaseous HI to $H_2(g)$ and $I_2(g)$ at 25° is given by Rate = $2.4 \times 10^{-21}$ $[HI]^2$. What is the equilibrium constant for the formation of gaseous HI from the gaseous elements at 25°?

**Solution**

The equilibrium constant may be written as

$$K = \frac{k_{\text{forward}}}{k_{\text{reverse}}}$$

since at equilibrium, $\text{Rate}_1 = \text{Rate}_2$, or

$$k_{\text{forward}}\ [\text{H}_2][\text{I}_2] = k_{\text{reverse}}\ [\text{HI}]^2$$

This may be expressed as

$$\frac{k_{\text{forward}}}{k_{\text{reverse}}} = \frac{[\text{HI}]^2}{[\text{H}_2][\text{I}_2]}$$

which is recognized as an equilibrium constant. Substitution gives

$$K = \frac{k_{\text{forward}}}{k_{\text{reverse}}} = \frac{1.7 \times 10^{-18}}{2.4 \times 10^{-21}} = 7.1 \times 10^2$$

16. A sample of $NH_3(g)$ was formed from $H_2(g)$ and $N_2(g)$ at 500°. If the equilibrium mixture was found to contain 1.35 mol $H_2$ per liter, 1.15 mol $N_2$ per liter and $4.12 \times 10^{-1}$ mol $NH_3$ per liter, what is the value of the equilibrium constant for the formation of $NH_3$?

**Solution**

The reaction may be written as

$$\text{N}_2 + 3\text{H}_2 \rightleftharpoons 2\text{NH}_3$$

The equilibrium constant for the reaction is

$$K_e = \frac{[\text{NH}_3]^2}{[\text{N}_2][\text{H}_2]^3} = \frac{[4.12 \times 10^{-1}\ \text{mol}\ \ell^{-1}]^2}{[1.15\ \text{mol}\ \ell^{-1}][1.35\ \text{mol}\ \ell^{-1}]^3}$$

$$= \frac{0.170\ \text{mol}^2\ \ell^{-2}}{(1.15\ \text{mol}\ \ell^{-1})(2.46\ \text{mol}^3\ \ell^{-3})}$$

$$= 0.0600\ \text{mol}\ \ell^{-1} = 6.00 \times 10^{-2}\ \text{mol}^{-2}\ \ell^2$$

18. A 0.72–mol sample of $PCl_5$ is put into a 1.00-ℓ vessel and heated. At equilibrium, the vessel contains 0.40 mol of $PCl_3$ (g) as well as $Cl_2$ (g) and undissociated $PCl_5$ (g). What is the equilibrium constant for the decomposition of $PCl_5$ to $PCl_3$ and $Cl_2$ at this temperature?

**Solution**

The reaction is

$$PCl_5 (g) \rightleftharpoons PCl_3 (g) + Cl_2 (g)$$

The equilibrium constant is

$$K_e = \frac{[PCl_3][Cl_2]}{[PCl_5]}$$

The amount of $PCl_5$ that had to decompose is 0.72 mol – 0.40 mol = 0.32 mol. This must also be the amount of $Cl_2$ present. Thus

$$K_e = \frac{[0.40 \text{ mol } ℓ^{-1}][0.40 \text{ mol } ℓ^{-1}]}{[0.32 \text{ mol } ℓ^{-1}]}$$

$$= 0.50 \text{ mol } ℓ^{-1}$$

20. The vapor pressure of water is 0.196 atm at 60°. What is the equilibrium constant for the transformation $H_2O(l) \longrightarrow H_2O(g)$?

**Solution**

The equilibrium constant may be expressed in terms of concentrations or in terms of pressures. For the transformation $H_2O(l) \longrightarrow H_2O(g)$ the equilibrium may easiest be expressed in terms of pressures. The equilibrium constant depends only on the substance in the gaseous phase at equilibrium. Thus

$$K_p = p(H_2O(g))$$

$$= 0.196 \text{ atm}$$

22. The equilibrium constant for the reaction represented by $CO + H_2O \rightleftharpoons CO_2 + H_2$ is 5.0 at a given temperature.

(a) Upon analysis, an equilibrium mixture of the substances present at the given temperature was found to contain 0.20 mol of CO, 0.30 mol of water vapor, and 0.90 mol of $H_2$ in a liter. How many moles of $CO_2$ were there in the equilibrium mixture?
(b) Maintaining the same temperature, additional $H_2$ was added to the system, and some water vapor removed by drying. A new equilibrium mixture was thereby established that contained 0.40 mol of CO, 0.30 mol of water vapor, and 1.2 mol of $H_2$ in a liter. How many moles of $CO_2$ were in the new equilibrium mixture? Compare the value with the quantity in part (a) and discuss whether the second value is reasonable. Explain how it is possible

139

for the water vapor concentration to be the same in the two equilibrium solutions even though some vapor was removed before the second equilibrium was established.

**Solution**

(a) For the above reaction,

$$K_e = \frac{[CO_2][H_2]}{[CO][H_2O]} = 5.0$$

The concentrations at equilibrium are 0.20 $M$ CO, 0.30 $M$ $H_2O$, 0.90 $M$ $H_2$. Substitution gives

$$K_e = 5.0 = \frac{[CO_2][0.90]}{[0.20][0.30]}$$

$$[CO_2] = \frac{5.0(0.20)(0.30)}{0.90} = 0.33\ M$$

No. moles $CO_2 = 0.33$ mol $\ell^{-1} \times 1\ \ell = 0.33$ mol

(b) At the particular temperature of reaction, $K_e$ remains constant at 5.0. The new concentrations are 0.40 $M$ CO, 0.30 $M$ $H_2O$, 1.2 $M$ $H_2$.

$$\frac{[CO_2][1.2]}{[0.40][0.30]} = 5.0$$

$$[CO_2] = [0.50\ M]$$

No. moles $CO_2 = 0.50$ mol $\ell^{-1} \times 1\ \ell = 0.50$ mol

25. The equilibrium constant, $K$, for the reaction $PCl_5(g) \rightleftharpoons PCl_3(g) + Cl_2(g)$ is 0.0211 at a certain temperature. What are the equilibrium concentrations of $PCl_5$, $PCl_3$, and $Cl_2$ starting with a concentration of $PCl_5$ of 1.00 $M$?

**Solution**

The concentrations of these substances at equilibrium depend on the initial amount of $PCl_5$. Let $x$ equal the amount of $PCl_5$ that dissociates. The amount of $PCl_5$ at equilibrium is 1.00 mol $\ell^{-1} - x$. Since the decomposition of one mole of $PCl_5$ produces one mole of $PCl_3$ and one mole of $Cl_2$, the amount of $PCl_3$ formed is $x$ and the amount of $Cl_2$ formed is $x$. Substitution into the equilibrium constant and solving for $x$ follows the sequence

$$K_e = \frac{[PCl_3][Cl_2]}{[PCl_5]} = \frac{(x)(x)}{1-x} = 0.0211$$

$$x^2 = 0.0211(1-x)$$

$$x^2 + 0.0211\,x - 0.0211 = 0$$

See page 151 and problem 3, page 154 for information on how to solve a quadratic equation. Use the quadratic equation to solve for $x$:

$$x = \frac{-b \pm \sqrt{b^2 - 4ac}}{2a} = \frac{-0.0211 \pm \sqrt{(0.0211)^2 + (0.0844)}}{2}$$

$$x = \frac{-0.0211 \pm \sqrt{0.0848}}{2} = \frac{-0.0211 + .2912}{2} = 0.135 \text{ mol } \ell^{-1}$$

The final concentrations are

$$PCl_5 = 1.00 - 0.135 = 0.865 \ M$$

$$Cl_2 = PCl_3 = 0.135 \ M$$

27. The equilibrium constant, $K_p$, for the decomposition of nitrosyl bromide $[2NOBr(g) \rightleftharpoons 2NO(g) + Br_2\,(g)]$ is $1.0 \times 10^{-2}$ atm at $25°$. What per cent of NOBr is decomposed at $25°$ and a total pressure of 0.25 atm?

**Solution**

The equilibrium constant in terms of pressures for the above reaction is

$$K_p = \frac{(p_{NO})^2 \ (p_{Br_2})}{(p_{NOBr})^2} = 1.0 \times 10^{-2} \text{ atm}$$

Since $K_e < 1$, the reaction favors the reactants, that is, much of the initial amount of NOBr will remain undissociated at equilibrium. From the chemical equation we find that for each mole of NOBr decomposed, 1 mole of NO and $\frac{1}{2}$ mole of $Br_2$ are formed. Since all of the components are gases, the pressure of each component will vary as its number of moles. Let $x =$ the pressure in atm of the NOBr decomposed. Then, in terms of pressure, the partial pressures of the species at equilibrium are

$$p_{NOBr} = 0.25 \text{ atm} - x - 0.5 \ x = 0.25 \text{ atm} - 1.5 \ x \text{ atm}$$

$$p_{NO} = x \text{ atm} \qquad p_{Br_2} = 0.5 \ x \text{ atm}$$

Substitution into the equilibrium expression gives

$$K_p = \frac{[x]^2 \ [0.5 \ x]}{[0.25 - 1.5 \ x]^2} = 1.0 \times 10^{-2} \text{ atm}$$

Solving for $x$, we have

$$x^3 - 4.5 \times 10^{-2} \ x^2 + 1.5 \times 10^{-2} \ x - 1.25 \times 10^{-3} = 0$$

This is a cubic equation, which may be solved in several ways. One technique involves using a cubic formula, but this formula is not readily available nor always applicable, as is the familiar quadratic equation. The method chosen for use here is one of successive approximations. This technique for quadratic equations is discussed in Chapter 16 of the textbook. The method is based on the idea that the value of $x$ that solves this equation will give a value of the equation exactly equal to zero. Values of $x$ that are too large will be positive and those too small will be negative. In order to shorten the process as much as possible, the best choice of $x$ should be made using the information available. In this case, no more than 0.25 nor less than 0.0 can be dissociated, and, therefore, the range of $x$ must be 0 to 0.25. We pick a value of 0.1 for $x$ and substitute into the equation. Thus

$$x^3 - 4.5 \times 10^{-2}\, x^2 + 1.5 \times 10^{-2}\, x - 1.25 \times 10^{-3} = 0$$

for $x = 0.10$

$$10^{-3} - 4.5 \times 10^{-4} + 1.5 \times 10^{-3} - 1.25 \times 10^{-4} \qquad f(x) = 8.00 \times 10^{-4}$$

The value obtained from this guess is close to zero but is positive. This means that we are on the high side of the true value of $x$. A negative value will mean that the value chosen is too low. Additional choices of $x$ give the following values:

| $x$ | $f(x)$, value of cubic equation expression above |
|---|---|
| 0.10 | $8.00 \times 10^{-4}$ |
| 0.05 | $-4.875 \times 10^{-4}$ |
| 0.08 | $1.74 \times 10^{-4}$ |
| 0.07 | $-7.75 \times 10^{-5}$ |
| 0.073 | $+1.118 \times 10^{-3}$ |
| 0.071 | $-5.39 \times 10^{-5}$ |
| 0.072 | $-3.03 \times 10^{-5}$ |
| 0.0725 | $-1.8 \times 10^{-5}$ |

From these values obtained, we see that the values for $x$ of 0.072 and 0.073 bracket the transition from negative values to positive values. Consequently, the value 0.0725 is chosen to narrow the value of $x$ still closer. By comparison of the values $f(x)$ for 0.0725 and 0.073, the value of $x$ that solves the cubic equation (that is, gives a value of zero) is close to 0.0725. This value could be refined further still, but this last value is sufficiently accurate to substitute and to determine the value of the partial pressures. Thus,

$$p_{NO} = 0.0725 \text{ atm}$$
$$p_{Br_2} = 0.0362 \text{ atm}$$
$$p_{NOBr} = 0.250 - 0.109 = 0.141 \text{ atm}$$

Total pressure at equilibrium = 0.0725 atm + 0.0362 atm + 0.141 atm
= 0.250 atm

Substitution of these values into the original equation proves that $x = 0.0725$ atm is a solution and that the amount that decomposes is responsible for 0.109 atm of the total pressure.

Our problem does not end here. To determine the amount of NOBr originally present, needed in order to calculate the per cent decomposition, we must consider that had the NOBr not decomposed, the total pressure due to it alone would have been larger than the 0.141 atm present at equilibrium. That is, the original pressure is 0.141 atm plus the pressure that would have been present had NOBr not decomposed. Using the values above, the original pressure is 0.141 atm + 0.0725 atm = 0.213 atm. Thus the per cent decomposition is

$$\frac{\text{Amount decomposed}}{\text{original amount}} \times 100 = \frac{0.0725 \text{ atm}}{0.213 \text{ atm}} \times 100 = 34\%$$

28. A 1.00-ℓ vessel at 400° contains the following equilibrium concentrations: $N_2$, 1.00 $M$; $H_2$, 0.50 $M$; and $NH_3$, 0.50 $M$. How many moles of hydrogen must be removed from the vessel in order to increase the concentration of nitrogen to 1.2 $M$?

**Solution**

The reaction is $N_2 + 3H_2 \rightleftharpoons 2NH_3$. The equilibrium constant for this equilibrium is calculated from the original data.

$$K_e = \frac{[NH_3]^2}{[N_2][H_2]^3} = \frac{(0.50)^2}{(1.00)(0.50)^3} = 2.0 \text{ mol}^{-2} \text{ ℓ}^2$$

The concentration of $N_2$ increases by 1.2 $M$ − 1.0 $M$ = 0.2 $M$. From the balanced equation, 1 mol $N_2 \longrightarrow 2$ mol $NH_3$. Thus 0.2 $M$ $N_2$ must have come from the decomposition of 2(0.2 $M$ $NH_3$) = 0.4 $M$ $NH_3$. The amount of $NH_3$ remaining is 0.5 $M$ − 0.4 $M$ = 0.1 $M$ $NH_3$. In addition to the nitrogen formed, hydrogen was also formed. Since $NH_3 \longrightarrow \frac{3}{2} H_2$, the decomposition of 0.4 $M$ $NH_3$ results in the formation of 0.60 $M$ $H_2$. Thus a total of 0.50 $M$ + 0.60 $M$ = 1.10 $M$ $H_2$ is the total amount of $H_2$.

In order to maintain equilibrium, hydrogen must be removed from the reaction mixture to allow the concentration of $N_2$ to increase to 1.2 $M$. Let $x$ = the amount of $H_2$ in the final mixture. Then

$$K_e = \frac{[0.1 \text{ mol ℓ}^{-1}]^2}{[1.20 \text{ mol ℓ}^{-1}][x]^3} = 2.0 \text{ mol}^{-2} \text{ ℓ}^2$$

$$2.4 \ x^3 \text{ mol}^{-1} \text{ ℓ}^1 = 0.01 \text{ mol}^2 \text{ ℓ}^{-2}$$

$$x^3 = 4.17 \times 10^{-3} \text{ mol}^3 \text{ ℓ}^{-3}$$

$$x = 0.16 \text{ mol ℓ}^{-1}$$

Since only 0.16 $M$ remains,

$$1.10 \, M - 0.16 \, M = 0.94 \, M \, H_2 \text{ were removed}$$

This is not unreasonable even though more hydrogen was removed than originally present, since the decomposition of $NH_3$ formed additional $H_2$·

## RELATED PROBLEMS

1. Hemoglobin thermally denatures in a first-order reaction that has been found to take 3460 sec at 60.0°C and 530 sec at 65.0°C. Assume that the Arrhenius Law governs the reaction. Calculate the energy of activation at 60.0°C. *Answer: $E_a = 35.1 \, kJ$*

2. A certain reaction

$$2X^- + A + 2H^+ \longrightarrow X_2 + 2HA$$

occurs in several stages. The rate equation is

$$\text{Rate} = k[A][H^+][X^-]$$

(a) If the concentration of A is increased by a factor of 4, by what factor is the rate of disappearance of $X^-$ ions increased?
(b) How is $k$ changed by increasing the concentration of $X^-$ ions?
(c) If the rate of disappearance of $X^-$ ions is $3.8 \times 10^{-3} \, mol \, \ell^{-1} \, sec^{-1}$, what is the rate of appearance of $X_2$?
*Answer: (a) 3; (b) none; (c) $1.9 \times 10^{-3} \, mol \, \ell^{-1} \, sec^{-1}$*

3. The following rate data for the formation of C were taken for the reaction

$$A + 2B \longrightarrow C$$

| $[A]/mol \, \ell^{-1}$ | $[B]/mol \, \ell^{-1}$ | $Rate/mol \, \ell^{-1} \, sec^{-1}$ |
|---|---|---|
| $3.50 \times 10^{-2}$ | $2.3 \times 10^{-2}$ | $5.0 \times 10^{-7}$ |
| $7.0 \times 10^{-2}$ | $4.6 \times 10^{-2}$ | $2.0 \times 10^{-6}$ |
| $7.0 \times 10^{-2}$ | $9.2 \times 10^{-2}$ | $4.0 \times 10^{-6}$ |

What are $m$ and $n$ in the rate equation

$$\text{Rate} = k[A]^m [B]^n$$

and what is the rate constant $k$? *Answer: $m = 1, n = 1$; $k = 6.21 \times 10^{-4} \, \ell \, mol^{-1} \, sec^{-1}$*

4. A 1.00-$\ell$ vessel contains at equilibrium 0.300 mol of $N_2$, 0.400 mol of $H_2$, and 0.100 mol of $NH_3$. If the temperature is maintained constant, how many moles of $H_2$ must be introduced into the vessel in order to double the equilibrium concentration of $NH_3$? *Answer: 0.425 M*

5. At a certain temperature, the gas-phase reaction $N_2O_4(g) \rightleftharpoons 2NO_2(g)$ has a $K_e$ of $1.1 \times 10^{-5}$. If 0.20 mol of $N_2O_4$ is dissolved in 400 ml of chloroform and the reaction allowed to come to equilibrium, (a) what is the new $NO_2$ concentration, and (b) what will be the per cent dissociation of the original $N_2O_4$?

*Answer: (a) $2.3 \times 10^{-3}$ mol $\ell^{-1} NO_2$; (b) 0.23% dissociation*

# Chapter 16: Ionic Equilibria
## of Weak Electrolytes

## INTRODUCTION

Weak electrolytes are substances, such as acids, bases, and salts, that only slightly conduct an electric current in aqueous solution. Examples include the various substances that carbonates form in the oceans, in ground water, and even in blood; organic acids that make up the fats of plants and animals; and the vast amount of sulfides and sulfites formed by the oxidation of sulfur. One important aspect of weak electrolytes is that they have a major role in the control of acidity in our natural environment.

   In water, certain weak electrolytes function as either weak acids or weak bases that undergo dissociation, thereby reaching an equilibrium that contains both ions of the electrolyte and the undissociated electrolyte molecules. Aqueous solutions of weak acids, HA, and weak bases, WB, are represented by the following equilibria:

$$HA(aq) \rightleftharpoons H_3O^+(aq) + A^-(aq) \qquad K_i \ll 1$$

$$WB(aq) \rightleftharpoons WBH^+(aq) + OH^-(aq) \qquad K_i \ll 1$$

In general, the fraction of electrolyte molecules so dissociated at equilibrium ranges from a high of about 20% to a low of less than 1%.

   The salts formed by the reaction of weak acids with weak bases are themselves weak bases or weak acids: They are called the *conjugate base* or *conjugate acid* of the respective acid or base. These salts form solutions called *buffer solutions*, that, in combination with the parent acid or base, are resistant to changes in acidity. If these salts are dissolved by themselves in water, they hydrolyze: that is, react with water to form solutions that are acidic or basic depending on their origin.

The discussion in this chapter treats the equilibria of weak electrolytes in aqueous solution. Specifically, the equilibria include weak electrolytes, buffer solutions, and hydrolytic solutions. Problems are included to represent each type of equilibrium.

## FORMULAS AND DEFINITIONS

**Ionization constants** $(K_i)$: weak acids, weak bases   An ionization constant is a measure of the dissociation of an acid or base in aqueous solution into $H_3O^+(aq)$ or $OH^-(aq)$. In general, aqueous solutions of weak acids and weak bases are ionized according to the reactions

$$HA(aq) + H_2O \rightleftharpoons H_3O^+(aq) + A^-(aq)$$

$$WB(aq) + H_2O \rightleftharpoons WBH^+(aq) + OH^-(aq)$$

where HA stands for a weak acid and WB stands for a weak base. The corresponding expressions for $K_i$ values are

$$K_i = \frac{[H_3O^+][A^-]}{[HA]} \quad ; \quad K_i = \frac{[WBH^+][OH^-]}{[WB]}$$

where the brackets indicate molar concentrations of the ions or molecular species in solution. Typical values for $K_i$ are considerably less than 1 (See Appendices G and H). The larger the value of $K_i$ the greater the extent of ionization or dissociation; hence the acid or base is correspondingly stronger.

**Buffer solution**   A buffer solution contains either a weak acid or a weak base that is in solution with a salt having an ion common to the weak acid or weak base. Such solutions resist changes in acidity produced by the addition of more acid or base. This is accomplished by reaction of the acid or base with either the ions $A^-$, $WBH^+$, or with the molecular acid or base already in solution. The reactions that can occur upon the addition of acid or base to a buffer solution are the following.
   *Weak acid-salt*:

$$A^-(aq) + H^+(aq) \longrightarrow HA(aq)$$

$$HA(aq) + OH^-(aq) \longrightarrow A^-(aq) + H_2O$$

   *Weak base-salt*:

$$WBH^+(aq) + OH^-(aq) \longrightarrow WB(aq) + H_2O$$

$$WB(aq) + H^+(aq) \longrightarrow WBH^+(aq)$$

Buffer solutions are described algebraically in terms of the $K_i$ defining the weak acid or weak base. The general expressions defining buffers are

Weak acid-salt:$\qquad\qquad K_i = [H^+]\dfrac{[salt]}{[acid]}$

Weak base-salt:$\qquad\qquad K_i = [OH^-]\dfrac{[salt]}{[base]}$

Typical buffer solutions are composed of weak acids and their sodium salts or weak bases and their chlorides. Examples are acetic acid-sodium acetate and ammonia-ammonium chloride.

**Ion-product constant for water $(K_w)$** The equilibrium constant that describes the relation between the hydronium ion and hydroxyl ion concentrations in aqueous solution is

$$K_w = [H_3O^+][OH^-] = 1 \times 10^{-14}\qquad \text{at } 25°C$$

In pure water, the concentration of $H_3O^+$ and of $OH^-$ equals $1 \times 10^{-7}\ M$ at $25°$ C.

**pH** The pH of a solution is a measure of the hydronium ion concentration in solution, and is defined as

$$pH = -\log[H_3O^+]$$

The pH values of most aqueous solutions range from a low of about 0 to a high of about 14; at a pH of 0, $[H_3O^+] = 1.0$, and at 14, $[H_3O^+] = 1 \times 10^{-14}$.

*Example 1*: Calculate the pH of a solution that has a hydronium ion concentration of 0.0025 $M$.

**Solution**

If you use a calculator with logarithm capability, merely enter the concentration value, take the log, and change the sign to get pH. If, however, you use log tables, the $[H_3O^+]$ should be rewritten in scientific notation and the log taken as follows:

$$pH = -\log 0.0025 = -\log 2.5 \times 10^{-3}$$
$$= -[\log 2.5 + \log 10^{-3}]$$
$$= -[0.3979 + (-3)]$$
$$= -(-2.60) = 2.60$$

The numbers to the right of the decimal point are the significant figures in the pH value; the 2, in this case, represents the power of 10 in the log function.

Hydronium ion concentrations are frequently needed in calculations involving equilibrium constants. Given the $pH$ of a solution, the $[H_3O^+]$ can be calculated by using the definition of $pH$.

$$pH = -\log[H_3O^+]$$
$$\log[H_3O^+] = -pH$$
$$[H_3O^+] = 10^{-pH}$$

By use of a calculator with log capability, you should be able to enter the exponent, $-pH$, and compute directly. Log tables, however, contain only positive values, and negative log values must be rewritten as a product of two exponential base-10 terms for conversion to a rational term.

   *Example*: Calculate the hydronium ion concentration in a solution with a $pH$ of 9.26.

**Solution**

$[H_3O^+] = 10^{-pH} = 10^{-9.26}$. To evaluate this exponential, rewrite $10^{-9.26}$ as a product of two log base-10 exponentials, one with a positive decimal exponent, the other with a negative integer exponent. In order to maintain the same value as the original term, calculate the difference between $-9.26$ and the next smaller integer exponent. The result gives

$$10^{-9.26} = 10^{0.74} \times 10^{-10}$$

The $[H_3O^+]$ is the antilog of 0.74 times $10^{-10}$:

$$10^{0.74} = 5.5$$

and therefore

$$[H_3O^+] = 5.5 \times 10^{-10}$$

*pOH*   The $pOH$ of a solution is a measure of the hydroxide ion ($OH^-$) concentration in solution and is defined as

$$pOH = -\log[OH^-]$$

The expression for $K_w$ relates $pOH$ and $pH$ through the concentration of $OH^-$ and $H_3O^+$ in the following way:

$$K_w = [H_3O^+][OH^-] = 1 \times 10^{-14}$$

Take logs of both sides and multiply by $(-1)$.

$$-\log[H_3O^+] + (-\log[OH^-]) = -(-14)$$

Substitution from the definitions above yields

$$pH + pOH = 14$$

This relation is especially useful when working with basic solutions in which the $OH^-$ is known or is to be calculated.

**Hydrolysis** Salts formed from weak acids or weak bases interact with water to form solutions that are acidic or basic depending on the nature of the parent substance. The conjugate bases of weak acids and the conjugate acids of weak bases are relatively strong bases and acids, respectively. For the general case these substances undergo hydrolysis with water in the following ways:

$$A^-(aq) + H_2O \rightleftharpoons HA(aq) + OH^-(aq) \tag{1}$$

$$WBH^+(aq) + H_2O \rightleftharpoons WB(aq) + H_3O^+(aq) \tag{2}$$

Water functions as an acid in the reaction with $A^-$ and as a base with $WBH^+$.

**Hydrolysis ionization constant $(K_h)$** This constant describes the equilibrium established in a reaction involving hydrolysis. For the reactions shown above in the definition of hydrolysis, the expressions for $K_h$ are

For (1), $\qquad A^-(aq) + H_2O \rightleftharpoons HA(aq) + OH^-(aq)$

$$K_h = \frac{[HA][OH^-]}{[A^-]}$$

Substitution of

$$[OH^-] = \frac{K_w}{[H_3O^+]}$$

gives

$$K_h = \frac{[HA]K_w}{[A^-][H_3O^+]} = \frac{K_w}{K_i(\text{weak acid})}$$

*Example*: Calculate the hydrolysis constant for the cyanide ion, $CN^-$.

**Solution**

The ion, $CN^-$, is the conjugate base of the weak acid, HCN, $K_i = 4 \times 10^{-10}$. Hydrolysis will occur as follows:

$$CN^-(aq) + H_2O \rightleftharpoons HCN(aq) + OH^-(aq)$$

$$K_h = \frac{[HCN][OH^-]}{[CN^-]} = \frac{[HCN]K_w}{[CN^-][H_3O^+]} = \frac{1 \times 10^{-14}}{4 \times 10^{-10}} = 2 \times 10^{-5}$$

For (2), $WBH^+(aq) + H_2O \rightleftharpoons WB(aq) + H_3O^+(aq)$

$$K_h = \frac{[WB][H_3O^+]}{[WBH^+]}, \qquad \text{where} \qquad [H_3O^+] = \frac{K_w}{[OH^-]}$$

Then

$$K_h = \frac{[WB]K_w}{[WBH^+][OH^-]} = \frac{K_w}{K_i(\text{weak base})}$$

*Example*: Calculate the hydrolysis constant for the methyl ammonium ion, $CH_3NH_3^+$.

**Solution**

The ion, $CH_3NH_3^+$, is the conjugate acid of the weak base, $CH_3NH_2$, $K_i = 4.4 \times 10^{-4}$. Hydrolysis will occur as follows:

$$CH_3NH_3^+(aq) + H_2O \rightleftharpoons CH_3NH_2(aq) + H_3O^+(aq)$$

$$K_h = \frac{[CH_3NH_2][H_3O^+]}{[CH_3NH_3^+]} = \frac{[CH_3NH_2]K_w}{[CH_3NH_3^+][OH^-]}$$

$$= \frac{1.0 \times 10^{-14}}{4.4 \times 10^{-4}} = 2.3 \times 10^{-11}$$

To summarize,

$$K_h = K_w/K_i(\text{weak acid})$$
$$K_h = K_w/K_i(\text{weak base})$$

**Quadratic equations**  A quadratic equation is defined as any equation that can be written in the form

$$ax^2 + bx + c = 0$$

in which $a$, $b$, and $c$ are constants and $a \neq 0$. Since these equations are second order, $x^2$, two solutions are possible, that is, a negative and a positive solution. In chemistry, reactions involve real amounts of substance; hence equations rarely are written in such a way that negative values of $x$ are plausible.

Several methods can be used to solve quadratic equations, but the most convenient method for solving equations dealing with chemical processes is to use the quadratic formula (shown below) which is based on the general form of the quadratic equation.

$$x = \frac{-b \pm \sqrt{b^2 - 4ac}}{2a}$$

**PROBLEMS**

*Note*: Unless otherwise stated, assume that water is the solvent used in each of the problems.

1. Calculate the concentration of each of the ions in the following solutions of strong electrolytes:

   (a)  0.0090 $M$ HBr
   (c)  0.0033 $M$ $[Al(H_2O)_6]_2(SO_4)_3$

**Solution**

(a) Strong electrolytes are assumed to be completely dissociated or ionized in solution; HBr will ionize as

$$HBr \rightleftharpoons H^+ + Br^-$$

or

$$HBr(aq) \rightleftharpoons H_3O^+(aq) + Br^-(aq)$$

$$0.0090 \, \frac{mol}{\ell} \, HBr \longrightarrow 0.0090 \, \frac{mol}{\ell} \, H^+ + 0.0090 \, \frac{mol}{\ell} \, Br^-$$

(c) $[Al(H_2O_6)]_2(SO_4)_3 \rightleftharpoons 2 \, Al(H_2O)_6{}^{3+}(aq) + 3 \, SO_4{}^{2-}(aq)$

$[Al(H_2O)_6]^{3+} = 2(0.0033 \, M) = 0.0066 \, M = 6.6 \times 10^{-3} \, M$

$[SO_4{}^{2-}] = 3(0.0033 \, M) = 0.0099 \, M = 9.9 \times 10^{-3} \, M$

2. Using the ionization constants in Appendix B, calculate the hydrogen ion concentration and the per cent ionization in each of the following solutions:

(a) 0.0092 M HClO
(c) 0.417 M HCO$_2$H

**Solution**

(a) The hydrogen ion concentration must be calculated from the ionization constant of hypochlorous acid, HClO. The acid ionizes as

$$HClO(aq) \rightleftharpoons H_3O^+(aq) + ClO^-(aq)$$

$$K_i = \frac{[H_3O^+][ClO^-]}{[HClO]} = 3.5 \times 10^{-8}$$

The small value of $K_i$ indicates that only a small fraction of the initial HClO ionizes in solution. Perhaps it is helpful to set up a tabular arrangement as shown below to better visualize the concentrations of the solution components present initially and at equilibrium.

|  | [HClO] | [H$_3$O$^+$] | [ClO$^-$] |
|---|---|---|---|
| initial | 0.0092 | 0 | 0 |
| equilibrium | 0.0092 - x | x | x |

In most cases involving weak acids or bases, and certainly strong acids or bases, the amount of hydrogen ion or hydroxide ion in solution that is contributed by water is negligibly small and can be ignored. How much HClO remains at equilibrium? Let x equal the amount of HClO that ionizes; therefore,

$$x = [H_3O^+] = [ClO^-]$$
$$[HClO] = 0.0092 - x$$

Substitute these values into the expression for $K_i$ and solve for $x$.

$$K_i = 3.5 \times 10^{-8} = \frac{(x)(x)}{(0.0092 - x)}$$

In the factor $(0.0092 - x)$, $x$ is very small relative to 0.0092 and can be neglected, which greatly simplifies the calculation. In general, if the initial concentration of the ionizing substance and $K_i$ for the substance differ by an exponential factor of 3 or more, $x$ can be neglected in the denominator. In this case, the [HClO] is $9.2 \times 10^{-3}$ and $K_i$ is $3.5 \times 10^{-8}$; the exponents differ by 5. Hence $x$ can be neglected. This generalization is premised on the fact that $K$ values usually have two significant figures, and the factor of $x$ in the rigorous solution of the quadratic equation does not significantly add or subtract from the equation. Solving the equation for $x$ and neglecting the $x$ in the term $(0.0092 - x)$

$$\frac{x^2}{0.0092} = 3.5 \times 10^{-8}$$

or

$$x^2 = 0.0092 \, (3.5 \times 10^{-8})$$
$$= 3.22 \times 10^{-10}$$

Taking the square root of both sides gives

$$x = \pm 1.8 \times 10^{-5}$$

Notice that the negative value of $x$ is not a plausible solution to the equation; only real amounts of substance can be ionized.

$$x = 1.8 \times 10^{-5} \, M = [H^+] = [ClO^-]$$

The per cent of the initial HClO ionized at equilibrium is

$$\% \text{ ionization} = \frac{x}{[HClO] \text{ initial}} \times 100$$
$$= \frac{1.8 \times 10^{-5}}{0.0092} \times 100 = 0.20\%$$

(c) The ionization of formic acid, $HCO_2H$, is more easily visualized from its structural formula:

$$\overset{\displaystyle O}{\underset{\displaystyle \|}{HC}} - OH(aq) \rightleftharpoons H_3O^+(aq) + \overset{\displaystyle O}{\underset{\displaystyle \|}{HC}} - O^-(aq)$$

Employ the procedure used in (a) above to calculate the hydrogen ion concentration.

$$K_i = 1.8 \times 10^{-4} = \frac{[H_3O^+][HCOO^-]}{[HCO_2H]}$$

|  | [HCO₂H] | [H₃O⁺] | [HCOO⁻] |
|---|---|---|---|
| initial | 0.417 | 0 | 0 |
| equilibrium | 0.417-x | x | x |

Let $x$ equal the number of moles of $HCO_2H$ that ionize. At equilibrium, the concentrations of $[H_3O^+]$ and of $[HCOO^-]$ equal $x$ and the $[HCO_2H]$ equals $0.417 - x$. Substitute these values into the expression for $K_i$.

$$K_i = 1.8 \times 10^{-4} = \frac{(x)(x)}{(0.417 - x)}$$

Can $x$ in the denominator be neglected? Yes, but only barely. Solve for $x$.

$$x^2 = 1.8 \times 10^{-4} (0.417) = 7.51 \times 10^{-5}$$

Take square roots:

$$x = 8.7 \times 10^{-3} \text{ mol} = [H_3O^+] = [HCOO^-]$$

$$\% \text{ ionization} = \frac{8.7 \times 10^{-3}}{0.417} \times 100 = 2.1\%$$

3. Calculate the hydrogen ion concentration and per cent ionization of the weak acid in each of the following solutions. Note that the ionization constants may be such that the change in electrolyte concentration cannot be neglected and the quadratic equation or successive approximations may be required.

(a) 0.0184 $M$ HCNO    ($K_i = 3.46 \times 10^{-4}$)
(d) 0.02173 $M$ CH₂ClCO₂H    ($K_i = 1.4 \times 10^{-3}$)

**Solution**

The procedure for calculating the hydrogen ion concentration and per cent ionization for the weak acids in this problem is the same as in Problem 2 above; the same rules apply.

(a) 0.0184 $M$ HCNO    ($K_i = 3.46 \times 10^{-4}$)

$$HCNO(aq) \rightleftharpoons H_3O^+(aq) + CNO^-(aq)$$

$$K_i = 3.46 \times 10^{-4} = \frac{[H_3O^+][CNO^-]}{[HCNO]}$$

Let $x$ equal the number of moles of HCNO that ionize. At equilibrium the concentrations of the solution components are

$$x = [H_3O^+] = [CNO^-]$$
$$[HCNO] = 0.0184 - x$$

Substitution gives

$$K_i = 3.46 \times 10^{-4} = \frac{(x)(x)}{0.0184 - x}$$

Can the $x$ in $(0.0184 - x)$ be neglected?

$$[HCNO] = 1.84 \times 10^{-2} \quad \text{and} \quad K_i = 3.46 \times 10^{-4}$$

Exponential difference equals 2.

*Answer:* $x$ cannot be neglected. Therefore, solve the equation for $x$ the quadratic formula. The process is as follows.

$$x^2 = 3.46 \times 10^{-4}(0.0184 - x)$$
$$= 6.37 \times 10^{-6} - 3.46 \times 10^{-4}\,x$$

Rearrangement to the standard quadratic form gives

$$x^2 + 3.46 \times 10^{-4}\,x - 6.37 \times 10^{-6} = 0$$

The equation is now in the form $ax^2 + bx + c = 0$, and the quadratic formula applies:

$$x = \frac{-b \pm \sqrt{b^2 - 4ac}}{2a}$$

Substitution into the formula gives

$$x = \frac{-3.46 \times 10^{-4} \pm \sqrt{(3.46 \times 10^{-4})^2 - 4(1)(-6.37 \times 10^{-6})}}{2(1)}$$

and

$$x = \frac{-3.46 \times 10^{-4} \pm \sqrt{1.197 \times 10^{-7} + 2.548 \times 10^{-5}}}{2}$$

$$x = \frac{-3.46 \times 10^{-4} \pm \sqrt{2.56 \times 10^{-5}}}{2} = \frac{-3.46 \times 10^{-4} \pm 5.06 \times 10^{-3}}{2}$$

The positive root of $x$ is

$$x = \frac{4.71 \times 10^{-3}}{2} = 2.36 \times 10^{-3}\, M = [H_3O^+] = [CNO^-]$$

If the simplification had been made, the value of $[H_3O^+]$ would have been $2.52 \times 10^{-3}$.

$$\% \text{ ionization} = \frac{2.36 \times 10^{-3}}{0.0184} \times 100 = 12.8\%$$

(d)  $0.02173 \ M \ CH_2 ClCO_2 H$     $(K_i = 1.4 \times 10^{-3})$

$$CH_2 ClCO_2 H(aq) \rightleftharpoons H_3 O^+(aq) + CH_2 ClCO_2^-(aq)$$

$$K_i = 1.4 \times 10^{-3} = \frac{[H_3 O^+][CH_2 ClCO_2^-]}{[CH_2 ClCO_2 H]}$$

Let $x$ = moles of $CH_2 ClCO_2 H$ that ionize at equilibrium:

$$x = [H_3 O^+] = [CH_2 ClO_2^-]$$

$$[CH_2 ClCO_2 H] = 0.02173 - x$$

and

$$K_i = 1.4 \times 10^{-3} = \frac{(x)(x)}{0.02173 - x}$$

Can $x$ in $(0.02173 - x)$ be neglected? No! Solving the equation for $x$ via the quadratic formula gives

$$x^2 = 1.4 \times 10^{-3} (0.02173 - x) = 3.042 \times 10^{-5} - 1.4 \times 10^{-3} x$$

$$x^2 + 1.4 \times 10^{-3} x - 3.042 \times 10^{-5} = 0$$

$$x = \frac{-1.4 \times 10^{-3} \pm \sqrt{(1.4 \times 10^{-3})^2 - 4(1)(-3.042 \times 10^{-5})}}{2(1)}$$

$$x = \frac{-1.4 \times 10^{-3} \pm \sqrt{1.236 \times 10^{-4}}}{2} = \frac{-1.4 \times 10^{-3} \pm 1.1 \times 10^{-2}}{2}$$

The positive root of $x$ is

$$x = 4.9 \times 10^{-3} \ M = [H_3 O^+]$$

$$\% \text{ ionization} = \frac{4.9 \times 10^{-3}}{0.02173} \times 100 = 22\%$$

4.  The ionization constant of lactic acid, $CH_3 CHOHCO_2 H$, is $1.36 \times 10^{-4}$. If 20.0 g of lactic acid is used to make a solution with a volume of 1.00 $\ell$, what is the concentration of hydrogen ion in the solution?

**Solution**

The hydrogen ion concentration can be calculated from the expression for $K_i$ after computing the concentration of lactic acid in terms of molarity.

$$\text{GFW } CH_3 CHOHCO_2 H = 3(12.01) + 6(1.01) + 3(16.0) = 90.1 \ g$$

$$\text{Molarity (lactic acid)} = 20.0 \ g \times \frac{1 \ mol}{90.1 \ g/1.00 \ \ell} = 0.222 \ M$$

Lactic acid ionizes as

$$CH_2 CHOHCO_2 H(aq) \rightleftharpoons CH_3 CHOHCO_2^-(aq) + H_3 O^+(aq)$$

$$LA(aq) \rightleftharpoons LA^-(aq) + H_3 O^+(aq)$$

$$K_i = 1.36 \times 10^{-4} = \frac{[H_3 O^+][LA^-]}{[LA]}$$

Let $x$ = no. of moles of LA that ionize.
*At equilibrium*:

$$x = [H_3 O^+] = [LA^-]$$

$$[LA] = 0.222 - x$$

and

$$K_i = 1.36 \times 10^{-4} = \frac{(x)(x)}{0.222 - x}$$

Can $x$ in $(0.222 - x)$ be neglected? This is a borderline situation since $K_i$ has 3 significant figures. The value of $x^2$ as determined from the equation after dropping $x$ in the denominator is

$$x^2 = (1.36 \times 10^{-4})(0.222) = 3.02 \times 10^{-5}$$

The positive root of $x^2$ is $5.49 \times 10^{-3}$. Without simplification, $x$ is $5.43 \times 10^{-3}$, a difference of only 1%. In most laboratory work involving measurements with a $pH$ meter, this small difference would not be detected.

7. Calculate the hydroxide ion concentration and the per cent ionization of the weak base in each of the following solutions. (In some cases it may prove necessary to use the quadratic equation or successive approximations.)

(a)  $0.0784\ M\ C_6 H_5 NH_2$     $(K_i = 4.6 \times 10^{-10})$
(c)  $4.113 \times 10^{-3}\ M\ CH_3 NH_2$     $(K_i = 4.4 \times 10^{-4})$

**Solution**
The hydroxide ion concentration in each of the examples is calculated from the $K_i$ expression in the same manner as was used to calculate $[H^+]$ in Problem 2.

(a)  $0.0784\ M\ C_6 H_5 NH_2$     $(K_i = 4.6 \times 10^{-10})$

$$C_6 H_5 NH_2 (aq) \rightleftharpoons C_6 H_5 NH_3^+(aq) + OH^-(aq)$$

$$K_i = 4.6 \times 10^{-10} = \frac{[C_6 H_5 NH_3^+][OH^-]}{[C_6 H_5 NH_2]}$$

Let $x$ = no. of moles of $C_6 H_5 NH_2$ that ionize at equilibrium:

$$x = [OH^-] = [C_6 H_5 NH_3^+]$$

$$[C_6 H_5 NH_2] = 0.0784 - x$$

Substitution into the expression for $K_i$ gives

$$K_i = 4.6 \times 10^{-10} = \frac{(x)(x)}{0.0784 - x}$$

Can $x$ in $(0.0784 - x)$ be neglected? Yes, $10^{-10}$ is more than 3 orders of magnitude smaller than $7.8 \times 10^{-2}$. Solving for the positive root of $x$ gives

$$x^2 = (0.0784)(4.6 \times 10^{-10}) = 3.61 \times 10^{-11}$$

$$x = [OH^-] = 6.0 \times 10^{-6} \ M$$

$$\% \text{ ionization} = \frac{6.0 \times 10^{-6}}{0.0784} \times 100 = 7.6 \times 10^{-3} \ \%$$

(c)  $4.113 \times 10^{-3} \ M \ CH_3 NH_2 \qquad (K_i = 4.4 \times 10^{-4})$

$$CH_3 NH_2 \, (aq) \rightleftharpoons CH_3 NH_2^+(aq) + OH^-(aq)$$

$$K_i = 4.4 \times 10^{-4} = \frac{[CH_3 NH_2^+][OH^-]}{[CH_3 NH_2]}$$

Let $x$ = no. of moles of $CH_3 NH_2$ that ionize.
  *At equilibrium*: $x = [OH^-] = [CH_3 NH_2^+]$.

$$[CH_3 NH_2] = 4.113 \times 10^{-3} - x$$

Substituting these values into $K_i$ gives

$$4.4 \times 10^{-4} = \frac{(x)(x)}{(4.113 \times 10^{-3} - x)}$$

Can $x$ in $(4.113 \times 10^{-3} - x)$ be neglected?  No. The positive root of $x$, as solved through use of the quadratic formula, is

$$x = [OH^-] = 1.14 \times 10^{-3} \ M$$

$$\% \text{ ionization} = \frac{1.14 \times 10^{-3}}{4.11 \times 10^{-3}} \times 100 = 28\%$$

8.  Calculate the $p$H and $p$OH of the following solutions:

(a)  0.100 $M$ HCl
(b)  1.45 $M$ NaOH
(c)  0.0071 $M$ Ba(OH)$_2$

**Solution**
Strong acids, such as HCl and HNO$_3$, and strong bases, such as NaOH and Ba(OH)$_2$, in relatively dilute solutions can be assumed to be completely ionized. The concentrations of [H$^+$] and of [OH$^-$] in these solutions approximately equal their strong acid and strong base molarities, respectively.

(a) 0.100 $M$ HCl

$$[H^+] = 0.100 \ M$$
$$pH = -\log[H^+] = -\log 0.100$$

If you are using a calculator equipped with a logarithm function, merely enter the concentration as 0.100, take the log, and change the sign; this value is the $pH$ of the solution. If, however, you are finding logs from a log table, the value of the molarity should be written in exponential notation and logs taken in the following way:

$$pH = -\log[H^+] = -\log 0.100 = -\log(1.00 \times 10^{-1})$$
$$= -[\log 1.00 + \log 10^{-1}] = -[0.000 + (-1.000)]$$
$$= 1.000$$

Here we have found the log of the rational term (1.00) in the log table and added it to the log of the exponential term, which is simply the value of the exponent. Then, since

$$pH + pOH = 14.000$$

or

$$pOH = 14.00 - pH$$

In this case substitution for $pH$ is

$$pOH = 14.000 - 1.000 = 13.000$$

(b) 1.45 $M$ NaOH. In a solution this concentrated, the $OH^-$ concentration will be slightly less than 1.45 $M$ due to ion activities; for our purposes, assume total ionization.

$$[OH^-] = 1.45 \ M$$
$$pOH = -\log 1.45 = -(0.161) = -0.161$$
$$pH = 14.000 - (-0.161) = 14.161$$

(c) 0.0071 $M$ Ba(OH)$_2$

$$[OH^-] = 2(0.0071) = (0.0142 \ M)$$
$$pOH = -\log 0.0142 = -\log 1.42 \times 10^{-2} = 1.85$$
$$pH = 14.00 - 1.85 = 12.15$$

12. Calculate the ionization constants for each of the following solutes from the per cent ionization and the concentration of the solute:

(a) 0.050 $M$ HClO, $8.4 \times 10^{-2}\%$ ionized
(b) 0.010 $M$ HNO$_2$, 19% ionized

**Solution**

The ionization constant for a weak acid or base can be calculated from the equilibrium concentrations of the various solution components.

159

Since the initial concentration of the ionizing substance is given in each of the following examples, the equilibrium concentration of each component can be calculated.

(a) 0.050 $M$ HClO, $8.4 \times 10^{-2}$% ionized

$$HClO(aq) \rightleftharpoons H_3O^+(aq) + ClO^-(aq)$$

*At equilibrium:*

$$[H_3O^+] = 8.4 \times 10^{-2}\% \text{ of } 0.050\,M = [ClO^-]$$
$$= (0.00084)(0.050) = 4.2 \times 10^{-5}\,M$$

Since one mole of HClO ionizes to produce one mole each of $H_3O^+$ and $ClO^-$, the equilibrium concentration of HClO is

$$[HClO] = [0.050 - 4.2 \times 10^{-5}]\,M$$

$$K_i(HClO) = \frac{[H_3O^+][ClO^-]}{[HClO]} \quad.$$

Substituting the concentrations into the expression gives

$$K_i = \frac{(4.2 \times 10^{-5})(4.2 \times 10^{-5})}{(0.050 - 4.2 \times 10^{-5})} = 3.5 \times 10^{-8}$$

(b) 0.010 $M$ $HNO_2$, 19% ionized

$$HNO_2\,(aq) \rightleftharpoons H_3O^+(aq) + NO_2^-(aq)$$

$$K_i = \frac{[H_3O^+][NO_2^-]}{[HNO_2]}$$

*At equilibrium:*

$$[H_3O^+] = [NO_2^-] = 19\% \text{ of } 0.010\,M$$
$$= 0.19(0.010)M = 0.0019\,M$$
$$[HNO_2] = (0.010 - 0.0019)M$$
$$K_i = \frac{(0.0019)(0.0019)}{(0.010 - 0.0019)} = 4.4 \times 10^{-4}$$

13. What is the concentration of acetic acid in a solution that is 0.30% ionized?

**Solution**

Given that the acetic acid in solution is ionized 0.30%, an expression for $K_i$ can be written that involves only the initial concentration of HOAc as the unknown.

$$HOAc(aq) \rightleftharpoons H_3O^+(aq) + OAc^-(aq)$$

$$K_i = 1.8 \times 10^{-5} = \frac{[H_3O^+][OAc^-]}{[HOAc]}$$

Let $x$ = initial concentration of HOAc.
  *At equilibrium*:

$$[H_3O^+] = [OAc^-] = 0.0030x$$
$$[HOAc] = x - 0.0030x$$

Substitution gives

$$\frac{(0.0030x)\,(0.0030x)}{x - 0.0030x} = 1.8 \times 10^{-5}$$

Clear the fraction to get

$$9.0 \times 10^{-6}\,x^2 = 1.8 \times 10^{-5}\,x - 5.4 \times 10^{-8}\,x$$

Divide both sides by $x$ and $9 \times 10^{-6}$

$$x = \frac{1.8 \times 10^{-5}}{9.0 \times 10^{-6}} = 2.0\ M$$

A 2.0 $M$ solution of acetic acid would be 0.30% ionized.

16. Calculate the $pH$ of each of the following solutions, which contain two solutes with the concentrations indicated.

(a)  0.50 $M$ HOAc, 0.50 $M$ NaOAc
(e)  0.125 $M$ NH$_3$, 1.00 $M$ NaOH
(f)  0.400 $M$ NaHSO$_4$, 0.400 $M$ Na$_2$SO$_4$

**Solution**

(a)  0.50 $M$ HOAc, 0.50 $M$ NaOAc

   This solution is a buffer solution containing the weak acid, HOAc, and a salt, NaOAc, containing the anion of the acid. The acetic acid equilibrium describes the solution, since the added NaOAc merely causes a shift in the equilibrium.

$$HOAc(aq) \rightleftharpoons H_3O^+ + OAc^-(aq)$$

Let $x$ = no. of moles of HOAc that ionize.
  *At equilibrium*:

$$[H_3O^+] = x$$

The total amount of OAc$^-$ in solution equals the amount of OAc$^-$ added by way of NaOAc plus the amount $x$ produced by the ionization of HOAc:

$$[OAc^-] = (x + 0.50)\,M$$
$$[HOAc] = (0.50 - x)\,M$$
$$K_i = \frac{[H_3O^+]\,[OAc^-]}{[HOAc]} = 1.8 \times 10^{-5}$$

Substituting the concentrations into the equation gives

$$K_i = 1.8 \times 10^{-5} = \frac{(x)\,(x + 0.50)}{(0.50 - x)}$$

The rules for neglecting $x$ in the denominator also apply to buffer or hydrolysis problems. Can $x$ be neglected? Yes. Since $x$ is small relative to 0.50 in $(0.50 - x)$, it also is small relative to 0.50 in $(x + 0.50)$. The expression is simplified to

$$1.8 \times 10^{-5} = \frac{(x)\,(0.50)}{(0.50)}$$

Solving for $x$ gives

$$x = 1.8 \times 10^{-5} = [H_3O^+]$$

Also,

$$pH = -\log\,[H_3O^+] = -\log\,(1.8 \times 10^{-5})$$
$$= -[\log 1.8 + \log 10^{-5}]$$
$$= -[0.2553 + (-5)]$$
$$= 4.74$$

(e) $0.125\,M\;NH_3$, $1.00\,M\;NaOH$

This solution is a combination of the weak base, $NH_3$, and the strong base, NaOH. At equilibrium in a solution containing $0.125\,M\;NH_3$ only, the $OH^-$ concentration is approximately $1.5 \times 10^{-3}\,M$. Addition of one mole of NaOH (1.0 mole of $OH^-$) to the solution simply overwhelms the equilibrium, and the $[OH^-]$ approximately equals the $[OH^-]$ from NaOH.

*At equilibrium:*

$$NH_3\,(aq) \rightleftharpoons NH_4^+(aq) + OH^-(aq)$$
$$[OH^-] \simeq [NaOH] = 1.00\,M$$
$$pOH = -\log 1.00 = 0.00$$
$$pH = 14.00$$

(f) $0.400\,M\;NaHSO_4$, $0.400\,M\;Na_2SO_4$

In this solution $NaHSO_4$ is a moderately strong acid that ionizes as

$$HSO_4^-(aq) \rightleftharpoons H_3O^+(aq) + SO_4^{2-}(aq)$$
$$K_i = \frac{[H_3O^+]\,[SO_4^{2-}]}{[HSO_4^-]} = 1.2 \times 10^{-2}$$

Let $x$ = no. of moles of $HSO_4^-$ that ionize.

*At equilibrium*:

$$[H_3O^+] = x$$

$$[SO_4{}^{2-}] = (x + 0.400) M$$

$$[HSO_4{}^-] = (0.400 - x) M$$

Substituting the concentrations into the expression gives

$$\frac{(x)(x + 0.400)}{(0.400 - x)} = 1.2 \times 10^{-2}$$

Can $x$ in $(0.400 - x)$ be neglected? No. Clear the fraction and transpose terms to get

$$x^2 + 0.412 x - 0.0048 = 0$$

Solving for $x$ by way of the quadratic formula gives

$$x = \frac{-0.412 \pm \sqrt{(0.412)^2 - 4(1)(-0.0048)}}{2}$$

$$= \frac{-0.412 \pm 0.435}{2} = 0.0113 = [H_3O^+]$$

$$pH = -\log(0.0113) = -\log 1.13 \times 10^{-2} = 1.95$$

17. What relative number of moles of sodium acetate and acetic acid in water must be used to prepare a buffer with a $pH$ of 5.08?

**Solution**

A buffer solution of NaOAc and HOAc is defined in terms of $K_i$ (HOAc).

$$HOAc(aq) \rightleftharpoons H_3O^+(aq) + OAc^-(aq)$$

$$K_i = 1.8 \times 10^{-5} = \frac{[H_3O^+][OAc^-]}{[HOAc]}$$

The ratio of $OAc^-$ to HOAc is calculated from the expression after substitution of the $[H_3O^+]$. This is found from the $pH$:

$$pH = 5.08 = -\log[H_3O^+]$$

$$[H_3O^+] = 10^{-pH} = 10^{-5.08}$$

If you use log tables to find the number that corresponds to $10^{-5.08}$, the exponential should be rewritten as a product of two exponential terms; one term should contain a positive value that can be located in the log table and the other, a whole number with a negative value used to establish the decimal point. (You may wish to consult the programmed instruction unit on logs in Part 2 of this manual.)

163

$$10^{-5.08} = 10^{0.92} \times 10^{-6}$$
$$= 8.32 \times 10^{-6}$$

Now,

$$1.8 \times 10^{-5} = 8.32 \times 10^{-6} \left( \frac{[OAc^-]}{[HOAc]} \right)$$

$$\frac{[OAc^-]}{[HOAc]} = \frac{1.8 \times 10^{-5}}{8.32 \times 10^{-6}} = 2.2$$

This is interpreted as

$$\frac{No.\ moles}{\ell} (OAc^-) = 2.2 \left( \frac{no.\ moles}{\ell} \right) HOAc$$

19. A buffer solution is made up of equal volumes of 0.100 $M$ acetic acid and 0.500 $M$ sodium acetate. (a) What is the $pH$ of this solution? (b) What is the $pH$ that results from adding 1.00 ml of 0.100 $M$ HCl to 0.200 $\ell$ of the buffer solution? (Use $1.80 \times 10^{-5}$ for the ionization constant of acetic acid.)

**Solution**

0.100/2 $M$ HOAc and 0.500/2 $M$ NaOAc

(a) The equilibrium expression for HOAc defines this buffer system.

$$HOAc(aq) \rightleftharpoons H_3O^+(aq) + OAc^-(aq)$$

$$K_i = 1.80 \times 10^{-5} = \frac{[H_3O^+][OAc^-]}{[HOAc]}$$

Let $x$ = moles of HOAc that ionize.
*At equilibrium*:

$$[H_3O^+] = x$$
$$[HOAc] = (0.0500 - x) M$$
$$[OAc^-] = (0.250 + x) M$$

Substitution into the $K_i$ expression gives

$$K_i = 1.80 \times 10^{-5} = \frac{(x)(0.250 + x)}{(0.0500 - x)}$$

The value of $x$ in $(0.0500 - x)$ may be dropped on the basis of our guidelines. However, the value of $x$ is even smaller in a buffer solution than in a solution containing only the acid because there is a shift in the equilibrium toward HOAc. By the same reasoning, $x$ can be neglected in $(0.250 + x)$. Rearranging and clearing the fraction gives

$$x = [H_3O^+] = \frac{1.80 \times 10^{-5}}{5} = 3.60 \times 10^{-6}$$

$$pH = -\log 3.6 \times 10^{-6} = 5.444$$

(b) Because a buffer solution contains both an acidic substance and a basic substance, the solution has the capacity to react with either added acid or base. In this case HCl is being added to the buffer system. The effect on the equilibrium and, subsequently, the pH may be found as follows. First, the HCl exists as ions in aqueous solution and the NaOAc dissociates.

$HCl(aq) \longrightarrow H_3O^+(aq) + Cl^-(aq)$   $Cl^-(aq)$ and $Na^+(aq)$ remain

$NaOAc(aq) \longrightarrow Na^+(aq) + OAc^-(aq)$   unchanged in the next step.

The hydronium ion then reacts quantitatively with acetate ions forming an equilibrium leaving only small amounts of $H_3O^+$ and $OAc^-$ in solution.

$$H_3O^+(aq) + OAc^-(aq) \rightleftharpoons HOAc(aq) + H_2O$$

1 mole    + 1 mole    $\longrightarrow$ 1 mole

Again letting $x$ equal the number of moles of HOAc that ionize according to the above sequence, the initial amounts of the solution components are

No. moles HCl $= (0.00100 \, \ell)\left(\dfrac{0.100 \, \text{mol}}{\ell}\right) = 0.0010$ mol

No. moles $OAc^- = (0.200 \, \ell)\left(0.250 \, \dfrac{\text{mol}}{\ell}\right) + x = 0.0500$ mol $+ x$

No. moles HOAc $= (0.200 \, \ell)\left(0.0500 \, \dfrac{\text{mol}}{\ell}\right) - x = 0.0100$ mol $- x$

After the reaction with HCl, the equilibrium is reestablished, and the concentrations are

$$[HCl] = 0; \quad [H_3O^+] = x$$

$$[OAc^-] = \frac{(0.0500 + x - 0.00010) \, \text{mol}}{0.201 \, \ell} \simeq 0.248 \, M$$

$$[HOAc] = \frac{(0.0100 - x + 0.00010) \, \text{mol}}{0.201 \, \ell} \simeq 0.0502 \, M$$

Quite clearly, the concentrations of $OAc^-$ and HOAc are only slightly different after the addition of a small amount of HCl. The value of $[H_3O^+]$ is found from the expression

$$K_i = 1.80 \times 10^{-5} = \frac{[H_3O^+][OAc^-]}{[HOAc]} = \frac{(x)(0.248)}{(0.0502)} = x(4.94)$$

$$x = \frac{1.80 \times 10^{-5}}{4.94} = 3.64 \times 10^{-6} = [H_3O^+]$$

Therefore

$$pH = -\log 3.64 \times 10^{-6} = 5.438$$

Thus the $pH$ of the solution is only very slightly changed as shown.

21. Calculate the $pH$ of each of the following solutions:

(a) 0.4735 $M$ NaCN
(d) 0.333 $M$ $[(CH_3)_2NH_2]_2SO_4$

**Solution**

The solute in each of these solutions is a salt composed of ions in which one of the ions originated from either a weak acid or a weak base. These ions undergo hydrolysis to produce acidic or basic solutions depending on their origin.

(a) 0.4735 $M$ NaCN. This salt dissociates in water, yielding

$$NaCN(aq) \rightleftharpoons Na^+(aq) + CN^-(aq)$$

Hydrolysis of the $CN^-$ occurs because it is the anion of a *weak* acid. Similar hydrolysis of $Na^+$ does not occur since $Na^+$ is a cation of a *strong* base and is fully dissociated in aqueous solution. Thus

$$CN^-(aq) + H_2O \rightleftharpoons HCN(aq) + OH^-(aq)$$

The hydroxide ion is a strong base and HCN is a weak acid; the reaction increases the concentration of hydroxide ion, thereby causing the solution to be basic. The equilibrium constant for this process is called $K$-hydrolysis and is written $K_h$. Its value is

$$K_h = \frac{[HCN][OH^-]}{[CN^-]}$$

where the concentration of water is absorbed into the value of $K_h$. Since $[OH^-] = K_w/[H_3O^+]$, substitution gives

$$K_h = \frac{[HCN]K_w}{[CN^-][H_3O^+]} = \frac{K_w}{K_i(HCN)}$$

where

$$K_i(HCN) = \frac{[H_3O^+][CN^-]}{[HCN]} = 4 \times 10^{-10}$$

Therefore

$$K_h = \frac{1 \times 10^{-14}}{4 \times 10^{-10}} = 2.5 \times 10^{-5}$$

166

If in our reaction $x$ equals the number of moles of $CN^-$ that hydrolyze, then, at equilibrium, $x = [HCN] = [OH^-]$ and

$$[CN^-] = (0.4735 - x)\, M$$

$$K_h = 2.5 \times 10^{-5} = \frac{(x)(x)}{0.4735 - x}$$

Neglect $x$ in $(0.4735 - x)$.

$$x^2 = 1.18 \times 10^{-5} \quad \text{or} \quad x = 3.44 \times 10^{-3} = [OH^-]$$

$$pOH = -\log 3.44 \times 10^{-3} = 2.46$$

$$pH = 14.00 - pOH = 14.00 - 2.46 = 11.5$$

(d) $0.333\ M\ [(CH_3)_2 NH_2]_2 SO_4$ (dimethylamine sulfate). The dimethylammonium ion will hydrolyze as

$$(CH_3)_2 NH_2^+(aq) + H_2 O \rightleftharpoons (CH_3)_2 NH(aq) + H_3 O^+(aq)$$

$$K_h = \frac{K_w}{K_i((CH_3)_2 NH)} = \frac{1.0 \times 10^{-14}}{7.4 \times 10^{-4}} = \frac{[(CH_3)_2 NH][H_3 O^+]}{[(CH_3)_2 NH_2^+]}$$

$$= 1.35 \times 10^{-11}$$

Let $x$ = no. of moles of $(CH_3)_2 NH_2^+$ that hydrolyze.
*At equilibrium*:

$$x = [H_3 O^+] = [(CH_3)_2 NH]$$

Since the dissociation of the sulfate produces 2 ions of $(CH_3)_2 NH_2^+$,

$$[(CH_3)_2 NH_2^+] = 2(0.333) - x$$

$$K_h = 1.35 \times 10^{-11} = \frac{(x)(x)}{(0.666 - x)}$$

$x$ is sufficiently small compared to 0.666 that it can be neglected.

$$1.35 \times 10^{-11} = \frac{x^2}{0.666}$$

$$x^2 = 8.99 \times 10^{-12}$$

$$x = 3.00 \times 10^{-6} = [H_3 O^+]$$

$$pH = -\log (3.00 \times 10^{-6})$$

$$= 5.52$$

24. Calculate the $pH$ of a $0.470\ M$ solution of $Li_2 CO_3$.

**Solution**

The hydrolysis of $CO_3^{2-}$ occurs in two steps as described by the following equations:

$$CO_3{}^{2-}(aq) + H_2O \rightleftharpoons HCO_3{}^-(aq) + OH^-(aq) \qquad (1)$$

$$HCO_3{}^-(aq) + H_2O \rightleftharpoons H_2CO_3(aq) + OH^-(aq) \qquad (2)$$

The hydrolysis constants for the two steps are

$$K_{h_1} = \frac{[HCO_3{}^-][OH^-]}{[CO_3{}^{2-}]} = \frac{K_w}{K_i(HCO_3{}^-)} = \frac{1 \times 10^{-14}}{7 \times 10^{-11}} = 1.4 \times 10^{-4}$$

$$K_{h_2} = \frac{[H_2CO_3][OH^-]}{[HCO_3{}^-]} = \frac{K_w}{K_i(H_2CO_3)} = \frac{1 \times 10^{-14}}{4.3 \times 10^{-7}} = 2.3 \times 10^{-8}$$

The $pH$ of the solution is controlled by the $OH^-$ generated by reaction (1). Only a small amount of $HCO_3{}^-$ is produced by reaction (1) and, in turn, $HCO_3{}^-$ hydrolyzes only slightly to produce a negligible amount of $OH^-$. Let $x$ = moles of $CO_3{}^{2-}$ that hydrolyze.

*At equilibrium:*

$$x = [OH^-] = [HCO_3{}^-]$$

$$[CO_3{}^{2-}] = (0.470 - x)\,M$$

$$K_h = 1.4 \times 10^{-4} = \frac{(x)(x)}{(0.470 - x)}$$

Can $x$ in $(0.470 - x)$ be neglected? Yes. Barely.

$$x^2 = 6.58 \times 10^{-5} \quad \text{and} \quad x = 8.1 \times 10^{-3} = [OH^-]$$

$$pOH = -\log 8.1 \times 10^{-3} = 2.1$$

$$pH = 11.9$$

29. In many detergents, phosphates have been replaced with silicates as water conditioners. If 125 g of a detergent that contains 8.0% $Na_2SiO_3$ by weight is used in 4.0 ℓ of water, what is the $pH$ and hydroxide ion concentration in the wash water?

$$SiO_3{}^{2-} + H_2O \rightleftharpoons SiO_3H^- + OH^- \qquad K_i = 1.6 \times 10^{-3} \qquad (1)$$

$$SiO_3H^- + H_2O \rightleftharpoons SiO_3H_2 + OH^- \qquad K_i = 3.1 \times 10^{-5} \qquad (2)$$

**Solution**

The hydrolysis of $SiO_3{}^{2-}$ occurs in two steps. However, due to the small amount of $SiO_3H^-$ produced in reaction (1) and the low $K_i$ in (2), the amount of $OH^-$ in the final solution is due almost entirely to the first hydrolysis. Calculate the molarity of $Na_2SiO_3$ and let $x$ equal the number of moles of $SiO_3{}^{2-}$ that hydrolyze.

$$\text{Molarity } Na_2SiO_3 = 0.080(125 \text{ g}) \times \frac{1 \text{ mol}/122.1 \text{ g}}{4.0 \text{ ℓ}} = 0.0205 \, M$$

*At equilibrium:*

$$x = [OH^-] \simeq [SiO_3 H^-]$$

$$[SiO_3{}^{2-}] \simeq (0.0205 - x)$$

$$K_i = 1.6 \times 10^{-3} = \frac{(x)(x)}{(0.0205 - x)}$$

or

$$x^2 = 1.6 \times 10^{-3}(0.0205 - x)$$

$$x^2 + 1.6 \times 10^{-3}\, x - 3.28 \times 10^{-5} = 0$$

$$x = \frac{-1.6 \times 10^{-3} \pm \sqrt{2.56 \times 10^{-6} + 4(3.28 \times 10^{-5})}}{2}$$

$$= \frac{-1.6 \times 10^{-3} \pm 1.16 \times 10^{-2}}{2} = \frac{10.0 \times 10^{-3}}{2} = [OH^-] = 5.0 \times 10^{-3}$$

$$pOH = -\log 5.0 \times 10^{-3} = 2.30$$

$$pH = 11.70$$

38. Calculate the $pH$ of a solution resulting from mixing 0.10 ℓ of 0.10 $M$ NaOH with 0.40 ℓ of 0.025 $M$ HF.

**Solution**

This is a neutralization reaction with the strong base NaOH reacting with the weak acid HF. The reaction is

$$NaOH(aq) + HF(aq) \longrightarrow NaF(aq) + H_2 O$$

1 mole $\quad$ + 1 mole $\longrightarrow$ 1 mole

Does the reaction reach the end point?

$$\text{No. moles NaOH} = (0.10\ \ell)\left(0.10\ \frac{mol}{\ell}\right) = 0.010\ mol$$

$$\text{No. moles HF} = (0.40\ \ell)\left(0.025\ \frac{mol}{\ell}\right) = 0.010\ mol$$

Equal molar amounts of NaOH and HF have reacted and only the salt solution containing NaF remains; $F^-$ will hydrolyze as

$$F^-(aq) + H_2 O \rightleftharpoons HF(aq) + OH^-(aq)$$

The $pH$ of the solution is calculated from the hydrolysis expression. Let $x$ equal the number of moles of $F^-$ hydrolyzing.

$$\frac{[HF][OH^-]}{[F^-]} = \frac{K_w}{K_i(HF)} = \frac{1 \times 10^{-14}}{7.2 \times 10^{-4}} = 1.4 \times 10^{-11}$$

At the end point and at equilibrium,

$$x = [HF] = [OH^-]; \quad [F^-] = \frac{0.010 \text{ mol}}{0.40 \text{ } \ell + 0.10 \text{ } \ell} = 0.020 \text{ } M$$

$$K_h = 1.4 \times 10^{-11} = \frac{(x)(x)}{(0.020 - x)}$$

and

$$x^2 = 2.8 \times 10^{-13}$$

$$x = [OH^-] = 5.3 \times 10^{-7}$$

$$pOH = 6.28$$

$$pH = 7.72$$

52. Lime juice is among the most acidic of fruit juices with a $pH$ of 1.92. If the acidity is due to citric acid, which we can abbreviate as $H_3$ Cit, what is the ratio of $[H_3 \text{ Cit}]$ and $[H_2 \text{ Cit}]$ and$[HCit^{2-}]$ to $[Cit^{3-}]$?

$$H_3 \text{ Cit} \rightleftharpoons H^+ + H_2 \text{ Cit}^- \qquad K_i = 8.4 \times 10^{-4} \qquad (1)$$

$$H_2 \text{ Cit}^- \rightleftharpoons H^+ + HCit^{2-} \qquad K_i = 1.8 \times 10^{-5} \qquad (2)$$

$$HCit^{2-} \rightleftharpoons H^+ + Cit^{3-} \qquad K_i = 4.0 \times 10^{-6} \qquad (3)$$

**Solution**

Since the $pH$ of the solution and the $K_i$ values for the three ionization steps are known, a series of ratios written in terms of $[Cit^{3-}]$ can be written. Starting with reaction (3),

$$pH = 1.92; \quad [H_3 O^+] = 10^{-1.92} = 1.20 \times 10^{-2} \text{ } M$$

$$\frac{[H^+][Cit^{3-}]}{[HCit^{2-}]} = 4.0 \times 10^{-6}$$

and

$$[HCit^{2-}] = \frac{(1.20 \times 10^{-2})[Cit^{3-}]}{4.0 \times 10^{-6}} = 3.0 \times 10^3 [Cit^{3-}]$$

For reaction (2),

$$\frac{[H^+][HCit^{2-}]}{[H_2 \text{ Cit}^-]} = 1.8 \times 10^{-5}$$

$$[H_2 \text{ Cit}^-] = \frac{(1.20 \times 10^{-2})[HCit^{2-}]}{1.8 \times 10^{-5}} = 6.67 \times 10^2 [HCit^{2-}]$$

$$= (6.67 \times 10^2)(3.0 \times 10^3)[Cit^{3-}] = 2.0 \times 10^6 [Cit^{3-}]$$

For reaction (1),

$$\frac{[H^+][H_2 Cit^-]}{[H_3 Cit]} = 8.4 \times 10^{-4}$$

$$[H_3 Cit] = \frac{1.20 \times 10^{-2}}{8.4 \times 10^{-4}} [H_2 Cit^-] = 14.3[H_2 Cit^-]$$

$$= (14.3)(2.0 \times 10^6)[Cit^{3-}]$$

$$= 2.9 \times 10^7 [Cit^{3-}]$$

$$[H_3 Cit] : [H_2 Cit^-] : [HCit^{2-}] : [Cit^{3-}]$$

| | | | |
|---|---|---|---|
| $2.9 \times 10^7$ | $2 \times 10^6$ | $3 \times 10^3$ | $1$ |

## RELATED PROBLEMS

1. Calculate the $pH$ of each of the following solutions.

   (a) 35.00 ml of 1.000 $M$ KOH mixed with 65.00 ml of 0.7500 $M$ HCl.
   (b) 20.0 g of NaCN diluted with distilled water to 500.0 ml.
   (c) 15.0 g of benzoic acid, $C_6 H_5 COOH$, in 1.00 ℓ of solution.

   $$K_i(C_6 H_5 COOH) = 6.46 \times 10^{-5}$$

   (d) 3.00 g of $CH_3 NH_2$ in 250. ml of solution.
   *Answer: (a) 0.86; (b) 8.7; (c) 2.5; (d) 11.5*

2. The procedure for the preparation of a buffer solution directs that 83.33 ml of 6.00 $M$ acetic acid be dissolved with 205.0 g of sodium acetate and the mixture diluted with distilled water to 1.00 ℓ. Calculate the $pH$ of this buffer solution. *Answer: pH = 5.44*

3. Although several buffer combinations exist in human blood, the blood is mainly buffered by the $H_2 CO_3 - HCO_3^-$ system. Calculate the ratio of $HCO_3^-$ to $H_2 CO_3$ in blood given that the $pH$ of blood is 7.4.
   *Answer: $HCO_3 - H_2 CO_3 = 10.8 : 1$*

4. Urine produced by a human whose diet has been only fruits and vegetables will have a $pH$ that is basic, about 7.6. Given that normal elimination of urine is about 1300 ml per day, calculate the number of equivalents of hydrogen ion eliminated per day.
   *Answer: No. equiv $H^+ = 3.3 \times 10^{-8}$*

5. At one point in the titration of a 20.0-ml sample of vinegar, the $pH$ of the solution is 5.10. Given that the initial $pH$ of the vinegar (acetic acid in water) was 2.80, calculate the number of moles of NaOH required to produce this change in $pH$.
   *Answer: No. moles NaOH = 1.93 \times 10^{-3} mol*

# Chapter 17: The Solubility Product Principle

## INTRODUCTION

Many ionic substances function as strong electrolytes in water although they are only slightly soluble in it. These substances include carbonates, such as limestone, $CaCO_3$, and sulfides, such as pyrite, $FeS_2$, and cinnabar, HgS. Mercury(II) sulfide, HgS, is one of the least soluble ionic substances: Only about $1.3 \times 10^{-24}$ g will dissolve in one liter of water. Because of their slight solubility in water such substances often form mineral deposits that are valuable to miners.

The occurrence of mineral deposits can be understood by considering the mode of formation of slightly soluble salts. In reactions involving the formation of a slightly soluble substance, the solubility is usually exceeded and a precipitate forms. For example, the salt $BaSO_4$ exists in water as $Ba^{2+}(aq)$ and $SO_4^{2-}(aq)$, but the maximum concentration at 25°C is only $1 \times 10^{-5}$ M. When a solution containing barium ions, such as $BaCl_2$, is added to one containing sulfate ions, such as $H_2SO_4$, the solubility limit is exceeded and a white precipitate of $BaSO_4$ forms and settles to the bottom. The solid $BaSO_4$ is then in equilibrium with the ions in solution. This equilibrium is defined in terms of the product of ion concentrations, that is, the solubility product, $K_{sp}$.

$$BaSO_4(s) \rightleftharpoons Ba^{2+}(aq) + SO_4^{2-}(aq)$$

$$K_{sp} = [Ba^{2+}][SO_4^{2-}] = 1.08 \times 10^{-10}$$

Thus a precipitate will form when the ion concentrations in the solubility product expression exceed the $K_{sp}$. Precipitation will continue until the product of the concentrations equals the $K_{sp}$.

Slightly soluble substances that contain ions derived from weak acids or weak bases dissolve and undergo hydrolysis or association depending upon the $pH$ of the solution. Two or more simultaneous equilibria that exist in solution may compete for the ions. In such cases all equilibria must be considered in the determination of the solubility.

Several concepts involving solubility are treated in this chapter of the textbook. Solubility product constants with several examples are presented and should be studied carefully before attempting to solve problems at the end of the chapter. The $K_{sp}$ concept is extended to the dissolution of precipitates through the formation of complex ions, which ultimately involve simultaneous equilibria. Many examples that involve $K_{sp}$ also involve the concepts of weak acids, buffers, and hydrolysis as treated in Chapter 16.

## FORMULAS AND DEFINITIONS

**Saturated solution**  A saturated solution contains a slightly soluble solute in a two-phase system in which dissolved solute is in contact with undissolved solute. The system is at equilibrium, meaning that undissolved solute continues to dissolve while simultaneously, and at the same rate, ions in solution associate and crystallize.

**Solubility product constant ($K_{sp}$)**  An equilibrium constant based on the molar concentrations of ions in a saturated solution containing a slightly soluble electrolyte. Each ion concentration is raised to the power corresponding to its stoichiometric coefficient as shown in the equilibrium expression. In general, the expression for $K_{sp}$ is written as

$$A_x B_y (s) \rightleftharpoons xA(aq)^{(positive)} + yB(aq)^{(negative)}$$

$$K_{sp} = [A^{positive}]^x [B^{negative}]^y$$

Solubility product constants are published without units for the sake of brevity. But always keep in mind that units for constants are in terms of concentrations raised to some power and sometimes must be used in conjunction with equilibrium calculations.

**Complex ion-formation constant**  Certain metal ions associate with ligands to form ions containing two or more species. Examples include $Ag(NH_3)_2^+$, $Cu(CN)_2^-$, $Al(OH)_4^-$, and $Sn(OH)_3^-$. Many of the complex ions are quite soluble in water, and they provide a mechanism for dissolving precipitates of slightly soluble electrolytes.

In solution ions associate reversibly to form complex ions and to reach an equilibrium defined by the formation constant, $K_{form}$. The value of

$K_{form}$ is a measure of the tendency to form the complex ion and the chemical stability of the complex. Typical values for formation constants are very large as indicated for the formation of $Ag(NH_3)_2^+$.

$$Ag^+(aq) + 2NH_3(aq) \rightleftharpoons Ag(NH_3)_2^+$$

$$K_{form} = \frac{[Ag(NH_3)_2^+]}{[Ag^+][NH_3]^2} = 1.6 \times 10^7$$

Calculations involving formation constants are similar to those for ionic equilibria.

## PROBLEMS

1. Calculate the solubility product constants of each of the following from the solubility given:

(a) $AgBr$, $5.7 \times 10^{-7}$ mol/$\ell$
(c) $PbF_2$, $2.1 \times 10^{-3}$ mol/$\ell$
(d) $Ag_2CrO_4$, $4.3 \times 10^{-2}$ g/$\ell$

**Solution**

(a) $AgBr$, $5.7 \times 10^{-7}$ mol/$\ell$. Silver bromide, AgBr, is a very slightly soluble salt that dissociates in water as

$$AgBr(s) \rightleftharpoons Ag^+(aq) + Br^-(aq)$$

The $K_{sp}$ expression includes only the ions in the solution phase and is written as

$$K_{sp} = [Ag^+][Br^-]$$

In a solution of a 1:1 electrolyte such as AgBr, the concentration of $Ag^+$ and of $Br^-$ equals the solubility of AgBr. The concentration of AgBr that dissolves is $5.7 \times 10^{-7}$ mol/$\ell$ and, therefore, the concentration of $Ag^+$ and $Br^-$ is $5.7 \times 10^{-7}$ mol/$\ell$. Substitution into the $K_{sp}$ expression gives

$$K_{sp}(AgBr) = (5.7 \times 10^{-7})(5.7 \times 10^{-7}) = 3.2 \times 10^{-13}$$

(c) $PbF_2$, $2.1 \times 10^{-3}$ mol $\ell^-$. This salt dissociates in water to produce

$$PbF_2(s) \rightleftharpoons Pb^{2+}(aq) + 2F^-(aq)$$

From the solubility of $PbF_2$, the concentrations of $Pb^{2+}$ and of $F^-$ are determined:

$$[Pb^{2+}] = 2.1 \times 10^{-3} \text{ mol/}\ell; \quad [F^-] = 2(2.1 \times 10^{-3} \text{ mol/}\ell)$$
$$= 4.2 \times 10^{-3} \text{ mol/}\ell$$

$$K_{sp} = [Pb^{2+}][F^-]^2$$
$$= (2.1 \times 10^{-3})(4.2 \times 10^{-3})^2 = 3.7 \times 10^{-8}$$

(d) $Ag_2CrO_4$, $4.3 \times 10^{-2}$ g $\ell^{-1}$. Since equilibrium values are calculated in terms of molar quantities, the solubility must be in terms of molarity.

$$\text{GFW } Ag_2CrO_4 = 2(107.9) + 52.0 + 4(16.0) = 331.8 \text{ g}$$

$$\text{Molar solubility} = 4.3 \times 10^{-2} \frac{g}{\ell} \times \frac{1 \text{ mol}}{331.8 \text{ g}} = 1.3 \times 10^{-4} \text{ } M$$

Dissolving one formula unit of $Ag_2CrO_4$ produces 2 $Ag^+$ and 1 $CrO_4{}^{2-}$. Therefore

$$K_{sp} = [Ag^+]^2 [CrO_4{}^{2-}]$$
$$[Ag^+] = 2(1.3 \times 10^{-4}) = 2.6 \times 10^{-4}$$
$$[CrO_4{}^{2-}] = 1.3 \times 10^{-4}$$
$$K_{sp} = (2.6 \times 10^{-4})^2 (1.3 \times 10^{-4}) = 8.8 \times 10^{-12}$$

2. Calculate the concentrations of ions in a saturated solution of each of the following. (See Appendix D for solubility product constants.)

(a) $AgI$
(b) $Ag_2SO_4$
(e) $Sr(OH)_2 \cdot 8 H_2O$

**Solution**

(a) The dissolution of $AgI$ produces one each of the ions $Ag^+$ and $I^-$.

$$AgI(s) \rightleftharpoons Ag^+(aq) + I^-(aq)$$
$$K_{sp} = [Ag^+][I^-] = 1.5 \times 10^{-16}$$

Let $x$ equal the solubility of $AgI$ in moles per liter.

$$x = [Ag^+] = [I^-]$$
$$K_{sp} = (x)(x) = 1.5 \times 10^{-16}$$
$$x^2 = 1.5 \times 10^{-16}$$
$$[Ag^+] = [I^-] = x = 1.2 \times 10^{-8} \text{ } M$$

(b) Dissolution of $Ag_2SO_4$ occurs as

$$Ag_2SO_4(s) \rightleftharpoons 2Ag^+(aq) + SO_4{}^{2-}(aq)$$

Let $x$ equal the molar solubility of $Ag_2SO_4$. Since dissolving $Ag_2SO_4$ produces 2 $Ag^+$ and 1 $SO_4{}^{2-}$, the concentrations in terms of $x$ are

$$[Ag^+] = 2x; \quad [SO_4{}^{2-}] = x$$
$$K_{sp} = [Ag^+]^2 [SO_4{}^{2-}] = 1.18 \times 10^{-5}$$

$$(2x)^2 (x) = 4x^3 = 1.18 \times 10^{-5}$$
$$x^3 = 2.95 \times 10^{-6}$$
$$x = 1.4 \times 10^{-2}$$
$$[Ag^+] = 2.8 \times 10^{-2}\ M; \quad [SO_4^{2-}] = 1.4 \times 10^{-2}\ M$$

(e) Dissolution of $Sr(OH)_2 \cdot 8H_2O$ occurs as

$$Sr(OH)_2 \cdot 8H_2O \rightleftharpoons Sr^{2+}(aq) + 2OH^-(aq) + 8H_2O$$

Let $x$ equal the molar solubility of $Sr(OH)_2 \cdot 8H_2O$. Dissolving 1 mole of $Sr(OH)_2 \cdot 8H_2O$ produces 1 mole of $Sr^{2+}$ and 2 moles of $OH^-$.

$$K_{sp} = [Sr^{2+}][OH^-]^2 = 3.2 \times 10^{-4}$$

The ion concentrations in terms of $x$ are

$$x = [Sr^{2+}]; \quad [OH^-] = 2x$$
$$(x)(2x)^2 = 3.2 \times 10^{-4}$$
$$4x^3 = 3.2 \times 10^{-4}$$
$$x^3 = 8.0 \times 10^{-5}$$
$$[Sr^{2+}] = x = 0.043 = 4.3 \times 10^{-2}\ M$$
$$[OH^-] = 8.6 \times 10^{-2}\ M$$

3. Calculate the concentration of $Sr^{2+}$ ion when strontium fluoride starts to precipitate from a solution that is 0.0025 $M$ in fluoride ion ($K_{sp} = 3.7 \times 10^{-12}$).

**Solution**

Precipitation of $SrF_2$ will begin when the concentration of the ions $Sr^{2+}$ and $F^-$ exceed the $K_{sp}$ of $SrF_2$.

$$SrF_2 \rightleftharpoons Sr^{2+}(aq) + 2F^-(aq)$$
$$K_{sp} = [Sr^{2+}][F^-]^2 = 3.7 \times 10^{-12}$$

The maximum concentration of $Sr^{2+}$ that will remain in solution is

$$[Sr^{2+}] = \frac{3.7 \times 10^{-12}}{(0.0025)^2} = 5.9 \times 10^{-7}\ M$$

12. A solution of 0.075 $M$ $CoBr_2$ is saturated with $H_2S$ ($[H_2S] = 0.1\ M$). What is the minimum $pH$ at which $CoS$ ($K_{sp} = 5.9 \times 10^{-21}$) will precipitate?

**Solution**

Two equilibria are in competition for the ions and must be considered simultaneously. Precipitation of $CoS$ will occur when the concentration of $S^{2-}$ in conjunction with 0.075 $M$ $Co^{2+}$ exceeds the $K_{sp}$ of $CoS$.

But the $[S^{2-}]$ must come from the ionization of $H_2S$ as defined by the equilibrium:

$$H_2S(aq) \rightleftharpoons 2H^+(aq) + S^{2-}(aq)$$

$$\frac{[H^+]^2[S^{2-}]}{[H_2S]} = K_1K_2(H_2S) = 1.3 \times 10^{-20}$$

Since a saturated solution of $H_2S$ is $0.10\ M$, this expression becomes

$$[H^+]^2[S^{2-}] = 1.3 \times 10^{-21}$$

From the equilibrium of CoS, the minimum concentration of $S^{2-}$ required to cause precipitation is calculated as

$$CoS(s) \rightleftharpoons Co^{2+}(aq) + S^{2-}(aq)$$

$$K_{sp} = [Co^{2+}][S^{2-}] = 5.9 \times 10^{-21}$$

$$[S^{2-}] = \frac{5.9 \times 10^{-21}}{0.075} = 7.87 \times 10^{-20}$$

This amount of $S^{2-}$ will exist in solution at a $pH$ defined by the $H_2S$ equilibrium.

$$[H^+]^2 (7.87 \times 10^{-20}) = 1.3 \times 10^{-21}$$

$$[H^+]^2 = 1.65 \times 10^{-2}$$

$$[H^+] = 1.29 \times 10^{-1}$$

$$pH = -\log 1.29 \times 10^{-1} = 0.89$$

16. What is the concentration of $Ca^{2+}$ and $CO_3{}^{2-}$ in a saturated solution of calcium carbonate ($K_{sp} = 4.8 \times 10^{-9}$)?

**Solution**

The dissolution of $CaCO_3$ is highly dependent on the $pH$ of the aqueous medium. Assume that association of $CO_3{}^{2-}$ with $H_3O^+$ from water is insignificant, meaning that the $[Ca^{2+}]$ at equilibrium equals $[CO_3{}^{2-}]$.

$$CaCO_3(s) \rightleftharpoons Ca^{2+}(aq) + CO_3{}^{2-}(aq)$$

$$K_{sp} = 4.8 \times 10^{-9} = [Ca^{2+}][CO_3{}^{2-}]$$

Let $x$ equal the number of moles of $CaCO_3$ dissolving.

$$x = [Ca^{2+}] = [CO_3{}^{2-}]$$

$$K_{sp}(x)(x) = 4.8 \times 10^{-9}$$

$$x = 6.9 \times 10^{-5}\ M$$

17. What is the concentration of $Ca^{2+}$ and $CO_3{}^{2-}$ in a buffer solution with a $pH$ of 4.55, in contact with an excess of $CaCO_3$?

## Solution

The dissolution of $CaCO_3$ produces one ion each of $Ca^{2+}$ and $CO_3^{2-}$. The carbonic acid is a weak acid and $CO_3^{2-}$ will associate with $H_3O^+$ according to the following reactions.

$$CO_3^{2-} + H_3O^+ \rightleftharpoons HCO_3^- + H_2O \qquad (1)$$

$$HCO_3^- + H_3O^+ \rightleftharpoons H_2CO_3 + H_2O \qquad (2)$$

The concentration of $Ca^{2+}$ at equilibrium equals the total concentration of the species containing carbonate.

$$\text{Solubility} = [Ca^{2+}] = [CO_3^{2-}] + [HCO_3^-] + [H_2CO_3] \qquad (3)$$

$$K_{sp}(CaCO_3) = [Ca^{2+}][CO_3^{2-}] = 4.8 \times 10^{-9} \qquad (4)$$

Since the solubility expression involves four unknowns, four simultaneous equations are needed for solving the expression for $[Ca^{2+}]$. Equations (1) and (2) are merely the reverse of the successive ionizations of $H_2CO_3$, and the $K$ values for $H_2CO_3$ can be used.

$$H_2CO_3(aq) \rightleftharpoons H_3O^+(aq) + HCO_3^-(aq) \qquad K_1 = 4.3 \times 10^{-7} \qquad (5)$$

$$HCO_3^-(aq) \rightleftharpoons H_3O^+(aq) + CO_3^{2-}(aq) \qquad K_2 = 7 \times 10^{-11} \qquad (6)$$

Equations (5) and (6) can be rearranged and expressed in terms of $[CO_3^{2-}]$. At a $pH$ of 4.55 the $[H_3O^+]$ is $2.8 \times 10^{-5}$.

$$\frac{[H_3O^+][CO_3^{2-}]}{[HCO_3^-]} = 7 \times 10^{-11}$$

$$[HCO_3^-] = \frac{2.8 \times 10^{-5}}{7 \times 10^{-11}} [CO_3^{2-}] = 4 \times 10^5 [CO_3^{2-}]$$

and

$$\frac{[H_3O^+][HCO_3^-]}{[H_2CO_3]} = 4.3 \times 10^{-7}$$

$$[H_2CO_3] = \frac{2.8 \times 10^{-5}}{4.3 \times 10^{-7}} [HCO_3^-] = 6.5 \times 10^1 [HCO_3^-]$$

$$= 6.5 \times 10^1 (4 \times 10^5)[CO_3^{2-}] = 2.6 \times 10^7 [CO_3^{2-}]$$

These values for $[HCO_3^-]$, $[H_2CO_3]$, and $[CO_3^{2-}]$ can be substituted in Equation (3), which yields

$$[Ca^{2+}] = [CO_3^{2-}] + 4 \times 10^5 [CO_3^{2-}] + 2.6 \times 10^7 [CO_3^{2-}]$$

$$[Ca^{2+}] = 2.6 \times 10^7 [CO_3^{2-}]$$

or

$$[CO_3^{2-}] = \frac{[Ca^{2+}]}{2.6 \times 10^7}$$

Substitution into the expression for $K_{sp}$ yields

$$K_{sp} = [Ca^{2+}][CO_3{}^{2-}] = [Ca^{2+}] \frac{[Ca^{2+}]}{2.6 \times 10^7} = 4.8 \times 10^{-9}$$

$$[Ca^{2+}]^2 = 1.25 \times 10^{-1}$$

$$[Ca^{2+}] = 0.35 \text{ mol/}\ell = 0.35 \ M$$

19. Fifty milliliters of $1.8 \ M$ $NH_3$ is mixed with an equal volume of a solution containing 0.95 g of $MgCl_2$. What mass of $NH_4Cl$ must be added to the resulting solution to prevent the precipitation of $Mg(OH)_2$?

**Solution**

The hydroxide ion concentration in solution depends on two simultaneous equilibria. The maximum allowable $[OH^-]$ can be calculated from the $K_{sp}$ of $Mg(OH)_2$ based on the $[Mg^{2+}]$.

$$Mg(OH)_2 \rightleftharpoons Mg^{2+}(aq) + 2OH^-(aq) \qquad K_{sp} = 1.5 \times 10^{-11}$$

$$[Mg^{2+}] = [MgCl_2]$$

$$[Mg^{2+}] = \frac{0.95 \text{ g } MgCl_2 \times \dfrac{1 \text{ mol}}{95.3 \text{ g}}}{0.10 \ \ell} = 0.0997 \ M$$

$$[Mg^{2+}][OH^-]^2 = 1.5 \times 10^{-11}$$

$$[OH^-]^2 = \frac{1.5 \times 10^{-11}}{0.0997} = 1.50 \times 10^{-10}$$

$$[OH^-] = 1.22 \times 10^{-5} \ M$$

The $[OH^-]$ produced from $NH_3$ must be suppressed to $1.2 \times 10^{-5}$ by buffering the solution through the addition of $NH_4Cl$. The required $[NH_4{}^+]$ can be calculated from the equilibrium constant expression for ammonia.

$$NH_3(aq) \rightleftharpoons NH_4{}^+(aq) + OH^-(aq)$$

$$K_i = 1.8 \times 10^{-5} = \frac{[NH_4{}^+][OH^-]}{[NH_3]}$$

At equilibrium, the $[NH_3]$ approximately equals $1.8 \ M/2 = 0.90 \ M$ since $1.22 \times 10^{-5}$ is small with respect to 0.90. Therefore the $[NH_4{}^+]$ is

$$1.8 \times 10^{-5} = \frac{[NH_4{}^+](1.22 \times 10^{-5})}{0.90}$$

$$[NH_4{}^+] = \frac{(0.90)(1.8 \times 10^{-5})}{1.22 \times 10^{-5}} = 1.33 \ M$$

Mass $NH_4Cl$ required $= \left(1.33 \dfrac{mol}{\ell}\right)\left(53.5 \dfrac{g}{mol}\right)(0.10\ \ell) = 7.1\ g$

22. The calcium ions in human blood serum are necessary for coagulation of the blood. In order to prevent this coagulation when a sample is drawn for laboratory tests, an anticoagulant is added to the sample. Potassium oxalate, $K_2C_2O_4$, can be used as an anticoagulant because, in the proper amounts, it removes the calcium as a precipitate of $CaC_2O_4 \cdot H_2O$. In order to prevent coagulation it is necessary to remove all but 1.0% of the calcium ion in the serum. If normal blood serum with a buffered $pH$ of 7.40 contains 9.5 mg of $Ca^{2+}$ per 100 ml of serum, what mass of $K_2C_2O_4$ is required to prevent the coagulation of a 10-ml blood sample that is 55% serum and 45% red blood cells (a solid)? (All volumes are accurate to two significant figures. Note that the volume of fluid in a 10-ml blood sample is 5.5 ml.)

**Solution**

Although oxalic acid is a weak acid, the oxalate ions, $C_2O_4^{2-}$, do not associate significantly with $H_3O^+$ at the $pH$ of blood. The amount of $K_2C_2O_4$ required equals the equivalent of 99% of the available $Ca^{2+}$ plus the amount needed to maintain the equilibrium defined by the solubility product.

$$K_{sp}(CaC_2O_4) = [Ca^{2+}][C_2O_4^{2-}] = 2.27 \times 10^{-9}$$

The amount of available $Ca^{2+}$ in 5.5 ml of serum is

$$\text{No. moles } Ca^{2+} = 5.5\ ml \times \frac{9.5\ mg}{100\ ml} \times \frac{1.0\ g}{1000\ mg} \times \frac{1\ mol}{40.08\ g}$$

$$= 1.304 \times 10^{-5}\ mol$$

No. moles $Ca^{2+}$ to be precipitated $= (0.99)(1.304 \times 10^{-5}\ mol)$

$$= 1.291 \times 10^{-5}\ mol$$

At equilibrium the $[Ca^{2+}]$ is 1% of the original:

$$[Ca^{2+}] = \frac{(0.01)(1.304 \times 10^{-5}\ mol)}{0.055\ \ell} = 2.371 \times 10^{-6}\ \frac{mol}{\ell}$$

From the $K_{sp}$ expression,

$$[C_2O_4^{2-}] = \frac{2.27 \times 10^{-9}}{2.371 \times 10^{-6}} = 9.574 \times 10^{-4}\ \frac{mol}{\ell}$$

No. moles $C_2O_4^{2-}$ in 5.5 ml $= 9.574 \times 10^{-4}\ \dfrac{mol}{\ell} \times 0.055\ \ell$

$$= 5.266 \times 10^{-5}\ mol$$

Total no. moles $C_2O_4^{2-}$ required $= 5.266 \times 10^{-5}$ mol $+ 1.304 \times 10^{-5}$ mol

$$= 6.57 \times 10^{-5} \text{ mol}$$

$$\text{Mass } K_2C_2O_4 = 6.57 \times 10^{-5} \text{ mol} \times 166.2 \frac{g}{mol} = 0.011 \text{ g}$$

23. About 50% of all urinary calculi (kidney stones) consist of calcium phosphate, $Ca_3(PO_4)_2$. The normal midrange calcium content excreted in the urine is 0.10 g of $Ca^{2+}$ per day. The normal midrange amount of urine passed may be taken as 1.4 ℓ per day. What is the maximum concentration of phosphate ion possible in urine before a calculus begins to form?

**Solution**

The dissolution of $Ca_3(PO_4)_2$ yields

$$Ca_3(PO_4)_2(s) \rightleftharpoons 3Ca^{2+}(aq) + 2PO_4^{3-}(aq)$$

Given the concentration of $Ca^{2+}$ in solution, the maximum $[PO_4^{3-}]$ can be calculated by using the $K_{sp}$ expression for $Ca_3(PO_4)_2$.

$$K_{sp} = 1 \times 10^{-25} = [Ca^{2+}][PO_4^{3-}]^2$$

$$[Ca^{2+}]_{urine} = \frac{0.10 \text{ g} \times \dfrac{1 \text{ mol}}{40.1 \text{ g}}}{1.4 \text{ ℓ}} = 1.8 \times 10^{-3} \, M$$

$$[PO_4^{3-}]^2 = \frac{1 \times 10^{-25}}{(1.8 \times 10^{-3})^3} = 1.7 \times 10^{-17}$$

$$[PO_4^{3-}] = 4 \times 10^{-9} \, M$$

24. If the pH of a normal urine sample is 6.30 and the total phosphate concentration ($[PO_4^{3-}] + [HPO_4^{2-}] + [H_2PO_4^-] + [H_3PO_4]$) is 0.020 $M$, what is the minimum concentration of $Ca^{2+}$ necessary to induce calculus formation? (See Problem 23 for additional information.)

**Solution**

The concentration of $Ca^{2+}$ depends on the concentration of $PO_4^{3-}$ in solution. But the $[PO_4^{3-}]$ is dependent on pH and the $H_3PO_4$ equilibrium. Since the total phosphate concentration is 0.020 $M$, the $[PO_4^{3-}]$ must be calculated from the three expressions involving $H_3PO_4$. These expressions, solved in terms of $[PO_4^{3-}]$, yield a ratio of $[PO_4^{3-}]$ to the other components.

$$H_3PO_4 \rightleftharpoons H^+ + H_2PO_4^- \qquad K_1 = 7.5 \times 10^{-3} \qquad (1)$$

$$H_2PO_4^- \rightleftharpoons H^+ + HPO_4^{2-} \qquad K_2 = 6.2 \times 10^{-8} \qquad (2)$$

$$HPO_4{}^{2-} \rightleftharpoons H^+ + PO_4{}^{3-} \qquad K_3 = 3.6 \times 10^{-13} \qquad (3)$$

At a $pH$ of 6.3, the $[H^+] = 5.01 \times 10^{-7}$. For Equation (3),

$$\frac{[H^+][PO_4{}^{3-}]}{[HPO_4{}^{2-}]} = 1 \times 10^{-12}$$

$$[HPO_4{}^{2-}] = \frac{5.01 \times 10^{-7}}{3.6 \times 10^{-13}} [PO_4{}^{3-}]$$

$$= 1.39 \times 10^6 [PO_4{}^{3-}]$$

For Equation (2),

$$\frac{[H^+][HPO_4{}^{2-}]}{[H_2PO_4{}^-]} = 6.2 \times 10^{-8}$$

$$[H_2PO_4{}^-] = \frac{5.01 \times 10^{-7}}{6.2 \times 10^{-8}} [HPO_4{}^{2-}]$$

$$= 8.08(1.39 \times 10^6)[PO_4{}^{3-}] = 1.12 \times 10^7 [PO_4{}^{3-}]$$

For Equation (1),

$$\frac{[H^+][H_2PO_4{}^-]}{[H_3PO_4]} = 7.5 \times 10^{-3}$$

$$[H_3PO_4] = \frac{5.01 \times 10^{-7}}{7.5 \times 10^{-3}} [H_2PO_4{}^-]$$

$$= 6.7 \times 10^{-5}(1.12 \times 10^7)[PO_4{}^{3-}]$$

$$= 750[PO_4{}^{3-}]$$

$$[PO_4{}^{3-}]:[HPO_4{}^{2-}]:[H_2PO_4{}^-]:[H_3PO_4]$$

$$1:1.39 \times 10^6 : 1.12 \times 10^7 : 750$$

The fraction of $PO_4{}^{3-}$ in solution is

$$\frac{[PO_4{}^{3-}]}{[PO_4{}^{3-}] + [HPO_4{}^{2-}] + [H_2PO_4{}^-] + [H_3PO_4]} = \frac{1}{1.26 \times 10^7}$$

$$= 7.94 \times 10^{-8}$$

The concentration of $PO_4{}^{3-}$ in urine at $pH$ 6.3 is

$$[PO_4{}^{3-}] = 7.94 \times 10^{-8} (0.020) = 1.59 \times 10^{-9}$$

Use the $K_{sp}$ of $Ca_3(PO_4)_2$ to calculate the minimum $[Ca^{2+}]$ present. For the reaction $Ca_3(PO_4)_2 \rightleftharpoons 3Ca^{2+} + 2PO_4{}^{3-}$,

$$K_{sp} = [Ca^{2+}]^3 [PO_4{}^{3-}]^2$$

$$[Ca^{2+}]^3 = \frac{K_{sp}}{[PO_4{}^{3-}]^2} = \frac{1 \times 10^{-25}}{(1.59 \times 10^{-9})^2} = 3.96 \times 10^{-8} \ M$$

$$[Ca^{2+}] = (3.96 \times 10^{-8})^{1/3} = 3.4 \times 10^{-3} \ M$$

27. Calculate the cadmium ion concentration in a solution prepared by mixing 0.100 ℓ of 0.0100 $M$ $Cd(NO_3)_2$ solution with 0.150 ℓ of 0.100 $M$ $NH_3 (aq)$.

**Solution**

Cadmium ions associate with ammonia molecules in solution to form the complex ion, $[Cd(NH_3)_4]^{2+}$, which is defined by the following equilibrium:

$$Cd^{2+}(aq) + 4NH_3(aq) \rightleftharpoons [Cd(NH_3)_4]^{2+}(aq) \qquad K_{form} = 4.0 \times 10^6$$

The formation of the complex requires 4 moles of $NH_3$ for each mole of $Cd^{2+}$. Let us first calculate the initial amounts of $Cd^{2+}$ and of $NH_3$ available for association.

$$[Cd^{2+}] = \frac{(0.100 \ \ell)(0.0100 \ mol/\ell)}{0.250 \ \ell} = 4.00 \times 10^{-3} \ M$$

$$[NH_3] = \frac{(0.150 \ \ell)(0.100 \ mol/\ell)}{0.250 \ \ell} = 6.00 \times 10^{-2} \ M$$

For the reaction, $4.00 \times 10^{-3}$ mol/ℓ of $Cd^{2+}$ would require $4(4.00 \times 10^{-3}$ mol/ℓ) of $NH_3$ or $1.6 \times 10^{-2}$ mol. Due to the large value of $K_{form}$ and the substantial excess of $NH_3$, we can assume that the reaction goes to completion with only a small amount of the complex dissociating to form the ions. After reaction, concentrations of the species in solution are

$$[NH_3] = 6.00 \times 10^{-2} \ \frac{mol}{\ell} - 1.6 \times 10^{-2} \ \frac{mol}{\ell} = 4.4 \times 10^{-2} \ M$$

$[Cd^{2+}]$ = equilibrium concentration from the dissociation of the complex

$$[Cd(NH_3)_4]^{2+} \simeq 4.00 \times 10^{-3} \ M$$

*At equilibrium:* Let $x$ = moles of $[Cd(NH_3)_4]^{2+}$ that dissociate.

$$x = [Cd^{2+}]$$

$$[NH_3] = 4.4 \times 10^{-2} + x$$

$$K_{form} = 4.0 \times 10^6 = \frac{[Cd(NH_3)_4{}^{2+}]}{[Cd^{2+}][NH_3]^4}$$

$$4.0 \times 10^6 = \frac{(4.00 \times 10^{-3} - x)}{(x)(4.4 \times 10^{-2} + x)^4}$$

The expression can be simplified to

$$4.0 \times 10^6 = \frac{(4.00 \times 10^{-3})}{(x)(4.4 \times 10^{-2})^4}$$

Rearranging and solving for $x$ yields

$$1.50 \times 10^1 \, x = 4.00 \times 10^{-3}$$

$$x = 2.7 \times 10^{-4} \, M = [Cd^{2+}]$$

32. (a) What mass of AgCl will dissolve in 1.0 ℓ of 1.0 $M$ NH$_3$?

**Solution**

Silver ion from dissolved AgCl complexes with ammonia to form a diaminesilver complex as follows:

$$AgCl(s) + 2NH_3(aq) \rightleftharpoons Ag(NH_3)_2^+(aq) + Cl^-(aq) \qquad (1)$$

The formation constant for this equilibrium is

$$K_{form} = \frac{[Ag(NH_3)_2^+]}{[Ag^+][NH_3]^2} = 1.6 \times 10^7 \qquad (2)$$

A small amount of AgCl dissolves according to the equilibrium

$$AgCl(s) \rightleftharpoons Ag^+(aq) + Cl^-(aq) \qquad K_{sp} = 1.8 \times 10^{-10} \qquad (3)$$

At equilibrium both equilibria, Ag(NH$_3$)$_2^+$ and AgCl, must be satisfied simultaneously. The Ag$^+$ in solution applies to both equilibria when AgCl and Ag(NH$_3$)$_2^+$ are present. At equilibrium, let $x$ equal the number of moles of AgCl that dissolve. According to Eq. (1), $x$ equals the [Cl$^-$] in solution and the amount of Ag$^+$ available for producing the complex, the [Ag(NH$_3$)$_2^+$]. By using Eq. (3), the [Ag$^+$] in terms of $K_{sp}$ is

$$[Ag^+](x) = 1.8 \times 10^{-10}$$

$$[Ag^+] = \frac{1.8 \times 10^{-10}}{x}$$

The formation constant for the complex is very large; hence essentially all the available Ag$^+$ is complexed with only a small amount remaining in solution. Since the formation of the complex requires two moles of NH$_3$ for each Ag$^+$, the concentration of NH$_3$ at equilibrium is $1.0 - 2x$. Substitution into Eq. (2) gives

$$\frac{x}{\left(\dfrac{1.8 \times 10^{-10}}{x}\right)(1.0 - 2x)^2} = 1.6 \times 10^7$$

Clearing the fraction and rearranging to standard quadratic form gives

$$x^2 = 2.88 \times 10^{-3} (1 - 4x + 4x^2)$$

$$0.988x^2 + 1.15 \times 10^{-2}x - 2.88 \times 10^{-3} = 0$$

Substitution into the quadratic formula and calculation of the value of the radical gives

$$x = \frac{-1.15 \times 10^{-2} \pm 0.107}{1.98}$$

The positive root of x is $4.8 \times 10^{-2}$ mol.

$$\text{Mass AgCl dissolved} = 4.8 \times 10^{-2} \text{ mol} \times 143.4 \frac{g}{mol} = 6.9 \text{ g}$$

34. Calculate the minimum concentration of ammonia needed in one liter of solution to dissolve $3.0 \times 10^{-3}$ moles of AgBr.

**Solution**

The dissolving of $3.0 \times 10^{-3}$ moles of AgBr in a solution containing ammonia produces $3.0 \times 10^{-3}$ moles of $Br^-$ and $3.0 \times 10^{-3}$ moles of $Ag(NH_3)_2^+$.

$$AgBr(s) + 2NH_3 \rightleftharpoons Ag(NH_3)_2^+ + Br^-$$

Two equilibria are involved since the $Ag^+$ in solution applies to both the $K_{sp}$ expression for AgBr and the formation constant expression for $Ag(NH_3)_2^+$. The maximum $[Ag^+]$ allowable before precipitation of AgBr occurs is

$$AgBr(s) \rightleftharpoons Ag^+(aq) + Br^-(aq) \qquad K_{sp} = 3.3 \times 10^{-13}$$

$$[Ag^+] = \frac{3.3 \times 10^{-13}}{3.0 \times 10^{-3}} = 1.1 \times 10^{-10} M$$

Any amount of $Ag^+$ greater than this value must be complexed with ammonia. The $[NH_3]$ required for the equilibrium is calculated from the formation constant expression.

$$Ag^+(aq) + 2NH_3(aq) \rightleftharpoons Ag(NH_3)_2(aq)$$

$$K_{form} = \frac{[Ag(NH_3)_2^+]}{[Ag^+][NH_3]^2} = 1.6 \times 10^7$$

Since $K_{form}$ is very large, the dissociation of $Ag(NH_3)_2^+$ can be neglected. Substitution into the expression for $K_{form}$ gives

$$\frac{(3.0 \times 10^{-3})}{(1.1 \times 10^{-10})[NH_3]^2} = 1.6 \times 10^7$$

Rearranging and solving for $[NH_3]$ gives

$$[NH_3]^2 = 1.7$$

$$[NH_3] = 1.3 M$$

## RELATED PROBLEMS

1. Calculate the concentration of silver ion required to initiate precipitation of AgI from a 0.010 $M$ KI solution.

   *Answer: $[Ag^+] = 1.5 \times 10^{-14}\ M$*

2. Silver plating can be accomplished through the electrolysis of a solution containing silver cyanide. The equilibrium of AgCN is represented as

   $$2AgCN(s) \longrightarrow Ag^+ + Ag(CN)_2^- \quad K_{sp} = 4.0 \times 10^{-12}$$

   Calculate the concentration of free $Ag^+$ at equilibrium in a saturated solution.

   *Answer: $[Ag^+] = 2.0 \times 10^{-6}\ M$*

3. Sea water contains a substantial amount of dissolved magnesium salts. Calculate the concentration of hydroxide ion necessary to remove 60% of the $Mg^{2+}$ from sea water that is 0.050 $M$ in $Mg^{2+}$.

   *Answer: $[OH^-] = 2.7 \times 10^{-5}\ M$*

4. Calculate the mass of lead(II) fluoride required to prepare 2.0 ℓ of saturated solution.

   *Answer: 1.0 g*

5. The inside walls of cooking ware often become encrusted with a variety of slightly soluble compounds. Calculate the volume of water that would be required to dissolve 10.0 g of crust composed of pure $CaCO_3$. Assume that $CaCO_3$ dissolves and does not undergo hydrolysis.

   *Answer: $1.4 \times 10^3$ ℓ*

# Chapter 18: Chemical Thermodynamics

The beginnings of modern thermodynamics can be traced to Benjamin Thompson, better known as Count Rumford of the Holy Roman Empire. His observations of the boring of cannon barrels in the early 1800s convinced him that the heat liberated in the machining resulted from the dissipation of mechanical work. Later, in the 1840s, James Joule made quantitative measurements of the conversion of mechanical energy into heat. His value was close to the modern value of the equivalency of heat and work: 1 calorie of heat = 4.184 joules of work.

This interconvertibility of heat and work makes it possible to define energy as the ability to produce heat or to do work. The First Law of Thermodynamics interrelates these two quantities and is basically an outgrowth of the human experience that energy can neither be created nor destroyed. Mathematically stated, the First Law is

$$\Delta E = q - w$$

where $\Delta E$ is the change in internal energy, $q$ is the heat absorbed by the system, and $w$ is the work done *by* the system.

This concept is important in chemistry because chemists generally are interested in three basic questions that ultimately deal with energy: (1) Will two or more substances react? (2) If a reaction does occur, what is the associated energy change? (3) If the reaction occurs, what will be the equilibrium concentrations of the reactants and products?

The application of the First Law of Thermodynamics to chemical systems is immediately evident if we consider a reaction involving a phase change, where the work done may be ignored. Thus ice at 0°C may be converted to water at 0°C solely by the addition of heat $q$. In this reaction we find that the energy content of ice has increased from that initially present by the amount of heat necessary to make this transition. We may write

$$\Delta E = q - w = q - 0 = q$$

The heat change in this reaction is therefore the change in the internal energy of the system.

In general, during the course of *any* chemical reaction, the internal energy of the system will change by a specific amount because of a change in heat or work. The enthalpy ($H$), a new function related to the internal energy, is introduced to simplify the study of the energy changes that occur in chemical reactions. The study of these heat effects is called *thermochemistry* and constitutes one important aspect of thermodynamics. This field answers our second question above.

In order to answer the other two questions, two more functions must be introduced. These are also the result of the study of fundamental laws in nature, namely: (1) systems tend to attain a state of minimum potential energy, and (2) systems tend toward a state of maximum disorder.

The first of these functions, entropy ($S$), is historically an outgrowth of the study of steam engines by the Frenchman Sadi Carnot. Carnot's study dates from 1824, but it was Clausius who first introduced the term entropy in 1840. Entropy, a measure of the disorder in a system, when properly combined with the enthalpy under the two constraints above, leads to a new function that conveniently allows us to determine whether or not a reaction will occur. The American J. Willard Gibbs introduced this new function originally known as the free energy, but now called the Gibbs energy $G$.

The Gibbs energy is an extremely powerful tool, for it not only allows us to determine whether a reaction will occur based only upon the knowledge of the state of the system, but it also allows us to predict the concentrations of the reacting substances at equilibrium through the expression

$$\log K = \frac{\Delta G^\circ}{-2.303\, RT}$$

where $K$ is the equilibrium constant. Thus the three questions of interest to chemists posed earlier can be answered through the application of several simple concepts.

The problems in this chapter deal with the calculation of internal energy, enthalpy, entropy, and Gibbs energy changes as well as the determination of the equilibrium constant.

## FORMULAS AND DEFINITIONS

**Chemical thermodynamics**   That branch of chemistry that studies the energy transformations and transfers that accompany chemical and physical changes.

**System** That part of the universe on which we focus our attention and with whose properties we are concerned.

**Surroundings** All of the universe except the system we are studying.

**State** The condition of the system, defined by $n$, $P$, $V$, and $T$.

**State function** A function that depends only on the particular state of a system and not on how the system got to that state.

**First Law of Thermodynamics** A statement of the law of conservation of energy: The total amount of energy in the universe is constant. Mathematically, $\Delta E = E_2 - E_1 = q - w$. Here $\Delta E$ is the internal energy change of the system due to a change in state, $q$ is heat, and $w$ is work.

**Heat** ($q$) A form of energy. A positive sign indicates a heat increase in the system; a negative sign corresponds to loss of heat from the system.

**Work** ($w$) A positive sign indicates work done by the system; a negative sign corresponds to work done on the system. Work has a pressure-volume equivalent defined as $w = P(V_2 - V_1)$, where $P$ is the pressure restraining the system, $V_1$ is the initial volume, and $V_2$ is the final volume.

**Enthalpy** ($H$) The heat content or enthalpy of the system. The change in enthalpy $\Delta H$ is the quantity of heat absorbed or liberated by the system when a reaction takes place at constant pressure; therefore $\Delta H = q$. If a reaction is endothermic, $q$ is positive; if exothermic, $q$ is negative. By definition, $\Delta H = \Delta E + \Delta(PV)$, or $\Delta H = \Delta E + P\Delta V$ for a constant-pressure process.

**Standard state** An agreed upon specific set of conditions designed to facilitate the handling of data. The standard state of a pure substance is taken as $25°C$ ($298.15$ K) and 1 atm pressure.

**$\Delta H°_{f298}$** Standard molar enthalpy of formation. This is the change in enthalpy when one mole of a pure substance is formed from the free elements in their most stable state under standard conditions. For any free element in its most stable form, the value of the standard molar enthalpy is zero.

**Hess's law** For any process that can be considered the sum of several stepwise processes, the enthalpy change for the total process must equal the sum of the enthalpy changes for the various steps.

**Bond energy** A measure of the strength of the chemical bonds in a compound. It is determined through the summation of the heats of dissociation of all the individual chemical bonds in a compound.

**Entropy** ($S$) The entropy is a measure of the order or randomness of a system. The smaller the value of the entropy, the more ordered is the system; the larger the entropy, the greater the disorder or randomness of the system. The entropy is also a function of the temperature; it decreases as the temperature decreases and increases as the temperature increases. The importance of entropy lies in our ability to predict the direction of a chemical process if both the entropy of the system and the entropy of the surroundings are known.

**Second Law of Thermodynamics**  In any spontaneous change, the entropy of the universe increases.

**Third Law of Thermodynamics**  The entropy of any pure, perfectly crystalline substance at the absolute zero of temperature (0 K) equals zero. Basically, this law allows the establishment of a beginning point, or zero point, for entropy measurements.

**Gibbs energy change (free energy) ($\Delta G$)**  Perhaps the most useful function of thermodynamics. It is the maximum amount of useful work that can be accomplished by a reaction at constant temperature and pressure. The Gibbs energy can also be used to predict the direction of a chemical process using only information about the system. These predictions are possible since reactions tend to proceed to a state of maximum disorder (positive $\Delta S$) and minimum energy (negative $\Delta H$). The sign that accompanies $\Delta G$ derived from the Gibbs energy expression, $\Delta G = \Delta H - T \Delta S$, is used to determine the spontaneity of the reaction: A negative sign indicates a spontaneous reaction as written, a positive value indicates a nonspontaneous reaction, and a value of zero indicates a reaction at equilibrium.

**Relation of the Gibbs energy ($\Delta G$) to the equilibrium constant $K_e$**  The relalation between the standard Gibbs energy and the equilibrium constant is given by the equation

$$\Delta G^\circ = -RT \ln K_e$$

where the term $\ln K_e$ is the natural or Naperian logarithm of $K_e$. Natural logarithms (ln) occur in calculus and are defined in terms of the base $e$, where $e = 2.71828$. If we are interested in the ln of the number $x$, we can express $x$ as $e$ raised to some power $a$. Thus

$$x = e^a$$

Then $a$ is called the natural logarithm of $x$ and

$$a = \ln x$$

Tables are available in handbooks to calculate $a$. However, we are more accustomed to working with numbers to the base 10. These are called common or Briggsian logarithms (log) and written

$$x = 10^b$$

where $b$ is called the common logarithm of $x$. This is expressed as $b = \log x$. (If you are unfamiliar with the fundamental rules for using logs, you should work through the programmed instruction section on logs in Part 2 of this manual.)

A relation between these two bases can be derived so that equations written in terms of natural logarithms can be expressed in terms of common logarithms. This is done in the following manner. Since

$$x = e^a \quad \text{and} \quad x = 10^b$$

$$e^a = 10^b$$

Taking logs to the base $e$ of both sides gives

$$\ln e^a = \ln 10^b$$

Since the ln of $e$ raised to any power is simply that power

$$a = b \ln 10$$

However, as we have already seen, $a = \ln x$; therefore substitution is again possible since $b = \log x$. Consequently,

$$\ln x = \log x \ln 10$$

or

$$\ln x = 2.303 \log x$$

The Gibbs energy expression can, therefore, be written as

$$\Delta G° = -2.303 \, RT \log K_e$$

Note that the *standard* Gibbs energy for the reaction is used. The Gibbs energy by itself will not allow the calculation of the equilibrium constant.

## PROBLEMS

1. Calculate the missing value of $\Delta E$, $q$, or $w$ for a system given the following data:

   (b) $\Delta E = -7500 \text{ J}; w = -4500 \text{ J}$
   (d) One kilojoule of heat energy is absorbed by the system and the system does 650 J of work on the surroundings.

   ### Solution

   (b) The internal energy change $\Delta E$ of a system is a balance between the heat and work. This reaction is given by the First Law of Thermodynamics, $\Delta E = q - w$. Solving for the unknown $q$, we have

   $$q = \Delta E + w = -7500 \text{ J} + (-4500 \text{ J}) = -12,000 \text{ J}$$

   (d) Heat absorbed by the system is considered to be positive and work done by the system is considered positive. From the First Law,

   $$\Delta E = q - w = 1000 \text{ J} - (+650 \text{ J}) = 350 \text{ J}$$

2. Calculate the work involved in compressing a system consisting of one mole of $H_2O$ as it changes from a gas at 373 K (volume = 30.6 ℓ) to a

liquid at 373 K (volume = 18.9 ml) under a constant pressure of 1 atm. Does this work increase or decrease the internal energy of the system?

**Solution**

For pressure-volume work done at constant pressure, the work is given by $P(V_2 - V_1)$. In order to have the work in joules, we must express the pressure in pascals and the volume in (meter)$^3$. We recall that 1 atm = 101,325 Pa, and since $1\ \ell = 10^{-3}\ m^3$, the two volumes may be expressed as

$$V_1 = 30.6\ \ell \times \frac{10^{-3}\ m^3}{\ell} = 3.06 \times 10^{-2}\ m^3$$

and

$$V_2 = 18.9\ ml \times \frac{1\ \ell}{10^3\ ml} \times \frac{10^{-3}\ m^3}{\ell} = 1.89 \times 10^{-5}\ m^3$$

From $P(V_2 - V_1)$ the work is

$$w = P(V_2 - V_1) = 101,325\ Pa\ (1.89 \times 10^{-5} - 3.06 \times 10^{-2})\ m^3$$
$$= -3.10 \times 10^3\ Pa\ m^3 = -3.10 \times 10^3\ J = -3.10\ kJ$$

Hence 3.10 kJ of work would be involved. The work done on the system has a negative value. From the First Law, $\Delta E = q - w$ and since $w$ enters the equation as a negative quantity, the negative sign in the equation causes an overall increase in the internal energy.

4. (a) Using the data in Appendix J, calculate the standard enthalpy change for each of the following reactions:

   (1) $Fe_2 O_3 (s) + 13CO(g) \longrightarrow 2Fe(CO)_5 (g) + 3CO_2 (g)$
   (3) $CH_4 (g) + N_2 (g) \longrightarrow HCN(g) + NH_3 (g)$

**Solution**

   (1) $\Delta H = \Delta H(\text{products}) - \Delta H(\text{reactants})$   ($\Delta H°$ values in kJ)

   $\Delta H° = 2\ \Delta H°_{Fe(CO)_5 (g)} + 3\ \Delta H°_{CO_2 (g)} - \Delta H°_{Fe_2 O_3 (s)} - 13\ \Delta H°_{CO(g)}$

   $= 2(-733.9) + 3(-393.5) - (-824.2) - 13(-110.5)$

   $= -387.6\ kJ$

   (3) $\Delta H° = \Delta H°_{HCN(g)} + \Delta H°_{NH_3 (g)} - \Delta H°_{CH_4 (g)} - \Delta H°_{N_2 (g)}$

   $= (135) + (-46.11) - (-74.81) - (0)$

   $= 164\ kJ$

5. How many kilocalories of heat energy will be liberated when 49.70 g of manganese are burned to form $Mn_3 O_4 (s)$ at standard state conditions? $\Delta H°_{f298}$ of $Mn_3 O_4$ is equal to $-1388\ kJ\ mol^{-1}$.

**Solution**

First write the overall reaction

$$3Mn(s) + 2O_2(g) \longrightarrow Mn_3O_4(s)$$

Next calculate the number of moles of $Mn_3O_4(s)$ that will be formed by the reaction of 49.70 g of Mn. Based on the balanced equation,

$$3 \text{ moles Mn} \longrightarrow 1 \text{ mole } Mn_3O_4$$

Therefore

$$\text{No. moles } Mn_3O_4 = \frac{\text{no. moles Mn}}{3} = \frac{\text{Mass Mn}}{3(\text{at. wt Mn})}$$

$$= \frac{49.70 \text{ g}}{3(54.94 \text{ g/mol})} = 0.3015 \text{ mol}$$

We now multiply the number of moles of $M_3O_4$ produced by the heat released per mole to obtain the heat liberated. Since $\Delta H^\circ_{f298Mn_3O_4} = -1388 \text{ kJ mol}^{-1}$,

$$\text{Heat} = 0.3015 \text{ mol} \times -1388 \text{ kJ mol}^{-1} = 418.5 \text{ kJ}$$

6. The heat of formation of $OsO_4(s)$, $\Delta H^\circ_{f_{OsO_4(s)}}$, is $-391$ kJ mol$^{-1}$ at 298 K and the heat of sublimation is 56.4 kJ mol$^{-1}$. What is $\Delta H^\circ_{298}$ for the process $Os(s) + 2O_2(g) \longrightarrow OsO_4(g)$ under standard state conditions?

**Solution**

Sublimation is the process of the direct conversion of a solid to a gas. The sublimation process is endothermic and requires heat, as shown by the positive sign for the heat of sublimation. On the other hand, the negative sign for the heat of formation of $OsO_4(s)$ indicates that the formation is exothermic. For the overall reaction, heat is liberated by the formation of $OsO_4(s)$ and absorbed by its sublimation. Thus

$$Os(s) + 2O_2(g) \longrightarrow OsO_4(s) \qquad \Delta H^\circ_f = -391 \text{ kJ}$$

followed by

$$OsO_4(s) \longrightarrow OsO_4(g) \qquad \Delta H^\circ_{sub} = 56.4 \text{ kJ}$$

The sum of the two reactions gives the heat of formation of $OsO_4(g)$.

$$Os(s) + 2O_2(g) \longrightarrow OsO_4(g)$$

$$\Delta H^\circ_{f_{OsO_4(g)}} = \Delta H^\circ_{f_{OsO_4(s)}} + \Delta H^\circ_{sub}$$

$$= -391 \text{ kJ} + 56.4 \text{ kJ} = -335 \text{ kJ}$$

7. Calculate the standard molar enthalpy of formation of $NO(g)$ from the following data:

$$N_2(g) + 2O_2(g) \longrightarrow 2NO_2(g) \qquad \Delta H^\circ_{f298} = 66.4 \text{ kJ}$$

$$2NO(g) + O_2(g) \longrightarrow 2NO_2(g) \qquad \Delta H^\circ = -114.1 \text{ kJ}$$

### Solution

Hess's Law can be applied to the two equations above by reversing the sense of the second equation.

$$N_2(g) + 2O_2(g) \longrightarrow 2NO_2(g) \qquad\qquad \Delta H^\circ_{f298} = 66.4 \text{ kJ}$$

$$2NO_2(g) \longrightarrow 2NO(g) + O_2(g) \qquad \Delta H^\circ_{f298} = 114.1 \text{ kJ}$$

Adding,

$$N_2(g) + 2O_2(g) \longrightarrow 2NO(g) + O_2(g) \qquad \Delta H^\circ_{f298} = 180.5 \text{ kJ}$$

The heat of formation per mole of NO,

$$\Delta H^\circ_{f298} = \frac{180.5 \text{ kJ}}{2} = 90.3 \text{ kJ per mole of NO}$$

9. The heat of combustion of a hydrocarbon (a compound of carbon and hydrogen) is the standard state enthalpy change for the reaction of the compound with oxygen to give $CO_2(g)$ and $H_2O(l)$. Determine the heats of combustion of (a) octane [$C_8H_{18}$, $\Delta H^\circ_f = -208.4 \text{ kJ mol}^{-1}$], a major component of gasoline and (b) methane [$CH_4(g)$, $\Delta H^\circ_f = -74.81 \text{ kJ mol}^{-1}$], the major component of natural gas. Which has the higher heat content per gram?

### Solution

(a) The reaction for the combustion of octane may be written with $\Delta H^\circ_f$ values in kJ mol$^{-1}$. Thus

$$C_8H_{18}(l) + \frac{25}{2}O_2(g) \longrightarrow 8CO_2(g) + 9H_2O(l)$$

$$\Delta H^\circ_{comb} = 8\Delta H^\circ_{f298CO_2} + 9\Delta H^\circ_{f298H_2O} - \Delta H^\circ_{f298C_8H_{18}} - \Delta H^\circ_{f298O_2}$$

$$\Delta H^\circ_{comb} = 8(-393.5) + 9(-285.8) - (-208.4) - (0)$$

$$= -3148 - 2572.2 + 208.4 = -5512 \text{ kJ}$$

(b) For methane, the combustion process is

$$CH_4(g) + 2O_2(g) \longrightarrow CO_2(g) + 2H_2O(l)$$

$$\Delta H^\circ_{comb} = \Delta H^\circ_{f298CO_2} + 2\Delta H^\circ_{f298H_2O} - \Delta H^\circ_{f298CH_4} - 2\Delta H^\circ_{f298O_2}$$

$$= -393.5 + 2(-285.8) - (-74.81) - 2(0)$$

$$= -393.5 - 571.6 + 74.81 = -890.3 \text{ kJ mol}^{-1}$$

The substance with the larger amount of heat released per gram is calculated by dividing the individual heats released through combustion by the molecular weight of the respective organic compound.

For octane, $\dfrac{5512 \text{ kJ mol}^{-1}}{114 \text{ g mol}^{-1}} = 48.4 \text{ kJ g}^{-1}$

For methane, $\dfrac{890.3 \text{ kJ mol}^{-1}}{16 \text{ g mol}^{-1}} = 55.6 \text{ kJ g}^{-1}$

Thus methane has a higher heat content per unit mass.

10. Calculate, using the data in Appendix J, the bond energies of $F_2$, $Cl_2$, and FCl. All are gases in their most stable form at standard conditions.

**Solution**

The bond energy, $D$, for a diatomic molecule equals the change in standard enthalpy for the dissociation of the molecule. In general, the reaction can be expressed as

$$XY(g) \longrightarrow X(g) + Y(g) \qquad \Delta H^\circ (\text{reaction}) = D$$

For F – F,

$$F_2(g) \longrightarrow F(g) + F(g)$$

$$D = \Delta H^\circ = 2\Delta H^\circ_{f298\,F(g)} - \Delta H^\circ_{f298\,F_2(g)} = 2(78.99 \text{ kJ}) - 0 \text{ kJ}$$

$$= 158.0 \text{ kJ per mole of bonds}$$

For Cl – Cl,

$$Cl_2(g) \longrightarrow Cl(g) + Cl(g)$$

$$D = \Delta H^\circ = 2\Delta H^\circ_{f298\,Cl(g)} - \Delta H^\circ_{f298\,Cl_2(g)} = 2(121.68 \text{ kJ}) - 0 \text{ kJ}$$

$$= 243.36 \text{ kJ per mole of bonds}$$

For F – Cl,

$$FCl(g) \longrightarrow F(g) + Cl(g)$$

$$D = \Delta H^\circ = \Delta H^\circ_{f298\,F(g)} + \Delta H^\circ_{f298\,Cl(g)} - \Delta H^\circ_{f298\,FCl}$$

$$= 78.99 + 121.68 - (-54.48) \text{ (units of kJ per mole of bonds)}$$

$$= 255.15 \text{ kJ per mole of bonds}$$

13. (a) Using the bond energies given in Section 18.6, determine the approximate enthalpy change for the formation of ethylene from ethane which is described in Section 15.14; $C_2H_6(g) \longrightarrow C_2H_4(g) + H_2(g)$. (b) Compare this with the standard state of enthalpy change.

**Solution**

(a) Heats of reaction can be calculated from bond energies by using the the same procedure as we have with enthalpies:

Δ bond energy = bond energy products − bond energy reactants

Each bond in every compound involved in the reaction must be considered. First write the structural formula of the compounds to better determine the bonds involved,

$$
\begin{array}{c}
\text{H}\quad\text{H} \\
\text{\textbackslash}\quad\text{/} \\
\text{H–C–C–H} \\
\text{/}\quad\text{\textbackslash} \\
\text{H}\quad\text{H}
\end{array}
\longrightarrow
\begin{array}{c}
\text{H}\qquad\text{H} \\
\text{\textbackslash}\qquad\text{/} \\
\text{C=C} \\
\text{/}\qquad\text{\textbackslash} \\
\text{H}\qquad\text{H}
\end{array}
\;+\;
\text{H–H}
$$

and then write the number of bond types:

| Ethane | Ethylene + hydrogen | |
|--------|---------------------|--------|
| 6 C–H | 4 C–H | 1 H–H |
| 1 C–C | 1 C=C | |

The change in bond energies is obtained by taking the value of the bond energies of the products minus the values of those of the reactants. Since the change in bond energies is negative, more energy is required to break the bonds in ethane than is released on the formation of $C_2H_4$. Consequently, the heat of reaction is positive and equals the change in bond energy but is of opposite sign.

$$
\Delta \text{ bond energy} = \overbrace{[4(415) + 611] + [436]}^{\text{Products}} \overbrace{- [6(415) + 345]}^{-\text{ Reactants}}
$$

$$
\Delta D = \Delta \text{ bond energy} = -128 \text{ kJ mol}^{-1}
$$

The heat of reaction is $-\Delta D = +128$ kJ mol$^{-1}$.

(b) The standard enthalpy change is calculated from

$$
\Delta H = \Delta H^{\circ}_{\text{f298}_{\text{ethylene}}} + \Delta H^{\circ}_{\text{f298}_{\text{H}_2}} - \Delta H^{\circ}_{\text{f298}_{\text{ethane}}}
$$

$$
= 52.26 + 0 - (-84.68) = 136.9 \text{ kJ mol}^{-1}
$$

16. What is the entropy change accompanying the evaporation of one mole of chloroform, $CHCl_3 (l) \longrightarrow CHCl_3 (g)$, under standard state conditions?

**Solution**

For this process, which occurs at 298 K,

$\Delta S^\circ$ = absolute entropy for $CHCl_3(g)$ (final state)

— absolute entropy for $CHCl_3(l)$ (initial state)

$$= S^\circ_{CHCl_3(g)_{298}} - S^\circ_{CHCl_3(l)_{298}}$$

$$= 295.6 - 202 = 94 \text{ J K}^{-1} \text{ mol}^{-1}$$

18. (a) Using the data in Appendix J, calculate the standard free energy changes for the reactions given in Problem 4.
    (b) Which of these reactions are spontaneous? Why?

**Solution**

(a) (1) $Fe_2O_3(s) + 13CO(g) \longrightarrow 2Fe(CO)_5(g) + 3CO_2(g)$

$\Delta G^\circ = \Delta G^\circ(\text{products}) - \Delta G^\circ(\text{reactants})$     ($\Delta G^\circ$ values in kJ mol$^{-1}$)

$\Delta G^\circ = 2\Delta G^\circ_{Fe(CO)_5(g)} + 3\Delta G^\circ_{CO_2(g)} - \Delta G^\circ_{Fe_2O_3(s)} - 13\Delta G^\circ_{CO(g)}$

$= 2(-697.26) + 3(-394.36) - (-742.2) - 13(-137.15)$

$= -52.4 \text{ kJ}$

(3) $CH_4(g) + N_2(g) \longrightarrow HCN(g) + NH_3(g)$

$\Delta G^\circ = \Delta G^\circ_{HCN(g)} + \Delta G^\circ_{NH_3(g)} - \Delta G^\circ_{CH_4(g)} - \Delta G^\circ_{N_2(g)}$

$= +124.7 + (-16.48) - (-50.75) - (0)$

$= 159.0 \text{ kJ}$

(b) Of the two reactions above, (1) is spontaneous because the sign of $\Delta G$ is negative.

19. The standard enthalpies of formation of $NO(g)$, $NO_2(g)$, and $N_2O_3(g)$ are 90.25 kJ mol$^{-1}$, 33.2 kJ mol$^{-1}$, and 83.72 kJ mol$^{-1}$, respectively. Their standard entropies are 210.65, 239.9, and 312.2 J mol$^{-1}$ K$^{-1}$, respectively.

(a) Use the data above to calculate the free energy change for the following reaction at 25.0°C.

$$N_2O_3(g) \longrightarrow NO(g) + NO_2(g)$$

**Solution**

We apply the equation

$$\Delta G^\circ = \Delta H^\circ - T\Delta S^\circ$$

$\Delta H^\circ = \Delta H^\circ_{fNO(g)} + \Delta H^\circ_{fNO_2(g)} - \Delta H^\circ_{fN_2O_3(g)}$     ($\Delta H^\circ_f$ values in kJ mol$^{-1}$)

$= 90.25 + 33.2 - 83.72 = 39.7 \text{ kJ}$

$$\Delta S° = \Delta S°_{NO(g)} + \Delta S°_{NO_2(g)} - \Delta S°_{N_2O_3(g)} \quad (\Delta S° \text{ values in J mol}^{-1} \text{ K}^{-1})$$

$$= 210.65 + 239.9 - 312.2 = 138.4 \text{ J mol}^{-1} \text{ K}^{-1}$$

Then,

$$\Delta G° = 39,700 \text{ J} - 298.2(138.4) \text{ J}$$

$$= -1570 \text{ J} = -1.6 \text{ kJ mol}^{-1}$$

20. Consider the reaction

$$I_2(g) + Cl_2(g) \longrightarrow 2ICl(g)$$

(a) For this reaction $\Delta H°_{298} = -26.9$ kJ, and $\Delta S°_{298} = 11.3$ J K$^{-1}$. Calculate $\Delta G°_{298}$ for the reaction.

(b) Calculate the equilibrium constant for this reaction at 25.0°C.

**Solution**

(a) $\Delta G°_{298} = \Delta H°_{298} - T \Delta S°_{298}$

$$= -26.9 \text{ kJ} - 298.2 \, (11.3 \text{ J K}^{-1})$$

$$= -26,900 - 3370 = -30,270 \text{ J} = -30.3 \text{ kJ}$$

(b) The equilibrium constant for the reaction at 25°C is related to Gibbs energy (free energy) by the equation

$$\Delta G° = -2.303 \, RT \log K$$

Thus the value of the standard state Gibbs energy (free energy) for a reaction can be used to determine the equilibrium constant $K$ for the reaction. The value of $\Delta G°$ is $-30.3$ kJ; therefore,

$$-30,300 \text{ J} = (-2.303)(8.314 \text{ J K}^{-1})(298 \text{ K}) \log K$$

$$\log K = \frac{30,300}{(2.303)(8.314)(298.2)} = 5.307$$

$$K = 2.03 \times 10^5$$

22. (a) For the vaporization of bromine liquid to bromine gas, calculate the change in enthalpy and the change in entropy at standard state conditions.

(c) Estimate the value of $\Delta G°_{298}$ for the vaporization of bromine from the data in Appendix J.

(d) State what you can about the spontaneity of the process from the value you obtained for $\Delta G°_{298}$ in (c).

(e) Estimate the temperature at which liquid and gaseous Br$_2$ are in equilibrium with each other at 1 atm (assume $\Delta H°$ and $\Delta S°$ are independent of temperature).

**Solution**

(a) For Br$_2$ $(l) \longrightarrow$ Br$_2$ $(g)$,

$$\Delta H^\circ_{298} = \Delta H^\circ_{f298\,Br_2(g)} - \Delta H^\circ_{f298\,Br_2(l)}$$

$$= 30.91\ kJ - 0\ kJ = 30.91\ kJ\ mol^{-1}$$

$$\Delta S^\circ_{298} = \Delta S^\circ_{298\,Br_2(g)} - \Delta S^\circ_{298\,Br_2(l)}$$

$$= 245.35 - 152.23 = 93.12\ J\ mol^{-1}\ K^{-1}$$

(c)  For vaporization, $\Delta G^\circ_{298} = \Delta H^\circ_{298} - T\,\Delta S^\circ_{298}$

$$\Delta G^\circ_{298} = 30{,}910\ J - 298.2(93.12)\ J$$

$$= 3140\ J = 3.14\ kJ\ mol^{-1}$$

(d)  The vaporization should not be a spontaneous process at 1 atm of pressure and 298 K.

(e)  For equilibrium to occur, $\Delta G^\circ_T$ must equal zero.

Therefore

$$\Delta G^\circ_T = 0 = \Delta H^\circ - T\,\Delta S^\circ$$

or
$$\Delta H^\circ = T\,\Delta S^\circ$$

Assuming that $\Delta H^\circ$ and $\Delta S^\circ$ do not change significantly with a change in temperature, we write

$$T = \frac{\Delta H^\circ_{298}}{\Delta S^\circ_{298}} = \frac{30910}{93.12} = 331.9\ K\ \text{or}\ 58.7^\circ C$$

24.  (a)  If you wish to decompose $CaCO_3\,(s)$ into $CaO(s)$ and $CO_2\,(g)$ at atmospheric pressure, estimate the minimum temperature at which you would conduct the reaction.

**Solution**

Write the balanced chemical reaction:

$$CaCO_3\,(s) \longrightarrow CaO(s) + CO_2\,(g)$$

Decomposition will occur spontaneously when the system is at equilibrium: $\Delta G$ for the reaction is zero. In order to determine the equilibrium temperature, first calculate $\Delta H^\circ$ and $\Delta S^\circ$ for the reaction.

$$\Delta H^\circ = \Delta H^\circ_{298\,CaO(s)} + \Delta H^\circ_{298\,CO_2(s)} - \Delta H^\circ_{298\,CaCO_3(s)}$$

$$= -635.5 + (-393.5) - (-1206.9)\quad (\Delta H^\circ\ \text{in}\ kJ\ mol^{-1})$$

$$= 177.9\ kJ$$

$$\Delta S^\circ = \Delta S^\circ_{298\,CaO(s)} + \Delta S^\circ_{298\,CO_2(g)} - \Delta S^\circ_{298\,CaCO_3(s)}$$

$$= 40. + 213.6 - 92.9\quad (\Delta S^\circ\ \text{in}\ J\ mol^{-1}\ K^{-1})$$

$$= 160.7\ J\ K^{-1}$$

Then, from

$$\Delta G = \Delta H - T\,\Delta S = 0$$

on the assumption that $\Delta H = \Delta H°$ and $\Delta S = \Delta S°$, we have

$$T = \frac{\Delta H°}{\Delta S°} = \frac{177{,}900\text{ J}}{160.7\text{ J K}^{-1}}$$

$$= 1107\text{ K} = 834°C$$

This calculation is based on the assumption that $\Delta H$ and $\Delta S$ are independent of temperature over the range from 298 K to the temperature of dissociation. This is not strictly true, and the actual values of $\Delta H$ and $\Delta S$ near the calculated temperature should be used to obtain a more accurate value.

25. If the enthalpy of vaporization of $CH_2Cl_2$ is 29.0 kJ $mol^{-1}$ at 25.0°C and the entropy of vaporization is 92.5 J $mol^{-1}$ $K^{-1}$, calculate a value for the normal boiling point temperature of $CH_2Cl_2$.

**Solution**

The wording of this problem seems quite different from the two previous problems. However, the same basic idea applies: $\Delta G$ is equal to zero at equilibrium (the boiling point in this case). Thus

$$\Delta G = \Delta H - T\,\Delta S = 0$$

$$T = \frac{\Delta H}{\Delta S} = \frac{29{,}000\text{ J}}{92.5\text{ J K}^{-1}}$$

$$= 313.5\text{ K or }40.3°C$$

27. The equilibrium constant, $K_p$, for the reaction $N_2O_4(g) \rightleftharpoons 2NO_2(g)$ is 0.142 at 298 K. What is $\Delta G°$ for the reaction?

**Solution**

$$\Delta G° = -2.303\,RT \log K_p$$

$$= -2.303(8.314\text{ J K}^{-1}\text{ mol}^{-1})(298.2\text{ K})(\log 0.142)$$

$$= -5709.7\text{ J mol}^{-1}\ (-0.8477)$$

$$= 4840\text{ J mol}^{-1} = 4.84\text{ kJ mol}^{-1}\ N_2O_4$$

29. Acetic acid, $CH_3CO_2H$, can form a dimer, $(CH_3CO_2H)_2$, in the gas phase.

$$2CH_3CO_2H(g) \rightleftharpoons (CH_3CO_2H)_2(g)$$

The dimer is held together by two hydrogen bonds

$$CH_3-C\underset{O-H\cdots O}{\overset{O\cdots H-O}{\Big\langle\quad\Big\rangle}}C-CH_3$$

with a total strength of 66.5 kJ per mole of dimer. At 25°C the equilibrium constant for the dimerization is $1.3 \times 10^3$ (pressure in atmospheres). What is $\Delta S°$ for the reaction at 25°?

**Solution**

Two items of information are given to use in this problem. The equilibrium constant will allow us to calculate $\Delta G°_{298}$. The strength of the bond (66.5 kJ) allows us to say that it requires 66.5 kJ to pull one mole of bonds apart. In other words, $\Delta H°_{f298} = -66.5$ kJ. The values of $\Delta G°_{298}$ and $\Delta H°_{f298}$ then allow us to calculate $\Delta S°_{298}$ by use of the equation

$$\Delta G°_{298} = \Delta H°_{f298} - T \Delta S°_{298}$$

First calculate $\Delta G°_{298}$:

$$\Delta G°_{298} = -2.303 \, RT \log K$$

$$= -2.303(8.314 \text{ J K}^{-1} \text{ mol}^{-1})(298.2 \text{ K})(\log 1.3 \times 10^3)$$

$$= -17.78 \text{ kJ mol}^{-1}$$

$$S°_{298} = -\frac{\Delta G°_{298} - \Delta H°_{298}}{T}$$

Then

$$\Delta S°_{298} = -\frac{(-17,780) - (-66,500)}{298.2}$$

$$= -163 \text{ J K}^{-1} \text{ mol}^{-1}$$

30. At 1000 K the equilibrium constant for the reaction $Br_2 (g) \longrightarrow 2Br$ is $2.8 \times 10^4$ (pressure in atmospheres). What is $\Delta G°$ for the reaction? Assume that the bond energy of $Br_2$ does not change between 298 K and 1000 K and calculate $\Delta S°$ for the reaction at 1000 K.

**Solution**

$$\Delta G° = -2.303 \, RT \log K$$

$$\Delta G°_{1000} = -2.303(8.314)(1000)(\log 2.8 \times 10^4)$$

$$= -19,147(4.447)$$

$$= -85 \text{ kJ mol}^{-1}$$

The value of the change in enthalpy of the reaction $Br_2 (g) \longrightarrow 2Br(g)$ may be calculated from the $\Delta H_f$'s at 298 K on the assumption that the value of $\Delta H$ will not change with temperature. Over such a large temperature range this is a first approximation. Techniques are developed in a course in physical chemistry to treat this situation. As an approximation, then,

$$\Delta H = 2\Delta H^{\circ}_{f Br(g)} - \Delta H^{\circ}_{f Br_2(g)}$$

$$= 2(111.88) - 30.91 \qquad (\Delta H^{\circ}_f \text{ in kJ mol}^{-1})$$

$$= 192.85 \text{ kJ mol}^{-1}$$

Then, from

$$\Delta G = \Delta H - T \Delta S$$

or

$$\Delta S = -\frac{\Delta G - \Delta H}{T}$$

$$= -\frac{-85,000 - 192,850}{1000 \text{ K}} = \frac{277,860 \text{ J mol}^{-1}}{1000 \text{ K}}$$

$$= 278 \text{ J K}^{-1} \text{ mol}^{-1}$$

## RELATED PROBLEMS

1. Boron compounds have been investigated extensively in recent years because of peculiarities that sometimes occur in their bonding. Diborane, $B_2 H_6$, exhibits such bonding in which the two boron atoms are joined indirectly to each other through two hydrogen atoms, one located on each side of the center line between the two boron atoms. Calculate the standard heat of formation of diborane if the combustion of diborane is, at constant pressure,

$$B_2 H_6 (g) + 3O_2 (g) \longrightarrow B_2 O_3 (s) + 3H_2 O(g)$$

The combustion proceeds with the liberation of 2020 kJ per mole. Combustion of elemental boron produces $B_2 O_3$ with the liberation of 1264 kJ mol$^{-1}$. $(\Delta H^{\circ}_{f298 H_2O(g)} = -241.8 \text{ kJ mol}^{-1})$

*Answer: +30.6 kJ mol$^{-1}$*

2. The enthalpies of individual ions in solution may be developed using the heat of formation of hydrogen ion as an arbitrary reference set at 0. All other heats are then compared to this standard. If the standard enthalpy of formation of the fumarate ion is $-777.4$ kJ mol$^{-1}$, calculate the enthalpy of formation of the succinate ion. The standard enthalpy change of the reaction

$$\text{fumarate}^{2-}(aq) + H_2 \longrightarrow \text{succinate}^{2-}(aq)$$

is $-131.4$ kJ. *Answer: $-908.8$ kJ mol$^{-1}$*

3. It is estimated that the human brain consumes the equivalent of 10 g of glucose, $C_6 H_{12} O_6$, per hour. The metabolism of glucose produces $CO_2$ and $H_2 O$ and proceeds in aqueous solution, where the standard state is

taken at a concentration of 1 molal at 25°C. We find from references that

$$\Delta H^{\circ}_{f298_{(glucose)}} (aq) = -1263.1 \text{ kJ mol}^{-1}$$

and

$$\Delta H^{\circ}_{f298_{(CO_2)}} (aq) = -413.8 \text{ kJ mol}^{-1}$$

Estimate (a) the energy utilized per hour and (b) the power output of the brain in watts [1 watt (W) = 1 J sec$^{-1}$.]

*Answer: (a) 163.0 kJ/hr; (b) 45 W*

4.  Calculate the enthalpy change accompanying the conversion of 1 mol of glucose into maltose according to the reaction

$$2C_6 H_{12} O_6 (s) \longrightarrow C_{12} H_{22} O_{11} (s) + H_2 O(l)$$

The heats of combustion are ($\Delta H^{\circ}_{comb}$ /kJ mol$^{-1}$)

$\alpha$-D-glucose, $C_6 H_{12} O_6 (s)$:   $-2809$

maltose, $C_{12} H_{22} O_{11} (s)$:   $-5645$

*Answer: 13.6 kJ mol$^{-1}$ (glucose)*

5.  The heat of sublimation of graphite to carbon atoms [$C_{graphite} \longrightarrow C(g)$] is estimated as 715 kJ mol$^{-1}$. The dissociation of molecular hydrogen into atoms [$H_2 (g) \longrightarrow 2H(g)$] has $\Delta H^{\circ} = 436$ kJ mole. Using $\Delta H^{\circ}_{f_{CH_4}} = -74.9$ kJ mol$^{-1}$, estimate $\Delta H^{\circ}$ for the reaction

$$C(g) + 4H(g) \longrightarrow CH_4 (g)$$

One-fourth of this value is a measure of the C–H bond strength in methane.                    *Answer: –1662 kJ or –415.5 kJ per C–H bond*

# Chapter 20: Electrochemistry
and
Oxidation-Reduction

## INTRODUCTION

Historically, the terms oxidation and reduction came from the field of metallurgy. Oxidation referred to reactions involving the addition of oxygen to a metal. Reduction, on the other hand, referred to the removal of oxygen from a reacting metal oxide by the passage of hydrogen over or through it. Today these terms are used in chemistry in a much broader sense to describe reactions involving the transfer of electrons from one substance to another.

Reactions involving oxidation and reduction are called *oxidation-reduction* or *redox* reactions. Such reactions are quite common. For example, the energy that is required for you to assimilate your thoughts while you read this page is derived from foods that have undergone a variety of complex biochemical oxidation-reduction reactions. Another example may be drawn from industry. The extraction of aluminum from bauxite ore is accomplished by a redox reaction in which an electric current is passed through a molten mixture of the ore. These examples by no means exhaust the diverse forms possible in redox reactions.

The first evidence of a relationship between chemical reactions and electricity was the result of work done by Luigi Galvani on the twitching of frog legs caused by an electrical shock. The results of further work by Galvani set the stage in 1800 for the development by Allesandro Volta of a practical battery based on a silver-zinc couple. This discovery made it possible for the first time in history to obtain a continuous source of electric current. In 1807, Sir Humphry Davy discovered the elements sodium and potassium by electrolyzing fused mixtures of their solid hydroxides. Bear in mind that all this work was accomplished prior to the discovery of subatomic particles—protons, electrons, and neutrons.

The development of this chapter treats the quantitative relationships between chemical change and electrical phenomena. The fundamental laws of electrochemical work were discovered by Michael Faraday during the years 1832 and 1833. Faraday's work showed that the decomposition that occurs in a quantity of substance brought about by electrical means is proportional to the electrical current passing through that substance and to the time the current is applied. He further extended his research to show that the masses of substances deposited at the electrodes in electrolysis cells are proportional to their chemical equivalent weights. Faraday's laws are now widely applied in research and industry.

The problems included in this chapter involve application of electrochemical principles to computing cell potentials or voltages, equilibrium constants, Gibbs energies (free energies), and the quantities appearing in Faraday's laws.

## FORMULAS AND DEFINITIONS

**Oxidation**  Oxidation involves the removal or loss of electrons from a substance. The element(s) undergoing oxidation are determined from changes in oxidation states or numbers in the following way. The number zero (called an oxidation number) is assigned to neutral species. For each electron in excess of the number in the neutral species, the state is decreased by $-1$, and for each electron less than that occurring in the neutral species, the state is increased by $+1$. Thus $Cl^{-1}$ indicates a gain of one electron; its oxidation number is $-1$. On the other hand, $Cu^{2+}$ indicates a loss of two electrons; its oxidation number is $+2$. By use of this convention, the substance undergoing oxidation shows a net increase in oxidation number. Examples include

$$Sn^{2+} - 2e^- \longrightarrow Sn^{4+}$$

$$Fe^0 - 2e^- \longrightarrow Fe^{2+}$$

$$O^{2-} - 2e^- \longrightarrow O^0$$

**Reduction**  The reduction of a substance involves the absorption or gain of electrons. By the convention used to assign oxidation numbers to reactants, the substance undergoing reduction shows a net decrease in oxidation number. Examples include

$$Fe^{+3} + e^- \longrightarrow Fe^{2+}$$

$$Cl^0 + e^- \longrightarrow Cl^-$$

$$Ag^+ + e^- \longrightarrow Ag^0$$

**Oxidizing agent**  The substance in a reaction causing the oxidation of a substance.

**Reducing agent**  The substance in a reaction causing the reduction of a substance.

In the following reaction,

$$Fe^0 + Sn^{2+} \longrightarrow Fe^{2+} + Sn^0$$

iron (0) is oxidized to iron (2+) and tin (2+) is reduced to tin (0).  Tin (2+) is the oxidizing agent and iron (0) is the reducing agent.

**Anode**  The electrode toward which negatively charged ions are attracted; electrons are withdrawn from the electrolytic liquid causing oxidation.

**Anions**  Negatively charged ions.

**Cathode**  The electrode toward which positively charged ions are attracted; electrons enter the electrolytic liquid causing reduction.

**Cations**  Positively charged ions.

**Electrolytic cell**  A chemical reaction system in which electrical energy is consumed to bring about desired chemical changes.  Such chemical changes are by definition nonspontaneous.  In the process, electrons are forced from an outside source on to the cathode, making it negatively charged, and electrons are withdrawn from the anode, making it positively charged.

**Electrolysis**  An oxidation-reduction reaction taking place in an electrolytic cell.

**Electromotive series**  An ordering of the elements according to their tendency to form positive ions.  In terms of reduction potentials, potassium has the largest negative value, $-2.925$ volts for the reaction $K^+ + e^- \longrightarrow K$.

**emf**  An acronym for electromotive force, a force or potential causing an electron flow.  It is normally measured in volts.

**Faraday's Law**  During electrolysis, 96,487 coulombs (1 faraday) of electricity reduce one gram-equivalent of the oxidizing agent and oxidize one gram-equivalent of the reducing agent.  In other words, the amount of substance reacted at each electrode during electrolysis is directly proportional to the quantity of electricity passed through the electrolytic cell.

**Nernst equation**  The equation is defined for reactions and for half-reactions having the general form

$$aA + bB \rightleftharpoons cC + dD \tag{1}$$

and

$$xM + ne^- \rightleftharpoons yN \tag{2}$$

as

$$E = E° - \frac{0.05915}{n} \log Q$$

where

$$Q = \frac{[C]^c[D]^d}{[A]^a[B]^b}$$

for Equation (1) and

$$Q = \frac{[N]^y}{[M]^x}$$

for Equation (2).

$E$ = emf for the reaction or half-reaction.

$E°$ = standard electrode potential for the cell reaction or the half-reaction.

$n$ = number of electrons required in the redox transfer process according to the balanced equation or half-reactions.

**Standard hydrogen electrode**  Prepared by bubbling hydrogen gas at 25°C and a pressure of 1 atm around a platinized platinum electrode immersed in a solution in which hydrogen ions are at unit activity (approximately 1 $M$).

**Standard potential**  Potential of the electrode measured at 25°C, when the concentration of the ions in the solution are at unit activity ($\sim$1 $M$) and the pressure of any gas involved is 1 atm.

**Thermodynamic functions and their relation to $E°$**  Several relations are possible:

$$\Delta G° = -nFE°$$

$$E° = \frac{RT}{nF} \ln K_e$$

$$= \frac{0.05915}{n} \log K_e$$

where $n$ is the number of electrons transferred and $F$ is the faraday, a constant in units of kilojoules per volt ($F = 96.487$ kJ/V and the temperature is defined at 298.15 K.

**Voltaic cells**  Commonly thought of as batteries, voltaic cells have as their negative terminal the anode, where oxidation occurs. Reduction occurs at the cathode, but in contrast to the situation in electro-chemical cells, the cathode is the positive terminal.

# BALANCING EQUATIONS: TECHNIQUES FOR OXIDATION-REDUCTION REACTIONS

Several methods are commonly used to balance equations involving oxidation and reduction. Regardless of the method used to balance equations, electrons lost through oxidation must be absorbed through reduction; no net gain or net loss of electrons can occur in a reaction. Further, for an equation to be balanced, the total of the ion charges on both sides of the equation must be equal. The two methods most used for balancing equations are presented here for your study.

*Change in oxidation number method*: This is based on the concept that in a redox reaction the total increase in units of positive oxidation number must equal the total decrease in units of negative oxidation number. Consider the following reaction as an example:

$$MnO_4^- + C_2O_4^{2-} + H^+ \longrightarrow Mn^{2+} + CO_2 + H_2O$$

Assign oxidation numbers to each element, determine those elements that undergo oxidation or reduction, and then write half-reactions that indicate the oxidation number changes (sometimes these are half-reactions for the overall reaction). In this case, the half-reactions are

$$C_2^{3+} \longrightarrow 2C^{4+} + 2e^- \quad \text{(gain in positive oxidation number, 2)}$$

$$Mn^{7+} \longrightarrow Mn^{2+} - 5e^- \quad \text{(decrease in positive oxidation number, 5)}$$

To balance the equation, we must select the proper number of manganese-containing and carbon-containing ions so that the total increase of electrons will equal the total decrease. This can be done by choosing the smallest factor common to both 2 and 5 and multiplying each half-reaction by the multiple of each in the factor. For these half-reactions, 10 is the common factor, and the half-reactions must be multiplied by 5 and 2, respectively.

$$5[C_2^{3+} \longrightarrow 2C^{4+} + 2e^-] \quad 5 \times 2e^- = 10e^-$$

$$2[Mn^{7+} \longrightarrow Mn^{2+} - 5e^-] \quad 2 \times 5e^- = 10e^-$$

The proper coefficients for those substances changing oxidation state become

$$2MnO_4^- + 5C_2O_4^{2-} + H^+ \longrightarrow Mn^{2+} + 10CO_2 + H_2O$$

The remaining factors in the equation can be balanced by inspection, yielding

$$2MnO_4^- + 5C_2O_4^{2-} + 16H^+ \longrightarrow 2Mn^{2+} + 10CO_2 + 8H_2O$$

*Ion-electron method*: Based on combining half-reactions, one half of which represents the oxidation step and the other, the reduction step. This method is very useful in electrochemical cells, for which, generally, the half-reactions are known. The same reaction used in the change in oxidation number method will be used to illustrate this method.

The oxalate ion is oxidized to carbon dioxide

$$C_2O_4^{2-} \longrightarrow 2CO_2 + 2e^- \tag{1}$$

and is balanced by inspection. The oxidizing agent in this reaction, permanganate, is reduced in acid solution to manganous ion and water:

$$MnO_4^- + 8H^+ + 5e^- \longrightarrow Mn^{2+} + 4H_2O \qquad (2)$$

Again the balancing is done by inspection.

It is now obvious that multiplying Equation (1) by 5 and Equation (2) by 2 will make the number of electrons lost by oxalate the same as the number gained by permanganate. The two equations are added to give the following:

$$5C_2O_4^{2-} \longrightarrow 10CO_2 + 10e^-$$

$$\underline{2MnO_4^- + 16H^+ + 10e^- \longrightarrow 2Mn^{2+} + 8H_2O}$$

$$2MnO_4^- + 5C_2O_4^{2-} + 16H^+ \longrightarrow 2Mn^{2+} + 10CO_2 + 8H_2O$$

Both methods give the same result, as we should expect.

## QUESTIONS

24. (a) $IF_5 + Fe \longrightarrow FeF_3 + IF_3$

$$3[I^{5+} \longrightarrow I^{3+} - 2e^-]$$

$$\underline{2[Fe^0 \longrightarrow Fe^{3+} + 3e^-]}$$

$$3I^{5+} + 2Fe^0 \longrightarrow 3I^{3+} + 2Fe^{3+}$$

$$3IF_5 + 2Fe \longrightarrow 2FeF_3 + 3IF_3$$

(c) $H_2S + Hg_2^{2+} \longrightarrow Hg + S + H^+$

$$S^{2-} \longrightarrow S^0 + 2e^-$$

$$\underline{Hg_2^{2+} \longrightarrow 2Hg^0 - 2e^-}$$

$$Hg_2^{2+} + S^{2-} \longrightarrow S^0 + 2Hg^0$$

$$H_2S + Hg_2^{2+} \longrightarrow 2Hg + S + 2H^+$$

(e) $Zn + BrO_4^- + OH^- + H_2O \longrightarrow Zn(OH)_4^{2-} + Br^-$

$$4[Zn^0 \longrightarrow Zn^{2+} + 2e^-]$$

$$\underline{Br^{7+} \longrightarrow Br^- - 8e^-}$$

$$4Zn^0 + Br^{7+} \longrightarrow 4Zn^{2+} + Br^-$$

$$4Zn + BrO_4^- + OH^- + H_2O \longrightarrow 4Zn(OH)_4^{2-} + Br^-$$

Charge balance is important and convenient here; the right side shows 9− and is fixed while $BrO_4^-$ is the only fixed negative charge on the left side. Hence 8 $OH^-$ are needed to balance the charge.

$$4Zn + BrO_4^- + 8OH^- + 4H_2O \longrightarrow 4Zn(OH)_4^{2-} + Br^-$$

(g) $MnO_4^- + S^{2-} + H_2O \longrightarrow MnO_2 + S + OH^-$

$$3[S^{2-} \longrightarrow S^0 + 2e^-]$$

$$\underline{2[Mn^{7+} \longrightarrow Mn^{4+} - 3e^-]}$$

$$3S^{2-} + 2Mn^{7+} \longrightarrow 3S^0 + 2Mn^{4+}$$

$$2MnO_4^- + 3S^{2-} + 4H_2O \longrightarrow 2MnO_2 + 3S + 8\,OH^-$$

(i) $Cu + H^+ + NO_3^- \longrightarrow Cu^{2+} + NO_2 + H_2O$

$$[Cu^0 \longrightarrow Cu^{2+} + 2e^-]$$

$$\underline{2[N^{5+} \longrightarrow N^{4+} - 1e^-]}$$

$$Cu^0 + 2N^{5+} \longrightarrow Cu^{2+} + 2N^{4+}$$

$$Cu + 4H^+ + 2NO_3^- \longrightarrow Cu^{2+} + 2NO_2 + 2H_2O$$

(k) $Cu + H^+ + NO_3^- \longrightarrow Cu^{2+} + NO + H_2O$

$$3[Cu^0 \longrightarrow Cu^{2+} + 2e^-]$$

$$\underline{2[N^{5+} \longrightarrow N^{2+} - 3e^-]}$$

$$3Cu^0 + 2N^{5+} \longrightarrow 3Cu^{2+} + 2N^{2+}$$

$$3Cu + 8H^+ + 2NO_3^- \longrightarrow 3Cu^{2+} + 2NO + 4H_2O$$

(m) $MnO_4^- + NO_2^- + H_2O \longrightarrow MnO_2 + NO_3^- + OH^-$

$$2[Mn^{7+} \longrightarrow Mn^{4+} - 3e^-]$$

$$\underline{3[N^{3+} \longrightarrow N^{5+} + 2e^-]}$$

$$2Mn^{7+} + 3N^{3+} \longrightarrow 2Mn^{4+} + 3N^{5+}$$

$$2MnO_4^- + 3NO_2^- + H_2O \longrightarrow 2MnO_2 + 3NO_3^- + 2OH^-$$

(o) $Br_2 + SO_2 + H_2O \longrightarrow H^+ + Br^- + SO_4^{2-}$

$$Br_2{}^0 \longrightarrow 2Br^- - 2e^-$$

$$\underline{S^{4+} \longrightarrow S^{6+} + 2e^-}$$

$$Br_2 + S^{4+} \longrightarrow 2Br^- + S^{6+}$$

$$Br_2 + SO_2 + 2H_2O \longrightarrow 4H^+ + 2Br^- + SO_4{}^{2-}$$

25. (a) $Al + Sn(OH)_4{}^{2-} \longrightarrow Al(OH)_4^- + Sn + OH^-$

$$2[Al^0 \longrightarrow Al^{3+} + 3e^-]$$

$$\underline{3[Sn^{2+} \longrightarrow Sn^0 - 2e^-]}$$

$$2Al^0 + 3Sn^{2+} \longrightarrow 2Al^{3+} + 3Sn^0$$

$$2Al + 3Sn(OH)_4{}^{2-} \longrightarrow 2Al(OH)_4^- + 3Sn + 4OH^-$$

(c) $H_2S + H_2O_2 \longrightarrow S + H_2O$

$$O_2^{2-} \longrightarrow 2O^{2-} - 2e^-$$

$$S^{2-} \longrightarrow S^0 + 2e^-$$

$$\overline{O_2^{2-} + S^{2-} \longrightarrow 2O^{2-} + S^0}$$

$$H_2S + H_2O_2 \longrightarrow S + 2H_2O$$

(f) $OH^- + NO_2 \longrightarrow NO_3^- + NO_2^- + H_2O$

$$N^{4+} \longrightarrow N^{5+} + e^-$$

$$N^{4+} \longrightarrow N^{3+} - e^-$$

$$\overline{2N^{4+} \longrightarrow N^{5+} + N^{3+}}$$

$$2OH^- + 2NO_2 \longrightarrow NO_3^- + NO_2^- + H_2O$$

(j) $C + HNO_3 \longrightarrow NO_2 + H_2O + CO_2$

$$C^0 \longrightarrow C^{4+} + 4e^-$$

$$4[N^{5+} \longrightarrow N^{4+} - 1e^-]$$

$$\overline{C^0 + 4N^{5+} \longrightarrow C^{4+} + 4N^{4+}}$$

$$C + 4HNO_3 \longrightarrow 4NO_2 + 2H_2O + CO_2$$

26. (a) $Zn + NO_3^- \longrightarrow Zn^{2+} + N_2$    (acidic)

$$5[Zn^0 \longrightarrow Zn^{2+} + 2e^-]$$

$$2N^{5+} \longrightarrow N_2^0 - 10e^-$$

$$\overline{5Zn^0 + 2N^{5+} \longrightarrow 5Zn^{2+} + N_2^0}$$

$$5Zn + 2NO_3^- + 12H^+ \longrightarrow 5Zn^{2+} + N_2 + 6H_2O$$

(c) $CuS + NO_3^- \longrightarrow Cu^{2+} + S + NO$    (acidic)

$$3[S^{2-} \longrightarrow S^0 + 2e^-]$$

$$2[N^{5+} \longrightarrow N^{2+} - 3e^-]$$

$$\overline{3S^{2-} + 2N^{5+} \longrightarrow 3S^0 + 2N^{2+}}$$

$$8H^+ + 3CuS + 2NO_3^- \longrightarrow 3Cu^{2+} + 3S + 2NO + 4H_2O$$

(f) $Cl_2 + OH^- \longrightarrow Cl^- + ClO_3^-$    (basic)

$$5[Cl^0 \longrightarrow Cl^- - e^-]$$

$$Cl^0 \longrightarrow Cl^{5+} - 5e^-$$

$$\overline{6Cl^0 \longrightarrow 5Cl^- + Cl^{5+}}$$

$$3Cl_2 + 6OH^- \longrightarrow 5Cl^- + ClO_3^- + 3H_2O$$

(h) $NO_2 \longrightarrow NO_3^- + NO_2^-$ (basic)

$$N^{4+} \longrightarrow N^{5+} + e^-$$
$$N^{4+} \longrightarrow N^{3+} - e^-$$
$$\overline{2N^{4+} \longrightarrow N^{5+} + N^{3+}}$$
$$2OH^- + 2NO_2 \longrightarrow NO_3^- + NO_2^- + H_2O$$

(j) $Fe^{3+} + I^- \longrightarrow Fe^{2+} + I_2$

$$2I^- \longrightarrow I_2^0 + 2e^-$$
$$2[Fe^{3+} \longrightarrow Fe^{2+} - e^-]$$
$$\overline{2Fe^{3+} + 2I^- \longrightarrow 2Fe^{2+} + I_2}$$
$$2Fe^{3+} + 2I^- \longrightarrow 2Fe^{2+} + I_2$$

(l) $P_4 \longrightarrow PH_3 + HPO_3^{2-}$ (acidic)

$$P^0 \longrightarrow P^{3+} + 3e^-$$
$$P^0 \longrightarrow P^{3-} - 3e^-$$
$$\overline{2[2P^0 \longrightarrow P^{3+} + P^{3-}]}$$
$$4P^0 \longrightarrow 2P^{3+} + 2P^{3-}$$
$$P_4 + 6H_2O \longrightarrow 2PH_3 + 2HPO_3^{2-} + 4H^+$$

## PROBLEMS

Standard reduction potentials for these problems may be found in Tables 20-1 and 20-2 and Appendix I.

1. Calculate the value of the Faraday constant, $F$, from the charge on a single electron, $1.6021 \times 10^{-19}$ coulombs.

**Solution**

The Faraday constant is the charge on one mole of electrons.

$$F = 1.6021 \times 10^{-19} \frac{\text{coulombs}}{e^-} \times \frac{6.022 \times 10^{23} \, e^-}{\text{mole}}$$

$$= 9.648 \times 10^4 \text{ coulombs}$$

2. How many moles of electrons are involved in the following electrochemical changes?

   (a) 1.0 mol of $Al^{3+}$ is converted to Al.
   (b) 0.800 mol of $I_2$ is converted to $I^-$.
   (d) 27.6 g of $SO_3$ is converted to $SO_3^{2-}$.
   (h) 15.80 ml of 0.1145 $M$ $MnO_4^-$ is converted to $Mn^{2+}$.

**Solution**

(a) The reduction of one mol of $Al^{3+}$ to Al requires 3.0 mol of electrons.

$$Al^{3+} + 3e^- \longrightarrow Al$$

(b) The reduction of one mol of $I_2$ molecules to 2 mol of $I^-$ ions requires 2 mol of electrons.

$$I_2 + 2e^- \longrightarrow 2I^-$$

$$\text{No. mol } e^- = \frac{2 \text{ mol } e^-}{\text{mol } I_2} \times 0.800 \text{ mol} = 1.60 \text{ mol } e^-$$

(d) The reduction of 1 mol of $SO_3$ to $SO_3{}^{2-}$ requires 2 mol of electrons.

$$SO_3 + 2e^- \longrightarrow SO_3{}^{2-}$$

$$\text{No. mol } e^- = 27.6 \text{ g } SO_3 \times \frac{1 \text{ mol}}{80.1 \text{ g}} \times \frac{2 \text{ mol } e^-}{\text{mol } SO_3} = 0.690 \text{ mol } e^-$$

(h) The reduction of 1 mol of $MnO_4^-$ to $Mn^{2+}$ requires 5 mol of electrons.

$$8H^+ + MnO_4^- + 5e^- \longrightarrow Mn^{2+} + 4H_2O$$

$$\text{No. mol } (MnO_4^-) = (0.01580 \text{ } \ell)\left(0.1145 \frac{\text{mol}}{\ell}\right)$$

$$= 1.809 \times 10^{-3} \text{ mol}$$

$$\text{No. mole } e^- = 1.809 \times 10^{-3} \text{ mol } MnO_4^- \times \frac{5 \text{ mol } e^-}{\text{mol } MnO_4^-}$$

$$= 9.046 \times 10^{-3} \text{ mol } e^-$$

3. How many faradays of electricity are involved in the electrochemical changes described in Problem 2?

**Solution**

One faraday of charge provides 1 mol of electrons for a reduction process.

(a) No. faradays $= 3.0$ mol $e^- \times \dfrac{1 \text{ faraday}}{\text{mol } e^-} = 3.0$ faradays

(b) No. faradays $= 1.6$ mol $e^- \times \dfrac{1 \text{ faraday}}{\text{mol } e^-} = 1.6$ faradays

(h) No. faradays $= 9.046 \times 10^{-1}$ mol $e^- \times \dfrac{1 \text{ faraday}}{\text{mol } e^-} = 9.046 \times 10^{-3}$ faraday

4. How many coulombs of electricity are involved in the electrochemical changes described in Problem 2?

**Solution**

One faraday of charge is equivalent to 96,487 coulombs.

(a) No. coulombs $= 3.0$ mol $e^- \times \dfrac{1 \text{ faraday}}{\text{mol } e^-} \times \dfrac{96{,}487 \text{ coulombs}}{\text{faraday}}$

$= 2.9 \times 10^5$

(b) No. coulombs $= 1.60$ mol $e^- \times \dfrac{1 \text{ faraday}}{\text{mol } e^-} \times \dfrac{96{,}487 \text{ coulombs}}{\text{faraday}}$

$= 1.54 \times 10^5$

(h) No. coulombs $= 9.046 \times 10^{-3}$ mol $e^- \times \dfrac{1 \text{ faraday}}{\text{mol } e^-} \times \dfrac{96{,}487 \text{ coulombs}}{\text{faraday}}$

$= 8.728 \times 10^2$

5. Calculate the emf for cells with the following net reactions run at standard conditions: (Consult Tables 20-1 and 20-2 for standard reduction potentials.)

(a) $Mn + Cd^{2+} \longrightarrow Cd + Mn^{2+}$
(c) $2Br^- + I_2 \longrightarrow Br_2 + 2I^-$

**Solution**

(a) The complete reaction represents the reduction of $Cd^{2+}$ to Cd and the oxidation of Mn to $Mn^{2+}$. At standard conditions, the emf for the cell equals the sum of the half-cell potentials.

$$E^\circ_{cell} = E^\circ_{Cd^{2+}/Cd} + E^\circ_{Mn/Mn^{2+}}$$

$$Cd^{2+} + 2e^- \longrightarrow Cd \qquad\qquad E^\circ = -0.50 \text{ V}$$

$$\underline{Mn - 2e^- \longrightarrow Mn^{2+} \qquad\qquad E^\circ = +1.18 \text{ V}}$$

$$E^\circ_{cell} = 0.68 \text{ V}$$

(c) The emf for the cell equals the sum of the half-cell potentials.

$$E^\circ_{cell} = E^\circ_{I_2/2I^-} + E^\circ_{2Br^-/Br_2}$$

$$2Br^- - 2e^- \longrightarrow Br_2 \qquad\qquad E^\circ = -1.0652 \text{ V}$$

$$\underline{I_2 + 2e^- \longrightarrow 2I^- \qquad\qquad E^\circ = +0.5355 \text{ V}}$$

$$E^\circ_{cell} = -0.5297 \text{ V}$$

6. Determine the standard emf for the following cells. (As is customary, the anode is written on the left.)

(a) $Co, Co^{2+}$ $(M = 1) \overset{\overset{e^-}{\longrightarrow}}{\|}$ $Cr^{3+}$ $M = 1, Cr$

**214**

**Solution**

(a) In this cell Co is oxidized to $Co^{2+}$ and $Cr^{3+}$ is reduced to Cr, both reactions occurring in 1 $M$ solutions. The emf of the cell is

$$E^\circ_{cell} = E^\circ_{Co/Co^{2+}} + E^\circ_{Cr^{3+}/Cr}$$

$$Co - 2e^- \longrightarrow Co^{2+} \qquad\qquad E^\circ = +0.277 \text{ V}$$

$$Cr^{3+} + 3e^- \longrightarrow Cr \qquad\qquad E^\circ = -0.740 \text{ V}$$

$$\overline{\qquad\qquad\qquad\qquad\qquad\qquad E^\circ_{cell} = -0.46 \text{ V}}$$

8. Calculate the standard free energy change and equilibrium constant for each net reaction in Problem 5.

**Solution**

(a) $\quad Mn + Cd^{2+} \longrightarrow Cd + Mn^{2+} \qquad E^\circ = 0.78 \text{ V}$

The change in free energy for this reaction at standard conditions is calculated from

$$\Delta G^\circ = -nFE^\circ$$

in which 2 mol of electrons are transferred from Mn to Cd per mole of reactant.

$$\Delta G^\circ = -(2)\left(96.487\,\frac{kJ}{V}\right)(0.78 \text{ V}) = -150 \text{ kJ}$$

The equilibrium constant can be calculated directly from $\Delta G^\circ$ or from $E^\circ$ equated to $K$. This latter method is preferred if a value for $E^\circ$ is available; the reason for this is that less chance for error due to rounding is involved. In this equation,

$$E^\circ = \frac{0.05915 \text{ V}}{n}\ \log K$$

the unit of $E^\circ$ is the volt, but the unit is conventionally deleted and the equation left as

$$E^\circ = \frac{0.05915}{n}\ \log K$$

with volt understood as the unit of measurement. In this problem the value of $K$ is calculated as

$$0.78 = \frac{0.05915}{2}\ \log K$$

$$\log K = \frac{2(0.78)}{0.05915} = 26.37$$

$$K = 10^{26.37} = 2.4 \times 10^{26}$$

(c) $2\,Br^- + I_2 \longrightarrow Br_2 + 2I^-$    $E° = -0.5297\,V$

$$\Delta G° = -nFE° = -(2)\left(96.487\,\frac{kJ}{V}\right)(-0.5297\,V) = 102.2\,kJ$$

And,

$$E° = \frac{0.05915}{n}\log K$$

$$-0.5297 = \frac{0.05915}{2}\log K$$

$$\log K = -17.9104$$

$$K = 10^{-17.9104} = 1.229 \times 10^{-18}$$

9. Calculate the emf for each of the following half-reactions.

(a)  $Sn^{2+}\,(0.0100\,M) + 2e^- \longrightarrow Sn$
(c)  $O_2\,(0.0010\,atm) + 4H^+\,(0.100\,M) + 4e^- \longrightarrow 2H_2O(l)$
(d)  $Cr_2O_6{}^{2-}\,(0.150\,M) + 14H^+\,(0.100\,M) + 6e^- \longrightarrow$
      $2Cr^{3+}\,(0.000100\,M) + 7H_2O(l)$

**Solution**

(a)  $Sn^{2+}\,(0.0100\,M) + 2e^- \longrightarrow Sn$. The emf for this half-cell is calcu-
     lated from the Nernst equation by assuming that the activity or con-
     centration of the free metal has a value of 1.  At unit concentration

$$E = E° - \frac{0.05915}{n}\log Q$$

the emf, $E°$, is $-0.136\,V$, but at a lower concentration of $Sn^{2+}$,
$0.0100\,M$, the cell potential is

$$E = -0.136\,V - \frac{0.05915}{2}\log\frac{[Sn]}{[Sn^{2+}]}$$

$$= -0.136\,V - \frac{0.05915}{2}\,V\left(\log\frac{1}{.01}\right)$$

$$= -0.136\,V - \frac{0.05915}{2}\,(2)\,V = -0.195\,V$$

(c)  $O_2\,(0.0010\,atm) + 4H^+\,(0.100\,M) + 4e^- \longrightarrow 2H_2O$

$$E = E° - \frac{0.05915}{n}\log Q$$

$$= 1.23\,V - \frac{0.05915}{4}\log\frac{[H_2O]^2}{pO_2\,[H^+]^4}$$

The water produced is pure and its concentration or activity is considered unity.

$$E = 1.23 \text{ V} - \frac{0.05915}{4} \log \frac{1}{(10^{-3})(10^{-1})^4}$$

$$= 1.23 \text{ V} - \frac{0.05915}{4} (7)\text{V} = 1.13 \text{ V}$$

(d) $Cr_2O_7^{2-}$ (0.150 $M$) + 14H$^+$ (0.100 $M$) + 6e$^-$ $\longrightarrow$ 2Cr$^{3+}$ (0.000100 $M$) + 7 H$_2$O($l$)

$$E = E° - \frac{0.05915}{n} \text{V}(\log Q)$$

$$= 1.33 \text{ V} - \frac{0.05915}{6} \text{V} \left( \log \frac{[Cr^{3+}]^2}{[Cr_2O_7^{2-}][H^+]^{14}} \right)$$

$$= 1.33 \text{ V} - \frac{0.05915}{6} \text{V} \left[ \log \frac{(1.00 \times 10^{-4})^2}{(0.150)(10^{-1})^{14}} \right]$$

$$= 1.33 \text{ V} - \frac{0.05915}{6} \text{V} (\log 6.67 \times 10^6)$$

$$= 1.33 \text{ V} - 0.0673 \text{ V} = 1.26 \text{ V}$$

11. How many grams of zinc will be deposited from a solution of zinc(II) sulfate by 3.40 faradays of electricity?

**Solution**

The reduction of 1 mol of zinc(II) ions requires 2 mol of electrons.

$$Zn^{2+} + 2e^- \longrightarrow Zn$$

And one faraday of charge furnishes 1 mol of electrons for the reaction. Hence, two faradays of charge reduce 1 mol of zinc(II) ions.

$$\text{Mass Zn} = 3.40 \text{ faradays} \times \frac{1 \text{ mol Zn}}{2 \text{ faradays}} \times \frac{65.4 \text{ g}}{\text{mol}} = 111 \text{ g}$$

13. How many grams of cobalt will be deposited from a solution of cobalt(II) chloride electrolyzed with a current of 20.0 A for 54.5 min?

**Solution**

The reduction of Co$^{2+}$ to Co requires two faradays of charge per mole of Co$^{2+}$ ions reduced.

$$Co^{2+} + 2e^- \longrightarrow Co$$

$$\text{No. coulombs} = (20 \text{ A}) \left( 54.5 \text{ min} \times 60 \frac{\text{sec}}{\text{min}} \right)$$

$$= 6.54 \times 10^4 \text{ coulombs}$$

$$\text{No. faradays} = 6.54 \times 10^4 \text{ coulombs} \times \frac{1 \text{ faraday}}{96,487 \text{ coulombs}} = 0.678$$

$$\text{Mass Co} = 0.678 \text{ faraday} \times \frac{1 \text{ mol Co}}{2 \text{ faradays}} \times \frac{58.9 \text{ g}}{\text{mol}} = 20.0 \text{ g}$$

16. A current of 10.0 A is applied to 1.0 ℓ of a solution containing 1.0 mol of HCl for 1.0 hr. Calculate the $pH$ of the solution at the end of this time. Assume that chlorine is produced at the anode.

**Solution**

The reduction of $H^+$ to produce $H_2$ at the cathode will produce a change in $pH$ as the reaction proceeds.

$$2H^+ + 2e^- \longrightarrow H_2$$

$$2Cl^- - 2e^- \longrightarrow Cl_2$$

The number of moles of $H^+$ consumed by the reaction is:

No. mol $H^+$ reduced = no. faradays passed

$$\text{No. faradays} = (10.0 \text{ A})\left(1.0 \text{ hr} \times 3600 \frac{\text{sec}}{\text{hr}}\right)\frac{1.0 \text{ faraday}}{96,487 \text{ coulombs}} = 0.37$$

No. mol $H^+$ reduced = 0.37 mol

$$[H^+] \text{ after reduction} = 1.0 \frac{\text{mol}}{\ell} - 0.37 \frac{\text{mol}}{\ell} = 0.63 \frac{\text{mol}}{\ell}$$

$$pH = -\log 0.63 = 0.20$$

23. What is the cell with the highest emf that could be constructed from the metals iron, nickel, copper, and silver?

**Solution**

The highest emf will result from the half-cell pair having the greatest potential difference. Of these metals-ions, silver ions are the most easily reduced. Then, what metal-ion pair has the greatest potential separation from silver?

$$Fe^{2+} + 2e^- \longrightarrow Fe \qquad E° = -0.440 \text{ V}$$

The greatest cell potential is

$$Fe - 2e^- \longrightarrow Fe^{2+} \qquad \qquad E° = 0.440 \text{ V}$$
$$Ag^+ + e^- \longrightarrow Ag \qquad \qquad E° = +.7991 \text{ V}$$
$$Fe, Fe^{2+} \parallel Ag^+, Ag \qquad \qquad E°_{cell} = 1.24 \text{ V}$$

24. Calculate the free energy change and equilibrium constant for the reaction $2Br^- + F_2 \longrightarrow 2F^- + Br_2$.

### Solution

The change in free energy for this reaction can be calculated from the emf of the cell:

$$\Delta G = -nFE°$$

$$2Br^- - 2e^- \longrightarrow Br_2 \qquad E° = -1.06\ V$$

$$\underline{F_2 + 2e^- \longrightarrow 2F^- \qquad E° = +2.87\ V}$$

$$E°_{cell} = 1.81\ V$$

$$\Delta G° = -2\left(96.487\ \frac{kJ}{V}\right)(1.81\ V) = -349\ kJ$$

and

$$E° = \frac{0.05915}{n}\log K$$

$$1.81 = \frac{0.05915}{2}\log K$$

$$\log K = 61.200$$

$$K = 10^{61.200} = 1.59 \times 10^{61}$$

27.  The standard reduction potentials for the reactions

$$Ag^+ + e^- \longrightarrow Ag$$

and

$$AgCl + e^- \longrightarrow Ag + Cl^-$$

are 0.7991 and 0.222 V, respectively.  From these data and the Nernst equation, calculate a value for the solubility product constant ($K_{sp}$) for AgCl.  Compare your answer to the value given in Appendix E.

### Solution

The solubility product constant for the dissolution of AgCl, is

$$AgCl(s) \longrightarrow Ag^+(aq) + Cl^-(aq)$$

$$K_{sp} = [Ag^+][Cl^-]$$

The two half-cells given in the problem can be rearranged to give the desired equilibrium.

$$Ag \longrightarrow Ag^+ + e^- \qquad E° = -0.7991\ V$$

$$\underline{AgCl + e^- \longrightarrow Ag + Cl^- \qquad E° = 0.222\ V}$$

$$AgCl \longrightarrow Ag^+ + Cl^- \qquad E°_{cell} = -0.557\ V$$

This value can be substituted into the equation relating $E°$ to $\log K$. We solve that equation to obtain

$$E° = \frac{0.05915}{n} \log K$$

$$-0.577 = \frac{0.05915}{1} \log K$$

$$\log K = \frac{-0.577}{0.05915} = -9.755$$

$$K = K_{sp} = 10^{-9.755} = 1.76 \times 10^{-10}$$

This is compared to $1.8 \times 10^{-10}$ as given in Appendix E.

## RELATED PROBLEMS

1. Calculate the number of faradays required to deposit 2.94 g of nickel at a cathode.                                                    *Answer: 0.10 faraday*

2. The potential for the cell

$$Zn\,|\,Zn^{2+}\ (1.70\ M)\,\|\,Cu^{2+}\ (M = ?)\,|\,Cu$$

   is 1.09 V. Calculate the concentration of $Cu^{2+}$ in this cell.
   *Answer: $[Cu^{2+}] = 0.779\ M$*

3. Given the following two half-cells, calculate the equilibrium constant for the cell combination that reacts spontaneously at standard conditions.

$$Ni^{2+} + 2e^- \longrightarrow Ni \qquad E° = -0.25\ V$$
$$Cu^{2+} + 2e^- \longrightarrow Cu \qquad E° = 0.34\ V$$

   *Answer: $K = 8.9 \times 10^{19}$*

4. The storage battery used for starting an automobile engine is designed to deliver a high current for a short period of time. Given that a current of 160 A is delivered for 2.5 sec, calculate the amount of lead that would be converted to lead(II) sulfate at each anode in a six-cell battery (cells are connected in series).                          *Answer: 0.43 g/cell*

5. Given the following cell,

$$Zn\,|\,Zn^{2+}\ (0.10\ M)\,\|\,Fe^{2+}\ (0.01\ M)\,|\,Fe$$

   Calculate the expected potential and the Gibbs energy for the cell.
   *Answer: $E = 0.29\ V;\ \Delta G = 56\ kJ$*

# Chapter 29: Nuclear Chemistry

## INTRODUCTION

In 1896, Henri Becquerel observed that ores containing the compound potassium uranyl sulfate, $K_2SO_4 \cdot UO_2SO_4 \cdot 2H_2O$, emitted high-energy rays similar to x rays. One of his students, Marie Sklodowska Curie, named this phenomenon radioactivity. Two years later, Marie and her husband Pierre were able to identify two new elements, polonium (Po), named after her native Poland, and radium (Ra), both of which were radioactive. The Nobel Prize was awarded to the Curies and Becquerel in 1903 for their work. Their efforts marked the beginning of the nuclear era.

Their discovery led to the understanding that certain atomic nuclei are unstable and spontaneously disintegrate, with the release of energy and penetrating radiations to produce new nuclei. These may be either nuclei of an element different from the original element or an isotope of the original element. About three-fourths of the more than 1000 known isotopes are unstable or radioactive and can exhibit the phenomena described. All isotopes with atomic number $Z$ greater than 83 are radioactive, and all elements beyond uranium, $Z = 92$, in the Periodic Table are artificially created as well as radioactive.

Atoms of stable isotopes can be made radioactive through bombardment of their nuclei with nuclear particles. Some of these nuclides so produced are useful in medicine, research, and in the generation of electrical energy. As an example, cobalt-60, an isotope widely used in cancer therapy, is prepared by bombarding stable cobalt-59 with neutrons according to the reaction

$$\mathrm{^{59}_{27}Co} + \mathrm{^{1}_{0}n} \longrightarrow \mathrm{^{60}_{27}Co}$$

But cobalt-60 is unstable and decays to stable nickel-60 as

$$\mathrm{^{60}_{27}Co} \longrightarrow \mathrm{^{60}_{28}Ni} + \mathrm{^{0}_{-1}\beta} + energy$$

This process requires 5.29 years for one-half of the original amount of cobalt to decompose. This time is known as the *half-life*. Some larger radioactive nuclei will split into two or more smaller nuclear fragments upon addition of another particle. This process, called *fission*, is exemplified by the splitting of uranium-235, which is used as an energy source for generating electricity. The reaction shown here is only one of many that have been observed in the fission of uranium-235.

$$\mathrm{^{235}_{92}U} + \mathrm{^{1}_{0}n} \longrightarrow \mathrm{^{236}_{92}U} \longrightarrow \mathrm{^{90}_{36}Kr} + \mathrm{^{144}_{56}Ba} + 2\,\mathrm{^{1}_{0}n}$$

The purpose of this chapter is to acquaint you with phenomena related to nuclear change. Specifically treated are characteristics of nuclear change, including natural and artificial nuclear reactions, nuclear stability, methods for detecting and accelerating particles, rates of nuclear reactions, energies associated with nuclear change, and some research and technological applications of radioactive isotopes.

## FORMULAS AND DEFINITIONS

**Binding energy** $(B)$   The mass of a nucleus is always less than the combined mass of its constituent particles. The mass difference, or mass defect, is related to energy through the equation $E = mc^2$. This energy, called the binding energy of the nucleus, is the energy required to break up the nucleus into its constituent particles. To calculate the binding energy, compute the mass difference between the mass of a nuclide and the mass of its components. This difference, the mass defect, is converted to energy through substitution into $E = mc^2$.

**Energy equivalences**   Energy produced by conversion of a mass equivalent to 1 amu, or $1.6605655 \times 10^{-27}$ kg, to energy through the Einstein equation, $E = mc^2$, is

$$E = (1.6605 \times 10^{-27}\ kg)(2.99792468 \times 10^8\ m/sec)^2 = 1.492442 \times 10^{-10}\ J$$

$$1\ joule = 6.24146 \times 10^{18}\ electron\ volts$$

$$= 6.24146 \times 10^{12}\ MeV$$

or

$$1\ MeV = 1.602189 \times 10^{-13}\ J$$

$$E = (1.49244 \times 10^{-10}\ J)(6.24146 \times 10^{12}\ MeV/J) = 931.450\ MeV$$

**Half-life** ($t_{1/2}$)  The amount of time required for one-half the number of nuclei in a radioactive sample to decay to new nuclei. Half-life values range from microseconds to billions of years.

**Isotopic mass**  The experimentally measured mass of an isotope (nuclide) relative to the mass of carbon-12.

**Mass number** ($A$)  Sum of the number of neutrons and protons in the nucleus of a specific nuclide.

**Nuclear reaction rate**  The rate of a nuclear reaction is kinetically of the first order. That is, the number of nuclei of a specific nuclide remaining in a sample after an elapsed time, $t$, is a function of the initial number of nuclei, $N_0$, and the half-life of the nuclide. The value $N_t$, or the number of nuclei at time $t$, is related to $N_0$ by the equation $N_t = N_0 e^{-kt}$, where $k$ is a proportionality constant called the decay constant. This equation is conveniently rearranged as

$$\log \frac{N_0}{N_t} = \frac{kt}{2.303} \quad \text{and} \quad k = \frac{0.693}{t_{1/2}}$$

## QUESTIONS

9. Complete the following equations:

(a) $^{27}_{13}\text{Al} + {}^{2}_{1}\text{H} \longrightarrow \quad + {}^{4}_{2}\text{He}$

(b) $^{7}_{3}\text{Li} + \quad \longrightarrow 2\,{}^{4}_{2}\text{He}$

(c) $^{9}_{4}\text{Be} + {}^{4}_{2}\text{He} \longrightarrow {}^{12}_{6}\text{C} +$

**Solution**

(a) $^{27}_{13}\text{Al} + {}^{2}_{1}\text{H} \longrightarrow {}^{25}_{12}\text{Mg} + {}^{4}_{2}\text{He}$

The mass and charge totals of both products and reactants must be equal in a correctly balanced equation.

(b) $^{7}_{3}\text{Li} + {}^{1}_{1}\text{H} \longrightarrow 2\,{}^{4}_{2}\text{He}$

(c) $^{9}_{4}\text{Be} + {}^{4}_{2}\text{He} \longrightarrow {}^{12}_{6}\text{C} + {}^{1}_{0}\text{n}$

10. Fill in the atomic number of the initial nucleus and write out the complete nuclear symbol for the product of the following nuclear reactions:

(a) $^{65}Cu$ (n, 2n)

(b) $^{54}Fe$ ($\alpha$, 2p)

(c) $^{33}S$ (n, p)

(g) $^{14}N$ (p, $\gamma$)

**Solution**

(a) $^{65}Cu$ (n, 2n)

$$^{65}_{29}Cu + ^{1}_{0}n \longrightarrow ^{64}_{29}Cu + 2\,^{1}_{0}n$$

(b) $^{54}Fe$ ($\alpha$, 2p)

$$^{54}_{26}Fe + ^{4}_{2}He \longrightarrow ^{56}_{26}Fe + 2\,^{1}_{1}H$$

(c) $^{33}S$ (n, p)

$$^{33}_{16}S + ^{1}_{0}n \longrightarrow ^{33}_{15}P + ^{1}_{1}H$$

(g) $^{14}N$ (p, $\gamma$)

$$^{14}_{7}N + ^{1}_{1}H \longrightarrow ^{15}_{8}O + \gamma$$

11. Complete the following notations by filling in the missing parts:

(a) $^{2}H$ (d, n)

(b) ($\alpha$, n) $^{30}P$

(e) $^{232}Th$ ( , n) $^{235}U$

**Solution**

(a) $^{2}H$ (d, n)

$$^{2}_{1}H + ^{2}_{1}H \longrightarrow ^{3}_{2}He + ^{1}_{0}n$$

(b) ($\alpha$, n) $^{30}P$

$$^{27}_{13}Al + ^{4}_{2}He \longrightarrow ^{30}_{15}P + ^{1}_{0}n$$

(e) $^{232}\text{Th}(\ ,n)\ ^{235}\text{U}$

$$^{232}_{90}\text{Th} + ^{4}_{2}\text{He} \longrightarrow ^{235}_{92}\text{U} + ^{1}_{0}\text{n}$$

## PROBLEMS

Atomic particle masses

Hydrogen atom (proton + electron) = 1.007825 amu = $1.673559 \times 10^{-27}$ kg

Neutron = 1.008665 amu = $1.6749543 \times 10^{-27}$ kg

Proton = 1.0072764 amu = $1.6726485 \times 10^{-27}$ kg

1 amu = $1.6605655 \times 10^{-27}$ kg

1. The isotopic mass of $^{27}_{13}\text{Al}$ is 26.98154. (a) Calculate its binding energy per atom in MeV. (b) Calculate its binding energy per nucleon. (See Appendix D.)

**Solution**

The binding energy per atom of $^{27}_{13}\text{Al}$ is calculated by computing the difference between the actual mass of the nuclide and its theoretical mass, and converting this mass to energy. An atom of Al-27 contains 14 neutrons and the equivalent of 13 hydrogen atoms (13 protons + 13 electrons in atomic orbitals).

Theoretical mass:

14 neutrons = 14 × 1.008665 amu = 14.121310 amu

13 H atoms = 13 × 1.007825 amu = 13.101725 amu

total = 27.223035 amu

Mass defect = (27.223035 − 26.98154)amu = 0.24150 amu

Binding energy = 0.24150 amu × 931.50 $\dfrac{\text{MeV}}{\text{amu}}$ = 224.96 MeV

(b) The binding energy per nucleon is calculated by dividing the binding energy per atom by the numbers of nucleons; in this case, 27. Binding energy/nucleon = 224.96 MeV/27 = 8.332 MeV.

3. The mass of deuteron $\left(^{2}_{1}\text{H}\right)$ is 2.01355 amu; that of an $\alpha$ particle, 4.00150 amu. How much energy per mole of $^{4}_{2}\text{He}$ produced is released by the reaction

$$^{2}_{1}\text{H} + ^{2}_{1}\text{H} \longrightarrow ^{4}_{2}\text{He}$$

225

**Solution**

Compute the mass change that occurs; then convert this mass to energy.

$$\text{Mass difference per } {}^4\text{He} = [2(2.01355) - 4.00150] \text{ amu}$$
$$= 0.02560 \text{ amu}$$

$$E({}^4\text{He}) = 0.02560 \text{ amu} \times 931.50 \text{ MeV/amu} = 23.846 \text{ MeV}$$
$$E({}^4\text{He}) = 23.846 \text{ MeV} \times 1.602189 \times 10^{-13} \text{ J/MeV}$$
$$= 3.821 \times 10^{12} \text{ J}$$

$$E(\text{mol } {}^4\text{He}) = 3.821 \times 10^{-12} \text{ J/atom} \times 6.022 \times 10^{23} \text{ atoms/mol}$$
$$= 2.301 \times 10^{12} \text{ J}$$
$$= 2.301 \times 10^{9} \text{ kJ}$$

4. What percentage of $^{212}_{82}\text{Pb}$ remains of a 1.00-g sample, 1.0 min after it is formed (half-life of 10.6 sec)? 10 min after it is formed?

**Solution**

The radioactivity of a sample is a function of the number of nuclei in the sample and time. The number of nuclei in a sample determines its mass, its concentration, and its activity. Therefore the formula

$$\log \frac{N_0}{N_t} = \frac{kt}{2.303}$$

is equally valid for concentration, activity, and mass.

$$\log \frac{C_0}{C_t} = \log \frac{A_0}{A_t} = \log \frac{M_0}{M_t} = \frac{kt}{2.303}$$

The time reference for $t$ and $k$ in the equation must be consistent. In this case, the half-life is given in seconds and the experimental time period in minutes. The same unit must be used for both measurements to satisfy the above equation:

$$k = \frac{0.693}{10.6 \text{ sec}} = \frac{0.0654}{\text{sec}} = 0.0654 \text{ sec}^{-1}$$

$$\log \frac{M_0}{M_t} = \frac{0.0654 \text{ sec}^{-1} \, t}{2.303}$$

$$= \frac{0.0654 \text{ sec}^{-1}(1 \text{ min} \times 60 \text{ sec/min})}{2.303}$$

$$= 1.704$$

$$\log M_0 - \log M_t = 1.704$$

226

Since $M_0 = 1.0$ g, the log $M_0 = 0$ and

$$\log M_t = -1.704$$

$$M_t = 10^{-1.704} = 0.02 \text{ g at } 1.0 \text{ min}$$

$$\% = \frac{0.020 \text{ g}}{1.0 \text{ g}} \times 100 = 2.0\%$$

5. The isotope of $^{208}$Tl undergoes $\beta$ decay with a half-life of 3.1 min.

(a) What isotope is the product of the decay?

(b) Is $^{208}$Tl more stable or less stable than an isotope with a half-life of 54.5 sec?

(c) How long will it take for 99.0% of a sample of pure $^{208}$Tl to decay?

(d) What percentage of a sample of pure $^{208}$Tl will remain undecayed after an hour?

**Solution**

(a) $^{208}_{81}\text{Tl} - ^{0}_{-1}\beta \longrightarrow ^{208}_{82}\text{Pb}$

(b) Tl-208 with a half-life of 3.1 min is considered to be more stable than a nuclide with a 54.5-sec half-life.

(c) The percentage of a sample remaining after a period of time is independent of mass. If 99% of the sample has decayed, 1%, or a fraction of 0.01 of the original remains (that is, $M_t = 0.01$ when $M_0 = 1$). The time is calculated from the first-order rate law.

$$k = \frac{0.693}{3.1 \text{ min}} = 0.224 \text{ min}^{-1}$$

$$\log \frac{M_0}{M_t} = \frac{kt}{2.303} = \frac{0.224 \text{ min}^{-1}}{2.303} t = 0.0973 \text{ min}^{-1} t$$

$$t = 10.3 \text{ min} \left(\log \frac{1}{0.01}\right) = 10.3 \, (-\log 0.01)$$

$$= (10.3 \text{ min}) \, (2) = 20.6 \text{ min}$$

(d) We let $M_0 = 1.00$ and then have upon substitution in

$$\log \frac{M_0}{M_t} = \frac{kt}{2.303} \qquad \log \frac{1.00}{M_t} = \frac{0.224 \text{ min}^{-1} \times 60 \text{ min}}{2.303}$$

$$\log M_t = -5.835 \quad \text{or} \quad M_t = 1.46 \times 10^{-6}$$

This is the amount remaining from one unit. We convert this percentage by dividing the part by the whole and multiplication by 100. Thus

$$\frac{1.46 \times 10^{-6}}{1} \times 100 = 1.46 \times 10^{-4} \%$$

6. Calculate the time required for 99.999% of each of the following radio-active isotopes to decay:

(a) $^{226}_{88}$Ra (half-life, 1590 years).

**Solution**

Consider the initial amount of Ra-226 to be 1.00. Therefore 0.001%, or a fraction of 0.00001, remains. Calculate $k$ and $t$ as in Problem 5(c).

$$k = \frac{0.693}{1590 \text{ y}} = 4.36 \times 10^{-4} \text{ y}^{-1}$$

$$\log \frac{1}{0.00001} = \frac{4.36 \times 10^{-4}}{2.303} \text{ y}^{-1} \, t$$

$$= 1.89 \times 10^{-4} \text{ y}^{-1} \, t$$

$$t = (5.28 \times 10^3 \text{ y}) \, (-\log 0.00001)$$

$$= (5.28 \times 10^3 \text{ y}) \, (5)$$

$$= 26,400 \text{ y}$$

7. The isotope $^{90}_{38}$Sr is an extremely hazardous isotope in the fallout from a nuclear fission explosion. A 0.500-g sample diminishes to 0.393 g in 10.0 years. Calculate the half-life.

**Solution**

Sufficient information is given in the problem to calculate the value of $k$, which in turn can be used to calculate the half-life of Sr-90.

$$\log \frac{M_0}{M_t} = \frac{kt}{2.303}$$

$$\log \frac{0.500 \text{ g}}{0.393 \text{ g}} = \frac{k(10 \text{ y})}{2.303} = k(4.3422 \text{ y})$$

$$\log 1.2723 = 4.3422 \text{ y}(k)$$

$$k = \frac{0.10459}{4.3422 \text{ y}} = 0.02409 \text{ y}^{-1}$$

$$\text{Half-life} = \frac{0.693}{0.02409 \text{ y}^{-1}} = 28.8 \text{ y}$$

## RELATED PROBLEMS

1. Which one of the following nuclear equations is incorrectly written?

   (a) $^{226}_{88}\text{Ra} \longrightarrow ^{222}_{86}\text{Rn} + ^{4}_{2}\text{He}$

   (b) $^{14}_{7}\text{N} + ^{4}_{2}\text{He} \longrightarrow ^{17}_{8}\text{O} + ^{1}_{0}\text{n}$

   (c) $^{10}_{5}\text{B} + ^{4}_{2}\text{He} \longrightarrow ^{13}_{7}\text{N} + ^{1}_{0}\text{n}$

   (d) $^{235}_{92}\text{U} + ^{1}_{0}\text{n} \longrightarrow ^{142}_{56}\text{Ba} + ^{91}_{36}\text{Kr} + 3\,^{1}_{0}\text{n}$

   *Answer: (b)*

2. The activity of carbon-12 in the ash remains of an ancient civilization is found to be 1/8 its original activity. Based on an archeological carbon-12 half-life of 5730 years, calculate the time elapsed since the demise of the civilization.        *Answer: 17,200 years*

3. The mass loss incurred as one mole of radium-226 decays to radon-222 is $2.4 \times 10^{21}$ amu. Calculate the energy produced by conversion of this mass to energy. Convert this mass loss from *amu* to *kg*. Given that the complete combustion of one mole of methane releases 882 kJ, calculate the mass of methane required to produce an energy equivalent to the decay of one mole of radium.
   *Answer: $3.6 \times 10^{11}$ J; $4 \times 10^{-6}$ kg; $6.5 \times 10^{3}$ kg*

4. The initial activity of a cobalt-60 source is $9.0 \times 10^{6}$ counts per second (cps). Given that the half-life of this nuclide is 5.2 years, calculate the activity that would remain 8.0 years hence.

   *Answer: $3.1 \times 10^{6}$ cps*

5. The Group I metals, potassium and sodium, are essential for the growth and maintenance of healthy plants and animals. Since cesium is in the same periodic group, one would expect it to be incorporated in living tissue in much the same manner as potassium and sodium. Cesium-137 is radioactive, has a half-life of 30 years, and is a significant radioactive waste. Given that the initial activity in 1980 of a 1.0-g sample of cesium-137 is $3.2 \times 10^{12}$ counts per second, calculate the activity of the sample in year 2500.        *Answer: Activity $= 1.9 \times 10^{7}$ cps*

# Part Two

---

# Exponential Notation and Logarithms

Part Two is a programmed unit designed as a comprehensive review of algebraic operations involving exponential numbers and logarithms. After a careful study of this unit, you should be able to

1. Write numbers in scientific notation or exponential form.
2. Multiply and divide numbers written in scientific notation.
3. Raise a number to a specified power.
4. Find a specified root of a number.
5. Perform logarithmic operations to calculate products, quotients, powers, and roots.

Make certain you are able to answer *correctly* all parts of the question in a frame before proceeding to the next frame. Answers to questions in this part begin on page 248.

## EXPONENTIAL NOTATION

[1] Scientific study involves writing and using numbers in the base 10 system. The use of exponential notation enables us to write very large and very small numbers with base 10 in a convenient manner. For example, 0.0000000007 can be written $7 \times 10^{-10}$ and 7,000,000,000,000,000 can be written $7 \times 10^{15}$. Operations with exponential numbers are easily performed with practice. Let us begin our study with some moderate-sized numbers as examples. The number 20 can be written $2 \times 10^1$; 40 can be written $4 \times$ _____ ; 400 can be written $4 \times$ _____ .

---------------------------------------------------------------------

[2] The number 100 can be thought of as $10 \times 10$ or as $10^1 \times 10^1$, both of which equal $10^2$. So the number 600 can be written $6 \times 10^2$. The number 750 can be written $7.5 \times$ _____. The number 625 can be written _____ $\times$ _____.

--------------------------------------------------------------------

[3] Just as 100 equals $10^2$, 1000 equals $10 \times 10 \times 10$, or $10^1 \times 10^1 \times 10^1$, or $10^3$. The number 4000 can be written $4 \times 10^3$. Rewrite the following numbers.

(a) 7700 is $7.7 \times 10^?$.
(b) 8250 is $8.25 \times 10^?$.
(c) 6255 is _____ $\times$ _____.

--------------------------------------------------------------------

[4] The number 100 is $10^2$, 1000 is $10^3$, 10,000 is $10^4$, and 1,000,000 is $10^6$. These numbers have a common factor. That is, 100 has two zeros and the exponent of 10 is 2; 100,000 has five zeros and the exponent of 10 is 5. It follows that the exponent of 10 for the number 1,000,000,000 should be _____.

--------------------------------------------------------------------

[5] Any number or expression with zero as an exponent has a value of one. For example: $10^0 = 1; a^0 = 1; (ab)^0 = 1$; etc. Calculate the values for the following exercises.

(a) $5^0 =$ ____                  (b) $100^0 =$ _____
(c) $5^0 \times 10^0 =$ _____          (d) $a^0 \times 10^0 \times b^0 =$ _____

--------------------------------------------------------------------

[6] In general, a number written in scientific or exponential form should be written with one nonzero digit to the left of the decimal point and all other significant figures to the right of the decimal point. Experimentally determined digits are referred to as significant figures. For example: 2254. contains 4 digits that have been experimentally determined and can be written exponentially as $2.254 \times 10^3$. The number 254,000 would be written exponentially as $2.54 \times 10^5$, since the 3 zeros are merely place holders. Complete the following exercises:

(a) $7655 = 7.655 \times 10^?$.
(b) $2,225,000,000 = 2.225 \times 10^?$.
(c) $786,000 = 7.86 \times 10^?$.

--------------------------------------------------------------------

[7] Write the following numbers in exponential form:

(a) 2250 _____          (b) 60,200,000,000 _____
(c) 5,575,000,000 _____

--------------------------------------------------------------------

[8]   Basically the same procedure as that outlined in frame 6 can be used
      to rewrite very small numbers in exponential form. Examine the
      accompanying group of numbers and note that the exponent of 10
      has a negative sign and represents the number of digits from the deci-
      mal point to the right of the first nonzero digit.

$$0.1 = 1 \times 10^{-1}$$
$$0.01 = 1 \times 10^{-2}$$
$$0.001 = 1 \times 10^{-3}$$
$$0.0001 = 1 \times 10^{-4}$$

With this concept in mind, study the following examples and rewrite
the exercises:

$$0.00000001 = 1 \times 10^{-8}$$
$$0.00025 = 2.5 \times 10^{-4}$$

(a)  $0.000007 = 7 \times 10^{?}$.
(b)  $0.0000425 = 4.25 \times 10^{?}$.
(c)  $0.0000608 = $ _____

- - - - - - - - - - - - - - - - - - - - - - - - - - - - - - - - - - - - - - - - - - -

[9]   By the same reasoning as in frame 8, the exponent of 10 for 0.000007
      is _____ and for 0.0000425 is _____.

- - - - - - - - - - - - - - - - - - - - - - - - - - - - - - - - - - - - - - - - - - -

[10]  The number 0.00000235 is correctly written $2.35 \times 10^{-6}$, and 506,000
      as $5.06 \times 10^{5}$. That is, the exponential form of each number contains
      all the significant figures in the number with one nonzero digit written
      to the left of the decimal point. In general, the exponent of 10 equals
      the number of digits from the decimal point of the number to the
      right of the first nonzero digit. The sign of the exponent is "+" if the
      number is greater than 1 and "−" if the number is less than 1. For
      the number 0.00000235, there are 6 digits from the decimal point to
      the right of 2, and for 506,000 there are 5 digits from the right of 5
      to the last digit. (No answer required).

- - - - - - - - - - - - - - - - - - - - - - - - - - - - - - - - - - - - - - - - - - -

[11]  Write the following numbers in scientific notation.

      (a)  0.003 _____
      (b)  0.0075 _____
      (c)  0.0002354 _____
      (d)  0.0000072 _____

- - - - - - - - - - - - - - - - - - - - - - - - - - - - - - - - - - - - - - - - - - -

[12]  Sometimes it is necessary to change the form a number is written in;
      care must be taken, however, not to change the magnitude of the
      number. The change in the value of the exponent must reflect the

change in position of the decimal point. For base 10 numbers, if the decimal point is moved 3 places to the left, the exponent of 10 must be increased by the same amount; it is decreased when the decimal point is moved to the right. Consider the following examples:

The number $2.25 \times 10^2$ can be written $22.5 \times 10^1$ or $225 \times 10^0$ without changing the value of the original number. Also, 0.00075 can be written $7.5 \times 10^{-4}$ or $75 \times 10^{-5}$. Using this concept, rewrite the following numbers as indicated.

(a) $235,000 = 23.5 \times 10^? = 2.35 \times 10^?$
(b) $0.00068 = 6.8 \times 10^? = 68 \times 10^?$

---

[13] The implication of the concept discussed in frame 12 is that all real base 10 numbers can be written as the product of a rational number and an exponential term. Therefore it follows that common arithmetical operations, such as multiplication and division, can be performed with numbers written in exponential form. Let us first consider the rules for multiplying exponential numbers. In multiplying expressions having the same number base system (in our case, base 10), the exponent of the product is merely the sum of the exponents of the multipliers. For example,

$$10^2 \cdot 10^3 = 10^{2+3} = 10^5 = \underline{100,000}$$

Determine the following products:

(a) $10^1 \cdot 10^5 = $ _____
(b) $10^3 \cdot 10^9 = $ _____
(c) $10^4 \cdot 10^{10} = $ _____

---

[14] The same rule applies when the exponents are negative. For example,

$$10^{-2} \cdot 10^{-3} = 10^{-5}$$

Determine the following products:

(a) $10^{-8} \cdot 10^{-10} = $ _____
(b) $10^{-5} \cdot 10^{-3} = $ _____
(c) $10^{-5} \cdot 10^{-5} = $ _____

---

[15] When both positive and negative exponents are present in the same expression, the same rule applies. Merely add the exponents algebracially. For example,

$$10^{-3} \cdot 10^5 = 10^2$$

(a) $10^{-15} \cdot 10^{12} = $ _____
(b) $10^{-2} \cdot 10^{-3} \cdot 10^6 = $ _____
(c) $10^{14} \cdot 10^{-12} \cdot 10^3 = $ _____

---

[16] Now consider the possibility of multiplying expressions written in scientific notation form. To find the product, add the exponents of the exponential terms and multiply the rational terms. For example,

$$(2 \times 10^5)(4 \times 10^6) = (2 \times 4)(10^5 \times 10^6) = 8 \times 10^{11}$$

Calculate the following:

(a) $(3.2 \times 10^4)(2.0 \times 10^5) = $ _____
(b) $(4.0 \times 10^6)(8.0 \times 10^{-5}) = $ _____
(c) $(8.0 \times 10^6)(9.1 \times 10^{-2}) = $ _____
(d) $(2.0 \times 10^3)(3.0 \times 10^{-5})(4.0 \times 10^2) = $ _____

- - - - - - - - - - - - - - - - - - - - - - - - - - - - - - - - - - - - - - - - - -

[17] The operations involved in dividing exponential expressions are just as simple as multiplication operations. With base 10 numbers (or any numbers having the same base), the exponent of the quotient is the algebraic difference between the exponent of the numerator and the exponent of the denominator. Study the following examples:

$$\frac{a^x}{a^y} = a^{x-y}$$

$$\frac{a^x}{a^{-y}} = a^{x-(-y)} = a^{x+y}$$

Now with numbers:

$$\frac{10^3}{10^2} = 10^{3-2} = 10^1$$

$$\frac{10^5}{10^{-2}} = 10^{5-(-2)} = 10^{5+2} = 10^7$$

(No answer required.)

- - - - - - - - - - - - - - - - - - - - - - - - - - - - - - - - - - - - - - - - - -

[18] Divide as indicated:

(a) $\dfrac{10^4}{10^1} = $ _____

(b) $\dfrac{10^6}{10^2} = $ _____

(c) $\dfrac{10^5}{10^{-5}} = $ _____

(d) $\dfrac{10^{1.2}}{10^{2.4}} = $ _____

- - - - - - - - - - - - - - - - - - - - - - - - - - - - - - - - - - - - - - - - -

[19] The procedure for dividing two expressions written in scientific notation is similar to multiplication. Let us consider dividing 4000 by 200. The numbers may be written as $4 \times 10^3$ and $2 \times 10^2$. Set up the division in the following manner:

$$\frac{4 \times 10^3}{2 \times 10^2}$$

Two division operations are required to obtain the quotient: first, division of the rational terms, and second, division of the exponential terms. The quotient should be left in scientific notation.

$$\frac{4}{2} = 2$$

$$\frac{10^3}{10^2} = 10^{3-2} = 10^1$$

The quotient is $2 \times 10^1$, or 20. Determine the quotient for each of the following examples.

(a) $\dfrac{5.0 \times 10^4}{2.0 \times 10^2} = $ _____

(b) $\dfrac{7.5 \times 10^{-1}}{3.8 \times 10^3} = $ _____

(c) $\dfrac{9.6 \times 10^{13}}{2.4 \times 10^{-12}} = $ _____

- - - - - - - - - - - - - - - - - - - - - - - - - - - - - - - - - - - - - - - - - - -

[20] Now consider the division of two numbers written in scientific notation in which the rational term in the numerator is smaller than the rational term in the denominator. The procedure for determining the quotient of the following expression is the same as in frame 19:

$$\frac{2.4 \times 10^1}{4.8 \times 10^2}$$

The quotient of 2.4/4.8 is 0.5 and of $10^1/10^2$ is $10^{-1}$, which can be combined as $0.5 \times 10^{-1}$. This answer is correct but it is not conventionally left in this form. The value should be rewritten as $5 \times 10^{-2}$. This type of change was considered briefly in frame 12. Since the expression $5 \times 10^{-2}$ is the product of two numbers, there is no change in the value of the expression when one factor is multiplied by a number and the other divided by the same number. To obtain $5 \times 10^{-2}$ from $0.5 \times 10^{-1}$, multiply and divide both terms by 10 as follows:

$$0.5 \times 10^{-1} \equiv (0.5)(10^1) \times \frac{10^{-1}}{10^1} \equiv 5 \times 10^{-1-(1)} = 5 \times 10^{-2}$$

Using the same logic, compute the quotient for each of the following expressions and leave the quotient in the proper form for scientific notation.

(a) $\dfrac{2.2 \times 10^{-2}}{6.6 \times 10^{-4}} = $ _____

(b) $\dfrac{8.1 \times 10^{14}}{9.0 \times 10^{-15}} = $ _____

(c) $\dfrac{1.42 \times 10^{-3}}{96.2 \times 10^{4}} = $ _____

Go to SELF-EVALUATION I.

## SELF-EVALUATION I

Complete the following self-evaluation of your skills in writing numbers in scientific notation and multiplying and dividing such terms. Answers to these questions are on page 250. If one of your answers does not agree with the answer listed, refer to the frame whose number appears in brackets with the answer and rework the problem(s) in that frame.

1. Write the number 7,070,000 in scientific notation.
2. Write the number $2.62 \times 10^5$ in rational form.
3. Write the number 0.0000785 in scientific notation.
4. Compute the product $(2 \times 10^6)(3.5 \times 10^8)$.
5. Compute the quotient $(1.9 \times 10^4)/(2.6 \times 10^5)$ and write the result in proper scientific notation.
6. Compute the product $(3.6 \times 10^{-1})(4.2 \times 10^{-7})(5.9 \times 10^8)$ and leave the answer in scientific notation.

Go to frame [21]

[21] Analyzing chemical data often requires calculations with powers and roots of numbers. We shall consider operations involving numbers written in scientific notation. In this frame, let us consider the general case for raising an exponential term to a power. The rule for raising a number to a power is to multiply exponents, as shown in the following examples:

$$(a^x)^y = a^{xy}$$
$$(a^2)^3 = a^{(2)(3)} = a^6$$

For base 10 terms, the rule is illustrated by the following:

$$(10^2)^3 = 10^6$$
$$(10^{-2})^4 = 10^{-8}$$

Using the rule given above, compute the following products:

(a) $(10^2)^5 = $ _____
(b) $(10^4)^{-2} = $ _____
(c) $(10^{1/2})^4 = $ _____
(d) $(10^{2.5})^2 = $ _____

-----

[22] Raising a number written in scientific notation to a power follows from the general rules in frame 21. In general, the product of two numbers raised to a power is merely the product of each term raised to the indicated power. Study the examples below and then make the indicated calculations.

$$(2 \times 10^2)^2 = 2^2 \times (10^2)^2 = 4 \times 10^4$$
$$(3.0 \times 10^3)^3 = 3.0^3 \times (10^3)^3 = 27 \times 10^9 = 2.7 \times 10^{10}$$
$$(2.50 \times 10^4)^2 = 2.50^2 \times (10^4)^2 = 6.25 \times 10^8$$
$$(3.0 \times 10^{-4})^3 = 3.0^3 \times (10^{-4})^3 = 27 \times 10^{-12} = 2.7 \times 10^{-11}$$

Evaluate the following expressions:

(a) $(4.0 \times 10^2)^3 = $ _____
(b) $(5.0 \times 10^5)^2 = $ _____
(c) $(2.50 \times 10^{-3})^3 = $ _____

-----

[23] The rule for extracting the root of a number is essentially the same as for raising the number to a power. The rule in frame 22 is rewritten for roots as follows. The root of a product involving two or more factors is merely the product of the root of each factor taken collectively. First, let us consider the extraction of roots for exponential terms. Recall that the square root of a given number is equivalent to the number raised to the power $\frac{1}{2}$ and the cube root of a given number is equivalent to the number raised to the power $\frac{1}{3}$. Study the following examples:

$$\sqrt{10^2} = (10^2)^{1/2} = 10^{2/2} = 10^1$$
$$\sqrt[3]{10^3} = (10^3)^{1/3} = 10^{3/3} = 10^1$$
$$\sqrt[4]{10^{-24}} = (10^{-24})^{1/4} = 10^{-24/4} = 10^{-6}$$

Use the rule for extracting roots to compute the values for the following expressions:

(a) $\sqrt{10^{-6}} = $ _____

(b) $\sqrt{10^4}$ =_____

(c) $\sqrt[3]{10^{-6}}$ =_____

(d) $\sqrt[5]{10^{-25}}$ =_____

----

[24] The exercises in frame 23 involved extracting roots of numbers whose exponents were evenly divisible by the root. For cases in which this is not true, the exponential term must be rewritten as a product of two numbers in which the rational term is greater than 1 and the exponent is evenly divisible by the root. As an example, $\sqrt{1.0 \times 10^3}$ is calculated in the following manner:

$$\sqrt{1.0 \times 10^3} = \sqrt{10. \times 10^2}$$

Now apply the general rule in frame 23:

$$\sqrt{10. \times 10^2} = \sqrt{10.} \times \sqrt{10^2} = (10.)^{1/2} \times (10^2)^{1/2}$$

$$(10.)^{1/2} = 3.2 \quad \text{and} \quad (10^2)^{1/2} = 10^1$$

Therefore $\sqrt{1.0 \times 10^3} = 3.2 \times 10^1$.

By using the procedure in this example calculate the value for each of the following expressions. An electronic calculator or a slide rule is essential for the computation work.

(a) $\sqrt{10^5}$ =_____

(b) $\sqrt[3]{10^7}$ =_____

(c) $\sqrt{10^7}$ = _____

(d) $\sqrt{1.0 \times 10^8}$ =_____

----

[25] Let us expand the concept developed in frames 23 and 24 to include numbers written in scientific notation. The cube root of 44,000 is calculated in the following manner. First, the number is written in exponential form, having the exponent of the exponential term evenly divisible by 3. That is,

$$44,000 = 44 \times 10^3$$

and

$$(44,000)^{1/3} = (44 \times 10^3)^{1/3}$$
$$= (44)^{1/3} \times (10^3)^{1/3}$$
$$= 3.5 \times 10^1$$

Apply the above procedure in calculating the following roots:

(a) $\sqrt{2500}$ = _____

(b) $\sqrt[3]{1440}$ =_____

(c) $\sqrt{26{,}200} =$_____

(d) $\sqrt[3]{18{,}000} =$_____

-------------------------------------------------------------------

[26]  Roots of small numbers are calculated in the same manner.  Study the
following examples and then calculate the roots for the exercises:

$$(0.000074)^{1/2} = (7.4 \times 10^{-5})^{1/2}$$
$$= (74 \times 10^{-6})^{1/2}$$
$$= 8.6 \times 10^{-3}$$
$$(0.00000081)^{1/3} = (8.1 \times 10^{-7})^{1/3}$$
$$= (810 \times 10^{-9})^{1/3}$$
$$= (810)^{1/3} \times (10^{-9})^{1/3}$$
$$= 9.3 \times 10^{-3}$$

(a)  $(0.000045)^{1/2} =$_____

(b)  $(0.00030)^{1/2} =$_____

(c)  $(0.00061)^{1/3} =$_____

(d)  $(9.6 \times 10^{-16})^{1/3} =$_____

-------------------------------------------------------------------

[27]  Fractional roots, such as $\frac{2}{3}$, 0.40, and $\frac{1}{3}$, will be considered in the discussion of logarithms.

-------------------------------------------------------------------

Go to SELF-EVALUATION II.

-------------------------------------------------------------------


## SELF-EVALUATION II

Complete the following self-evaluation of your skills in raising numbers to
powers and in extracting roots of numbers.  Answers to these questions are
on page 251.  If one of your answers does not agree with the answer listed,
refer to the frame whose number appears in brackets with the answer and
rework the problem(s) in that frame.

1.  The value of $(10^8)^3$ is_____.

2.  The value of $(2.5 \times 10^4)^2$ is_____.

3.  The cube root of 25,000 is_____.

4.  The square root of 36,800 is_____.

5.  Calculate the cube root of 0.000065.

6.  Calculate the square root of 0.000049.

-------------------------------------------------------------------

Go to LOGARITHMS and proceed with frame [28].

-------------------------------------------------------------------

# LOGARITHMS

[28] Here, we are concerned with arithmetical operations that involve using exponential numbers. We limit our study to operations involving base 10 numbers. Answers to questions in this part are on page 251.

First, let us define the term logarithm. The logarithm of a number is the exponent to which 10 must be raised to equal the number. For example, $100 = 10^2$; that is, the logarithm (abbreviated "log") of 100 is 2. A general interpretation of logs for base 10 numbers is

$$10^x = N$$

where $x$ is the log of the number $N$. This statement is conventionally rewritten in a form that is more useful for computational work, as shown.

$$\log_{10} N = x$$

The new statement is read in the following manner: "$x$ is the number to which 10 must be raised to equal $N$." Or alternatively, "$x$ is the base logarithm of $N$." Using this definition, one can find logs of numbers such as 10, 100, 0.1, and 0.01 as shown below:

$$\log 0.01 = \log 10^{-2} = -2$$
$$\log 0.1 \ = \log 10^{-1} = -1$$
$$\log 1 \quad = \log 10^0 \ = \ 0$$
$$\log 10 \quad = \log 10^1 \ = \ 1$$
$$\log 100 = \log 10^2 \ = \ 2$$

Find the log of each of the following numbers:

(a) $100,000 = $ _____   (b) $10,000 = $ _____
(c) $0.00001 = $ _____   (d) $0.000001 = $ _____

------------------------------------------------------------

[29] As illustrated in frame 28, logs of numbers are whole numbers when the numbers in question are integral powers of 10. But what about all other numbers? For instance, 25 is between 10 and 100. The exponent to which 10 must be raised to equal 25 is between 1 and 2. The log of 25 also is a number between 1 and 2. Perhaps it is obvious at this point that the log of 25 is 1 plus a decimal fraction. In fact, logs always consist of two parts. Consider the following example:

$$100 = 10^{2.0000}$$

The number 2 is called the characteristic and the decimal fraction is called the mantissa. Four decimal places are used after the 2 to establish the accuracy of the logarithm. The characteristic is defined as the whole number representing the lower limit of the exponential range within which a number is located. That is, 25 lies between $10^1$ and $10^2$ and the characteristic of 25 is 1; 3500 lies between $10^3$ and $10^4$ and the characteristic of 3500 is 3. Determine the characteristic of each of the following numbers.

(a)  175 = _____  (b)  7 = _____
(c)  1250 = _____  (d)  657,000 = _____

-----------------------------------------------------------------------

[30]  Mantissas for numbers have been computed and compiled into tables such as the table of logs inside the back cover of this book. Turn to the log table and locate the following numbers: the number 20 in the column headed by $N$ and the number 3010 under the heading 0 to the right of 20. The numbers are to be interpreted in the following manner. The number 20 should not be read "twenty" but rather "two-zero," which could represent the numbers 2, 20, 200, 2000, and so on. To use the table, mentally place a decimal point to the right of the first significant figure of the numbers under the heading $N$, thus assigning values ranging from 1.0 to 9.9 for numbers in the $N$ column. As a result of this assignment all the numbers in the columns headed by 0 through 9 become decimals ranging from .0000 to .9996.

   Now let us determine the logarithm of 250. First determine the characteristic to be 2. Next locate 25 in the $N$ column, and to the right in the 0 column find 3979. The log of 250 = 2.3979 to four decimal places. Also, $10^{2.3979}$ = 250. In the same manner, determine the logarithm for each of the following numbers.

(a)  log 3500 = _____
(b)  log 27,000 = _____
(c)  log 450,000 = _____

-----------------------------------------------------------------------

[31]  The $N$, or number, column of the log table in this book contains two-digit numbers, and to determine logs for numbers with three or more digits, the columns headed by 0 through 9 must be used as shown in the following example. Suppose we wish to find the log of 225. Since 225 lies between 100 and 1000, its characteristic is 2. Now locate 22 in the $N$ column; and to the right of 22 in the column headed by 5, find 3522. The log of 225 is 2.3522. The columns 0 to 9 effectively expand the $N$ column to a 3-digit column. Now determine logs as indicated below.

(a)  log 374 = _____  (b)  log 2410 = _____
(c)  log 1270 = _____  (d)  log 575,000 = _____

-----------------------------------------------------------------------

[32]  At this point you are able to find the log of a number; for logs to be useful you must also be able to find the number that corresponds to a

242

given log. This process is called finding the antilogarithm, and the procedure is just the reverse of finding the log of a number. As an example, find the number whose log is 2.9782. First, locate the mantissa, 9782, in the table. The mantissa is found to the right of 95 and in the 1 column. This number should be read "nine five one." Second, the magnitude of the number is established by recalling that 0.9782 is the log of 9.51 and the characteristic, 2, indicates that the decimal point is to be shifted two places to the right. That is, 2.9782 is the log of 951. Study the following two examples and then complete the exercises.

*Examples*:

$$\log x = 3.8779$$
$$.8779 \text{ corresponds to } 7.55$$
$$x = 7550$$

$$\log x = 6.7042$$
$$.7042 \text{ corresponds to } 5.06$$
$$x = 5,060,000$$

(a) $\log x = 4.8722$    $x =$ _____
(b) $\log x = 3.7745$    $x =$ _____
(c) $\log x = 2.4955$    $x =$ _____

- - - - - - - - - - - - - - - - - - - - - - - - - - - - - - - - - - - - - - - - -

[33] The table of logs in this book can be used to find logs of three-digit numbers directly, and a fourth place can be found by using the proportional parts (see last three columns of log table). Electronic calculators equipped with log circuits are convenient for working with logs. These calculators usually display logs to eight or nine places. With calculators, antilogs are computed directly by reversing the log function. Consult the instruction manual of your calculator for proper operation. Using proportional parts to determine logs or antilogs is good practice, but not necessary if you have an appropriate calculator. You should work the remaining exercises, with a calculator if you wish, to gain practice with the fundamental logarithm concepts.

The proportional parts table is used in the following manner. In frame 31, we found the log of 225. Now find the log of 225.4. Since 225.4 lies between 225 and 226, the log of 225.4 must lie between log of 225 and log of 226, that is, between 2.3522 and 2.3541. To find the log 225.4, go to the 4 column in the proportional parts section of the table on the same line as 22. There find the number 8. To the log 225, namely 2.3522, add 8 to the last digit to get 2.3530. As another example, the log of 3765 is found in a similar manner.

$\log 3760 = 3.5752$     $\log 3765 = ?$     $\log 3770 = 3.5763$

From proportional parts section, column 5, find that 6 must be added to get the log of 3765: log 3765 = 3.5758. Find the indicated logs.

(a) log 69340 = _____

(b) log 7469 = _____

---

[34]  The proportional parts table also is used to establish the fourth digit in the antilog procedure. In fact, the log-finding procedure is just reversed. The antilog of 2.6458 is found as follows:

$$2.6458 = \log x$$
$$2.6454 = \log 442$$

Diff.    .0004

Locate the 4 in the proportional parts table in the same line as 442. Note that the 4 is in the 4 column. Therefore, 2.6458 is the log of 442.4. Using the same procedure, find the antilogs as indicated.

(a) $\log x = 1.8989$        (b) $\log x = 2.7791$        (c) $\log x = 3.8429$

---

**Go to SELF-EVALUATION III.**

---

## SELF-EVALUATION III

Complete the following self-evaluation of your skills in finding logs of numbers and antilogs. Answers to these questions are on page 252. If one of your answers does not agree with the answer listed, refer to the frame whose number appears in brackets with the answer and rework the problem(s) in that frame.

1. The log of 0.00001 is _____ .
2. The log of 125 is _____ .
3. The antilog of 2.5502 _____ .
4. By using the proportional parts section of the log table, find the antilog of 1.9677.
5. Find the log of 56.78.

---

**Go to frame [35]**

---

[35]  Next, we consider the common arithmetic operations—multiplication, division, powers, and roots—through the use of logarithms. Rules for performing these operations with exponents were treated in the section on exponential numbers. Since logs are exponents, the rules for

operations with exponents apply to log operations, except that one more step is involved to determine answers. First, we shall treat multiplication.

Recall that the product of two exponential numbers to the same base is the base raised to the sum of the exponents. Therefore the log of a product is merely the sum of the logs of each factor. In general,

$$\log_{10} (x)(y) = \log_{10} x + \log_{10} y$$

With numbers,

$$\log (10^4)(10^5) = \log (10^4) + \log (10^5)$$
$$= 4 + 5 = 9$$

The log of the product equals 9; therefore the product equals $10^9$.

For the following indicated products, compute the logs.

(a)  log (44) (51) = _____

(b)  log (685) (72) = _____

(c)  log (65) (7850) = _____

(d)  log (45) (421) (7850) = ____

----------------------------------------------------------------

[36] Products can be computed by calculating the log of a product, then find the antilog. The table of proportional parts is invaluable at this point. The product of two numbers, such as (75) (85), is computed in the following manner:

$$\log (75)(85) = \log 75 + \log 85$$
$$= 1.8751 + 1.9294$$
$$= 3.8045$$

Therefore $(75)(85) = 10^{3.8045}$, or, from the antilog, 6376. If this product is computed by long-hand multiplication, its value is found to be 6375. The apparent discrepancy is due to rounding in the evaluation of logs. However, answers generally will be accurate to the number of allowable significant figures. In this case the product has two significant figures and should be left as 6400. Use the above procedure to compute the following products.

(a)  (44) (51)
(b)  (685) (72)
(c)  (65) (7850)
(d)  (45) (421) (7850)

----------------------------------------------------------------

[37] All examples involving logs encountered thus far have dealt with numbers greater than 1. The use of logs is confined to all positive numbers, that is, numbers greater than zero. Now consider finding the log of a number whose value is greater than 0 and less than 1. As an example, the

log of 0.5 is found in the following manner. First, rewrite the number in scientific notation as $5 \times 10^{-1}$. Now compute the log of the product.

$$\log 5 \times 10^{-1} = \log 5 + \log 10^{-1}$$
$$= 0.6990 + (-1) = -0.301$$

Therefore $0.5 = 10^{-0.301}$.

Compute the following logs:

(a)  log 0.0065               (b)  log 0.0043               (c)  log 0.000675

- - - - - - - - - - - - - - - - - - - - - - - - - - - - - - - - - - - - - - - - - - - - - -

[38]  Finding the antilog in which the log is negative requires one more step than if the log is positive. Although several methods can be used for this procedure, we consider one method, indicated in the following example: Find the number whose log is $-2.1871$.

Let $x$ be the number in question. Therefore

$$\log x = -2.1871$$
$$x = 10^{-2.1871}$$

Since all log values in the table are positive, the log must be rewritten as the sum of two numbers of which one is an integral power of 10 and the other is greater than 0 but less than 1, their sum equaling the value of the log. For the above case, the log can be written

$$10^{-2.1871} = 10^{3-2.1871} \times 10^{-3}$$
$$= 10^{0.8129} \times 10^{-3}$$

In other words, what value can be added to $-3$, the next-higher negative number, to get $-2.1871$? The value of $x$ is the antilog of 0.8129 times $10^{-3}$: $6.50 \times 10^{-3}$.

Find the antilog of the following log:

(a)  $-1.6884$             (b)  $-3.6590$             (c)  $-4.8652$

- - - - - - - - - - - - - - - - - - - - - - - - - - - - - - - - - - - - - - - - - - - - - -

[39]  Division operations with logs are in a sense opposite to multiplication operations; that is, as the log of the product of two terms is the sum of the logs, so the log of the quotient of two terms is the difference of the logs. In general,

$$\log_{10} \frac{x}{y} = \log_{10} x - \log_{10} y$$

$$\log \frac{10^4}{10^2} = \log 10^4 - \log 10^2 = 4 - 2 = 2$$

$$\log \frac{4}{2} = \log 4 - \log 2$$

$$= 0.6021 - 0.3010 = 0.3011$$

Then $\frac{4}{2} = 10^{0.3011} = 2$.

Applying the above procedure, calculate the quotient for the following exercises.

(a) $\dfrac{4650}{321}$

(b) $\dfrac{69,500}{225}$

--------------------------------------------------------------------

[40] Now consider a division operation with logs in which the numerator is smaller than the denominator. As an example, the quotient 2/4 is calculated in the following manner.

$$\log \frac{2}{4} = \log 2 - \log 4$$

$$= 0.3010 - 0.6021$$

$$= -0.3011$$

Then

$$\frac{2}{4} = 10^{-0.3011}$$

$$= 10^{0.6989} \times 10^{-1}$$

The antilog of 0.6989 is 5 and the quotient of 2/4 is $5 \times 10^{-1}$, or 0.5. Calculate the following quotients by using logs.

(a) $\dfrac{425}{575}$

(b) $\dfrac{1650}{18,250}$

(c) $\dfrac{(465)\,(830)}{960}$

--------------------------------------------------------------------

[41] Last, we consider the use of logs for raising numbers to powers and for extracting roots of numbers. Raising numbers to powers greater than 2 or 3 becomes cumbersome and time-consuming if one does not use a calculator or logs. Logs are exponents and the rules for raising exponential terms to a power or root apply to logs. That is,

$$\log_{10} (N)^x = x \log_{10} N$$

With numbers, we have

$$\log_{10} (2)^5 = 5 \log_{10} 2$$

$$= 5(0.3010) = 1.5050$$

Then

$$(2)^5 = 10^{1.5050} = 32$$

As another example, find the value of $(25)^{2.6}$.

$$\log (25)^{2.6} = 2.6 \log 25$$

$$= 2.6(1.3979) = 3.6345$$

$$(25)^{2.6} = 10^{3.6345} = 4310$$

Using logs, raise the following numbers to the powers indicated.

(a) $(1250)^4$                    (b) $(21)^{3.4}$                    (c) $(145)^{8.67}$

----------------------------------------------------------------

[42]  Extracting roots with logs involves exactly the same operations as raising numbers to powers. For example, the cube root of 265 is found in the following manner:

$$\log (265)^{1/3} = \frac{1}{3} \log 265$$

$$= \frac{1}{3} (2.4232) = 0.8077$$

antilog of $0.8077 = 6.42$

Calculate the indicated roots.

(a) $(475)^{1/5}$                    (b) $(1430)^{2/5}$

----------------------------------------------------------------
Go to SELF-EVALUATION IV.
----------------------------------------------------------------


## SELF-EVALUATION IV

Complete the following self-evaluation of your skills in using logs for multiplication, division, raising numbers to powers, and extracting roots of numbers. Answers to these questions are on page 254. If one of your answers does not agree with the answer listed, refer to the frame whose number appears in brackets with the answer and rework the problems(s) in that frame.

1. Calculate the product of (250) (325) (460).
2. Calculate the quotient of 4850/2320.
3. Calculate the cube root of 4365.
4. Calculate the quotient of 275/865.
5. Evaluate $(117)^4$.


## ANSWERS FOR PROGRAMMED UNITS

**1.**

$40 = 4 \times 10 = 4 \times 10^1$

$400 = 4 \times 100 = 4 \times 10^2$

**2.**

$750 = 7.5 \times 100 = 7.5 \times 10^2$

$625 = 6.25 \times 100 = 6.25 \times 10^2$

-------------------------------        -------------------------------

**3.**

(a) $7700 = 7.7 \times 1000 = 7.7 \times 10^3$

(b) $8250 = 8.25 \times 1000 = 8.25 \times 10^3$

(c) $6255 = 6.255 \times 1000 = 6.255 \times 10^3$

- - - - - - - - - - - - - - - - - - - - - - - - - - - -

**4.**

Since 1,000,000,000 contains 9 zeros, the exponent of 10 is 9. In exponential notation 1,000,000,000 is written $1 \times 10^9$.

- - - - - - - - - - - - - - - - - - - - - - - - - - - -

**5.**

(a) $5^0 = 1$

(b) $100^0 = 1$

(c) $5^0 \times 10^0 = 1 \times 1 = 1$

(d) $a^0 \times 10^0 \times b^0 = 1 \times 1 \times 1 = 1$

- - - - - - - - - - - - - - - - - - - - - - - - - - - -

**6.**

(a) $7655 = 7.655 \times 10^3$

(b) $2,225,000,000 = 2.225 \times 10^9$

(c) $786,000 = 7.86 \times 10^5$

- - - - - - - - - - - - - - - - - - - - - - - - - - - -

**7.**

(a) $2250 = 2.25 \times 10^3$

(b) $60,200,000,000 = 6.02 \times 10^{10}$

(c) $5,575,000,000 = 5.575 \times 10^9$

- - - - - - - - - - - - - - - - - - - - - - - - - - - -

**8.**

(a) $7 \times 10^{-6}$

(b) $4.25 \times 10^{-5}$

(c) $6.08 \times 10^{-5}$

- - - - - - - - - - - - - - - - - - - - - - - - - - - -

**9.**

$0.000007 = 7 \times 10^{-6}$

$0.0000425 = 4.25 \times 10^{-5}$

- - - - - - - - - - - - - - - - - - - - - - - - - - - -

**10.**

No answer required.

- - - - - - - - - - - - - - - - - - - - - - - - - - - -

**11.**

(a) $3 \times 10^{-3}$

(b) $7.5 \times 10^{-3}$

(c) $2.354 \times 10^{-4}$

(d) $7.2 \times 10^{-6}$

- - - - - - - - - - - - - - - - - - - - - - - - - - - -

**12.**

(a) $23.5 \times 10^4 = 2.35 \times 10^5$

(b) $6.8 \times 10^{-4} = 68 \times 10^{-5}$

- - - - - - - - - - - - - - - - - - - - - - - - - - - -

**13.**

(a) $10^1 \cdot 10^5 = 10^{1+5} = 10^6$

(b) $10^3 \cdot 10^9 = 10^{3+9} = 10^{12}$

(c) $10^4 \cdot 10^{10} = 10^{4+10} = 10^{14}$

- - - - - - - - - - - - - - - - - - - - - - - - - - - -

**14.**

(a) $10^{-8} \cdot 10^{-10} = 10^{-8+(-10)} = 10^{-18}$

(b) $10^{-5} \cdot 10^{-3} = 10^{-5+(-3)} = 10^{-8}$

(c) $10^{-5} \cdot 10^{-5} = 10^{-5+(-5)} = 10^{-10}$

- - - - - - - - - - - - - - - - - - - - - - - - - - - -

**15.**

(a) $10^{-15} \cdot 10^{12} = 10^{-15+12} = 10^{-3}$

(b) $10^{-2} \cdot 10^{-3} \cdot 10^6 = 10^{-2+(-3)+6} = 10^{-5+6} = 10^1$

(c) $10^{14} \cdot 10^{-12} \cdot 10^3 = 10^{14+(-12)+3} = 10^5$

- - - - - - - - - - - - - - - - - - - - - - - - - - - -

**16.**

(a) $(3.2 \times 10^4)(2.0 \times 10^5) = (3.2)(2.0)(10^4)(10^5) = 6.4 \times 10^9$

(b) $(4.0 \times 10^6)(8.0 \times 10^{-5}) = (4.0)(8.0)(10^6)(10^{-5}) = 32 \times 10^1$ or $3.2 \times 10^2$

(c) $(8.0 \times 10^6)(9.1 \times 10^{-2}) =$
$(8.0)(9.1)(10^6)(10^{-2}) = 7.3 \times 10^5$

(d) $(2.0 \times 10^3)(3.0 \times 10^{-5})(4.0 \times 10^2) =$
$2.4 \times 10^1$.

--------------------------------------------------

**17.**
No answer required.

--------------------------------------------------

**18.**

(a) $\dfrac{10^4}{10^1} = 10^{4-1} = 10^3$

(b) $\dfrac{10^6}{10^2} = 10^{6-2} = 10^4$

(c) $\dfrac{10^5}{10^{-5}} = 10^{5-(-5)} = 10^{5+5} = 10^{10}$

(d) $\dfrac{10^{1.2}}{10^{2.4}} = 10^{1.2-2.4} = 10^{-1.2}$

--------------------------------------------------

**19.**

(a) $\dfrac{5.0 \times 10^4}{2.0 \times 10^2} = \dfrac{5.0}{2.0} \times \dfrac{10^4}{10^2} =$

$2.5 \times 10^{4-2} = 2.5 \times 10^2$

(b) $\dfrac{7.5 \times 10^{-1}}{3.8 \times 10^3} = \dfrac{7.5}{3.8} \times \dfrac{10^{-1}}{10^3} =$

$2.0 \times 10^{-1-3} = 2.0 \times 10^{-4}$

(c) $\dfrac{9.6 \times 10^{13}}{2.4 \times 10^{-12}} = \dfrac{9.6}{2.4} \times \dfrac{10^{13}}{10^{-12}} =$

$4.0 \times 10^{13-(-12)} = 4.0 \times 10^{25}$

--------------------------------------------------

**20.**

(a) $\dfrac{2.2 \times 10^{-2}}{6.6 \times 10^{-4}} = \dfrac{2.2}{6.6} \times \dfrac{10^{-2}}{10^{-4}} =$

$0.33 \times 10^2$ ; This quotient should be left as $3.3 \times 10^1$, derived as follows:

$(0.33)(10^1) \times \dfrac{10^2}{10^1} = 3.3 \times 10^1$

(b) $\dfrac{8.1 \times 10^{14}}{9.0 \times 10^{-15}} = \dfrac{8.1}{9.0} \times \dfrac{10^{14}}{10^{-15}} =$

$0.90 \times 10^{29}$ and is left as $9.0 \times 10^{28}$, derived from

$(0.90)(10^1) \times \dfrac{10^{29}}{10^1} = 9.0 \times 10^{28}$

(c) $\dfrac{1.42 \times 10^{-3}}{96.2 \times 10^4} = \dfrac{1.42}{96.2} \times \dfrac{10^{-3}}{10^4} =$

$0.0148 \times 10^{-7} = 1.48 \times 10^{-9}$

as derived from

$(0.0148)(10^2) \times \dfrac{10^{-7}}{10^2} = 1.48 \times 10^{-9}$

--------------------------------------------------

**Self-evaluation I Answers**
1. $7.07 \times 10^6$  [1 through 7]
2. 262,000  [6 and 7]
3. $7.85 \times 10^{-5}$  [8, 9, and 10]
4. $7 \times 10^{14}$  [16]
5. $7.3 \times 10^{-2}$  [19] and [20]
6. $8.9 \times 10^1$  [20]

--------------------------------------------------

**21.**
(a) $(10^2)^5 = 10^{(2)(5)} = 10^{10}$
(b) $(10^4)^{-2} = 10^{-8}$
(c) $(10^{1/2})^4 = 10^{4/2} = 10^2$
(d) $(10^{2.5})^2 = 10^{(2.5)(2)} = 10^5$

--------------------------------------------------

**22.**
(a) $(4.0 \times 10^2)^3 = (4.0)^3(10^2)^3 =$
$64 \times 10^6 = 6.4 \times 10^7$

(b) $(5.0 \times 10^5)^2 = (5.0)^2(10^5)^2 =$
$25 \times 10^{10} = 2.5 \times 10^{11}$

(c) $(2.50 \times 10^{-3})^3 = (2.50)^3(10^{-3})^3 =$
$15.6 \times 10^{-9} = 1.56 \times 10^{-8}$

--------------------------------------------------

**23.**

(a) $\sqrt{10^{-6}} = (10^{-6})^{1/2} = 10^{-6/2} = 10^{-3}$

(b) $\sqrt{10^4} = 10^{4/2} = 10^2$

(c) $\sqrt[3]{10^{-6}} = (10^{-6})^{1/3} = 10^{-6/3} = 10^{-2}$

(d) $\sqrt[5]{10^{-25}} = 10^{-5}$

- - - - - - - - - - - - - - - - - - - - - - - - - - - - - -

**24.**

(a) $\sqrt{10^5} = (10^5)^{1/2} = (1 \times 10^5)^{1/2} = (10 \times 10^4)^{1/2} = 3 \times 10^2$

(b) $\sqrt[3]{10^7} = (1 \times 10^7)^{1/3} = (10 \times 10^6)^{1/3} = (10)^{1/3} \times (10^6)^{1/3} = 2 \times 10^2$

(c) $\sqrt{10^7} = (1 \times 10^7)^{1/2} = (10 \times 10^6)^{1/2} = 3 \times 10^3$

(d) $\sqrt[3]{1.0 \times 10^8} = (1.0 \times 10^8)^{1/3} = (100 \times 10^6)^{1/3} = (100)^{1/3} \times (10^6)^{1/3} = 4.6 \times 10^2$

- - - - - - - - - - - - - - - - - - - - - - - - - - - - - -

**25.**

(a) $\sqrt{2500} = (25 \times 10^2)^{1/2} = 5.0 \times 10^1$

(b) $\sqrt[3]{1440} = (1.44 \times 10^3)^{1/3} = (1.44)^{1/3} \times (10^3)^{1/3} = 1.13 \times 10^1$

(c) $\sqrt{26,200} = (2.62 \times 10^4)^{1/2} = 1.62 \times 10^2$

(d) $\sqrt[3]{18,000} = (18 \times 10^3)^{1/3} = 2.6 \times 10^1$

- - - - - - - - - - - - - - - - - - - - - - - - - - - - - -

**26.**

(a) $(0.000045)^{1/2} = (45 \times 10^{-6})^{1/2} = 6.7 \times 10^{-3}$

(b) $(0.00030)^{1/2} = (3.0 \times 10^{-4})^{1/2} = 1.7 \times 10^{-2}$

(c) $(0.00061)^{1/3} = (610 \times 10^{-6})^{1/3} = 8.5 \times 10^{-2}$

(d) $(9.6 \times 10^{-16})^{1/3} = (960 \times 10^{-18})^{1/3} = 9.9 \times 10^{-6}$

- - - - - - - - - - - - - - - - - - - - - - - - - - - - - -

**27.**

No answer required.

- - - - - - - - - - - - - - - - - - - - - - - - - - - - - -

**Self-evaluation II Answers**

1. $(10^8)^3 = 10^{24}$  [21]
2. $(2.5 \times 10^4)^2 = (2.5)^2 \times (10^4)^2 = 6.2 \times 10^8$  [22]
3. $(25,000)^{1/3} = 2.9 \times 10^1$  [25]
4. $(36,800)^{1/2} = 1.92 \times 10^2$  [25]
5. $(0.000065)^{1/3} = 4.0 \times 10^{-2}$  [26]
6. $(0.000049)^{1/2} = 7.0 \times 10^{-3}$  [26]

- - - - - - - - - - - - - - - - - - - - - - - - - - - - - -

**28.**

(a) $\log 100,000 = \log 10^5 = 5$

(b) $\log 10,000 = \log 10^4 = 4$

(c) $\log 0.00001 = \log 10^{-5} = -5$

(d) $\log 0.000001 = \log 10^{-6} = -6$

- - - - - - - - - - - - - - - - - - - - - - - - - - - - - -

**29.**

(a) $10^2 - 175 - 10^3$     $\underline{2}$

(b) $10^0 - 7 - 10^1$     $\underline{0}$

(c) $10^3 - 1250 - 10^4$     $\underline{3}$

(d) $10^5 - 657,000 - 10^6$     $\underline{5}$

- - - - - - - - - - - - - - - - - - - - - - - - - - - - - -

**30.**

(a) $3500 = 3.5 \times 10^3$
The characteristic is 3. The mantissa is .5441.
$\log 3500 = 3.5441$ or $10^{3.5441} = 3500$

(b) $27,000 = 2.7 \times 10^4$
Characteristic = 4; mantissa = .4314.
$\log 27,000 = 4.4314$ or $10^{4.4314} = 27,000$

(c) $450,000 = 4.5 \times 10^5$
Characteristic = 5; mantissa = .6532.
$\log 450,000 = 5.6532$ or $10^{5.6532} = 450,000$

- - - - - - - - - - - - - - - - - - - - - - - - - - - - - -

**31.**

(a) $374 = 3.74 \times 10^2$
Characteristic = 2; mantissa = .5729
$\log 374 = 2.5729$

- - - - - - - - - - - - - - - - - - - - - - - - - - - - - -

(b) $2410 = 2.41 \times 10^3$

Characteristic = 3; mantissa = .3820
$\log 2410 = 3.3820$ or $10^{3.3820} = 2410$

(c) $1270 = 1.27 \times 10^3$
Characteristic = 3; mantissa = .1038
$\log 1270 = 3.1038$ or $10^{3.1038} = 1270$

(d) $\log 575{,}000 = 5.7597$

- - - - - - - - - - - - - - - - - - - - - - - - - - - - -

**32.**

(a) $\log x = 4.8722$ or $x = 10^{4.8722}$

$10^{.8722} = 7.45$ so $10^{4.8722} = \underset{\text{4 places}}{7\underline{45}00.}$

(b) $\log x = 3.7745$ or $x = 10^{3.7745}$

$10^{.7745} = 5.95$ so $10^{3.7745} = \underset{\text{3 places}}{5\underline{95}0.}$

(c) $\log x = 2.4955$ or $x = 10^{2.4955}$

$10^{.4955} = 3.13$ so $10^{2.4955} = \underset{\text{2 places}}{3\underline{13}.}$

- - - - - - - - - - - - - - - - - - - - - - - - - - - - -

**33.**

(a) $\log 69340 = 4.8407 + .0002 = 4.8409$

(b) $\log 7469 = 3.8727 + .0005 = 3.8732$

- - - - - - - - - - - - - - - - - - - - - - - - - - - - -

**34.**

(a) From the tabled values, 8989 corresponds to $7920 + 3 = 7923$. The characteristic is 1; therefore $x = 79.23$.

(b) $x = 6010 + 3; 601.3$

(c) $x = 6960 + 5; 6965$

- - - - - - - - - - - - - - - - - - - - - - - - - - - - -

**Self-evaluation III Answers**

1. $-5$ [27]
2. 2.0969 [28]
3. 355 [32]
4. 92.83 [34]
5. 1.7542 [33]

- - - - - - - - - - - - - - - - - - - - - - - - - - - - -

**35.**

(a) $\log (44)(51) = \log 44 + \log 51$
$\log 44 = 1.6435$
$\log 51 = 1.7076$
$\log (44)(51) = 3.3511$

(b) $\log (685)(72) = \log 685 + \log 72$
$\log 685 = 2.8357$
$\log 72 = 1.8573$
$\log (685)(72) = 4.6930$

(c) $\log (65)(7850) = \log 65 + \log 7850$
$\log 65 = 1.8129$
$\log 7850 = 3.8949$
$\log (65)(7850) = 5.7078$

(d) $\log (45)(421)(7850) = \log 45 +$
$\quad \log 421 + \log 7850$
$\log 45 = 1.6532$
$\log 421 = 2.6243$
$\log 7850 = 3.8949$
$\log (45)(421)(7850) = 8.1724$

- - - - - - - - - - - - - - - - - - - - - - - - - - - - -

**36.**

(a) $\log (44)(51) = \log 44 + \log 51$
$\qquad\qquad = 1.6434 + 1.7076$
$\qquad\qquad = 3.3510$

Then

$\qquad (44)(51) = 10^{3.3510} = 2.2 \times 10^3$

(b) $\log (685)(72) = \log 685 + \log 72$
$\qquad\qquad = 2.8357 + 1.8573$
$\qquad\qquad = 4.6930$

Then

$\qquad (685)(72) = 10^{4.6930} = 4.9 \times 10^4$

(c) $\log (65)(7850) = \log 65 + \log 7850$
$\qquad\qquad = 1.8129 + 3.8949$
$\qquad\qquad = 5.7078$

Then

$\qquad (65)(7850) = 10^{5.7078} = 5.1 \times 10^5$

(d) $\log (45)(421)(7850) =$
$\quad \log 45 + \log 421 + \log 7850 =$
$\quad 1.6532 + 2.6243 + 3.8949 =$
$\quad 8.1724$

Then

$\qquad (45)(421)(7850) = 10^{8.1724}$
$\qquad\qquad\qquad\qquad = 1.5 \times 10^8$

**37.**

(a) $\log 0.0065 = \log 6.5 \times 10^{-3}$
$= \log 6.5 + \log 10^{-3}$
$= 0.8129 + (-3)$
$= -2.1871$

(b) $\log 0.0043 = \log 4.3 \times 10^{-3}$
$= \log 4.3 + \log 10^{-3}$
$= 0.6335 + (-3)$
$= -2.3665$

(c) $\log 0.000675 = \log 6.75 \times 10^{-4}$
$= \log 6.75 + \log 10^{-4}$
$= 0.8293 + (-4)$
$= -3.1707$

- - - - - - - - - - - - - - - - - - - - - - - - - - - - - -

**38.**

(a) $x = 10^{-1.6884}$
$= 10^{0.3410} \times 10^{-2}$
$= 2.05 \times 10^{-2}$

(b) $x = 10^{-3.6590}$
$= 10^{0.3410} \times 10^{-4}$
$= 2.19 \times 10^{-4}$

(c) $x = 10^{-4.8652}$
$= 10^{0.1348} \times 10^{-5}$
$= 1.36 \times 10^{-5}$

- - - - - - - - - - - - - - - - - - - - - - - - - - - - - -

**39.**

(a) $\log \dfrac{4650}{321} = \log 4650 - \log 321$
$= 3.6675 - 2.5065$
$= 1.1610$

Then

$\dfrac{4650}{321} = 10^{1.1610} = 14.5$

(b) $\log \dfrac{69,500}{225} = \log 69,500 - \log 225$
$= 4.8420 - 2.3522$
$= 2.4898$

Then

$\dfrac{69,500}{225} = 10^{2.4898} = 309$

- - - - - - - - - - - - - - - - - - - - - - - - - - - - - -

**40.**

(a) $\log \dfrac{425}{575} = \log 425 - \log 575$
$= 2.6284 - 2.7597$
$= -0.1313$

Then

$\dfrac{425}{575} = 10^{-0.1313} = 10^{0.8687} \times 10^{-1}$

antilog of $0.8687 = 7.391$

$\dfrac{425}{575} = 7.39 \times 10^{-1}$

(b) $\log \dfrac{1650}{18,250} = \log 1650 - \log 18,250$
$= 3.2175 - 4.2613$
$= -1.0438$

$\dfrac{1650}{18,250} = 10^{-1.0438}$

antilog $= 9.04 \times 10^{-2}$

(c) $\log \dfrac{(465)(830)}{960} = \log 465 + \log 830 -$
$\log 960$
$= 2.6675 + 2.9191 -$
$2.9823$
$= 2.6043$
antilog $= 402$

- - - - - - - - - - - - - - - - - - - - - - - - - - - - - -

**41.**

(a) $\log(1250)^4 = 4 \log 1250$
$= 4(3.0969) = 12.3876$
$(1250)^4 = 2.44 \times 10^{12}$

(b) $\log(21)^{3.4} = 3.4 \log 21$
$= 3.4(1.3222) = 4.4955$
$(21)^{3.4} = 3.1 \times 10^4$

(c) $(145)^{8.67} = 5.48 \times 10^{18}$

- - - - - - - - - - - - - - - - - - - - - - - - - - - - - -

**42.**

(a) $\log(475)^{1/5} = \dfrac{1}{5} \log 475$

$= \dfrac{1}{5}(2.6767) = 0.5353$

antilog of $0.5353 = 3.43$

(b) $\log(1430)^{2/5} = \frac{2}{5} \log 1430$

$$= \frac{2}{5}(3.1553) = 1.2621$$

antilog of $1.2621 = 18.3$

- - - - - - - - - - - - - - - - - - - - - - - - - - - - - - - -

**Self-evaluation IV Answers**
1. $3.7 \times 10^7$  [36]
2. 2.09  [37]
3. 16.34  [42]
4. 0.3179  [38 and 39]
5. $1.87 \times 10^8$  [41]

- - - - - - - - - - - - - - - - - - - - - - - - - - - - - - - -

# Appendices

## Appendix C
### Units of Measurement and Conversion Factors

#### Prefixes

| | |
|---|---|
| mega (M) | $1,000,000 \times$ or $10^6 \times$ |
| kilo (k) | $1000 \times$ or $10^3 \times$ |
| hecto (h) | $100 \times$ or $10^2 \times$ |
| deka (da) | $10 \times$ or $10^1 \times$ |
| deci (d) | $0.1 \times$ or $10^{-1} \times$ |
| centi (c) | $0.01 \times$ or $10^{-2} \times$ |
| milli (m) | $0.001 \times$ or $10^{-3} \times$ |
| micro ($\mu$) | $0.00001 \times$ or $10^{-6} \times$ |
| nano (n) | $0.000000001 \times$ or $10^{-9} \times$ |
| pico (p) | $0.000000000001 \times$ or $10^{-12} \times$ |

#### Base Units

| *Measurement* | *Unit* | *Symbol* |
|---|---|---|
| Length | meter | m |
| Mass | kilogram | kg |
| Time | second | sec |
| Electric current | ampere | A |
| Temperature | kelvin | K |
| Amount of substance | mole | mol |
| Luminous intensity | candela | cd |

Length

2.54 cm = 1 in.          1 m = 39.37 in.
1 km = 0.6215 mile   or   1 mile = 1.609 km

Volume

1 liter = 1.057 qt      or   1 qt = 0.946 liter
1 liter = 0.0353 ft$^3$    or   1 ft$^3$ = 28.32 liters
1 ml = 1 cm$^3$ = 0.001 $\ell$
1 m$^3$ = 10$^3$ $\ell$ = 10$^6$ cm$^3$ = 10$^9$ mm$^3$

Mass

453.6 g = 1 lb   or   1 g = 0.00220 lb
1 kg = 2.20 lb          28.35 g = 1 oz
1 metric ton = 10$^3$ kg $\simeq$ 2200 lb

Derived Units

Force ($f$) = mass $\times$ acceleration

$$= \text{kg} \times \frac{\text{m}}{\text{sec}^2} = \text{newton (N)}$$

$$= \text{g} \times \frac{\text{cm}}{\text{sec}^2} = \text{dyne}$$

Momentum = mass $\times$ velocity

$$= \text{kg} \times \frac{\text{m}}{\text{sec}}$$

Work = force $\times$ distance
   = N $\times$ m = (kg $\times$ m sec$^{-2}$) $\times$ m = joule (J)
   = dyne $\times$ cm = (g $\times$ cm sec$^{-2}$) $\times$ cm = erg

Energy units are equivalent to units of work.

Kinetic energy (KE) = $\frac{1}{2}$ mv$^2$

$$= \text{kg} \times \left(\frac{\text{m}}{\text{sec}}\right)^2 = \text{joule}$$

$$= \text{g} \times \left(\frac{\text{cm}}{\text{sec}}\right)^2 = \text{erg}$$

Potential energy (PE) = mass $\times$ acceleration $\times$ distance

$$= \text{kg} \times \frac{\text{m}}{(\text{sec})^2} \times \text{m} = \text{joule}$$

$$= \text{g} \times \frac{\text{cm}}{(\text{sec})^2} \times \text{cm} = \text{erg}$$

$$\text{Pressure} = \frac{\text{force}}{\text{area}} = \frac{N}{m^2} = \text{Pascal(Pa)}$$

Constants; Conversions

Atomic mass unit (amu) $= 1.6605655 \times 10^{-27}$ kg

Electron mass $9.1095 \times 10^{-31}$ kg $= 0.0005486$ amu

Neutron mass $1.6749 \times 10^{-27}$ kg $= 1.00866$ amu

Proton mass $1.6726 \times 10^{-27}$ kg $= 1.00728$ amu

Gas constant $(R)$ $0.082057 \dfrac{\ell \text{ atm}}{\text{mol K}} = 8.3143 \dfrac{J}{\text{mol K}} = 8314 \dfrac{\ell \text{ Pa}}{\text{mol K}}$

Joule $= 0.2390$ calorie or cal $= 4.184$ J

Temperature conversions

$$°C = \frac{5}{9}(°F - 32); \quad °F = \frac{9}{5}°C + 32; \quad K = °C + 273$$

Planck's constant $(h) = 6.626 \times 10^{-34}$ J s $= 6.626 \times 10^{-27}$ erg sec
$$= 1.584 \times 10^{-37} \text{ kcal sec}$$
Speed of light $(c) = 2.9979 \times 10^8$ m/sec $= 2.9979 \times 10^{10}$ cm/sec

# Appendix E

## Solubility Product Constants

| Substance | $K_{sp}$ at 25° | Substance | $K_{sp}$ at 25° |
|---|---|---|---|
| Aluminum | | FeS | $1 \times 10^{-19}$ |
| $Al(OH)_3$ | $1.9 \times 10^{-33}$ | $Fe(OH)_3$ | $1.1 \times 10^{-36}$ |
| Barium | | Lead | |
| $BaCO_3$ | $8.1 \times 10^{-9}$ | $Pb(OH)_2$ | $2.8 \times 10^{-16}$ |
| $BaC_2O_4 \cdot 2H_2O$ | $1.1 \times 10^{-7}$ | $PbF_2$ | $3.7 \times 10^{-8}$ |
| $BaSO_4$ | $1.08 \times 10^{-10}$ | $PbCl_2$ | $1.7 \times 10^{-5}$ |
| $BaCrO_4$ | $2 \times 10^{-10}$ | $PbBr_2$ | $6.3 \times 10^{-6}$ |
| $BaF_2$ | $1.7 \times 10^{-6}$ | $PbI_2$ | $8.7 \times 10^{-9}$ |
| $Ba(OH)_2 \cdot 8H_2O$ | $5.0 \times 10^{-3}$ | $PbCO_3$ | $1.5 \times 10^{-13}$ |
| $Ba_3(PO_4)_2$ | $1.3 \times 10^{-29}$ | PbS | $8.4 \times 10^{-28}$ |
| $Ba_3(AsO_4)_2$ | $1.1 \times 10^{-13}$ | $PbCrO_4$ | $1.8 \times 10^{-14}$ |
| Bismuth | | $PbSO_4$ | $1.8 \times 10^{-8}$ |
| BiO(OH) | $1 \times 10^{-12}$ | $Pb_3(PO_4)_2$ | $3 \times 10^{-44}$ |
| BiOCl | $7 \times 10^{-9}$ | Magnesium | |
| $Bi_2S_3$ | $1.6 \times 10^{-72}$ | $Mg(OH)_2$ | $1.5 \times 10^{-11}$ |
| Cadmium | | $MgCO_3 \cdot 3H_2O$ | $ca.\ 1 \times 10^{-5}$ |
| $Cd(OH)_2$ | $1.2 \times 10^{-14}$ | $MgNH_4PO_4$ | $2.5 \times 10^{-13}$ |
| CdS | $3.6 \times 10^{-29}$ | $MgF_2$ | $6.4 \times 10^{-9}$ |
| $CdCO_3$ | $2.5 \times 10^{-14}$ | $MgC_2O_4$ | $8.6 \times 10^{-5}$ |
| Calcium | | Manganese | |
| $Ca(OH)_2$ | $7.9 \times 10^{-6}$ | $Mn(OH)_2$ | $4.5 \times 10^{-14}$ |
| $CaCO_3$ | $4.8 \times 10^{-9}$ | $MnCO_3$ | $8.8 \times 10^{-11}$ |
| $CaSO_4 \cdot 2H_2O$ | $2.4 \times 10^{-5}$ | MnS | $5.6 \times 10^{-16}$ |
| $CaC_2O_4 \cdot H_2O$ | $2.27 \times 10^{-9}$ | Mercury | |
| $Ca_3(PO_4)_2$ | $1 \times 10^{-25}$ | $Hg_2O \cdot H_2O$ | $1.6 \times 10^{-23}$ |
| $CaHPO_4$ | $5 \times 10^{-6}$ | $Hg_2Cl_2$ | $1.1 \times 10^{-18}$ |
| $CaF_2$ | $3.9 \times 10^{-11}$ | $Hg_2Br_2$ | $1.26 \times 10^{-22}$ |
| Chromium | | $Hg_2I_2$ | $4.5 \times 10^{-29}$ |
| $Cr(OH)_3$ | $6.7 \times 10^{-31}$ | $Hg_2CO_3$ | $9 \times 10^{-17}$ |
| Cobalt | | $Hg_2SO_4$ | $6.2 \times 10^{-7}$ |
| $Co(OH)_2$ | $2 \times 10^{-16}$ | $Hg_2S$ | $1 \times 10^{-45}$ |
| $CoS(\alpha)$ | $5.9 \times 10^{-21}$ | $Hg_2CrO_4$ | $2 \times 10^{-9}$ |
| $CoS(\beta)$ | $8.7 \times 10^{-23}$ | HgS | $3 \times 10^{-53}$ |
| $CoCO_3$ | $1.0 \times 10^{-12}$ | Nickel | |
| $Co(OH)_3$ | $2.5 \times 10^{-43}$ | $Ni(OH)_2$ | $1.6 \times 10^{-14}$ |
| Copper | | $NiCO_3$ | $1.36 \times 10^{-7}$ |
| CuCl | $1.85 \times 10^{-7}$ | $NiS(\alpha)$ | $3 \times 10^{-21}$ |
| CuBr | $5.3 \times 10^{-9}$ | $NiS(\beta)$ | $1 \times 10^{-26}$ |
| CuI | $5.1 \times 10^{-12}$ | $NiS(\gamma)$ | $2 \times 10^{-28}$ |
| CuCNS | $4 \times 10^{-14}$ | Potassium | |
| $Cu_2S$ | $1.6 \times 10^{-48}$ | $KClO_4$ | $1.07 \times 10^{-2}$ |
| $Cu(OH)_2$ | $5.6 \times 10^{-20}$ | $K_2PtCl_6$ | $1.1 \times 10^{-5}$ |
| CuS | $8.7 \times 10^{-36}$ | $KHC_4H_4O_6$ | $3 \times 10^{-4}$ |
| $CuCO_3$ | $1.37 \times 10^{-10}$ | Silver | |
| Iron | | $\frac{1}{2}Ag_2O(Ag^+ + OH^-)$ | $2 \times 10^{-8}$ |
| $Fe(OH)_2$ | $7.9 \times 10^{-15}$ | AgCl | $1.8 \times 10^{-10}$ |
| $FeCO_3$ | $2.11 \times 10^{-11}$ | AgBr | $3.3 \times 10^{-13}$ |

| Substance | $K_{sp}$ at 25° | Substance | $K_{sp}$ at 25° |
|---|---|---|---|
| AgI | $1.5 \times 10^{-16}$ | Thallium | |
| AgCN | $1.2 \times 10^{-16}$ | TlCl | $1.9 \times 10^{-4}$ |
| AgCNS | $1.0 \times 10^{-12}$ | TlCNS | $5.8 \times 10^{-4}$ |
| $Ag_2S$ | $1.0 \times 10^{-51}$ | $Tl_2S$ | $1.2 \times 10^{-24}$ |
| $Ag_2CO_3$ | $8.2 \times 10^{-12}$ | $Tl(OH)_3$ | $1.5 \times 10^{-44}$ |
| $Ag_2CrO_4$ | $9 \times 10^{-12}$ | Tin | |
| $Ag_4Fe(CN)_6$ | $1.55 \times 10^{-41}$ | $Sn(OH)_2$ | $5 \times 10^{-26}$ |
| $Ag_2SO_4$ | $1.18 \times 10^{-5}$ | SnS | $8 \times 10^{-29}$ |
| $Ag_3PO_4$ | $1.8 \times 10^{-18}$ | $Sn(OH)_4$ | $ca. 1 \times 10^{-56}$ |
| Strontium | | Zinc | |
| $Sr(OH)_2 \cdot 8H_2O$ | $3.2 \times 10^{-4}$ | $ZnCO_3$ | $6 \times 10^{-11}$ |
| $SrCO_3$ | $9.42 \times 10^{-10}$ | $Zn(OH)_2$ | $4.5 \times 10^{-17}$ |
| $SrCrO_4$ | $3.6 \times 10^{-5}$ | ZnS | $1.1 \times 10^{-21}$ |
| $SrSO_4$ | $2.8 \times 10^{-7}$ | | |
| $SrC_2O_4 \cdot H_2O$ | $5.61 \times 10^{-8}$ | | |

# Appendix F

## Association (Formation) Constants for Complex Ions

| Equilibrium | $K_f$ |
|---|---|
| $Al^{3+} + 6F^- \rightleftharpoons [AlF_6]^{3-}$ | $5 \times 10^{23}$ |
| $Cd^{2+} + 4NH_3 \rightleftharpoons [Cd(NH_3)_4]^{2+}$ | $4.0 \times 10^6$ |
| $Cd^{2+} + 4CN^- \rightleftharpoons [Cd(CN)_4]^{2-}$ | $1.3 \times 10^{17}$ |
| $Co^{2+} + 6NH_3 \rightleftharpoons [Co(NH_3)_6]^{2+}$ | $8.3 \times 10^4$ |
| $Co^{3+} + 6NH_3 \rightleftharpoons [Co(NH_3)_6]^{3+}$ | $4.5 \times 10^{33}$ |
| $Cu^+ + 2CN^- \rightleftharpoons [Cu(CN)_2]^-$ | $1 \times 10^{16}$ |
| $Cu^{2+} + 4NH_3 \rightleftharpoons [Cu(NH_3)_4]^{2+}$ | $1.2 \times 10^{12}$ |
| $Fe^{2+} + 6CN^- \rightleftharpoons [Fe(CN)_6]^{4-}$ | $1 \times 10^{37}$ |
| $Fe^{3+} + 6CN^- \rightleftharpoons [Fe(CN)_6]^{3-}$ | $1 \times 10^{44}$ |
| $Fe^{3+} + 6SCN^- \rightleftharpoons [Fe(NCS)_6]^{3-}$ | $3.2 \times 10^3$ |
| $Hg^{2+} + 4Cl^- \rightleftharpoons [HgCl_4]^{2-}$ | $1.2 \times 10^{15}$ |
| $Ni^{2+} + 6NH_3 \rightleftharpoons [Ni(NH_3)_6]^{2+}$ | $1.8 \times 10^8$ |
| $Ag^+ + 2Cl^- \rightleftharpoons [AgCl_2]^-$ | $2.5 \times 10^5$ |
| $Ag^+ + 2CN^- \rightleftharpoons [Ag(CN)_2]^-$ | $1 \times 10^{20}$ |
| $Ag^+ + 2NH_3 \rightleftharpoons [Ag(NH_3)_2]^+$ | $1.6 \times 10^7$ |
| $Zn^{2+} + 4CN^- \rightleftharpoons [Zn(CN)_4]^{2-}$ | $1 \times 10^{19}$ |
| $Zn^{2+} + 4OH^- \rightleftharpoons [Zn(OH)_4]^{2-}$ | $2.9 \times 10^{15}$ |

# Appendix G

## Ionization Constants of Weak Acids

| Acid | Formula | $K_i$ at 25° |
|------|---------|--------------|
| Acetic | HOAc ($CH_3COOH$) | $1.8 \times 10^{-5}$ |
| Arsenic | $H_3AsO_4$ | $4.8 \times 10^{-3}$ |
| | $H_2AsO_4^-$ | $1 \times 10^{-7}$ |
| | $HAsO_4^{2-}$ | $1 \times 10^{-13}$ |
| Arsenous | $H_3AsO_3$ | $5.8 \times 10^{-10}$ |
| Boric | $H_3BO_3$ | $5.8 \times 10^{-10}$ |
| Carbonic | $H_2CO_3$ | $4.3 \times 10^{-7}$ |
| | $HCO_3^-$ | $7 \times 10^{-11}$ |
| Cyanic | HCNO | $3.46 \times 10^{-4}$ |
| Formic | HCOOH | $1.8 \times 10^{-4}$ |
| Hydrazoic | $HN_3$ | $1 \times 10^{-4}$ |
| Hydrocyanic | HCN | $4 \times 10^{-10}$ |
| Hydrofluoric | HF | $7.2 \times 10^{-4}$ |
| Hydrogen peroxide | $H_2O_2$ | $2.4 \times 10^{-12}$ |
| Hydrogen selenide | $H_2Se$ | $1.7 \times 10^{-4}$ |
| | $HSe^-$ | $1 \times 10^{-10}$ |
| Hydrogen sulfate ion | $HSO_4^-$ | $1.2 \times 10^{-2}$ |
| Hydrogen sulfide | $H_2S$ | $1.0 \times 10^{-7}$ |
| | $HS^-$ | $1.3 \times 10^{-13}$ |
| Hydrogen telluride | $H_2Te$ | $2.3 \times 10^{-3}$ |
| | $HTe^-$ | $1 \times 10^{-5}$ |
| Hypobromous | HBrO | $2 \times 10^{-9}$ |
| Hypochlorous | HClO | $3.5 \times 10^{-8}$ |
| Nitrous | $HNO_2$ | $4.5 \times 10^{-4}$ |
| Oxalic | $H_2C_2O_4$ | $5.9 \times 10^{-2}$ |
| | $HC_2O_4^-$ | $6.4 \times 10^{-5}$ |
| Phosphoric | $H_3PO_4$ | $7.5 \times 10^{-3}$ |
| | $H_2PO_4^-$ | $6.2 \times 10^{-8}$ |
| | $HPO_4^{2-}$ | $3.6 \times 10^{-13}$ |
| Phosphorous | $H_3PO_3$ | $1.6 \times 10^{-2}$ |
| | $H_2PO_3^-$ | $7 \times 10^{-7}$ |
| Sulfurous | $H_2SO_3$ | $1.2 \times 10^{-2}$ |
| | $HSO_3^-$ | $6.2 \times 10^{-8}$ |

# Appendix H

## Ionization Constants of Weak Bases

| Base | Ionization Equation | $K_i$ at 25° |
|------|---------------------|--------------|
| Ammonia | $NH_3 + H_2O \rightleftharpoons NH_4^+ + OH^-$ | $1.8 \times 10^{-5}$ |
| Dimethylamine | $(CH_3)_2NH + H_2O \rightleftharpoons (CH_3)_2NH_2^+ + OH^-$ | $7.4 \times 10^{-4}$ |
| Methylamine | $CH_3NH_2 + H_2O \rightleftharpoons CH_3NH_3^+ + OH^-$ | $4.4 \times 10^{-4}$ |
| Phenylamine (aniline) | $C_6H_5NH_2 + H_2O \rightleftharpoons C_6H_5NH_3^+ + OH^-$ | $4.6 \times 10^{-10}$ |
| Trimethylamine | $(CH_3)_3N + H_2O \rightleftharpoons (CH_3)_3NH^+ + OH^-$ | $7.4 \times 10^{-5}$ |

# Appendix I

## Standard Electrode (Reduction) Potentials

| Half-Reactions | $E°$, volts |
|---|---|
| $Li^+ + e^- \longrightarrow Li$ | $-3.09$ |
| $K^+ + e^- \longrightarrow K$ | $-2.925$ |
| $Rb^+ + e^- \longrightarrow Rb$ | $-2.925$ |
| $Ra^{2+} + 2e^- \longrightarrow Ra$ | $-2.92$ |
| $Ba^{2+} + 2e^- \longrightarrow Ba$ | $-2.90$ |
| $Sr^{2+} + 2e^- \longrightarrow Sr$ | $-2.89$ |
| $Ca^{2+} + 2e^- \longrightarrow Ca$ | $-2.87$ |
| $Na^+ + e^- \longrightarrow Na$ | $-2.714$ |
| $La^{3+} + 3e^- \longrightarrow La$ | $-2.52$ |
| $Ce^{3+} + 3e^- \longrightarrow Ce$ | $-2.48$ |
| $Nd^{3+} + 3e^- \longrightarrow Nd$ | $-2.44$ |
| $Sm^{3+} + 3e^- \longrightarrow Sm$ | $-2.41$ |
| $Gd^{3+} + 3e^- \longrightarrow Gd$ | $-2.40$ |
| $Mg^{2+} + 2e^- \longrightarrow Mg$ | $-2.37$ |
| $Y^{3+} + 3e^- \longrightarrow Y$ | $-2.37$ |
| $Am^{3+} + 3e^- \longrightarrow Am$ | $-2.32$ |
| $Lu^{3+} + 3e^- \longrightarrow Lu$ | $-2.25$ |
| $\frac{1}{2}H_2 + e^- \longrightarrow H^-$ | $-2.25$ |
| $Sc^{3+} + 3e^- \longrightarrow Sc$ | $-2.08$ |
| $[AlF_6]^{3-} + 3e^- \longrightarrow Al + 6F^-$ | $-2.07$ |
| $Pu^{3+} + 3e^- \longrightarrow Pu$ | $-2.07$ |
| $Th^{4+} + 4e^- \longrightarrow Th$ | $-1.90$ |
| $Np^{3+} + 3e^- \longrightarrow Np$ | $-1.86$ |
| $Be^{2+} + 2e^- \longrightarrow Be$ | $-1.85$ |
| $U^{3+} + 3e^- \longrightarrow U$ | $-1.80$ |
| $Hf^{4+} + 4e^- \longrightarrow Hf$ | $-1.70$ |
| $SiO_3^{2-} + 3H_2O + 4e^- \longrightarrow Si + 6OH^-$ | $-1.70$ |
| $Al^{3+} + 3e^- \longrightarrow Al$ | $-1.66$ |
| $Ti^{2+} + 2e^- \longrightarrow Ti$ | $-1.63$ |
| $Zr^{4+} + 4e^- \longrightarrow Zr$ | $-1.53$ |
| $ZnS + 2e^- \longrightarrow Zn + S^{2-}$ | $-1.44$ |
| $Cr(OH)_3 + 3e^- \longrightarrow Cr + 3OH^-$ | $-1.3$ |
| $[Zn(CN)_4]^{2-} + 2e^- \longrightarrow Zn + 4CN^-$ | $-1.26$ |
| $Zn(OH)_2 + 2e^- \longrightarrow Zn + 2OH^-$ | $-1.245$ |
| $[Zn(OH)_4]^{2-} + 2e^- \longrightarrow Zn + 4OH^-$ | $-1.216$ |
| $CdS + 2e^- \longrightarrow Cd + S^{2-}$ | $-1.21$ |
| $[Cr(OH)_4]^- + 3e^- \longrightarrow Cr + 4OH^-$ | $-1.2$ |
| $[SiF_6]^{2-} + 4e^- \longrightarrow Si + 6F^-$ | $-1.2$ |
| $V^{2+} + 2e^- \longrightarrow V$ | $ca.\ -1.18$ |
| $Mn^{2+} + 2e^- \longrightarrow Mn$ | $-1.18$ |
| $[Cd(CN)_4]^{2-} + 2e^- \longrightarrow Cd + 4CN^-$ | $-1.03$ |
| $[Zn(NH_3)_4]^{2+} + 2e^- \longrightarrow Zn + 4NH_3$ | $-1.03$ |
| $FeS + 2e^- \longrightarrow Fe + S^{2-}$ | $-1.01$ |
| $PbS + 2e^- \longrightarrow Pb + S^{2-}$ | $-0.95$ |
| $SnS + 2e^- \longrightarrow Sn + S^{2-}$ | $-0.94$ |
| $Cr^{2+} + 2e^- \longrightarrow Cr$ | $-0.91$ |
| $Fe(OH)_2 + 2e^- \longrightarrow Fe + 2OH^-$ | $-0.877$ |
| $SiO_2 + 4H^+ + 4e^- \longrightarrow Si + 2H_2O$ | $-0.86$ |
| $NiS + 2e^- \longrightarrow Ni + S^{2-}$ | $-0.83$ |

## Standard Electrode (Reduction) Potentials (continued)

| Half-Reactions | $E°$, volts |
|---|---|
| $2H_2O + 2e^- \longrightarrow H_2 + 2OH^-$ | $-0.828$ |
| $Zn^{2+} + 2e^- \longrightarrow Zn$ | $-0.763$ |
| $Cr^{3+} + 3e^- \longrightarrow Cr$ | $-0.74$ |
| $HgS + 2e^- \longrightarrow Hg + S^{2-}$ | $-0.72$ |
| $[Cd(NH_3)_4]^{2+} + 2e^- \longrightarrow Cd + 4NH_3$ | $-0.597$ |
| $Ga^{3+} + 3e^- \longrightarrow Ga$ | $-0.53$ |
| $S + 2e^- \longrightarrow S^{2-}$ | $-0.48$ |
| $[Ni(NH_3)_6]^{2+} + 2e^- \longrightarrow Ni + 6NH_3$ | $-0.47$ |
| $Fe^{2+} + 2e^- \longrightarrow Fe$ | $-0.440$ |
| $[Cu(CN)_2]^- + e^- \longrightarrow Cu + 2CN^-$ | $-0.43$ |
| $Cr^{3+} + e^- \longrightarrow Cr^{2+}$ | $-0.41$ |
| $Cd^{2+} + 2e^- \longrightarrow Cd$ | $-0.403$ |
| $Se + 2H^+ + 2e^- \longrightarrow H_2Se$ | $-0.40$ |
| $[Hg(CN)_4]^{2-} + 2e^- \longrightarrow Hg + 4CN^-$ | $-0.37$ |
| $ClO_4^- + H_2O + 2e^- \longrightarrow ClO_3^- + 2OH^-$ | $-0.36$ |
| $PbSO_4 + 2e^- \longrightarrow Pb + SO_4^{2-}$ | $-0.356$ |
| $In^{3+} + 3e^- \longrightarrow In$ | $-0.342$ |
| $[Ag(CN)_2]^- + e^- \longrightarrow Ag + 2CN^-$ | $-0.31$ |
| $Co^{2+} + 2e^- \longrightarrow Co$ | $-0.277$ |
| $[SnF_6]^{2-} + 4e^- \longrightarrow Sn + 6F^-$ | $-0.25$ |
| $Ni^{2+} + 2e^- \longrightarrow Ni$ | $-0.250$ |
| $Sn^{2+} + 2e^- \longrightarrow Sn$ | $-0.136$ |
| $CrO_4^{2-} + 4H_2O + 3e^- \longrightarrow Cr(OH)_3 + 5OH^-$ | $-0.13$ |
| $Pb^{2+} + 2e^- \longrightarrow Pb$ | $-0.126$ |
| $MnO_2 + 2H_2O + 2e^- \longrightarrow Mn(OH)_2 + 2OH^-$ | $-0.05$ |
| $[HgI_4]^{2-} + 2e^- \longrightarrow Hg + 4I^-$ | $-0.04$ |
| $2H^+ + 2e^- \longrightarrow H_2$ | $0.00$ |
| $NO_3^- + H_2O + 2e^- \longrightarrow NO_2^- + 2OH^-$ | $+0.01$ |
| $[Ag(S_2O_3)_2]^{3-} + e^- \longrightarrow Ag^+ + 2S_2O_3^{2-}$ | $+0.01$ |
| $[Co(NH_3)_6]^{3+} + e^- \longrightarrow [Co(NH_3)_6]^{2+}$ | $+0.1$ |
| $S + 2H^+ + 2e^- \longrightarrow H_2S$ | $+0.141$ |
| $Sn^{4+} + 2e^- \longrightarrow Sn^{2+}$ | $+0.15$ |
| $Cu^{2+} + e^- \longrightarrow Cu^+$ | $+0.153$ |
| $Co(OH)_3 + e^- \longrightarrow Co(OH)_2 + OH^-$ | $+0.17$ |
| $[HgBr_4]^{2-} + 2e^- \longrightarrow Hg + 4Br^-$ | $+0.21$ |
| $AgCl + e^- \longrightarrow Ag + Cl^-$ | $+0.222$ |
| $Hg_2Cl_2 + 2e^- \longrightarrow 2Hg + 2Cl^-$ | $+0.27$ |
| $ClO_3^- + H_2O + 2e^- \longrightarrow ClO_2^- + 2OH^-$ | $+0.33$ |
| $Cu^{2+} + 2e^- \longrightarrow Cu$ | $+0.337$ |
| $[Fe(CN)_6]^{3-} + e^- \longrightarrow [Fe(CN)_6]^{4-}$ | $+0.36$ |
| $[Ag(NH_3)_2]^+ + e^- \longrightarrow Ag + 2NH_3$ | $+0.373$ |
| $O_2 + 2H_2O + 4e^- \longrightarrow 4OH^-$ | $+0.401$ |
| $[RhCl_6]^{3-} + 3e^- \longrightarrow Rh + 6Cl^-$ | $+0.44$ |
| $Ag_2CrO_4 + 2e^- \longrightarrow 2Ag + CrO_4^{2-}$ | $+0.446$ |
| $NiO_2 + 2H_2O + 2e^- \longrightarrow Ni(OH)_2 + 2OH^-$ | $+0.49$ |
| $Cu^+ + e^- \longrightarrow Cu$ | $+0.521$ |
| $TeO_2 + 4H^+ + 4e^- \longrightarrow Te + 2H_2O$ | $+0.529$ |
| $I_2 + 2e^- \longrightarrow 2I^-$ | $+0.5355$ |
| $[PtBr_4]^{2-} + 2e^- \longrightarrow Pt + 4Br^-$ | $+0.58$ |
| $MnO_4^- + 2H_2O + 3e^- \longrightarrow MnO_2 + 4OH^-$ | $+0.588$ |
| $[PdCl_4]^{2-} + 2e^- \longrightarrow Pd + 4Cl^-$ | $+0.62$ |

| Half-Reactions | $E°$, volts |
|---|---|
| $ClO_2^- + H_2O + 2e^- \longrightarrow ClO^- + 2OH^-$ | $+0.66$ |
| $[PtCl_6]^{2-} + 2e^- \longrightarrow [PtCl_4]^{2-} + 2Cl^-$ | $+0.68$ |
| $O_2 + 2H^+ + 2e^- \longrightarrow H_2O_2$ | $+0.682$ |
| $[PtCl_4]^{2-} + 2e^- \longrightarrow Pt + 4Cl^-$ | $+0.73$ |
| $Fe^{3+} + e^- \longrightarrow Fe^{2+}$ | $+0.771$ |
| $Hg_2^{2+} + 2e^- \longrightarrow 2Hg$ | $+0.789$ |
| $Ag^+ + e^- \longrightarrow Ag$ | $+0.7991$ |
| $Hg^{2+} + 2e^- \longrightarrow Hg$ | $+0.854$ |
| $HO_2^- + H_2O + 2e^- \longrightarrow 3OH^-$ | $+0.88$ |
| $ClO^- + H_2O + 2e^- \longrightarrow Cl^- + 2OH^-$ | $+0.89$ |
| $2Hg^{2+} + 2e^- \longrightarrow Hg_2^{2+}$ | $+0.920$ |
| $NO_3^- + 3H^+ + 2e^- \longrightarrow HNO_2 + H_2O$ | $+0.94$ |
| $NO_3^- + 4H^+ + 3e^- \longrightarrow NO + H_2O$ | $+0.96$ |
| $Pd^{2+} + 2e^- \longrightarrow Pd$ | $+0.987$ |
| $Br_2(l) + 2e^- \longrightarrow 2Br^-$ | $+1.0652$ |
| $ClO_4^- + 2H^+ + 2e^- \longrightarrow ClO_3^- + H_2O$ | $+1.19$ |
| $Pt^{2+} + 2e^- \longrightarrow Pt$ | $ca. +1.2$ |
| $ClO_3^- + 3H^+ + 2e^- \longrightarrow HClO_2 + H_2O$ | $+1.21$ |
| $O_2 + 4H^+ + 4e^- \longrightarrow 2H_2O$ | $+1.23$ |
| $MnO_2 + 4H^+ + 2e^- \longrightarrow Mn^{2+} + 2H_2O$ | $+1.23$ |
| $Cr_2O_7^{2-} + 14H^+ + 6e^- \longrightarrow 2Cr^{3+} + 7H_2O$ | $+1.33$ |
| $Cl_2 + 2e^- \longrightarrow 2Cl^-$ | $+1.3595$ |
| $HClO + H^+ + 2e^- \longrightarrow Cl^- + H_2O$ | $+1.49$ |
| $Au^{3+} + 3e^- \longrightarrow Au$ | $+1.50$ |
| $MnO_4^- + 8H^+ + 5e^- \longrightarrow Mn^{2+} + 4H_2O$ | $+1.51$ |
| $Ce^{4+} + e^- \longrightarrow Ce^{3+}$ | $+1.61$ |
| $HClO + H^+ + e^- \longrightarrow \frac{1}{2}Cl_2 + H_2O$ | $+1.63$ |
| $HClO_2 + 2H^+ + 2e^- \longrightarrow HClO + H_2O$ | $+1.64$ |
| $Au^+ + e^- \longrightarrow Au$ | $ca. +1.68$ |
| $NiO_2 + 4H^+ + 2e^- \longrightarrow Ni^{2+} + 2H_2O$ | $+1.68$ |
| $PbO_2 + SO_4^{2-} + 4H^+ + 2e^- \longrightarrow PbSO_4 + 2H_2O$ | $+1.685$ |
| $H_2O_2 + 2H^+ + 2e^- \longrightarrow 2H_2O$ | $+1.77$ |
| $Co^{3+} + e^- \longrightarrow Co^{2+}$ | $+1.82$ |
| $F_2 + 2e^- \longrightarrow 2F^-$ | $+2.87$ |

# Appendix J

## Standard Molar Enthalpies of Formation, Standard Molar Free Energies of Formation, and Absolute Standard Entropies [298.15 K (25°C), 1 atm]

| Substance | $\Delta H°_{f298.15}$, kJ/mol | $\Delta G°_{f298.15}$, kJ/mol | $S°_{298.15}$, J/K mol |
|---|---|---|---|
| Aluminum | | | |
| $Al(s)$ | 0 | 0 | 28.3 |
| $Al(g)$ | 326 | 286 | 164.4 |
| $Al_2O_3(s)$ | $-1676$ | $-1582$ | 50.92 |
| $AlF_3(s)$ | $-1504$ | $-1425$ | 66.44 |
| $AlCl_3(s)$ | $-704.2$ | $-628.9$ | 110.7 |
| $AlCl_3 \cdot 6H_2O(s)$ | $-2692$ | — | — |
| $Al_2S_3(s)$ | $-724$ | $-492.4$ | – |
| $Al_2(SO_4)_3(s)$ | $-3440.8$ | $-3100.1$ | 239 |

263

# Standard Molar Enthalpies of Formation, Standard Molar Free Energies of Formation, and Absolute Standard Entropies [298.15 K (25°C), 1 atm] (continued)

| Substance | $\Delta H^\circ_{f_{298.15}}$, kJ/mol | $\Delta G^\circ_{f_{298.15}}$, kJ/mol | $S^\circ_{298.15}$, J/K mol |
|---|---|---|---|
| **Antimony** | | | |
| Sb(s) | 0 | 0 | 45.69 |
| Sb(g) | 262 | 222 | 180.2 |
| $Sb_4O_6$(s) | −1441 | −1268 | 221 |
| $SbCl_3$(g) | −314 | −301 | 337.7 |
| $SbCl_5$(g) | −394.3 | −334.3 | 401.8 |
| $Sb_2S_3$(s) | −175 | −174 | 182 |
| $SbCl_3$(s) | −382.2 | −323.7 | 184 |
| SbOCl(s) | −374 | — | — |
| **Arsenic** | | | |
| As(s) | 0 | 0 | 35 |
| As(g) | 303 | 261 | 174.1 |
| $As_4$(g) | 144 | 92.5 | 314 |
| $As_4O_6$(s) | −1313.9 | −1152.5 | 214 |
| $As_2O_5$(s) | −924.87 | −782.4 | 105 |
| $AsCl_3$(g) | −258.6 | −245.9 | 327.1 |
| $As_2S_3$(s) | −169 | −169 | 164 |
| $AsH_3$(g) | 66.44 | 68.91 | 222.7 |
| $H_3AsO_4$(s) | −906.3 | — | — |
| **Barium** | | | |
| Ba(s) | 0 | 0 | 66.9 |
| Ba(g) | 175.6 | 144.8 | 170.3 |
| BaO(s) | −558.1 | −528.4 | 70.3 |
| $BaCl_2$(s) | −860.06 | −810.9 | 126 |
| $BaSO_4$(s) | −1465 | −1353 | 132 |
| **Beryllium** | | | |
| Be(s) | 0 | 0 | 9.54 |
| Be(g) | 320.6 | 282.8 | 136.17 |
| BeO(s) | −610.9 | −581.6 | 14.1 |
| **Bismuth** | | | |
| Bi(s) | 0 | 0 | 56.74 |
| Bi(g) | 207 | 168 | 186.90 |
| $Bi_2O_3$(s) | −573.88 | −493.7 | 151 |
| $BiCl_3$(s) | −379 | −315 | 177 |
| $Bi_2S_3$(s) | −143 | −141 | 200 |
| **Boron** | | | |
| B(s) | 0 | 0 | 5.86 |
| B(g) | 562.7 | 518.8 | 153.3 |
| $B_2O_3$(s) | −1272.8 | −1193.7 | 53.97 |
| $B_2H_6$(g) | 36 | 86.6 | 232.0 |
| $B(OH)_3$(s) | −1094.3 | −969.01 | 88.83 |
| $BF_3$(g) | −1137.3 | −1120.3 | 254.0 |
| $BCl_3$(g) | −403.8 | −388.7 | 290.0 |
| $B_3N_3H_6$(l) | −541.0 | −392.8 | 200 |
| $HBO_2$(s) | −794.25 | −723.4 | 40 |
| **Bromine** | | | |
| $Br_2$(l) | 0 | 0 | 152.23 |
| $Br_2$(g) | 30.91 | 3.142 | 245.35 |
| Br(g) | 111.88 | 82.429 | 174.91 |

| Substance | $\Delta H^\circ_{f\,298.15}$, kJ/mol | $\Delta G^\circ_{f\,298.15}$, kJ/mol | $S^\circ_{298.15}$, J/K mol |
|---|---|---|---|
| $BrF_3(g)$ | −255.6 | −229.5 | 292.4 |
| $HBr(g)$ | −36.4 | −53.43 | 198.59 |
| Cadmium | | | |
| $Cd(s)$ | 0 | 0 | 51.76 |
| $Cd(g)$ | 112.0 | 77.45 | 167.64 |
| $CdO(s)$ | −258 | −228 | 54.8 |
| $CdCl_2(s)$ | −391.5 | −344.0 | 115.3 |
| $CdSO_4(s)$ | −933.28 | −822.78 | 123.04 |
| $CdS(s)$ | −162 | −156 | 64.9 |
| Calcium | | | |
| $Ca(s)$ | 0 | 0 | 41.6 |
| $Ca(g)$ | 192.6 | 158.9 | 154.78 |
| $CaO(s)$ | −635.5 | −604.2 | 40 |
| $Ca(OH)_2(s)$ | −986.59 | −896.76 | 76.1 |
| $CaSO_4(s)$ | −1432.7 | −1320.3 | 107 |
| $CaSO_4\ 2H_2O(s)$ | −2021.1 | −1795.7 | 194.0 |
| $CaCO_3(s)$ (calcite) | −1206.9 | −1128.8 | 92.9 |
| $CaSO_3\ 2H_2O(s)$ | −1762 | −1565 | 184 |
| Carbon | | | |
| $C(s)$ (graphite) | 0 | 0 | 5.740 |
| $C(s)$ (diamond) | 1.897 | 2.900 | 2.38 |
| $C(g)$ | 716.681 | 671.289 | 157.987 |
| $CO(g)$ | −110.52 | −137.15 | 197.56 |
| $CO_2(g)$ | −393.51 | −394.36 | 213.6 |
| $CH_4(g)$ | −74.81 | −50.75 | 186.15 |
| $CH_3OH(l)$ | −238.7 | −166.4 | 127 |
| $CH_3OH(g)$ | −200.7 | −162.0 | 239.7 |
| $CCl_4(l)$ | −135.4 | −65.27 | 216.4 |
| $CCl_4(g)$ | −102.9 | −60.63 | 309.7 |
| $CHCl_3(l)$ | −134.5 | −73.72 | 202 |
| $CHCl_3(g)$ | −103.1 | −70.37 | 295.6 |
| $CS_2(l)$ | 89.70 | 65.27 | 151.3 |
| $CS_2(g)$ | 117.4 | 67.15 | 237.7 |
| $C_2H_2(g)$ | 226.7 | 209.2 | 200.8 |
| $C_2H_4(g)$ | 52.26 | 68.12 | 219.5 |
| $C_2H_6(g)$ | −84.68 | −32.9 | 229.5 |
| $CH_3COOH(l)$ | −484.5 | −390 | 160 |
| $CH_3COOH(g)$ | −432.25 | −374 | 282 |
| $C_2H_5OH(l)$ | −277.7 | −174.9 | 161 |
| $C_2H_5OH(g)$ | −235.1 | −168.6 | 282.6 |
| $C_3H_8(g)$ | −103.85 | −23.49 | 269.9 |
| $C_6H_6(g)$ | 82.927 | 129.66 | 269.2 |
| $C_6H_6(l)$ | 49.028 | 124.50 | 172.8 |
| $CH_2Cl_2(l)$ | −121.5 | −67.32 | 178 |
| $CH_2Cl_2(g)$ | −92.47 | −65.90 | 270.1 |
| $CH_3Cl(g)$ | −80.83 | −57.40 | 234.5 |
| $C_2H_5Cl(l)$ | −136.5 | −59.41 | 190.8 |
| $C_2H_5Cl(g)$ | −112.2 | −60.46 | 275.9 |
| $C_2N_2(g)$ | 308.9 | 297.4 | 241.8 |
| $HCN(l)$ | 108.9 | 124.9 | 112.8 |
| $HCN(g)$ | 135 | 124.7 | 201.7 |
| Chlorine | | | |
| $Cl_2(g)$ | 0 | 0 | 222.96 |
| $Cl(g)$ | 121.68 | 105.70 | 165.09 |

## Standard Molar Enthalpies of Formation, Standard Molar Free Energies of Formation, and Absolute Standard Entropies [298.15 K (25°C), 1 atm] (continued)

| Substance | $\Delta H^\circ_{f_{298.15}}$, kJ/mol | $\Delta G^\circ_{f_{298.15}}$, kJ/mol | $S^\circ_{298.15}$, J/K mol |
|---|---|---|---|
| ClF(g) | −54.48 | −55.94 | 217.8 |
| ClF₃(g) | −163 | −123 | 281.5 |
| Cl₂O(g) | 80.3 | 97.9 | 266.1 |
| Cl₂O₇(l) | 238 | — | — |
| Cl₂O₇(g) | 272 | — | — |
| HCl(g) | −92.307 | −95.299 | 186.80 |
| HClO₄(l) | −40.6 | — | — |
| Chromium | | | |
| Cr(s) | 0 | 0 | 23.8 |
| Cr(g) | 397 | 352 | 174.4 |
| Cr₂O₃(s) | −1140 | −1058 | 81.2 |
| CrO₃(s) | −589.5 | — | — |
| (NH₄)₂Cr₂O₇(s) | −1807 | — | — |
| Cobalt | | | |
| Co(s) | 0 | 0 | 30.0 |
| CoO(s) | −237.9 | −214.2 | 52.97 |
| Co₃O₄(s) | −891.2 | −774.0 | 103 |
| Co(NO₃)₂(s) | −420.5 | — | — |
| Copper | | | |
| Cu(s) | 0 | 0 | 33.15 |
| Cu(g) | 338.3 | 298.5 | 166.3 |
| CuO(s) | −157 | −130 | 42.63 |
| Cu₂O(s) | −169 | −146 | 93.14 |
| CuS(s) | −53.1 | −53.6 | 66.5 |
| Cu₂S(s) | −79.5 | −86.2 | 121 |
| CuSO₄(s) | −771.36 | −661.9 | 109 |
| Cu(NO₃)₂(s) | −303 | — | — |
| Fluorine | | | |
| F₂(g) | 0 | 0 | 202.7 |
| F(g) | 78.99 | 61.92 | 158.64 |
| F₂O(g) | −22 | −4.6 | 247.3 |
| HF(g) | −271 | −273 | 173.67 |
| Hydrogen | | | |
| H₂(g) | 0 | 0 | 130.57 |
| H(g) | 217.97 | 203.26 | 114.60 |
| H₂O(l) | −285.83 | −237.18 | 69.91 |
| H₂O(g) | −241.82 | −228.59 | 188.71 |
| H₂O₂(l) | −187.8 | −120.4 | 110 |
| H₂O₂(g) | −136.3 | −105.6 | 233 |
| HF(g) | −271 | −273 | 173.67 |
| HCl(g) | −92.307 | −95.299 | 186.80 |
| HBr(g) | −36.4 | −53.43 | 198.59 |
| HI(g) | 26.5 | 1.7 | 206.48 |
| H₂S(g) | −20.6 | −33.6 | 205.7 |
| H₂Se(g) | 30 | 16 | 218.9 |
| Iodine | | | |
| I₂(s) | 0 | 0 | 116.14 |
| I₂(g) | 62.438 | 19.36 | 260.6 |
| I(g) | 106.84 | 70.283 | 180.68 |

| Substance | $\Delta H^\circ_{f\,298.15}$, kJ/mol | $\Delta G^\circ_{f\,298.15}$, kJ/mol | $S^\circ_{298.15}$, J/K mol |
|---|---|---|---|
| IF(g) | 95.65 | −118.5 | 236.1 |
| ICl(g) | 17.8 | −5.44 | 247.44 |
| IBr(g) | 40.8 | 3.7 | 258.66 |
| IF₇(g) | −943.9 | −818.4 | 346 |
| HI(g) | 26.5 | 1.7 | 206.48 |
| Iron | | | |
| Fe(s) | 0 | 0 | 27.3 |
| Fe(g) | 416 | 371 | 180.38 |
| Fe₂O₃(s) | −824.2 | −742.2 | 87.40 |
| Fe₃O₄(s) | −1118 | −1015 | 146 |
| Fe(CO)₅(l) | −774.0 | −705.4 | 338 |
| Fe(CO)₅(g) | −733.9 | −697.26 | 445.2 |
| FeSeO₃(s) | −1200 | — | — |
| FeO(s) | −272 | — | — |
| FeAsS(s) | −42 | −50 | 120 |
| Fe(OH)₂(s) | −569.0 | −486.6 | 88 |
| Fe(OH)₃(s) | −823.0 | −696.6 | 107 |
| FeS(s) | −100 | −100 | 60.29 |
| Fe₃C(s) | 25 | 20 | 105 |
| Lead | | | |
| Pb(s) | 0 | 0 | 64.81 |
| Pb(g) | 195 | 162 | 175.26 |
| PbO(s) (yellow) | −217.3 | −187.9 | 68.70 |
| PbO(s) (red) | −219.0 | −188.9 | 66.5 |
| Pb(OH)₂(s) | −515.9 | — | — |
| PbS(s) | −100 | −98.7 | 91.2 |
| Pb(NO₃)₂(s) | −451.9 | — | — |
| PbO₂(s) | −277 | −217.4 | 68.6 |
| PbCl₂(s) | −359.4 | −314.1 | 136 |
| Lithium | | | |
| Li(s) | 0 | 0 | 28.0 |
| Li(g) | 155.1 | 122.1 | 138.67 |
| LiH(s) | −90.42 | −69.96 | 25. |
| Li(OH)(s) | −487.23 | −443.9 | 50.2 |
| LiF(s) | −612.1 | −584.1 | 35.9 |
| Li₂CO₃(s) | −1215.6 | −1132.4 | 90.4 |
| Manganese | | | |
| Mn(s) | 0 | 0 | 32.0 |
| Mn(g) | 281 | 238 | 173.6 |
| MnO(s) | −385.2 | −362.9 | 59.71 |
| MnO₂(s) | −520.03 | −465.18 | 53.05 |
| Mn₂O₃(s) | −959.0 | −881.2 | 110 |
| Mn₃O₄(s) | −1388 | −1283 | 156 |
| Mercury | | | |
| Hg(l) | 0 | 0 | 76.02 |
| Hg(g) | 61.317 | 31.85 | 174.8 |
| HgO(s) (red) | −90.83 | −58.555 | 70.29 |
| HgO(s) (yellow) | −90.46 | −57.296 | 71.1 |
| HgCl₂(s) | −224 | −179 | 146 |
| Hg₂Cl₂(s) | −265.2 | −210.78 | 192 |
| HgS(s) (red) | −58.16 | −50.6 | 82.4 |
| HgS(s) (black) | −53.6 | −47.7 | 88.3 |
| HgSO₄(s) | −707.5 | — | — |

## Standard Molar Enthalpies of Formation, Standard Molar Free Energies of Formation, and Absolute Standard Entropies [298.15 K (25°C), 1 atm] (continued)

| Substance | $\Delta H^\circ_{f_{298.15}}$, kJ/mol | $\Delta G^\circ_{f_{298.15}}$, kJ/mol | $S^\circ_{298.15}$, J/K mol |
|---|---|---|---|
| **Nitrogen** | | | |
| $N_2(g)$ | 0 | 0 | 191.5 |
| $N(g)$ | 472.704 | 455.579 | 153.19 |
| $NO(g)$ | 90.25 | 86.57 | 210.65 |
| $NO_2(g)$ | 33.2 | 51.30 | 239.9 |
| $N_2O(g)$ | 82.05 | 104.2 | 219.7 |
| $N_2O_3(g)$ | 83.72 | 139.4 | 312.2 |
| $N_2O_4(g)$ | 9.16 | 97.82 | 304.2 |
| $N_2O_5(g)$ | 11 | 115 | 356 |
| $NH_3(g)$ | −46.11 | −16.5 | 192.3 |
| $N_2H_4(l)$ | 50.63 | 149.2 | 121.2 |
| $N_2H_4(g)$ | 95.4 | 159.3 | 238.4 |
| $NH_4NO_3(s)$ | −365.6 | −184.0 | 151.1 |
| $NH_4Cl(s)$ | −314.4 | −201.5 | 94.6 |
| $NH_4Br(s)$ | −270.8 | −175 | 113 |
| $NH_4I(s)$ | −201.4 | −113 | 117 |
| $NH_4NO_2(s)$ | −256 | — | — |
| $HNO_3(l)$ | −174.1 | −80.79 | 155.6 |
| $HNO_3(g)$ | −135.1 | −74.77 | 266.2 |
| **Oxygen** | | | |
| $O_2(g)$ | 0 | 0 | 205.03 |
| $O(g)$ | 249.17 | 231.75 | 160.95 |
| $O_3(g)$ | 143 | 163 | 238.8 |
| **Phosphorus** | | | |
| $P(s)$ | 0 | 0 | 41.1 |
| $P(g)$ | 58.91 | 24.5 | 280.0 |
| $P_4(g)$ | 314.6 | 278.3 | 163.08 |
| $PH_3(g)$ | 5.4 | 13 | 210.1 |
| $PCl_3(g)$ | −287 | −268 | 311.7 |
| $PCl_5(g)$ | −375 | −305 | 364.5 |
| $P_4O_6(s)$ | −1640 | — | — |
| $P_4O_{10}(s)$ | −2984 | −2698 | 228.9 |
| $HPO_3(s)$ | −948.5 | — | — |
| $H_3PO_2(s)$ | −604.6 | — | — |
| $H_3PO_3(s)$ | −964.4 | — | — |
| $H_3PO_4(s)$ | −1279 | −1119 | 110.5 |
| $H_3PO_4(l)$ | −1267 | — | — |
| $H_4P_2O_7(s)$ | −2241 | — | — |
| $POCl_3(l)$ | −597.1 | −520.9 | 222.5 |
| $POCl_3(g)$ | −558.48 | −512.96 | 325.3 |
| **Potassium** | | | |
| $K(s)$ | 0 | 0 | 63.6 |
| $K(g)$ | 90.00 | 61.17 | 160.23 |
| $KF(s)$ | −562.58 | −533.12 | 66.57 |
| $KCl(s)$ | −435.868 | −408.32 | 82.68 |
| **Silicon** | | | |
| $Si(s)$ | 0 | 0 | 18.8 |
| $Si(g)$ | 455.6 | 411 | 167.9 |
| $SiO_2(s)$ | −910.94 | −856.67 | 41.84 |

| Substance | $\Delta H^\circ_{f298.15}$, kJ/mol | $\Delta G^\circ_{f298.15}$, kJ/mol | $S^\circ_{298.15}$, J/K mol |
|---|---|---|---|
| $SiH_4(g)$ | 34 | 56.9 | 204.5 |
| $H_2SiO_3(s)$ | −1189 | −1092 | 130 |
| $H_4SiO_4(s)$ | −1481 | −1333 | 190 |
| $SiF_4(g)$ | −1614.9 | −1572.7 | 282.4 |
| $SiCl_4(l)$ | −687.0 | −619.90 | 240 |
| $SiCl_4(g)$ | −657.01 | −617.01 | 330.6 |
| $SiC(s)$ | −65.3 | −62.8 | 16.6 |
| Silver | | | |
| $Ag(s)$ | 0 | 0 | 42.55 |
| $Ag(g)$ | 284.6 | 245.7 | 172.89 |
| $Ag_2O(s)$ | −31.0 | −11.2 | 121 |
| $AgCl(s)$ | −127.1 | −109.8 | 96.2 |
| $Ag_2S(s)$ | −32.6 | −40.7 | 144.0 |
| Sodium | | | |
| $Na(s)$ | 0 | 0 | 51.0 |
| $Na(g)$ | 108.7 | 78.11 | 153.62 |
| $Na_2O(s)$ | −415.9 | −377 | 72.8 |
| $NaCl(s)$ | −411.00 | −384.03 | 72.38 |
| Sulfur | | | |
| $S(s)$ (rhombic) | 0 | 0 | 31.8 |
| $S(g)$ | 278.80 | 238.27 | 167.75 |
| $SO_2(g)$ | −296.83 | −300.19 | 248.1 |
| $SO_3(g)$ | −395.7 | −371.1 | 256.6 |
| $H_2S(g)$ | −20.6 | −33.6 | 205.7 |
| $H_2SO_4(l)$ | −813.989 | 690.101 | 156.90 |
| $H_2S_2O_7(s)$ | −1274 | — | — |
| $SF_4(g)$ | −774.9 | −731.4 | 291.9 |
| $SF_6(g)$ | −1210 | −1105 | 291.7 |
| $SCl_2(l)$ | −50 | — | — |
| $SCl_2(g)$ | −20 | — | — |
| $S_2Cl_2(l)$ | −59.4 | — | — |
| $S_2Cl_2(g)$ | −18 | −32 | 331.4 |
| $SOCl_2(l)$ | −246 | — | — |
| $SOCl_2(g)$ | −213 | −198 | 309.7 |
| $SO_2Cl_2(l)$ | −394 | — | — |
| $SO_2Cl_2(g)$ | −364 | −320 | 311.8 |
| Tin | | | |
| $Sn(s)$ | 0 | 0 | 51.55 |
| $Sn(g)$ | 302 | 267 | 168.38 |
| $SnO(s)$ | −286 | −257 | 56.5 |
| $SnO_2(s)$ | −580.7 | −519.7 | 52.3 |
| $SnCl_4(l)$ | −511.2 | −440.2 | 259 |
| $SnCl_4(g)$ | −471.5 | −432.2 | 366 |
| Titanium | | | |
| $Ti(s)$ | 0 | 0 | 30.6 |
| $Ti(g)$ | 469.9 | 425.1 | 180.19 |
| $TiO_2(s)$ | −944.7 | −889.5 | 50.33 |
| $TiCl_4(l)$ | −804.2 | −737.2 | 252.3 |
| $TiCl_4(g)$ | −763.2 | −726.8 | 354.8 |
| Tungsten | | | |
| $W(s)$ | 0 | 0 | 32.6 |
| $W(g)$ | 849.4 | 807.1 | 173.84 |
| $WO_3(s)$ | −842.87 | −764.08 | 75.90 |

## Standard Molar Enthalpies of Formation, Standard Molar Free Energies of Formation, and Absolute Standard Entropies [298.15 K (25°C), 1 atm] (continued)

| Substance | $\Delta H^\circ_{f298.15}$, kJ/mol | $\Delta G^\circ_{f298.15}$, kJ/mol | $S^\circ_{298.15}$, J/K mol |
|---|---|---|---|
| **Zinc** | | | |
| Zn(s) | 0 | 0 | 41.6 |
| Zn(g) | 130.73 | 95.178 | 160.87 |
| ZnO(s) | −348.3 | −318.3 | 43.64 |
| ZnCl$_2$(s) | −415.1 | −369.43 | 111.5 |
| ZnS(s) | −206.0 | −201.3 | 57.7 |
| ZnSO$_4$(s) | −982.8 | −874.5 | 120 |
| ZnCO$_3$(s) | −812.78 | −731.57 | 82.4 |
| **Complexes** | | | |
| [Co(NH$_3$)$_4$(NO$_2$)$_2$]NO$_3$, *cis* | −898.7 | — | — |
| [Co(NH$_3$)$_4$(NO$_2$)$_2$]NO$_3$, *trans* | −896.2 | — | — |
| NH$_4$[Co(NH$_3$)$_2$(NO$_2$)$_4$] | −837.6 | — | — |
| [Co(NH$_3$)$_6$][Co(NH$_3$)$_2$(NO$_2$)$_4$]$_3$ | −2733 | — | — |
| [Co(NH$_3$)$_4$Cl$_2$]Cl, *cis* | −997.0 | — | — |
| [Co(NH$_3$)$_4$Cl$_2$]Cl, *trans* | −999.6 | — | — |
| [Co(en)$_2$(NO$_2$)$_2$]NO$_3$, *cis* | −689.5 | — | — |
| [Co(en)$_2$Cl$_2$]Cl, *cis* | −681.1 | — | — |
| [Co(en)$_2$Cl$_2$]Cl, *trans* | −677.4 | — | — |
| [Co(en)$_3$](ClO$_4$)$_3$ | −762.7 | — | — |
| [Co(en)$_3$]Br$_2$ | −595.8 | — | — |
| [Co(en)$_3$]I$_2$ | −475.3 | — | — |
| [Co(en)$_3$]I$_3$ | −519.2 | — | — |
| [Co(NH$_3$)$_6$](ClO$_4$)$_3$ | −1035 | −227 | 636 |
| [Co(NH$_3$)$_5$NO$_2$](NO$_3$)$_2$ | −1089 | −418.4 | 350 |
| [Co(NH$_3$)$_6$](NO$_3$)$_3$ | −1282 | −530.5 | 469 |
| [Co(NH$_3$)$_5$Cl]Cl$_2$ | −1017 | −582.8 | 366 |
| [Pt(NH$_3$)$_4$]Cl$_2$ | −728.0 | — | — |
| [Ni(NH$_3$)$_6$]Cl$_2$ | −994.1 | — | — |
| [Ni(NH$_3$)$_6$]Br$_2$ | −923.8 | — | — |
| [Ni(NH$_3$)$_6$]I$_2$ | −808.3 | — | — |

# Appendix K

## Composition of Commercial Acids and Bases

| Acid or Base | Specific Gravity | Percentage by Mass | Molarity | Normality |
|---|---|---|---|---|
| Hydrochloric | 1.19 | 38 | 12.4 | 12.4 |
| Nitric | 1.42 | 70 | 15.8 | 15.8 |
| Sulfuric | 1.84 | 95 | 17.8 | 35.6 |
| Acetic | 1.05 | 99 | 17.3 | 17.3 |
| Aqueous ammonia | 0.90 | 28 | 14.8 | 14.8 |

# Appendix L

## Half-Life Times for Several Radioactive Isotopes

(Symbol in parentheses indicates type of emission; E.C. = K-electron capture, S.F. = spontaneous fission; $y$ = years, $d$ = days, $h$ = hours, $m$ = minutes, $s$ = seconds.)

| | | | | | | |
|---|---|---|---|---|---|---|
| $^{14}_{6}C$ | 5770 $y$ | $(\beta^-)$ | | $^{226}_{88}Ra$ | 1590 $y$ | $(\alpha)$ |
| $^{13}_{7}N$ | 10.0 $m$ | $(\beta^+)$ | | $^{228}_{88}Ra$ | 6.7 $y$ | $(\beta^-)$ |
| $^{24}_{11}Na$ | 15.0 $h$ | $(\beta^-)$ | | $^{228}_{89}Ac$ | 6.13 $h$ | $(\beta^-)$ |
| $^{32}_{15}P$ | 14.3 $d$ | $(\beta^-)$ | | $^{228}_{90}Th$ | 1.90 $y$ | $(\alpha)$ |
| $^{40}_{19}K$ | $1.3 \times 10^9$ $y$ | $(\beta^-$ or E.C.) | | $^{232}_{90}Th$ | $1.39 \times 10^{10}$ $y$ | $(\alpha, \beta^-,$ or S.F.) |
| $^{60}_{27}Co$ | 5.2 $y$ | $(\beta^-)$ | | $^{233}_{90}Th$ | 23 $m$ | $(\beta^-)$ |
| $^{87}_{37}Rb$ | $4.7 \times 10^{10}$ $y$ | $(\beta^-)$ | | $^{234}_{90}Th$ | 24.1 $d$ | $(\beta^-)$ |
| $^{90}_{38}Sr$ | 28 $y$ | $(\beta^-)$ | | $^{223}_{91}Pa$ | 27 $d$ | $(\beta^-)$ |
| $^{115}_{49}In$ | $6 \times 10^{14}$ $y$ | $(\beta^-)$ | | $^{233}_{92}U$ | $1.62 \times 10^5$ $y$ | $(\alpha)$ |
| $^{131}_{53}I$ | 8.05 $d$ | $(\beta^-)$ | | $^{234}_{92}U$ | $2.4 \times 10^5$ $y$ | $(\alpha$ or S.F.) |
| $^{142}_{58}Ce$ | $5 \times 10^{15}$ $y$ | $(\alpha)$ | | $^{235}_{92}U$ | $7.3 \times 10^8$ $y$ | $(\alpha$ or S.F.) |
| $^{198}_{79}Au$ | 64.8 $h$ | $(\beta^-)$ | | $^{238}_{92}U$ | $4.5 \times 10^9$ $y$ | $(\alpha$ or S.F.) |
| $^{208}_{81}Tl$ | 3.1 $m$ | $(\beta^-)$ | | $^{239}_{92}U$ | 23 $m$ | $(\beta^-)$ |
| $^{210}_{82}Pb$ | 21 $y$ | $(\beta^-)$ | | $^{239}_{93}Np$ | 2.3 $d$ | $(\beta^-)$ |
| $^{212}_{82}Pb$ | 10.6 $h$ | $(\beta^-)$ | | $^{239}_{94}Pu$ | 24,360 $y$ | $(\alpha$ or S.F.) |
| $^{214}_{82}Pb$ | 26.8 $m$ | $(\beta^-)$ | | $^{240}_{94}Pu$ | $6.58 \times 10^3$ $y$ | $(\alpha$ or S.F.) |
| $^{206}_{83}Bi$ | 6.3 $d$ | $(\beta^+$ or E.C.) | | $^{241}_{94}Pu$ | 13 $y$ | $(\alpha$ or $\beta^-)$ |
| $^{210}_{83}Bi$ | 5.0 $d$ | $(\beta^-)$ | | $^{241}_{95}Am$ | 458 $y$ | $(\alpha)$ |
| $^{212}_{83}Bi$ | 60.5 $m$ | $(\alpha$ or $\beta^-)$ | | $^{242}_{96}Cm$ | 163 $d$ | $(\alpha$ or S.F.) |
| $^{207}_{84}Po$ | 5.7 $h$ | $(\alpha, \beta^+,$ or E.C.) | | $^{243}_{97}Bk$ | 4.5 $h$ | $(\alpha$ or E.C.) |
| $^{210}_{84}Po$ | 138.4 $d$ | $(\alpha)$ | | $^{245}_{98}Cf$ | 350 $d$ | $(\alpha$ or E.C.) |
| $^{212}_{84}Po$ | $3 \times 10^{-7}$ $s$ | $(\alpha)$ | | $^{253}_{99}Es$ | 20.0 $d$ | $(\alpha$ or S.F.) |
| $^{216}_{84}Po$ | 0.16 $s$ | $(\alpha)$ | | $^{254}_{100}Fm$ | 3.24 $h$ | (S.F.) |
| $^{218}_{84}Po$ | 3.0 $m$ | $(\alpha$ or $\beta^-)$ | | $^{255}_{100}Fm$ | 22 $h$ | $(\alpha)$ |
| $^{215}_{85}At$ | $10^{-4}$ $s$ | $(\alpha)$ | | $^{256}_{101}Md$ | 1.5 $h$ | (E.C.) |
| $^{218}_{85}At$ | 1.3 $s$ | $(\alpha)$ | | $^{254}_{102}No$ | 3 $s$ | $(\alpha)$ |
| $^{220}_{86}Rn$ | 54.5 $s$ | $(\alpha)$ | | $^{257}_{103}Lr$ | 8 $s$ | $(\alpha)$ |
| $^{222}_{86}Rn$ | 3.82 $d$ | $(\alpha)$ | | $^{263}_{106}(106)$ | 0.9 $s$ | $(\alpha)$ |
| $^{224}_{88}Ra$ | 3.64 $d$ | $(\alpha)$ | | | | |

# Appendix M

## Vapor Pressure of Ice and Water at Various Temperatures

| Temperature, °C | Pressure, mm Hg | Temperature, °C | Pressure, mm Hg | Temperature, °C | Pressure, mm Hg |
|---|---|---|---|---|---|
| -10 | 2.1 | 18 | 15.5 | 80 | 355.1 |
| - 5 | 3.2 | 19 | 16.5 | 90 | 525.8 |
| - 2 | 4.0 | 20 | 17.5 | 95 | 633.9 |
| - 1 | 4.3 | 21 | 18.7 | 96 | 657.6 |
| 0 | 4.6 | 22 | 19.8 | 97 | 682.1 |
| 1 | 4.9 | 23 | 21.1 | 98 | 707.3 |
| 2 | 5.3 | 24 | 22.4 | 99 | 733.2 |
| 3 | 5.7 | 25 | 23.8 | 99.1 | 735.9 |
| 4 | 6.1 | 26 | 25.2 | 99.2 | 738.5 |
| 5 | 6.5 | 27 | 26.7 | 99.3 | 741.2 |
| 6 | 7.0 | 28 | 28.3 | 99.4 | 743.9 |
| 7 | 7.5 | 29 | 30.0 | 99.5 | 746.5 |
| 8 | 8.0 | 30 | 31.8 | 99.6 | 749.2 |
| 9 | 8.6 | 31 | 33.7 | 99.7 | 751.9 |
| 10 | 9.2 | 32 | 35.7 | 99.8 | 754.6 |
| 11 | 9.8 | 33 | 37.7 | 99.9 | 757.3 |
| 12 | 10.5 | 34 | 39.9 | 100.0 | 760.0 |
| 13 | 11.2 | 35 | 42.2 | 100.1 | 762.7 |
| 14 | 12.0 | 40 | 55.3 | 100.2 | 765.5 |
| 15 | 12.8 | 50 | 92.5 | 100.3 | 768.2 |
| 16 | 13.6 | 60 | 149.4 | 100.5 | 773.7 |
| 17 | 14.5 | 70 | 233.7 | 101.0 | 787.5 |

2 3 4 5 6 7 8 9 0